OUT OF THE BLACK BOX

OUT OF THE BLACK BOX

CONVERSATIONS WITH GLOBAL MAJORITY ACTORS VOLUME 1

Edited by
Pamela Jikiemi

methuen | drama
LONDON • NEW YORK • OXFORD • NEW DELHI • SYDNEY

METHUEN DRAMA
Bloomsbury Publishing Plc, 50 Bedford Square, London, WC1B 3DP, UK
Bloomsbury Publishing Inc, 1359 Broadway, New York, NY 10018, USA
Bloomsbury Publishing Ireland, 29 Earlsfort Terrace, Dublin 2, D02 AY28, Ireland

BLOOMSBURY, METHUEN DRAMA and the Methuen Drama logo are
trademarks of Bloomsbury Publishing Plc

First published in Great Britain 2026

Copyright © Pamela Jikiemi and Contributors, 2026

Pamela Jikiemi and Contributors have asserted their right under the Copyright,
Designs and Patents Act, 1988, to be identified as Authors of this work.

For legal purposes the Acknowledgements on pp. xi–xii constitute an extension of this copyright page.

Photo © Adam Pearson

All rights reserved. No part of this publication may be: i) reproduced or transmitted in any form, electronic or mechanical, including photocopying, recording or by means of any information storage or retrieval system without prior permission in writing from the publishers; or ii) used or reproduced in any way for the training, development or operation of artificial intelligence (AI) technologies, including generative AI technologies. The rights holders expressly reserve this publication from the text and data mining exception as per Article 4(3) of the Digital Single Market Directive (EU) 2019/790.

Bloomsbury Publishing Plc does not have any control over, or responsibility for, any third-party websites referred to or in this book. All internet addresses given in this book were correct at the time of going to press. The author and publisher regret any inconvenience caused if addresses have changed or sites have ceased to exist, but can accept no responsibility for any such changes.

A catalogue record for this book is available from the British Library.

Library of Congress Control Number: 2025936199

ISBN: HB: 978-1-3502-6436-6
       PB: 978-1-3502-6435-9
       ePDF: 978-1-3502-6437-3
       eBook: 978-1-3502-6438-0

Typeset by Integra Software Services Pvt. Ltd.
Printed and bound in India

For product safety related questions contact productsafety@bloomsbury.com.

To find out more about our authors and books visit
www.bloomsbury.com and sign up for our newsletters.

*To all the young, not so young, those wrestling with giving up or going on,
Black and Global Majority actors, artists, creatives, if you can see it, you can be it,
go confidently in the direction of your dreams. Be kind to yourself.
Treat yourself as you would someone you have been asked to look after.*

CONTENTS

Foreword   ix
Dr Sharrell D. Luckett
Acknowledgements   xi

Introduction – Pamela Jikiemi   1

1   **James Earl Jones, Paterson Joseph, David Oyelowo OBE and Priyanga Burford**   5
    James Earl Jones   6
    Paterson Joseph   13
    David Oyelowo OBE   21
    Priyanga Burford   30

2   **Lucian Msamati, Noma Dumezweni, Jenny Jules and Colin Salmon**   37
    Lucian Msamati   38
    Noma Dumezweni   45
    Jenny Jules   52
    Colin Salmon   58

3   **Aliyah Odoffin, Phoebe Campbell, Jamael Westman, Caleb Obediah and Shakeel Haakim**   67
    Aliyah Odoffin   68
    Phoebe Campbell   76
    Jamael Westman   82
    Caleb Obediah   91
    Shakeel Haakim   97

4   **Ronkẹ Adékọluéjọ́, Fisayo Akinade, Francesca Amewudah-Rivers and Martins Imhangbe**   107
    Ronkẹ Adékọluéjọ́   108
    Fisayo Akinade   120
    Francesca Amewudah-Rivers   129
    Martins Imhangbe   140

5   **Nicole Brewer, Dr Karen Tomlin, Indhu Rubasingham MBE, Josette Bushell-Mingo OBE, Joel Trill and Heather Basten**   151
    Nicole Brewer   152
    Dr Karen Tomlin   158
    Indhu Rubasingham MBE   165

Contents

	Josette Bushell-Mingo OBE	170
	Joel Trill	177
	Heather Basten	188
6	**Sheila Atim MBE, Kit Young, Sara Zwangobani and Abraham Popoola**	**193**
	Sheila Atim MBE	194
	Kit Young	204
	Sara Zwangobani	217
	Abraham Popoola	226
7	**Jennifer Lim, Cyril Nri, Cornell John and Leo Wringer**	**237**
	Jennifer Lim	238
	Cyril Nri	247
	Cornell John	257
	Leo Wringer	265
	Epilogue	279

FOREWORD
Dr Sharrell D. Luckett

When working on *Black Acting Methods: Critical Approaches*, I knew that I wanted to give a gift to Black actors and creatives everywhere. I wanted to inspire, to uplift, but most importantly, I wanted to catalyse a movement to address the serious neglect of contributions to actor training from Black artists and artists of the Global Majority. This work opened doors for myriad texts to join the movement and *Out of the Black Box: Conversations with Global Majority Actors Volume 1* is, rightfully so, next in line.

Out of the Black Box: Conversations with Global Majority Actors Volume 1, edited by Pamela Jikiemi, is a collection of interviews that highlight actors' journeys in the field of performing arts. Infused with a serious respect for the craft and words of wisdom that actors should heed, insights from James Earl Jones to Josette Bushell-Mingo OBE to David Oyelowo OBE delight readers with responses to questions that delve deep into the craft of acting. In total, this book provides personal reflections on what it takes to 'make it' in this industry.

Out of the Black Box is right on time as actors, young and senior alike, are calling for greater visibility in classroom materials and in what are considered foundational texts – right on time for those participating in an ever-changing, fast-paced industry that is calling for more representation on the stage and screen, more 'meaty' roles for actors of the Global Majority, and more opportunities behind the scenes.

Ensconced in a deep and abiding passion for performance, Jikiemi has woven together thoughts from actors that should be read by actor-artists everywhere. The voices within acknowledge that acting is challenging, fun and eventful. This is clear. But what is also clear is the path-making that artists of the Global Majority are involved in. Read and woven as a unique tapestry of reflections on craft and community, there is great joy in learning about the journeys of Black and Global Majority artists as they can be familiar and unfamiliar at the same time. The treasure trove of insights provide nuggets of wisdom for all to add to their 'tool box'.

This anthology has the potential to augment classroom resources in a way that highlights representation, career crafting, and genius theatre-making all at once.

The conversations add to a still burgeoning canon of books that specifically uplift creative voices of the Global Majority, an ever-pressing necessity in acting and performance spaces. With this work, Jikiemi does not waver in her understanding that voices from the Global Majority are critical in the current conversations surrounding equity and artistry.

There is no doubt in my mind that *Out of the Black Box* will become a staple resource in classrooms and studios for years to come as it speaks to the seismic current of change that is taking place across the globe in acting classrooms – a change that ushers *Out of the Black Box* to a space where it enters the canon of required materials.

Foreword

When I'm engaged in selecting my next writing projects, I often ask myself what types of writing I would have wanted access to in the earlier parts of my acting career. Of course, *Out of the Black Box* is a book that I would have wanted to be able to read and share sooner. Navigating a career in the performing arts is not easy, so it's always a blessing – a gift – when a resource comes along that could prove critical to enhancing one's career. *Out of the Black Box: Conversations with Global Majority Actors Volume 1* is that resource.

Saluting all parties involved in this excellent volume that speaks to resilience, belonging, and artistic way-making – a volume that enhances our craft and one that should be read through the ages.

Dr Sharrell D. Luckett, author, professor, and lead editor of
Black Acting Methods: Critical Approaches

ACKNOWLEDGEMENTS

Creating, conducting and curating this book of conversations has been a journey filled with moments of inspiration, challenge and growth and I am profoundly grateful to all those who have supported me along the way.

First and foremost, I want to express my deepest gratitude to my children Esmie, Beeban and Aphra and my husband Adam. Their unwavering love, encouragement, patience and understanding have been my anchor throughout this process. They have pushed me to be brave, picked me up when all seemed lost, listened to my raves and rants, held me close and tight, and have given me the strength to keep asking questions and engaging with my craft.

To Stefanie Kenyon who I have known since we worked together for SBS Television in Australia. Stef was Head of Graphics extraordinaire and became a true friend and ally. She has designed and formatted, not only this book with patience and care, but several award-winning short films I have produced and directed. Stef has guided me in the ways of font, kerning and accessibility, and reminded me of the vagaries of Australian politics and her love of sport and kept me on track. Stef, you really are always there for me, thank you.

To my family, friends, colleagues and mentors Natasha Jules Catnott, Dr Karen Tomlin, Dr Hilary Baxter, Dr Sharrell D. Luckett, Professor Julian Meyrick, Amanda Brennan, Sandra Bates the former Governing and Artistic Director of the Ensemble Theatre in Australia, Josette Bushell-Mingo OBE, Diane Flowers, Stella Flowers, Yemisi Mokuolu, Helene Gaha, David Byrne, Cherry Cole, Geoff Colman, Tony Kaye, Ray Lyttleton, Sara Wiener, Professor Malcolm Quinn, Yvonne Tomlin-Miller, Emily Stillman, Professor Michael Worton CBE, Maxine Martin, Mrs Stoker, Mwenya Kawesha and Professor John Higgins (RIP) who are all fellow travellers I have met on this road of life, who have been in my corner through thick and thin, who saw something in me, provided me with wings when I had forgotten how to fly, revealed opportunities when it seemed there were none, who shared insights as to their experience of coming of age in the UK, and who continue to share, listen, guide and most importantly laugh at all of my jokes when our paths intersect on this sometimes fraught, often challenging, but ultimately joyful journey called life. Thank you for starting a conversation, lending an ear, offering feedback, giving me hard talk when I needed it most, lifting me up when all seemed lost and sharing your wisdom and restorative laughter. Your belief and trust in my abilities have been a source of strength, motivation and encouragement; thank you for being there for me, I am looking forward to the next conversation.

A special thank you to Ronkẹ Adékọluéjọ́, Fisayo Akinade, Francesca Amewudah-Rivers, Sheila Atim MBE, Heather Basten, Nicole Brewer, Priyanga Burford, Josette Bushell-Mingo OBE, Phoebe Campbell, Noma Dumezweni, Cornell John, James Earl Jones who ten years ago listened, laughed and shared his wonderful story with me, Shakeel Haakim, Martins Imhangbe, Paterson Joseph, Jenny Jules, Jennifer Lim, Lucian Msamati, Cyril Nri, Caleb Obediah, Aliyah Odoffin, David Oyelowo OBE, Abraham Popoola, Indhu Rubasingham MBE, Colin Salmon, Joel Trill, Dr Karen Tomlin, Jamael Westman, Leo Wringer, Kit Young, and Sara Zwangobani, whose his and her stories, wit, empathy, insights, kindness and experiences have been

Acknowledgements

instrumental in shaping this project. Your collective wisdom, patience and resilience have made a lasting impact, and I am incredibly fortunate to have had the opportunity to talk with you and capture a snapshot of the love, laughter, dedication, disappointment, pain, reflection and joy that you embrace in unequal measure to continue building and developing your artistic craft, vision, hopes and ambitions. I am eternally grateful for sharing a space with you.

I would like to acknowledge my editor Anna Brewer, and assistant editor Dr Aanchal Vij at Bloomsbury for believing in, and supporting, the vision for this project, whose insight, dedication and professionalism have helped bring this book to life. Your hard work and commitment to excellence are truly appreciated.

I would also like to acknowledge Zoe Cross and Olivia Davies at United Agents for understanding and believing in the idea that these conversations need to be chronicled much more openly and for their encouragement and support.

I am indebted to my mum, Esmie Jane Jikiemi (née Notice), my dad, Chief Olugbenga Jikiemi, my aunt Aduke Sonuga and my uncle Herbert Leopold Notice, who all passed away much too soon; there are still too many conversations we never got to have. Their love, strength, kindness, laughter and wisdom taught me that the art of a good conversation is listening; they would remind me 'to see blind and hear deaf' and would always reiterate the importance of our culture and our responsibility to pass on our oral history through parables, stories and life lessons – to never be afraid to take up space.

There is that great proverb – that until the lions have their own historians, the history of the hunt will always glorify the hunter ... I had to be that historian. It's not one man's job. It's not one person's job. But it is something we have to do, so that the story of the hunt will also reflect the agony, the travail – the bravery, even, of the lions.
(Chinua Achebe 1994. 'The Art of Fiction' No. 139, *The Paris Review*)

My dad spoke in parables, and he would say 'an African will always carry his culture in a suitcase', we all have stories, our job is to keep those stories alive to ensure that everyone's part in those stories is told with equal investment, feeling and imagination. We must never stop telling our stories, and above all we need tell them not only well, but often.

Sun Re O.

INTRODUCTION

When creative artists come together and talk to a fellow creative artist, something significant happens. Black and Global Majority artists contribute and create a significant body of artistic, performance, directorial, change-making work that represents the past, present and future; it is important that we are acknowledged in all our creative contributions and not erased or sidelined from the narrative. It is important that the notion of exceptionalism is challenged, whereby Black and Global Majority contributions are only recorded because of the notable nature of their proximity to white Western European society. With the conversations that follow, my aim was to provide the opportunity to talk to actors, artists and practitioners as individuals, to explore deeper aspects of their creative lived experience, to discuss how they have found ways to wield their agency and refute the limited expectations suggested of them in relation to their identity and representation and how they perceive themselves and their relationship to their art.

When I started to realize the idea behind this book, I understood that conversations specifically with Black and Global Majority actors and creatives about how to gain a start and develop life in the industry and creative choices as standalone subjects, were few and far between.

As these conversations evolved, the challenges of navigating identity and success in the entertainment industry, particularly for Black and Global Majority artists, became a recurring subtextual theme. All the artists shared their personal experiences of training, entering the profession, facing rejection, self-doubt and hierarchical structures, and emphasized the importance of developing craft, focus, being prepared to put in the groundwork, creating safe spaces for support and growth. They also discussed the deep value of self-care, self-reflection, and seeking help when needed.

Paterson Joseph offered in his interview that 'we are artists in the open', and that resonated with me and underpinned the importance of these conversations. Black and Global Majority creatives are very much in the open, but wrestle with really being seen and heard in a meaningful, representative and ongoing way. Lucian Msamati asserted in our conversation that when he set out to establish his career in the United Kingdom he 'came here for the throne'; his self-affirmation and self-belief left no doubt as to his creative determination and mission.

These wide-ranging conversations highlighted not only the need for a more inclusive and equitable industry that values representational perspectives and experiences, but more insistently asked, when will presence equal power and visibility? As I reflexively considered and edited these conversations I thought, when, indeed? So, what better place to start than with James Earl Jones? But I have jumped a bit, that comes later.

***

Capturing the words and reflections of Black and Global Majority artists as they discussed craft, choice and ambition, I realized that these viewpoints were rarely, if ever, fully explored. In 1992, writer Buchi Emecheta, along with other fellow New Zealander, African, Caribbean and South American writers, explored similar themes in relation to their craft in *Interviews with Writers of the Post Colonial World* edited by Feroza Jussawalla and Reed Way Dasenbrock.

Sharell D. Luckett with Tia M. Shaffer (2017) created an explosive shift in their seminal book *Black Acting Methods: Critical Approaches*, as they captured through their own experiences and pedagogical practices, through the contributions of a veritable list of distinguished artists, directors, scholars, actor trainers, and practitioners/academics, Afrocentric processes and aesthetics in relation to actor training in the United States.

Out of the Black Box continues that journey of reclaiming, reaffirming and reframing the role and contributions of Black and Global Majority artists to the creative culture of the live and recorded arts.

My dad used to say, 'If you are going to eat a frog, eat a fat one'. This was the advice most often shared in moments of indecision. When caught between the worlds of conflicting choice, do we accept the ongoing discriminatory situation and the very limited range of stereotypical choices only ever on offer, and be grateful? Or do we choose the road less travelled and take the risk of setting out to clear and redefine the narrow path that has been carved culturally and creatively through the blood, sweat and tears of those who have gone before? The road less travelled is always a risky and challenging option, but worth the adventure if we stay the course, maintain a visible path, share the load when we encounter adversity, and unite as a community to provide strength and support as we discover unconventional solutions and celebrate the gains.

'You're telling people don't let them tell you – don't let them dictate how you do your thing.'

'We're family. We have to be. That'd be my advice.' Ronkẹ Adékọluéjọ́, Chapter 4.

∗∗∗

In 2011, I had been invited to attend an interview that James Earl Jones was to give at Royal Central School of Speech and Drama. During the course of this interview, he spoke of his upbringing, his professional life and approach to acting – the gains and the experiences he still felt he had yet to have and how he continued to prevail in this most fickle of professions. I was captivated and wanted to interview him as part of my MA dissertation that I was exploring at Royal Central at the time. I approached his son after the event and asked if there would be any possibility of James Earl Jones considering being interviewed by me, one-to-one over the telephone, and left him with my number. Two days later I was heading home with my children in the car, with the usual mayhem round of 'when will we get home?', 'what's for dinner?', 'is it bad to like to One Direction?' 'I still can't find my Kumon sheets', when the phone rang. I answered it on speaker phone, expecting it to be my husband asking me to pick up something for the dinner he was cooking, I said 'hello' and what came back was the most beautiful, mellifluous 'Hello, am I speaking to Pamela Jikiemi?' – there was a collective gasp from the children and they said 'Mum! It's Mufasa!' – I nearly crashed the car. I pulled over, didn't have to worry about the kids – they were sitting in stunned, wide-eyed, open-mouthed silence and stayed that way for the duration of the call. He told me he would love to do the interview and we then set about agreeing a date and time. The call ended and we drove the rest of the way home in complete and utter 'remember who you are Simba' style silence. Best car journey ever!

The interview took place and the seed of the idea of interviewing Black and Global Majority creatives grew, developed and strengthened. I wanted to talk to other actors, as an actor myself, and capture their stories and feelings about their journeys, choices, representation, and the creative industries.

When I started this journey of conversations I wanted to connect with as many Black and Global Majority actors, creatives, and makers as I possibly could. This proved in many ways quite a challenging task. While there seems to be an appetite for mining the struggle of our individual and collective trauma, talking directly about their creative endeavour, focus and journey, solely as artists, is not something Black and Global Majority creatives are very often, if at all, invited to do in a meaningful way.

Introduction

I realized through these conversations that whether looking back at the past, standing and reflecting in the present, or gazing to the future, these direct first-hand personal experiences are all too often overlooked and under-explored. I wanted this book to act as a kind of a transactional memory repository.

The conversations in this book provide a snapshot of the lived experiences of all the creatives who gave me their valuable time and energy to share their histories and recollections on how they are, where they are at this point and who they are at this time. Each interview is completed by a moment that represents community. In diasporic communities, food is the tie that binds. We have spent time together, shared and passed on valuable information through stories, life lessons and laughter, so let's eat, break bread, chop, touch the heart – Dim Sum, with a choice that reflects a myriad of connections and the multi-faceted nature of where we are, who we be and why we like it. When in Nigeria, my cousins would visit us where we lived in Ikeja, Lagos. Usually at a crucial point, to diffuse what had characteristically become a heated debate over primogeniture, age, gender and familial naming rights, they would loudly declare, 'abeg come make we chop hunga dey catch me oh' and it would temporarily stop the debate in its tracks, we would all laugh and head off in search of either fried plantain (dodo) or Chin Chin, still arguing hotly on the way.

Out of the Black Box: Conversations with Global Majority Actors Volume 1, though conducted and curated by me, is talking directly to you, about acting, artistry, craft resilience, perseverance and bravery.

Aim high.
Unity is strength.
Pamela Jikiemi, 2025

CHAPTER 1
JAMES EARL JONES, PATERSON JOSEPH, DAVID OYELOWO OBE AND PRIYANGA BURFORD

Keywords/concepts: Emotion → choices → race → training → people → imagination

If you're going to eat a frog, eat a fat one.

Chief Olugbenga Jikiemi (1929–2009) Sun Re O

James Earl Jones

Forest Whitaker and James Earl Jones at the 15th Annual Screen Actors Guild Awards. Photographer: S Bukely.

James Earl Jones (1931–2024) needs no introduction from me. He passed away on 9 September 2024, just as I completed this book. Though our initial conversation provided the inspiration for this book, I am forever indebted to him for his candid sharing, selfless acts and insights to the impact of the past. James Earl Jones was considered one of the leading lights of the acting industry nationally and internationally. He is still held in such high regard that there is nothing I could add that would match the contribution he made by his work ethic of lifelong learning and creative generosity.

This conversation varies in format from the other conversations due to the fact that it took place a number of years ago when I first started my research journey into under representation.

Pamela Jikiemi – PJ I've compiled a few questions here, just to talk to you about your process a bit, your career and you know, who's exerted the strongest influence on you and what motivates you to act?

Since we last spoke, I've had more of an idea of what I'd like to explore with the interviews that I'm doing. It's more to examine how an actor prepares for a role at the different stages of their career, whether it's stage, film or voice-over. How do you relate to the director? Is training necessary? And is there such a thing as genius?

James Earl Jones – JEJ Those are some wonderful questions, what do you say we have them individually?

PJ When I had the pleasure of listening to your talk at Central, you said that you were not society raised but raised by your grandmother?

JEJ Being a rural person, a farm person, there weren't many peers, that's what I meant, yes that's exactly the case. It wasn't just my grandmother; she had the strongest influence in terms of the way I dealt with other people outside the family.

PJ Okay, so how did you come to be an actor? Were you trained?

JEJ I would say that one thing really has nothing to do with the other. My early beginning was about – to mistrust the outside. I'll give you an example of both my grandparents who were my guardians, my adopted parents.

My grandmother was a staunch racist, and taught me not only to mistrust other races, especially the white race, but to automatically discount and dislike them. Distrust, discount, dislike, all the negatives that come with racism. I now understand racism to be a disease, in fact it can affect anybody. I've heard Black people in my country say, 'Black people are not racist'. But that's not true. The disease can infect anyone. And it did her, she was part Choctaw Native American, Choctaw, Cherokee, Native American. And when she discovered that the Native Americans held Black slaves themselves, she felt betrayed by that part of her blood. She felt betrayed by the Black part of her blood for letting it happen.

She felt betrayed certainly by the white, her husband was part Irish, she felt betrayed by that, the white blood. She converted all that betrayal into a form of racism, that I think she thought was defensive because they were the power, certainly in the South where we were raised, where we first began.

My grandfather however, although he might have held many of the same views, he didn't express them. He didn't indoctrinate his children or grandchildren, she indoctrinated. But my grandfather just led by examples, for the most part, his examples were fair. He was a very fair person, a very balanced person.

But when we had the confrontation with the neighbour's children, and they were white farmers, as poor as we were, we were sharecroppers. And the neighbour's kids borrowed our wagon to hold wood in and when they brought the wagon back it was all beaten up because they had used the wagon to chop wood, to break blocks of wood into. And we didn't understand why my grandfather didn't chastise them and he explained it. We let that pass, it was up to the parents to chastise them, he could not chastise white children.

Later on, there was a dispute between his children, the Black children and the neighbour's children who were white over the plum orchard that straddled both properties. His solution was to go down with his axe and cut down all the plum trees to end the dispute. That impressed me, there was a dramatic act on his part, he destroyed good, healthy fruit to end a potentially explosive confrontation between children, and I am still impressed by that. He, in a way, has always been my hero. I adore my grandmother. And an example is that when I started acting, she was the first person in the front row to see me do plays. Because she more than anyone understood drama in a very personal subjective way. She had witnessed murder, lynchings, natural disasters, hurricanes and floods, to witness all the horrors of life in her own simple life and understood drama. Now she didn't share that with us, except for a few of her stories. But she responded when I became an actor. She responded very fully and I think in a very healthy way.

PJ So, your progression to becoming an actor, how did that come about? Were you trained? Or was it something that you doggedly pursued?

JEJ Well, I don't believe that you are an actor unless you're on stage or in front of a camera acting. At this point I am not an actor, in about two hours I will be an actor. (James Earl Jones had joined Vanessa Redgrave in the West End transfer production of Alfred Uhry's *Driving Miss Daisy* at the Wyndham Theatre.) Because I'll be engaged in the act of acting. Right now, I'm just a bloke sitting here talking to a nice person on the phone. Forgive me for using a phrase that I don't use at home, bloke. I say guy, fella, dude.

PJ Well, I spent quite a few years living in Australia and they use bloke and mate all the time, whether they're referring to the inanimate objects, women, children or animals, it's mate.

JEJ Where in Australia?

PJ Sydney, and I worked with the Sydney Theatre Company and the Sandra Bates-led Ensemble Theatre Company and the Belvoir Theatre, also worked for SBS Television.

JEJ I went to Australia for a visit once and I liked it a lot. All the people who looked to be of colour, would refer to me as brother.

PJ Yes, that's 'Choice bro', more New Zealand, but not in the African-American sense.

JEJ Well, in the ethnic sense. And I never liked that. I have a brother, a half-brother, I don't have a real brother and I resent people putting themselves in the shoes of 'brother' first of all because they don't know me.

PJ That reminds me of a story my father once told me, that he was almost mugged in Nigeria, which is where he was from, a proud Yoruba man from Sagamu. One night while on his way home, this figure suddenly stepped out from the shadows and said to him, 'Hello, brother'. And my father's response was, 'and that's what your mother told you, is it?' Because he said, 'you are not my brother, how do I know you, you don't know me?' And it was the same sort of thought, he took exception to that familial assertion. Because, he said, this guy, he's about to relieve me of my personal possessions. And he's calling me brother!

JEJ I think I would have liked your father.

PJ I think so too. I'll always remember that story because he said he was horrified at the attempted persuasion in the immediate circumstance, it is exactly what you said, that feeling that we're brothers. We're not brothers, you're about to do me a sort of mortal harm and you are calling me 'brother'.

JEJ It's a phrase to disarm the other person, isn't it?

PJ Yes, that's right. Which leads me on to the next question, what motivated you to want to act?

JEJ My father is an actor. He's dead now but I still say he is. I wasn't close to him. I didn't meet him until I was twenty-five. I wasn't allowed to meet him. By that same grandmother who was fierce, because she felt he had betrayed her daughter.

PJ Okay, did he abandon her?

JEJ Yes, but it was more complex than that, it was 1931. The depression was ravaging the country. And I'm really fortunate that I was not raised by my parents. Because they were incapable of raising a child. They were incapable of fulfilling their own growth, and my grandparents were quite capable.

PJ So they became your parents, in a sense?

JEJ They were my parents. I still call them and recognize them as Mama and Papa even today.

PJ Okay, was it your father that sort of motivated you to act?

JEJ No, not really.

PJ I feel that there's sort of something missing. Prior to that. You said you met him late. But it wasn't necessarily him that provided the primary motivation for you to enter into the acting profession?

JEJ There was an absence. But I did meet him when I was an adult. And I wanted to explore acting myself. I can't say he drew me to it. He simply said I would have to love it if I am going to take up that as a profession, because it is difficult. He resorted with, not only Black, but the blacklisted. Because of his association with people like Paul Robeson, he, himself was called before the House Un-American Activities Committee, and pretty much blocked from any employment. Certainly, in film and television he could not work. It was a tactic, a practice to deny people an opportunity of making a living, it was a form of emasculation.

PJ And in view of that, or in spite of that, which actor or actors have exerted the strongest influence on you?

JEJ None, not even my father. I think he was a good actor. And we worked a lot together. But I in no way wanted to be like anyone. Although I admired many people. I admire Sidney Poitier, I admired Marlon Brando, and the Book, showed the path to certain choices. I did not want to be a disciple of men. I resented people of the former generation being godfather to the 'new' crop of actors. There were teachers that were trained to teach acting and I don't think other actors should do that job.

They could show by example perhaps, or they can aspire, but they should train as a teacher. I tend not to listen to them. Directors I listen to. I can't say I have a role model, nor do I intend to be a role model ever.

PJ Why is that?

JEJ I don't believe in it. I think if you put a role model up for yourself, you have blocked your own light, your own energy. Because every person, every human being has within him the light to be very unique and if you pattern yourself after someone else that can set you back. I came up in the generation.

I'll mention Marlon Brando. Two actors who were captive of his style for a while – Richard Harris, was raised over here (in the UK) and I've worked with, I love Richard, and Paul Newman, who was from America. They both were Marlon Brando clones for a while. Then they found their own stride, their own style, they bloomed, they blossomed, but not until they stopped being Marlon Brando clones, you know.

PJ We had a similar couple of actors like that generation here in the UK with Olivier, they wanted to be like him, rather than finding their own way and the training was modified around that.

JEJ Who wanted to be like Olivier?

PJ Certain actors of that generation. Yes, they did the same thing.

There's another actor, Sir John Gielgud, who didn't want to be like him, and he carved his own niche by being himself, he trained at the Royal Academy of Dramatic Art. And there were other actors of that generation who did the same thing. And it took them a while to find their feet because everything was couched in terms of what did Olivier do, then, if you want to be considered a serious actor they you must 'act' like that also.

JEJ Do you think the casting had a lot to with that? That the casting director would say I want an Olivier type or I want a Brando type?

PJ Yes, I think very much so.

JEJ I think you are right.

PJ Especially in the classics. And I think that sort of held back some great actors, held them back professionally, because of that limitation. Black British actors did not even get a look in. There are quite a number of actors now, older actors that are saying that there was more than one way to skin a cat, but I wasn't prepared to say that at the time because I would have risked professional suicide. So, it's quite an interesting point that you make. What has been your most challenging role to date?

JEJ Well, I don't like the word challenge, because I think it is more fun than a struggle. It is play and you play with yourself, you play with your feelings you play with your mind. You let your mind play with the dialogue. The dialogue is fairly sacred, I believe, but it's also not set in stone. And you have to learn how to break it up. If you memorize it, go into it and break up the sentences as they are structured, just to see what it sounds like. To break up a pattern, because then maybe something else hidden in the pattern appears to be on the page. I guess Tyrone Guthrie came from this country (UK), but he had a big influence on the US and Canada.

He founded the Stratford Shakespeare festival in Canada, the theatre in Minneapolis, the Tyrone Guthrie theatre. He once gave a lecture in New York I had the good fortune to attend. And he just said that a play as written is like the tip of the iceberg. And every iceberg has beneath the surface of the water a mass. And if it's a play, that means its a mass of humanity that barely gets touched. So every director, every actor that goes into that play is in touch with that mass. Although it's not on the page, you have meaning, you have words, you have ideas that are not on the page, but they exist in the mass of humanity. And your relating to that, as you say, the dialogue was simple, singular character, nothing is alone, none of us are alone.

PJ My dad used to say 'I was born alone. What's your problem?' when we used to rail against life and its vicissitudes.

JEJ Okay yeah, I wouldn't argue with him about that. Yet at the same time, we're not alone. One piece of advice my father gave me about the role of Othello, for instance. If you take that role on that it's a very moral man, in spite of how the play ends he is a very endowed human being. Probably the most spiritually, mentally evolved human being in the whole universe of the play. Of the business at the time, he is better than anyone on that stage and the problem is he knows it. Therefore, he is responsible for everyone on that stage. He's like a sun God. So, when he falls apart, he's taking his whole universe with him. And the actor has to be aware of that responsibility, my father would advise me before taking the role on. He would say clean up your act. If you're involved in anything negative either by the way you behave or the way you treat other people, clean it up, because they will block your ability to play that character.

PJ Going on from that then, how would you define acting?

JEJ Trying to track with your person the life of an imaginary person and trying to make him as real as you can and that's quite a task. Not just the realism, but to bring to life a human being that also has conceived the old folk presentation of a God in Adam, he moulded the clay and then he blew the breath of life into Adam. Well, the actors are the breath of life.

PJ You have spent the last few months living and working in London. Have you found performing in the UK different to performing in America, how much research do you do for a role?

JEJ I love it, I love it. Right now I'm reading a lot about personas of the Cold War period in America. The political characters because I've done a play about that period of professional American politics. It's all I can do is to read those books. Other wonderful books are like records, wonderful books come out in the reviews everyday, and I can't keep up with them.

PJ Do you find it difficult to move between live performance film and voice-over work?

JEJ I don't know. I just try to learn how to do both the best I can. I'm trained for the stage. And I'm still really a novice at film acting. And I say that sincerely. I don't know quite what I'm doing and I really rely on a good director.

PJ What would you say are your strengths?

JEJ I don't know yet … I don't know if I have a strength.

PJ Do you have any acting ambitions?

JEJ I don't hanker, there aren't any roles that I am dying to do, that I hanker to do. They'll come along or not and I'll be ready for them as they do.

PJ Is there anyone you'd particularly like to work with who you haven't had an opportunity to yet, a role and or a director?

JEJ I can't know a director unless I work with them. I can't read about a director in a review and know him enough to say I would like to work with them. There are people I admire from their work. But not enough to say yeah, that's the one for me, or I don't know if this one is for me.

I've had experiences on the stage, not in film, I've had no experiences in film yet. I worked with a director once in a little movie called *Soul Man*.

That was done quite a while ago. And I was able to confess to him that I didn't know what I was doing on close-ups, I tended to really fall apart on close-ups to freeze. He said well, all I know what to do to help you is to do a lot of close-ups, to do more than usual to see if that would help. And it did, it did indeed help.

All I know is if I could be as unselfconscious as Robert De Niro or Al Pacino, I think could be happy doing a film. But that same lack of self-consciousness would work as well on the stage, except you can't be as unconscious on stage because you have to make sure you're talking loud enough for people to hear you and yet be aware of light. On film they'll fix the light for you.

PJ That's right, they'll even fix the shot too. You've worked and been incredibly successful with your voice and the quality of your voice, and what you can do with it. Do you feel that that's something actors really should focus on more?

JEJ I don't know, I think we're all going to sound different if we are trying to be as strict with ourselves as we can. But we'll all be unique I hope, but our main job is to be clear and that's my best advice for young people who come from ethnic cultures.

There was a time when I didn't speak at all. And that was the time of listening. I was very young and it was a good time to be a listener. And then there was a time when I really wanted to say something to express myself and also to say wonderful things that other people wrote like Shakespeare. I had my uncle, we were farmers, we were out in the field one day and I heard my uncle recite Anthony's funeral speech for Caesar. I had never heard Shakespeare before and he made it very musical, he didn't put it in the vernacular of Black farmers, he made it very clear and I loved it and I was curious about Shakespeare from then on. It's such a great speech, it's designed to make you mad, to arouse, to move you to action. That play is often completely misunderstood when it comes to performance and study. You asked about an actor's focus; as I said earlier, I was raised by my grandparents, not society raised, in pursuing my career I didn't expect to change people's minds, I worked hard to change their hearts, the way they feel.

Paterson Joseph

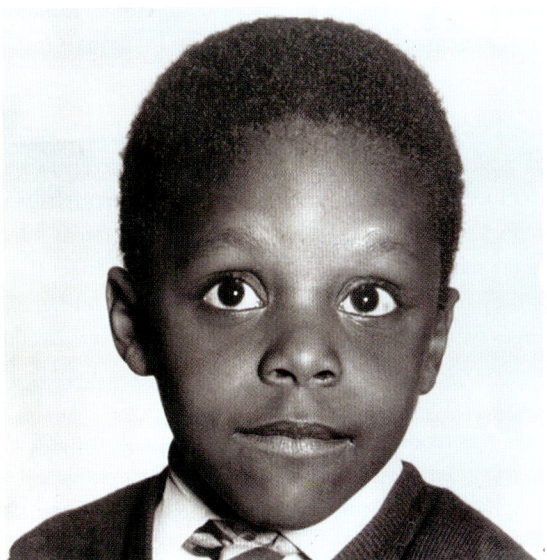 

Left: School 1970. Picture credit unavailable. *Right*: Photographer: Paterson Joseph.

Paterson Joseph is an actor and writer. He has performed extensively on British and American stages and on television, in *Vigil* and *Noughts and Crosses*, *Peep Show*, *Timeless* and as Samuel Wells in the BBC thriller *Boat Story,* and on film as Arthur Slugworth in Paul King's (2023) *Wonka*. Writing includes *Sancho – An Act of Remembrance*, *Julius Caesar and Me – Exploring Shakespeare's African Play* and his debut novel *The Secret Diaries of Charles Ignatius Sancho*.

Pamela Jikiemi Tell me about your journey to becoming an actor.

Paterson Joseph Wow. Gosh. It should be an easy answer, shouldn't it?

No, there's a lot of ins and outs and jiggery pokery. I would just advise anybody if they actually are interested in the details of my story to read a book that I wrote, called *Julius Caesar and Me – Exploring Shakespeare's African* play (published Bloomsbury 2018).

It was written for younger people to see the journey that I was on, I'm a son of two people who had come from St Lucia in the Caribbean in 1956/57. And we lived in decent circumstances, we were working class, had decent council housing, in Willesden Green, which is in north-west London.

I got kind of obsessed with language for two reasons. I've got older siblings – not that much older, my elder brother's five years older and then I've got three sisters between me and him, and a sister who's ten years younger than me.

But at the time, when I was about three – I didn't know this till later – my mother sat us down and said no more Creole in the house. So, I became obsessed, I think, with language. I have a couple of memories of running around and saying, mummy, how do you say table in Patois? Mummy, how do you say this in Patois? Mummy, how – and her getting annoyed and me clocking that even at three and a half, this is preschool.

And then I got to school, and I remember being asked 'what did you have for Sunday lunch?' and I went 'rice and peas' and they all laughed. Because, you know, Irish kids they don't know about rice and peas. But I carried on anyway, with a little fierceness in me. And I went, yeah, then we had salad with lettuce, tomato, kukumba – cucumber. And I didn't even know what kukumba meant. I don't even know why I said kukumba. But kukumba is Creole, St Lucian Creole, for cucumber.

I became language obsessed (with language), word obsessed in particular. Although I could read very early, I was part of that generation, that if you watch *Subnormal: A British Scandal* (available on BBC iPlayer) it is a crystal clear documentary by Lyttanya Shannon (Steve McQueen is Executive Producer), about how African and Caribbean kids in Britain in the 1960s and 70s were labelled 'educationally subnormal' and then as part of an unofficial segregation policy moved out of mainstream schools by the state. Regardless of the fact that they hadn't been tested or they came from a land where they had different languages. They were bilingual. But it wouldn't have been recognized because their languages weren't respected by the colonial powers in the Caribbean.

Pamela That happened to me, Paterson. At three years old I was reading, my mum was a language obsessive, my dad was a mathematical genius so we were drilled from a very early age on the expected direction of career travel and what would be required to get there. I was coached by my dad for the 11+ to within an inch of my life and the lives of quite a few wooden spoons, we all were. Yet I somehow managed to be labelled Educationally Sub-Normal (ESN) and segregated out to a 'special school' and the white kids in my junior state school class, some who still could not actually read somehow managed to avoid the same fate and get offered a place at a local comprehensive. My parents were not having any of it and they took on additional jobs and I did the entrance exam for a number of prestigious senior schools, which was very stressful at eleven, especially while carrying a deep sense of failure, that I had somehow let my parents down. But I knew I had aced those verbal and non-verbal papers, I knew it, but the school I was sent to, I would not have needed to take the test in the first place. No grammer school, but the ESN special school. I was accepted into all of private/independent schools I took entrance exams for. The formidable headmistress of the boarding school I then went to which had been opened by Queen Mary in 1925 and granted a royal charter in 1928, Mrs Freda Hatton, told me and my mother that my English essay was one of the best she had ever read.

Watching my parents work around the clock, sometimes doing three jobs to educate us all, sacrificing so much so that we could have choices in life via education, took me thirty years to process and recognize the educational apartheid that was taking place and how much it cost my parents, who, as a team, reeled from the injustice of it with all their might, so that we could survive, thrive and have a future, to be better than them.

Pamela Training around learning 'the craft'; did you go to a conservatoire drama school? Talk about your creative career and your commitment towards pursuing it.

Paterson I got to about eighteen, and I decided to go to a youth theatre called The Cockpit, which is in Marylebone. And I was very grateful for that place, this is in the early 80s.

Because a body which was called the London Education Authority (LEA) used to give money to youth theatres, and youth projects. I met people like – well, I met Lenny there. Lenny James. He was about seventeen, I think, when we first met, and we just did plays that summer and I got the bug.

I left my job which was at the Royal Free in Hampstead Heath as a trainee cook, because they were messing me about a bit. And I thought, let me do this. Let me try this.

I knew nothing. I opened *The Stage*, this is the stupidity of a man, I was trying to get at, I opened *The Stage* newspaper at the bit that I knew had drama schools in it. And they weren't all the great drama schools, by the way, who advertised in *The Stage*. And I closed my eyes, Pamela, and I put my finger on Studio 68 of Theatre Arts. And that's where I went for about a year and a half. Now, I advise anybody to just go talk to somebody. Don't do what I did. When I left the Studio 68, and I worked for a bit as a clerk for solicitors, which was just fascinating. Because you go to the Inns of Court, and it's theatre in the Inns of Court in London, just go in there. You can walk in there. It's another world. So, I did that for a year.

I applied for London Academy of Music and Dramatic Art (LAMDA), because I liked its Alexander technique. And because I was obsessed with people like Constantin Stanislavski and Jerzy Grotowski. The idea of working with my body really helped me – persuaded me to do it. So, I applied for them and another drama school that I also think doesn't exist any more. I can't even remember what it was called.

So, I know nothing. I know nobody. I've just gone to youth theatre. And I've just decided I'm going to go to drama school because I've heard people talking about drama school. So, I want to go to drama school. One of my sisters, Pam says, 'oh, don't go to drama school, you'll just end up playing slaves and servants'. And of course that bit in me was like, well, really. Let me just have a look at this. I thought, let me do it, let me do it. And then if they stop me, they're going to have to stop me because I'm good. Not because I'm not – I can do these things.

And so, you hear all the things that people say about Black actors, 'oh, they can't do the classics', and, 'oh, they don't have the physiognomy', 'you see, their tongues are too big', 'their lips are too big', 'their mouth shape is wrong', 'they don't have the same timbre', 'they can't do Shakespeare'. I've heard that, I heard that when I was coming through.

But anyway, I went to LAMDA, and I got in. So, that was me. I purposefully didn't apply to the Royal Academy of Dramatic Art (RADA). Why? Because I thought people who go to RADA, are like people who go to Oxford. Just put your certificate down. People go, oh, yeah, come in. Right. No, I wanted to be treated on my own merit. Anyway, I applied to LAMDA. And that's where I went.

Pamela What did you get from your actor training?

Paterson My confidence grew as a person; I became more and more articulate and bold about speaking out. And acting – even if I hadn't become an actor, if something had happened, and I decided not to do it. It gave me a voice that I would not have had otherwise, I'm certain of that. I was always told to be quiet, you know, we are that generation. And you're a Black kid, you don't want to stand out and all the rest of the nonsense that happens when you're in a society where you are the minority ethnicity, and a disparaged minority too, because I'm a child of the 80s. So, you get Thatcherite Britain, which is very heavily policing African Caribbean youths and people in general. We had the Deptford fire eighteen people died in the fire and, you know, 'eighteen dead, nothing said', was because the papers were all like, oh, they must have been criminals, it was just an eighteen-year-old's party and it ended in a tragedy, multiple tragedies. But we marched on the street. The Fleet Street newspapers, which used to be there screamed out of a window, abuse. I mean, we lived in a very dark time. We had the Brixton and general riots around the place. Because the police were oppressing us everywhere. So, I was very conscious politically about my position. And also conscious that there were certain places we were not meant to go. And we policed ourselves as well.

At LAMDA we had three Black kids, and one kid who didn't know he was half Black. He didn't find that out till he was about forty, I think. But we thought – Carl was half Indian. I think he thought he was just half Indian.

And then there was no other minority ethnicities. We did identify as Black. So, it was three of us, and, you know, yeah, you felt it, you did feel it. And the year above us, had no Black people in it. The year above that, had one, Patrick Robinson. And the year below us had two Black girls, and I think the year that came in next had none. So, that's the period. We're talking about the 1980s.

I went to LAMDA in '86. And all the way into – touching the 90s – because I left in '88 – it was pretty threadbare. And then you get the next generation coming in in the 90s. And they had already thankfully changed the regime there. So, they had it pretty good.

And as far as I know, they were all treated decently, apart from – well, one guy who left early, so I think he again suffered from the, not getting a certificate thing. But he – I don't think he would give a toss. But I don't know. You would have to ask him.

But I feel like that was a tough time. But at the same time, I knew that Lenny James was at Guildhall School of Music and Drama (Guildhall). I had a friend at Central, and a partner at Central School of Speech and Drama (Central) who had just left. The wonderful Cecilia Noble. Amazing. Cecilia, tremendous. She introduced me to Central kids. So, I sort of saw people like – Jimmy Nesbitt and various other sort of actors who became quite well known. But it was a really interesting to see them develop.

I remember I had another friend at RADA. So, we went to see people like David Harewood. He was like a big star already even though he hadn't left drama school. And Adrian came back two years later – but actually, it felt like we were a cohort, even though we never did any jobs together. Because there's only one, there's only ever allowed to be 'one'.

So – we never really worked together. But I knew they were there. And I hope they knew I was there. And we were pushing. We were pushing something. We were a little bit more gimme it, than the previous generation, of course. And the previous generation had suffered. They had suffered. Those kids who were late 70s, early 80s. They suffered. I was lucky. Yeah, I got some damage. But boy, they were devastated because drama school is hard.

Listen, you're a kid. Okay, I'm fifty-eight. So, I can say this, sorry, you're twenty something, your twenty and you are going to a place where you have already been self-examining because you're coming into your adult life. Who am I? What am I going to be? Am I going to be like my parents, or I'm going to do something different? What's happening? Where am I going? You're being influenced by these new friends that you're meeting who are from everywhere, when you go to university or – you are making major decisions, but you are also self-conscious. And you're an actor. Oh my gosh, what a terrible combination. Because now, not only are you going, is my nose too big? Are my ears in the wrong place? What are my eyes like? I wish my lips weren't like this. I wish my hair was better – and suddenly you've got a whole class of people doing the same thing to each other, not meanly. But oh, you're going up there doing Lady Macbeth. Oh, yeah. But she was walking awkwardly. Or the teacher might say, yes, why are you walking like that or why are you sitting like that. Why is your hair like this? Why are your hands moving? You're already self-conscious to the nth degree. And now you're putting yourself in this. That's why people went a bit bonkers at drama school. And then, you know, you might leave drama school and you're still young, and people are still doing it. Acting is a very vulnerable profession to be in. And we're not the strongest – we're not necessarily the strongest people on the planet. We are artists in the open. So, it's a quite a particular place. Nowadays there is a bit more pastoral care. But back in the day, my God.

Pamela What drives you? Looking at issues of employability, how do you navigate this?

Paterson Yeah, it's a difficult question because, look, it's an irrational profession as somebody wisely said. It doesn't work like any other business. It's not, oh, you've done that. So, therefore, you'll do this bigger thing. And then we'll do this bigger thing until you're doing this massive thing. No, you'll do this big thing. And then you'll do nothing for a while. And then you do this tiny thing, and then another big thing, then another bigger thing and then another tiny thing. Our profession is really erratic, it can't be trusted. Fashions come; fashions go. Oh, they want girls who are very pale and look like English roses. No, they want somebody with a little bit of colour in their skin. They want dark-haired girls; those are the ones. Oh, they want blondes, they want big girls, they want thin girls. They want tall girls; they want … you cannot second guess. So, all I've learned to do, when at my best, is go … this is what the role is. I – I've studied it. I've nailed it for myself, in my own room, like this is how I feel this character would be, this is how I would do it if I rehearsed it. Now, with what I know, with these two pages or with these – you know, half a script that they have given me. And I go and deliver that. What's going on the other side of the table, none of your business. What's happening to the observers, how are they observing it, none of your business. All you need to concentrate on is bringing your gift.

Pamela Is your preparation for a role different for theatre and screen?

Paterson No, I don't think so. I think I enjoy theatre more in terms of the preparation time because rehearsals are my favourite moment. Because in rehearsals, it's like kids in the nursery, you know, you're just making up stuff at its best. And again, I laugh a lot. And people laugh a lot when we work because that's the best place to create from in my opinion. Openness.

I don't fix much. I'll be where I need to be. But I tend to get into rehearsals, even if I had to – I've had to learn my lines, which people have asked me to do before because there is a short rehearsal period. I always make it malleable, so it's not fixed.

I don't know how I'm going to say it because I don't know what Cyril Nri, for example, in playing Cassius is going to give me. And by the way, when he started giving me what he gave me, it became a completely different domestic play to the, I am Brutus and I'm Cassius, it became like brothers. He was so passionate. And you can only get angry – if you have siblings, you'll know what I mean.

Only siblings can take you to that place where you lose your mind with anger, because you love them so much. But they're frustrated. And that I got with Cyril. But I wouldn't have got that if I had just gone, no, I've learned these lines and I know how he speaks. I know what this line says. And I'm going to do it.

So, I'm always open and malleable in rehearsals. That's my favourite moment. And then it sort of gets slightly spoilt for the week of tech and all of that, although I enjoy that too. But then the audience come in and they ruin it for a couple of days.

Pamela One of the recurring issues in the creative industry is the discussion around representation. How do you see your role in relation to that conversation?

Paterson I know Shakespeare, because I understood him without anybody telling me. So, he's actually for me, and he must be for everybody who can understand the English language, surely, because I understood it. And I hadn't even touched it. Nobody had ever talked to me about him. So, they're wrong about that. It isn't an Oxford Cambridge thing. It's a people thing. And then you find out more about Shakespeare and you find out that he loved to write for the people that they call the 'groundlings', the people – and there was like a double thing going on.

Out of the Black Box

A bit like *The Simpsons*, you know, the adults get one kind of humour, and the kids get another. And absolutely, he's undermining and making fun of that class difference all the time. He's addressing the groundlings. He's not leaving them out. Otherwise, they wouldn't come to the theatre would they?

So, give me Ibsen, even though Mike Leigh, our most famous, I suppose, director said to me during an interview when I was doing Torvald in Ibsen's *A Doll's House* with Anne Marie Duff at the Ambassador's, why are you doing that play? Huh. Why are you doing that play? Because it's a good play. It's *A Doll's House*. Yes, but why are you doing it? Oh, I thought in my head, oh, this is how this is going. I said, because it's a great role. Why, Mike? What do you mean? Well, you wouldn't be there would you, in Norway. I believe in people being and doing the things that they would be in and they would be there.

Now, because I did twenty years of research, I know that that's nonsense. There were Black people in Norway. In fact, there were Black people in every single European country. And I challenge you to defy that. And I can give you evidence, both artistic and historical. And in Norway, of course, and Sweden, there were some very famous Black people. But those were famous Black people. That doesn't mean that there weren't others. There would have been. Because every court in Europe had a Black servant or Black musicians or dancers, and are ignored by historians, because they're not important, but they're there.

But he didn't know that twenty years ago, and I didn't know enough by that point. I hadn't really gotten into my research.

And I said, listen, if you were playing Hamlet, you're not looking for someone who's Norwegian or Danish to look approximately like the Dane, you just get anybody. Ralph Fiennes isn't Danish. I was in his *Hamlet*. I played his Horatio. He's not Danish by any means. We suspend our disbelief, don't we? I mean, that's the whole point. It's not a documentary, we make believe, that's what we do. So, it doesn't matter as long as I'm capable of doing it. And that was the end of that conversation.

Then twenty years later, he called me back for an audition. And I went, does he know we had this conversation. Oh, no, he'll forget. First thing he said, so, I hear you have a problem with me. And I said, no, I don't have any problem with you. And by the way, I didn't want to have this conversation because we had this conversation twenty years ago, but I will tell you this, and because now I know twenty years of stuff, and I drilled it down. He was very silent and then went on to say, when I did *Peterloo* I purposefully didn't put any Black people in it. So, he had confessed to what many – and by the way, he's probably the more honest of them all. Well, over the thirty-odd years that I've been doing it, what many practitioners, white practitioners have said and Black people because they don't know, there weren't any Black people there. And so, this is the journey I've been on. It's, hey, I want to do this. Oh, you're not allowed. Well, I'm going to do it anyway. And I've done it. So, my thing is, there is a battle, but it's art. So, it's a difficult thing. Because if you go in with anger, and you act in fear or anger, that is not sustainable art. It is good for, you know, agitation propaganda, smack you in the face with something, I have no problem with that. But if you want something that's going to last, and we can watch it twenty years later, thirty to forty years later, it has to have a universal theme in it. And I want to do those plays, and – and hopefully see those plays written by all ethnicities, not just Europeans. And the problem really is the ignorance of our history, our world history, but definitely in Britain.

Pamela Thinking in terms of how you choose to identify, what do you think are the challenges in the acting/creative industry now?

Paterson So, you know the culture clash, class clash, all of that is part of our profession. Be real about it, it isn't easy. But you've got to find your way. And by the way, you will change, you must accept this, you will change. You will not be the same person from where you came from. So, if you don't want to change, then don't do it.

But my advice to you is, change can be good. It can be painful, but it can be good. And you can learn all sorts of things, that if you stayed where you were, you will not learn.

There'll be all sorts of adventures good or bad. But all sorts of adventures, mostly good that you will revel in by saying I'm going to be brave and let go of my fear – people say I shouldn't be – I'm not meant to be in here. I'm not – I'm not allowed to do this or that. Go for it.

Pamela What pitfalls should actors emerging from drama school aim to avoid?

Paterson Well, I suppose the idea that the profession is just going to open its doors and welcome you in. And here you are, and you'll be getting jobs all the time. You have to understand that that does happen to some people, and it will happen around you. But that doesn't mean anything because people can come bursting out and kill it for two or three years. And then they burst their bubble.

They've been seen. Or they're so young, that by the time they get to the place where they want to play mid-twenties people are like, we kind of see you as nineteen still. And so, take your time. There's plenty of time. This is a long career. It can be a long, long, long career, and curate it a little bit if you can. I know you're just trying to get a job, but curate it a little bit. If somebody says, oh, you know what; I really want to do a lot of classical plays. But oh, they've offered me this and it's money and it's telly.

Fine. Take it, take it, take it.

But if they go, oh, they've offered me these three years in *EastEnders*, I would question that. If you have just come out of drama school. Yeah, of course you can do it. Of course, you could do it. It would be fine; you'll probably be fine. But you'll learn a very specific set of skills for three whole years. Whereas if you're coming out, don't be in a rush, build yourself up. The longer you build yourself up, the longer you're going to be there. Longevity is key.

Pamela What motivates you to want to act and keep doing it?

Paterson I'm a laugher. I mean, I get on set and everybody's – we are laughing. I laugh – it might be you have to cry in the next scene. And I might be quiet for you know ten minutes before I have to do something. But otherwise, I'm just with people chatting, chatting, messing about, chatting. And then, oh, here we've got to do this.

Concentrate, do your thing. Do your thing. But I'm at work. I'm going to spend a third of my life here. Let me be relaxed. Let me be happy. Let me be with this community of people and – and we're lucky because we have a community of people who are so – oh, my gosh, open compared to many other professions.

And as long as you bring your skill and your excellence, you do your best that you can, you really don't have a lot to worry about. You know.

Pamela Who are the actors and directors that have inspired you?

Paterson I remember an older actor, Oscar James, a wonderful, wonderful Bajan actor. Previous generation. So, he would have been working in the 50s and 60s. Amazing. He said, 'huh, Black people, of course, we have to be – we have to be actors. We have to be actors, all of us actors init. We have to be. How else can we survive?'

Out of the Black Box

And I remember thinking, he is spot on. You adapt and survive in whatever environment you're in. It's ideal for being an actor. There's a kind of attention that you have when you're in that position.

Pamela If a young Black and Global Majority person of eighteen made the decision that they want to become an actor, what would your advice be?

Paterson I would say that is a great idea. But that it's very tough. And that you must be strong about rejection and do your research.

So, what kind of actor do you want to be? What do you mean? Do you want to do theatre stuff? Or are you not interested in theatre? Have you been to the theatre? Have you been to see good theatre?

Have you been to see theatre with people who you might connect with? Your age group, or you know, your ethnicity? Have you seen all sorts of theatre? Have you seen, you know, what you call posh theatre? Have you've been to the National Theatre?

Because they often have sometimes quite cheap tickets there.

I would say, get involved. Get into the world and see if you like it, get involved before you commit yourself to anything, obviously.

Look out for youth theatres. But just look them up online because they've got many courses. And you might be able to do a brief course, a short course.

Look at local courses; look at your local colleges. Just try it out first, because you might find what you really want to do is film because you like the way Denzel Washington acts or Viola Davis acts. But then you need to look at their story, read their autobiography or research them and see how they came through. Because a lot of people would have come through theatre.

Pamela Hard-dough bread, Sourdough bread, Chin Chin, Sweetbread, Roti, Sudsa, Bun and Cheese, Nai Wong Bao -奶黄包- Custard Bun or Naan?

Paterson I think if I was pushed, it would have to be Hard-dough and with some well-cooked baked beans. The trouble with people nowadays they just put the beans in the pan warm it up, that's not how our parents did it. They would cook that thing, like twice. So, it would be thick. It was like refried beans. It would taste good. So, yeah, that and a bit of Hard-dough. Maybe a little fried egg on top. Now, you've got me hungry. Am I hungry? I'm hungry. I have got to go.

David Oyelowo OBE

Photo: Austin Hargrave.

David Oyelowo OBE is a multiple Golden Globe, BAFTA, and Emmy-nominated actor and producer. Oyelowo made his directorial debut with the critically acclaimed *The Water Man*, in summer 2021. Oyelowo starred in the film, as well as produced under his Yoruba Saxon banner that he founded with his wife, Jessica. Yoruba Saxon is focused on creating values-based content, across all platforms and for all quadrants, with an aim to shift culture and colour outside the lines. Additionally, Oyelowo co-founded Mansa, the free streaming platform for curated global Black cultural content.

Pamela Jikiemi – PJ Tell me about your journey to becoming an actor.

David Oyelowo – DO My journey to becoming an actor was not the classic. It was very much framed by my Nigerian parents and their point of view in relation to the arts generally, but acting specifically around visibility.

They didn't see, I don't think enough evidence of success to warrant enthusiasm for me wanting to go into that. You know, in the early to mid-90s and, like most immigrant families or couples, they had moved to the UK for a better life, and a lot of that was tied to the future that they were hoping for their children.

I fell into acting, because I was invited to a theatre group by a girl in my church, I thought, you know, she was inviting me on a date and it was, unfortunately for me, not that. It was that they were low on boys at this theatre group and she was trying to basically get brownie points with the director by bringing boys to join the group.

I liked her enough that I kept on going. And, you know, a fateful tube strike is what led to the two guys who were being groomed to play the lead in this play that we were rehearsing, not being there. And I guess in the months that I'd been skulking in the corner, being very shy, I had been internalizing how I would do it, I guess. And so, the director just wanted a boy to stand up and do the male part. And I did it. And within a week, I was cast as the lead.

And that was the beginning of something that led to me going to drama school. But drama school, again, was not something I'd ever thought of. If I hadn't done that play, I wouldn't have taken theatre studies at A-level. I wouldn't have met Jill Foster, who saw in me an ability that she felt could be parlayed into a professional acting career.

And then she offered to help me with drama school application, which I didn't even know what that was, then I ended up getting a scholarship to London Academy of Music and Dramatic Art (LAMDA), which at least, was something to take to my parents who didn't understand the world of acting, but scholarship they at least understood.

So that became, oh, okay, so somebody's going to pay for your education for free. You know, that was like, get that. That's a win. And so, that's what led to me going to LAMDA. So, that was the sequence of events.

PJ Training around learning 'the craft'; did you go to a conservatoire drama school? Talk about your creative career and your commitment towards pursuing it.

DO I mean, auditioning, generally, I think is one of the hardest things and one of the most inefficient ways. In my opinion, it's the only way we have, and I haven't come up with a better way. But it's a pretty inefficient way at finding out who is truly gifted as an actor. But I do think – funnily enough, it was my audition at Rose Bruford, that was the most exhaustive one I can remember. Because it was the audition where you had to do a modern piece, a classical piece, a song, and then if you got called back, you had to do a workshop.

The workshop was truly terrifying because it felt like you were cattle in a pen that they were kind of whittling down to who is the thoroughbred.

Part of what is amazing about getting to act, especially if it's improvisation or you're doing a scene or whatever, is that you are there to serve the person that you are acting opposite, and hopefully that's reciprocated, which is what leads to a good scene.

But there was sort of this competitive edge to it, which is antithetical to what we're supposed to be doing. So, I did find that quite odd. But again, like I say, it's inefficient, but it was the way that process went.

Not everywhere did that. But yeah, you know, my recollection was that it was terrifying early on, but you sort of become a kind of a professional auditioner, you know, going from school to school and you know, pretty much the same pieces, the same song. And so that's the way it went. And, you know, I got into a few, which was a wonderful surprise.

But the true surprise was getting a scholarship to LAMDA. So, I think retrospectively – I'm looking at it through rose tinted glasses. I'm sure it was nightmarish at the time, but the fact that I got in, I think sort of makes it a little bit more palatable than it was.

PJ What did you get from your actor training?

DO I mean, again, looking at it retrospectively, I think if I hadn't got in anywhere, it would be indisputably a negative experience. But you know what I do remember, particularly in my LAMDA audition, getting that thing that isn't particularly useful as you go deeper into your career, i.e. you audition and it gets a very warm reception in the room and you're like, oh, yeah, this is happening. I've had plenty of auditions in my professional life where I thought it was a slam dunk. And no, that was not the case.

I did get a very warm reception, overtly so that was confidence inducing. And I think actually pretty soon after auditioning – it may even have been as I was walking out of the room; I was asked to come back.

So, it was instantaneously reciprocated with the feedback I thought I was getting.

I think it was pretty instant at LAMDA. So – so, yeah, it was – positive, definitely a positive experience.

PJ What drives you? Looking at issues of employability, how do you navigate this?

DO Well, you know, it's funny that we've kind of started this conversation talking about auditioning. I found the auditioning process earlier on in my career, especially moving out here to LA where it truly can feel like sort of a cattle call.

My drive was partly driven by never wanting to audition again. I was – I remember once going – walking into a waiting room and seeing several guys who of course look very demographically like me. And just feeling like this is humiliating, this is a nightmare. I know that there are people in this industry who get offers, that just must be so incredible. So, if you gave me twelve pages of dialogue to learn at 7 pm the night before a 9 am audition, I would stay up till 3 am, I would internalize the entire thing. I would be off book and I cannot hand on heart tell you that that was driven purely by wanting to get the job. It was about, you are going to give me this role, so that I get to the point where I never have to do this again. And that was a real thing for me. It was like a target because, you know, I've directed now and even as a director, I find that process just so debilitating for other people. We haven't found a better way of doing it.

But to your question, you know, early on in my career, those things were a driving force and then refusing to be boxed into whatever the notion of a Black role was, because I didn't see much evidence of anything that was Black.

So, especially on TV, that felt aspirational to me. You know, I had to look to America to see that. I had to see Denzel Washington or Will Smith or Jamie Foxx or Sidney Poitier or Morgan Freeman or Don Cheadle, to kind of go, that's the kind of role I want to play.

And early on in my career, I've said this before, but I read a formative interview with Denzel Washington where he said early on in his career, he said to his agents send me everything Harrison Ford is turning down and that became a mantra for me. Not send me anything that Harrison Ford is turning down, but the notion of, okay, where am I going to go to find three-dimensional, well-written, complex characters that are not hemmed in by the skin they are in.

And you know, I said to my reps, I want to see those scripts. I want the opportunity to go in and fight for those roles and colour-blind casting, as we now call it, was definitely not prevalent in the late 90s, early 2000s. But, you know, it culminated in me playing Danny Hunter in *Spooks*. And that was exactly the kind of opportunity I was looking for but, you know, it meant some door bashing to get there.

But, you know, I was at the RSC very early in my career, I was doing a play called *Oroonoko* which is an Aphra Behn play.

PJ I did that for BBC Radio 4 or 3 – I played Princess Imoinda with Leo Wringer as Oroonoko, one of my best experiences.

DO Oh, wow! Wow, wow, wow. Yeah. Nadine Marshall, I think, played that in our production. And, yeah, you know, I had an agent straight out of drama school. My agent became pregnant and decided to leave the business. So, I had to find a new agent. And my agent who has now been my agent for twenty-three/twenty-four years, and I love him to death. But our relationship began with him coming to see me in *Oroonoko* and me getting an answerphone message, with him saying, you know, what – just not looking to take on anyone right now. Enjoy the play but, you know, it's unfortunately going to be a pass for me.

I had really researched this, who I really wanted to be represented by, and I loved his list. I loved the boutique nature of the agency. And I had determined that he was going to be my agent. So, this was quite a shock for me. Because it was also a well-reviewed play. And I knew I was doing good work in it. And so, I called him. And I said, I think you're making a mistake. And I want the opportunity to prove to you that you are making a mistake. And he was so flummoxed by that, that he went, okay, let's give it a go. Let me send you up for a couple of things and see how that goes.

And like I said, he's been my agent ever since. And, that is the point I think you're making as well, which is that that's the dynamic, I'm not saying that's going to work every time. And you really have to have the goods for that to be how it plays out. But, you know – I think it's the Nigerian part of myself that was able to pick up the phone and do that. But if you're white and British, you have the luxury of being falsely humble. Like for us, you have just got to kick the door down. And that's what, you know, in working in America now for fifteen years. That's kind of innate here and celebrated actually.

PJ Is your preparation for a role different for theatre and screen?

DO Yeah, I mean, by virtue of the joy of being in a rehearsal room with fellow actors for weeks on end, going through the highs and the lows of discovering, then feeling like you don't know anything and then discovering again and feeling like there is no show. And then oh, my gosh, we may have a show. And then, oh, my goodness, we're about to show it to an audience. But that being a collaborative communal experience is why I think theatre is truly special.

The sheer amount of learning, if you are open to receiving it with theatre, I think you cannot compare it to film. Because every night you are gathering data as to what is working by virtue of the spiritual and emotional exchange between actor and story, and audience and their imbibing of what you're doing.

It's an unspoken thing, but it's what informs how you do it slightly differently the next night, and then how you do it when you have a cold, and how you do it when you really don't want to be there at all. And you know that muscle memory to me is what makes an actor.

Whereas with film, you are a lot of the time, combating things that depend on the environment you're in – but that really challenges your ability to do that same thing. Like theatre gives you a sacred space within which to tell a story, film often gives you a chaotic space in which you're supposed to somehow find the truth in a way that is intimate enough that this machine is going to capture and cut out any perception by the audience that it was captured in the midst of chaos, and distraction, and pressure tied to money and time.

That's why I truly believe some of the best film actors in the world have come from theatre, because they know from muscle memory, what a three-dimensional presentation of a character feels like, given that sacred space in which to do it. And then you go into this space where you have a light in your face, a boom in your face, a camera in your face. The gaffer is scratching his bum. There's someone, you know, talking over there. A plane went over in your best take, and you're supposed to still deliver.

That comes from, in my opinion, the kind of muscle memory an athlete has, when they know when the gun goes, their body goes into this sort of automatic thing. But they're also reacting to okay, I think I'm ahead, oh, I'm falling behind. You know, it's a combination of the two things, and theatre gives you that muscle memory.

So, you know, in terms of preparation, I take the best of what I learnt about preparing in theatre, apply it to film and TV in order to give myself the best shot at telling the truth, given the specifics of the challenges that both film and TV present.

PJ The industry and your place in it?

DO One of the things I enjoy the most about where I currently am in my career is being an advocate. Because I have been advocated for. I know, I'm standing on the shoulders of people who didn't get as much opportunity, as much notoriety, as much visibility, as I've been afforded by virtue of where they came in the timeline.

There is definitely a before and after, in relation to the George Floyd of it all.

And that's what I mean about the timeline. The amount of actors who came along to slowly erode the notion that – of what we can and can't do. And then it culminates for a moment in what I'm afforded the opportunity to do. Where I have a transcendent blessing of an experience to do a film with someone like Oprah Winfrey, who then becomes an advocate and an advisor, and a mother figure to me from that point on. Whereby she literally says to me, I want you to learn from my experiences, so that you don't make some of the mistakes I've made. I mean, I simply don't know another human being on the planet who you would rather say that to you than her. And that is something I've been afforded in my life as a person, as a man and as an artist. And so, having been a beneficiary of moments like that, that have had a direct correlation to my growth as an actor and an artist, what I'm now trying to do is as a producer, as someone who's been given a platform like who am I blowing the hinges off the door for, so that they can walk through. So, that's one of the things for me I enjoy the most. Directing a film like *The Water Man*, and having someone like Lonnie Chavis play the lead, an eleven-year old African-American boy, who when I was younger in those kinds of adventure fantasy films, I never saw someone who looked like me.

There is definitely a before and after, in relation to my own specific career, there was a before and after, in relation to playing Henry VI at the Royal Shakespeare Company, you know, in terms of a before and after.

Postscript: David Oyelowo was only two years out of drama school when he was approached by the Royal Shakespeare Company (RSC) to play the lead in *Henry VI*, *Parts I*, *II* and *III*, when the company continued its monumental two-year run through Shakespeare's Histories – entitled *This England*. The RSC cast David in the role of the English monarch for the first time in its forty-year history. This coincided with Adrian Lester (RADA Graduate) preparing to play one of the most coveted roles of Hamlet for the director Peter Brook in Paris. Lester at the time resided in America due to the dearth of roles for Black and Global Majority actors in the UK. Hugh Quarshie was the first Black Hotspur on a British stage when he took over from Timothy Dalton in *Henry IV* in 1983 for the RSC.

PJ One of the recurring issues in the creative industries is the discussion around representation. How do you see your role in relation to that conversation?

DO I think a world in which you see Leticia Wright, John Boyega, Daniel Kaluuya and you see Damson Idris, and then, a generation above, Idris Elba, that didn't exist in the 90s.

Out of the Black Box

From a global success point of view, from a big cinematic point of view, I go back to the UK, and I go to the theatre, and it's just amazing the amount of African names I will see in a theatre programme.

When I went out before I became an actor, that was an impossibility from an expectation point of view. And so, when my name started appearing in theatre programmes, you know, it was just complete brain damage for people to go, why are all these vowels and consonants bumping up against each other in this last name in a way that I've never seen before.

Because, again, they hadn't seen it before, necessarily. But now there is real evidence of success. And that I think that has really changed the dynamic. So, you know, I imagine if I was starting out, now, my parents would have a very different attitude, I think.

PJ Thinking in terms of how you choose to identify, what do you think are the challenges in the acting/creative industry now?

DO There is a difference between the Black and Brown actors and the white actors, by taking certain roles that deep in your heart, you know, you don't want to do or you shouldn't do.

Often those roles are erosive to the culture. They are erosive to the unfortunate circumstance we find ourselves in as Black people, which is that this incredibly potent and powerful medium that is screen storytelling is also informing people's perception about who we are as Africans, as Black people, as a Global Majority – majority is a word that has only recently in my world entered the lexicon. But it is certainly not how it plays out in western filmmaking and television. That is not the perception you would have if you were an alien who dropped on this earth.

PJ What pitfalls should actors emerging from drama school aim to avoid?

DO Oh, good question. Well, one of the things they don't teach you at drama school, which I don't know if it's changed, is like money. Like you've got to pay taxes, you got to manage your money.

And because drama school can sometimes be, or feel like, it's this kind of microcosm of what the industry is like. But it's not, it's a completely different thing. When I was at drama school, they weren't teaching you screen acting in the way that I believe they are doing more of now and you could come out of drama school, having done only theatre, and you spend the next five years on a movie set, or on a TV show.

You don't know what a mark is, you don't know where to look, you don't know what the lenses are. So, the pitfalls for me are just to try in some way if your drama school hasn't provided those things to get that knowledge. Money being one.

I've known so many people who just didn't realize that as a self-employed person, you have to put some money aside for tax. You know, you have to manage money. Then, you know, the pitfall that we've already talked about – your attitude towards your agents and auditioning.

Your job as an actor who's auditioning is to transport the director to the film set, that's your job – because no director likes auditioning actors. That's not what they became a director to do; they became a director to be on a set with the cameras there capturing lightning in a bottle and your job is to transport that lightning in a bottle that they're hoping to see on a film set or a TV set into the audition room.

You cannot do that if you don't know the lines, you cannot do that if you haven't done the work, if someone comes to audition for me, and they are holding pages in their hand, they are not getting the job. It's pure and simple. Because what you're telegraphing to me is that you're not going to be prepared and I may have to – I'm not saying it's fair, but I may have to give you new lines on the day.

I need to know that you can do that miraculous thing we as actors have to do, which is internalize those lines, and then convert them into something that is showable to a global audience. And so, that's also one of the pitfalls.

You think that you can just go in and, you know, be reading and like – like, I'm sorry – I remember once I was auditioning for a show, it was in the UK, and an actor who I had admired growing up, went in before me. So, that was already like my brain was melting at the fact that this dude was in there before me for this role and this was one of those instances where I'd stayed up till 3 am to learn the lines.

For whatever reason, they gave everyone the lines super late, and it was like kind of a nightmare. But I could hear his audition while I sat outside. And he didn't – not only did he not know the lines, but he was so frustrated at not knowing the lines, that he just kept on swearing in there at himself. I was like, damn, that's not the way to get the job and I ended up getting that job.

I simply should not have got that job in relation to who went in before me. If you showed 1,000 people my face and his face and ask them who would be getting the job. 1,000 people would say that guy who I've seen in all these other things is getting the job. But purely on the basis of performance in the room, I know, I got the job. So, that's, again, one of the pitfalls. You must be prepared; you must know that your job is to be the best version of yourself in this very competitive landscape all the time.

PJ What motivates you to want to act and keep doing it?

DO The indisputable cultural impact of storytelling. I mean, there's a reason why Barack Obama, 44th President of the United States, has a deal at Netflix.

You know, you go from being the most powerful man on the planet, to now being a storyteller. And as someone who is frustrated when humanity isn't learning from past lessons, as someone who is frustrated when I see prejudices being perpetuated and being the cause of so many of our problems. I know, I have felt first-hand how those prejudices – how that learning can break perceptions down in a way that actually, whether it'd be a drop in the ocean, or a bit of a bucket in the ocean, moves the needle when it comes to helping humanity be its best self.

I mean, I have literally seen that. I saw that with a film I did, Mira Nair's (2016) *Queen of Katwe*, I definitely saw that with Ava DuVernay's (2015) *Selma*, I saw that with a film I did Amma Asante's (2016) *A United Kingdom*.

I've done films where I've seen people's perception shift on the basis of showing them something that they didn't know exists like an eleven-year-old chess prodigy in a slum in Katwe, Uganda. And little white girls in Idaho, taking up chess because of that dark-skinned girl who they would never feel they had anything in common with.

That is the thing that really drives my continued passion for this – for this art form.

PJ What are your broad aims for the future of your screen acting presence?

DO I mean, there's a lot I haven't done that I still want to do. You don't know which way your career is going to go, and therefore what the perception about you is going to be so, I've built a reputation unwittingly of being a serious actor who does important roles. And so, when people see me in a comedy, it's always like, whoa, this is a different speed for you.

But people who know me know I'm a goof and it's not that much of a stretch to be in something a bit more light. So, you know, for me, it's to keep the audience guessing. I never want to be someone who goes, oh, they're a serious actor. They're a comedic actor. They're an action actor. They play historical figures. They do horror movies.

Christian Bale is one of my favourite actors as well because he can do the gamut and he can be excellent at the gamut, whether it's serious, comedic, action, drama, whatever it is. He's chameleonic. I think that's one of the main things, is keeping the audience guessing. And continuing the remit I've set myself; to contextualize Black life for a global audience.

The way to do that is to play a myriad of roles that maybe defy expectation of what someone like me is doing out in the world. I mean, who we are as Black people in the world is so much more complex, layered and fantastic than we get to see on the screen and to platform more of that. I mean, for me, global storytelling wise, Africa remains the sleeping giant.

Yes, we have Nollywood and all that kind of stuff. But between the landscape, the people, the untapped stories, the things we haven't seen yet, the oral traditions that have these amazing stories that we haven't yet found a way to give to a global audience, the history that isn't just tied to dictators and famine and civil war, but that are transcendent, aspirational love stories.

You know that continent for me, which I love so much and done some of the work I'm most proud of within, is a big target for me in terms of what I want to see going forward.

So, yeah, there's so much I still want to do. In some ways, I still feel like I'm at the beginning. But, you know, the reality is I'm probably very firmly in the middle of what will be my career.

PJ Who are the actors and directors that have inspired you?

DO I definitely looked up to Paterson Joseph, David Harewood and Lenny James, as great actors who I could see the quality of their work. But in my opinion, I didn't feel like they were being given roles commensurate with their talent.

Daniel Day-Lewis is my favourite actor of all time, Meryl Streep and Sidney Poitier. And, you know, with all of those actors, to me the reason why I love their work is because you can feel that they have gone to their character. They have yielded to something and what you are watching is something that is simply unattainable without giving yourself to something.

And that, to me is the difference between a true actor and a movie star. You know, movie stars, by and large tend to bring the character to them, in order to continue to exploit and monetize the persona that the audience has gravitated towards. They have that 'it' thing and that's fine. If that's a way to go.

But to me, the actors, whether it be Cate Blanchett, or Kate Winslet, or those guys I've just – just mentioned, or Saoirse Ronan, Andrew Garfield, Chadwick Boseman, when he was still with us. You know, these are actors who you can feel themselves, giving themselves over. Daniel Kaluuya is another. And that, to me is when you get transcendent work.

PJ If a young Black and Global Majority person of eighteen made the decision that they want to become an actor, what would your advice be?

DO I say this to everyone who asks that question of me, and I feel it more so now than I ever have done. It is such a difficult industry. It is such a competitive landscape in which to try to be an actor, especially with the explosion of social media and reality TV, and the cult of celebrity, where the lines are now blurred in relation to who's the storyteller.

Who's the person who should be in a movie or not? Should it be the pop star? Should it be the reality star? Should it be the social media influencer? Should it be the trained actor? It's only gotten more competitive.

Thankfully, there is more appetite for what we make. But there's also more competition.

So, my thing is, don't do it, unless it's the only thing you want to do. Because that is what keeps you going in the midst of the rejection, the frustration, the feelings of just being lost at times.

And that's not only tied to failure, it's tied to success; fame has its own challenges. The pressure of being in a big budget movie has its own downside or being in a play that is – playing Hamlet has its own completely unique difficulties of dealing with all the people who've gone before you, who've played that role.

It's not for the faint of heart. And if you're going to do it properly – and I always say to anyone who really wants to do it properly, please train. One of my sons is seriously considering an acting career, I've said, the one thing I ask of you is that you train.

Because it puts you in the top five – 2 to 5 per cent, in my opinion, especially out here in Hollywood, where you can be good-looking, and you can surf through for about five years before you get found out and they move onto the next good-looking person.

PJ Hard-dough bread, Sourdough bread, Chin Chin, Sweetbread, Roti, Sudsa, Bun and Cheese, Nai Wong Bao -奶黄包- Custard Bun or Naan?

DO Oh, Chin Chin, all day, every day. Now, I'm salivating – why would you do that to me?

Priyanga Burford

Photographer: Michael Shelford.

Priyanga Burford's film work includes *No Time to Die* and *Star Wars – The Last Jedi*. She was also cut from *Detective Pikachu* because her face was too distracting alongside a Pokémon … Theatre credits include leading roles at The Royal Court, The National Theatre, Chichester Festival Theatre, and the RSC. On television, Priyanga has worked long and hard to avoid playing the generic Asian doctor and has triumphantly played the Asian banker/lawyer instead. Most notably in HBO's *Industry, The Thick of It, Avenue 5*. Her work as a writer-director has garnered a Best Screenwriter and a nomination for Best Director at Rome's 2022 Prisma Film Festival. She is Co-founder and director of Dawn Chorus films.

Pamela Jikiemi – PJ Tell me about your journey to become an actor.

Priyanga Burford – PB I'm sure for a lot of people you've spoken to of my vintage it was tricky, because I didn't have that many – any people who look like me to watch.

I had never been inside a theatre before or watched a play. And that experience was the thing that made me want to be an actor. I'd always sort of done school plays and stuff like that, like a lot of people. I was really massively encouraged by my drama teacher at school. But it was never for me going to be considered as a viable career option.

My family were professionals, it's a fairly typical immigrant story of come over here and do well financially. So, that means you get your head down, be academic, work hard, get good grades, do something like a traditional kind of high-earning profession. And that was fine because I was academically pretty good at school and stuff.

But really, it was when I went to university that I really started doing drama in the university, drama societies and stuff, that I felt this huge pull. I felt that I could finally consider it as a real option.

So, going back to when I was seventeen. What happened was, I wasn't doing English A-level but my best friend was, and there was a spare place on the theatre trip for the A-level English students. And my friend said, do you want to come? And my English teacher who was really upset that I hadn't done English A-level said, you have got to come, you will love it. And I just went, yeah, okay. And then it was only after I had said yes that I found out they were going to see *Hamlet* at the National Theatre in London. I had done Shakespeare for GCSE. But I didn't know what *Hamlet* was. And then they told me it's going to be three hours. And I – my heart just sank. And I thought, oh God, this is going to be so boring.

And so, got there, watched and it was that famous production, which I found out later, was Ian Charleson, who had taken over from Daniel Day-Lewis, after he'd had what was allegedly quite a serious breakdown, directed by Richard Eyre. And I watched it, and it just completely blew me away. And that was such a powerful experience being in that theatre. It was such a moving and powerful experience that I had one of those massive moments that don't come very often in life where you just go, I am not coming back from this. I can't go home and pretend and go on, like I was before. So, I actually changed my A-levels or wanted to. I set off a bomb in my family. They were really unhappy. I was unhappy, because they were unhappy.

Anyway, I ended up carrying on with the same A-levels, and then took a year out and did two more A-levels in the subjects I actually wanted to do. Then I went to university and studied English Literature, which was not the original plan. It was at uni I started getting into drama. I also started applying to drama schools, I didn't tell anyone I was auditioning for drama schools.

PJ Training around learning 'the craft'; did you go to a conservatoire drama school? Talk about your creative career and your commitment towards pursuing it.

PB I went to my audition for Royal Academy of Dramatic Art (RADA) and London Academy of Music and Dramatic Art (LAMDA) and Royal Central School of Speech and Drama (Central), because those were the ones I knew about. I'd sent off for prospectuses to come to my uni address. So I took the coach down to London. And it was when I got through to the final round at RADA that I thought, oh, no, now I've got through to the last round, I had better tell my parents. So, I told them, I've been auditioning for drama schools, and it was, what are you talking about? And it was just a really difficult time. Because there were no artists in our family. This is not something we did. And then – yeah, so then I got into LAMDA. My parents are really lovely people, they were just coming from a totally different world.

PJ What did you get from your actor training?

PB I know, not everyone has this, but I had the most fantastic year of people that we are still in touch now. And I really couldn't have asked for a nicer bunch of people to be training with.

I made friends for life, definitely. And that was the other thing to – to meet other people, all with the same passion as me. But also, with very different skills. Like meeting people who were just – absolutely had funny bones, completely natural comedians, it was just pouring out of them. And for me, that was such a pleasure.

I thought, wow! Look at this person; they're clearly just made to do that thing. And then just incredibly talented singers, and people who just could do sword fighting, which I was absolutely terrible at. And so again, it was I had a peer group, a gifted peer group, which was also really, really valuable.

The other person who got the other scholarship was David Oyelowo. And we were in the same year together. So, he was there. And there was another mixed-race Pakistani British actress. And actually, in our year, that was pretty much it. I mean, yeah, for our year that was it. But actually, that seemed like quite good to me at the time.

PJ What drives you? Looking at issues of employability, how do you navigate this?

PB I think I'm still learning to navigate it. I'll tell you one of the things that really used to get to me until maybe about sort of five to ten years ago, was this thing of progression, right. So, I felt like the white contemporaries of mine spent the first ten years of their career, career building, and building on talent and success. And when they had proven themselves were given more to do. Whereas I felt for the first ten years of my career, I was always doing it for the first time and having to show people, no, I can actually do this, that it wasn't a fluke the last time. So, that feeling went on for a really long time, which I found really, really frustrating.

I think what I have discovered is writing my own stuff and trying to make my own stuff is really important even if it doesn't get made, it's like creatively, an outlet. And when I first left drama school, people were just not happy to listen. And I had a few experiences where people got really annoyed with me if I brought up, 'can I be seen for this role instead' sort of conversations, it was absolutely rejected out of hand. And I'm sure other people you've talked to have probably said, you know, I got the whole thing of like, oh, we don't think the audience is ready to see that. And if you pushed back on that with, well, who do you think your audience is then, you clearly don't think there are any Black or Brown people in your audience, they would get quite annoyed.

And as a woman as well. I was told really stupid, ridiculous things. Like I was once told by an early agent, dial down the intelligence when you go to auditions because it's intimidating for male directors, if you come across as too clever clogs. So, alright, you want me to pretend to be thick? Okay, I'll try.

PJ Is your preparation for a role different for theatre and screen?

PB No, not really. I do the same amount of work and the same kinds of stuff. And also depending on the role – you know, I don't have the same process for every role.

There are things which I learned back in drama school, and it's particular roles you'll go, oh yeah, that's what that – the animal thing we did is. Actually, that would work for this one. And it's probably not relevant for another one.

PJ How do you decide what roles to go for?

PB What I am offered. I do try – I mean, what's relevant for our conversation is I am very aware that there's been a very long tradition of South Asian women presented as being quiet, subservient, dainty, sort of fragile, and sort of exoticized and romanticized. And I am as aware as I can be in the choices I make that I want to sort of not do that if I can.

Just say, no, there's something else going on as well. And I also, if I can, I like to play the bad guy. Because I think that's also a weird thing about like, oh, well, if we're going to have a Black or Brown person, they have to be good. Which is also completely a misrepresentation, you know.

PJ The industry and your place in it?

Gosh, I don't know. I don't know about that. I would hope that the tiny blip that I've made on the timeline of life in the industry, means that people coming up behind me, might have seen me on the telly when they were little, or a teenager or something and gone, oh, okay. Yeah, alright.

Maybe I could do this. Yeah, perhaps the best thing I could have done thus far in my work is just shown that there are possibilities. And that those possibilities can become realities for people who look like me.

PJ One of the recurring issues in the creative industries is the discussion around representation. How do you see your role in relation to that conversation?

PB One of my things is sometimes when you're in a room, or in a place, you don't even have to say anything, is what I've found. Sometimes just turning up is the statement you need to make. So, there are some contexts in which just my face being there means that I don't even need to do anything or say anything.

There's just been a bunch of assumptions made that need to be let go of, not just about who can do what role, but also about who is watching. And who is consuming the material. I don't think it's okay to still assume that, for example, classical drama, classical theatre is consumed by one group of people. I don't think it's okay to assume that if you're going to do a Greek tragedy, the whole audience is going to be white. There's something wrong with that assumption.

PJ Thinking in terms of how you choose to identify, what do you think are the challenges in the acting/creative industry now?

PB Until very recently, there were very few stories where we were included. And the storylines were very samey. And biased – there's nothing wrong with them because they were about arranged marriages and stuff like that, which is part of the South Asian diaspora that does happen. But it, like, isn't the only thing that happens.

I think the challenges are still the same as they always were, just being seen as an equal, with equal potential, with equal talent, with equal ability to tackle a variety of different roles, a variety of different texts.

PJ What pitfalls should actors emerging from drama school aim to avoid?

PB Oh, my gosh, so many. Oh, dear.

That relationship with agents is so key. And yeah, it's important, there's a big balance to be struck between, you obviously want someone who's got connections and clout, and will be seeing the scripts, and have the contacts. But you also want someone who you can genuinely relate to. Because if you're unhappy, there's no point having someone who you can't talk to about that, on a professional level. If you're professionally unhappy.

And then an agent is more than that, as well. I mean, people have different ideas about agents. I mean, some people – some actors do have their agents as their best mate. Whereas for other people, they want to keep it very professional. And that's all fine. But the common denominator is you've got to be able to communicate. And you've got to be able to at least share a vision about what you want, and what's available and possible and all of that kind of thing.

PJ What motivates you to want to act and keep doing it?

PB The feat of sort of self-motivation, the engine that you have to drive inside to keep going, I don't think anyone fully appreciates the size that engine has to be to carry on in the face of that. Because what you're doing is you're really facing directly into the hurricane and there are not the voices or the sight of people around you, where you're looking at a screen or looking at a stage going, it's okay, there's – there's 300 of me that I've seen this week doing this.

You're looking and you're going, there is nobody like me doing this. And – and I'll tell you another odd kind of consequence of this, which is unintended, but it can go one of two ways I found, when there are very few of you.

Sometimes when there are very few of you, there's a real sense of camaraderie and support. And come on, man, it's just you and me; let's keep going together, let's support each other. Or – which I've also experienced, there's a real – there's only – there's only one.

PJ What are your broad aims for the future of your screen acting presences?

PB Well, I have completed making my first short film, which I wrote and directed recently and am on my way to completing my second. I would really like to carry on doing that. And making stories in that way. And for me, acting wise, it's all about the roles now, for me.

Everyone needs money, of course, that – that is always the case. But I am saying no to things, which I never really used to feel like I could do. But the odd one still comes along of would you like to play two scenes as a police officer interviewing someone. And I go, no. Why would I do that? It's not interesting. There are other roles in this which you could see me for? So, my hope is to do just what everyone else wants to do who's an actor, emotionally complex, layered characters, who give me something to chew on. And as an actor, give me something difficult to do. I want to do difficult roles. I want to do stuff which I find hard.

PJ Who are the actors and directors that have inspired you?

PB There are different kinds of inspiration that I've had from different kinds of people. So, in terms of artistry, I think of people like Anthony Hopkins who does the most amazing screen acting, I think.

But in terms of – of keeping going, I have to say it's mostly people younger than me, which is a funny thing to say. But I meet young actors, and they really inspire me. Or I see younger actors who are like fifteen to twenty years junior to me, and I find them truly inspiring.

Like Daniel Kaluuya, or people like that. And they're so strong and so full of energy and fire. And also hungry to be creatively different and complicated. They're making really interesting choices.

I find those guys and women really inspiring. I actually feed off their energy. Just watching them, watching what they're doing. And honestly, it's all the youngsters coming up who really inspire me.

PJ If a young Black and Global Majority person of eighteen made the decision that they want to become an actor, what would your advice be?

PB Do it, without fear or doubt. Do it! If you love it, do it. And work really hard.

Take all the opportunities. The real true opportunities that come to feed your creative artistry, to be challenged to nurture and hone your gift, to refine it. And go for it. Yeah, seriously, go for it. And don't be reticent or don't doubt yourself. You know that unlike me and you, they have many inspirational figures now or many more, at least, to look at.

The doors are opening. And one thing I would definitely say is, we belong everywhere. So, this impression of who belongs where, well, a Black actress that I was talking to a couple of years ago, when British Academy of Film and Television Arts (BAFTA) were doing this drive and I said you should – you should apply for BAFTA. And she said to me, oh, I don't know if I belong there. And I was so sad that she said that. And I just want people to feel like everyone belongs everywhere.

Everyone belongs everywhere. There is no room that we don't get to be in and there is no stage that we don't get to walk on and there is no role in terms of production, directing, writing, camera team, sound team, design/art department, producing, financing, we belong everywhere. So, I was trying to recruit diverse crew. And we think in front of the camera is bad, behind the camera is shocking. So, go everywhere. That's what I'd say.

PJ Hard-dough bread, Sourdough bread, Chin Chin, Sweetbread, Roti, Sudsa, Bun and Cheese, Nai Wong Bao -奶黄包- Custard Bun or Naan?

PB Yeah, Roti. I can't help it.

CHAPTER 2
LUCIAN MSAMATI, NOMA DUMEZWENI, JENNY JULES AND COLIN SALMON

Keywords/concepts: Curiosity → resilience → instincts → mentors → truthfulness → planning

No one is you and that's your super power.

Lucian Msamati

Photographer: John Holloway Photography.

Lucian Msamati is an award-winning actor, writer and director in theatre, film and television. His theatre work includes Salieri in the Oliver-Award winning revival of *Amadeus* (2017–18) at the National Theatre. On screen he is best known as J. L. B. Matekoni in the BBC/HBO adaptation of the beloved *No. 1 Ladies' Detective Agency* novels, pirate lord Salladhor Saan in HBO's era-defining hit *Game of Thrones*, George Chichester in the BBC/FX series *Taboo*, and mob boss Ed Dumani in the Emmy-award-winning Sky Atlantic/AMC action series *Gangs of London*. In 2019, Lucian won the Royal Television Society (RTS) Award for Best Actor and the Screen Nation Award for Best Actor for both his role in *Kiri* and the role of David Runihura in the BBC/Netflix series *Black Earth Rising*. Lucian is a founding member of Zimbabwe's acclaimed Over the Edge theatre company.

Pamela Jikiemi – PJ Tell me about your journey to become an actor.

Lucian Msamati – LM So my 'journey', quote, unquote, I suppose begins when, according to my mother and my late father, and when I was a toddler, three, four. And there was a family gathering that had some friends visiting and one of the uncles or visitors asked me as the little, talkative toddler, 'what do you want to be when you grow up?' And apparently, I turned around and said to him, I want to be an actor 'aaaargggghhhh' this said accompanied with the Incredible Hulk pose.

Little did they know. Little did they know. But, some of my earliest memories are of watching *Grease*, which is so vivid in my head. And I remember not only loving the music, but also going, these people are having such a good time. They're having such a good time. I want to do this. Another film, strangely, and I don't know what business my parents had letting me watch such a film at such an early age. But Roger Moore in *Live and Let Die*, I remember being completely terrified by the Baron Samedi character, you know, terrified, but also just 'Wow!' what is this? Also the scene where he has his magnetic watch. That's how young I was, watching, going,

Wow, what a cool thing you can do with a watch. Yes, you can take zip down! It was only years later, and I was like, oh, that's what's going on. So, those are the early, the earliest seeds of it.

But through all of this I remember at the age of about nine, at primary school in Zimbabwe, getting up on the dais at the front of the classroom. It was something to do with English, and we made up some sketch. And it was like, dare I be so so extra, as my daughter would say.

But there was a moment of me standing up there in front of the class, and I distinctly had the feeling of going I know how to do this. I've got this. This is where I'm supposed to be. And that was that. You know and it has been a lifelong love affair. It's a lifelong love affair.

It's a very something that, you know, once again, I cannot back you and praise you and support you enough, Pamela. Because I think the work you are doing with this is the beginning of an entire canon of work about the relationship, we the bastard children of the British Empire.

So much of it is ours. And yet we're told it's not ours. So much of it is, is wrong, and yet still a part of us believes that it's right.

And but that's also the truth of it. This is the ugly, complex spaghetti of truth. You know, it is intertwined and intermingled and you can't just pull out one strand and say, well, it's this, and ignore the rest of the bowl.

It's a company, it's appreciating that that mega dish.

My family is from Tanzania. I grew up in Zimbabwe. I was born in the UK, towards the end of my parents' time here. Interestingly, talking about the immigrant story, my mother and my late father lived and worked in the UK from approximately 1972 until 1983, so about ten to eleven years, they have never lived and worked in the UK since. They've visited, for work purposes, now that all of their children and grandchildren are here, there's been holidays. But in terms of the immigrant experience, this is another thing that doesn't get fully explored that there are a lot of people who come take their goods, go.

So I mean, that's a little sort of addendum to my story. We returned to Tanzania, in the early 80s. But that happened to coincide with Zimbabwe turning independent, and Zimbabwe was the boom town of Africa.

The front line against apartheid South Africa. And they were very adamant and very keen to have Black African expatriates. There's another story in that as well about those who went overseas, as it were, got their training, got the education got everything, came back home, to rebuild, and were rejected. It's the layers, the rejection, and these resentments, the jealousies, all of these delicious, dark, ugly human nuances.

But, as a result of that, when Zimbabwe came calling, we went. When people asked me where I was from, for decades, when I started to tell my story, people's eyes would glaze over. So it got to a point where I would say, Well, I'm Zimbabwean, even though those who have an eagle eye on an eagle ear, or who even bothered would go, Msamati, that's not Zimbabwean, it's not Zimbabwe.

That is where I grew up. I started high school in Zimbabwe. I was at university in Zimbabwe, I started my first jobs were in Zimbabwe, started my career in Zimbabwe, that is, my soul nation, that is my home. Of course, Tanzania is home in a sense, of course. England is home in a sense. But Zimbabwe is the country that has shaped me and formed me the most.

We are the golden generation, we were truly global citizens. At that time, the adult literacy rate of Zimbabwe was higher than that of the United States. I'm a beneficiary of that. Good schools, a good education, had cultural programmes, did school festivals and school plays, the facilities were there. I was a good student. I was exposed to a lot of things, we are the generation that had Zimbabwe at its best. Absolute best.

Of course, people don't want to hear that from an African point of view, it doesn't fit.

What do you mean the Mugabe of land reform? You are all supposed to be bare arsed, that's one side of the story. That's a little titbit of a strand of the spaghetti that you have picked out and gone, this is the one, I'm going to make this the entirety of the story. But at the same time, I'm trying to knit all these nuances together, please, excuse me. I think the generation of my parents were the liberation generation.

They were the first, who am I'm sure you've heard this countless times. It's such a typical lecture from my late father, who was an incredibly accomplished man. Before he died, he was inducted into the Tanzanian Academy of Sciences.

My parents were part are the deliberation generation. And whether actively or not, that generation were the first, they were the ones who, in some ways, bore the greatest, most brutal brunt. We, are, even though technically, in Zimbabwe terms, I'm not 'a born free' as in born after 1980, but as close as. We are sort of the first, the post-colonial generation, the, ones who reaped the benefit. And the problem is that I think you go from liberation. And the immediate desire is consolidation. Let us consolidate what we have. What we have won. What does that mean? It means that even though we are born with aspirations, no, no, no, here, here are your aspirations, doctor, lawyer, clerk, engineer, accountant, priests, like, hold on? What? What do you mean actor? That's a hobby, it's not a real job all that. And there are many friends, again, of my generation of people I grew up with who nowadays will come and see shows or get in touch, say, man, you know, seeing you not only am I proud, but there's that little bit of like, ah, I didn't, I didn't have the courage to pursue it as you did.

I'm appreciating that actually. I don't think that I have any more or less courage than anyone else. But what I did do was take the full brunt of the choice that I made.

And one goes through one's own journey of transformation and it was an incredible journey of learning for me, and I kind of had to go, well okay, if you want to make this your career, you're going to have to do it yourself. There are not going to be any hands that are going to help you, you're going to do it, have to do it yourself. We never know how the story is going to unfold. But it is in those moments that the resilience is built that the understanding that when you've been rejected seventeen times, you're like, fine, I can handle it. I can, you know, I was rejected by my family.

But of course, in later life, you come to realize that they will never, they will never be evil demons. No, it was all about them wanting you to be safe, to be happy, to be financially secure.

I will never forget my late father saying at the time that, you might as well have said that you wanted to go to the moon on foot. Because these things were so far removed. Yes, we all loved music. We watched our movies, we had our favourite, read magazines. But that was a world away from us. It was fantasyland. You know, that's not real. That's not something you do for a living, no, no.

PJ Training around learning 'the craft'; did you go to a conservatoire drama school? Talk about your creative career and your commitment towards pursuing it.

LM As a consequence of that I am not formally trained as an actor. But I've always said to people that when you are enthusiastic about something, when you have a passion, you are already looking with different eyes.

I remember sitting with my late brother, we'd be watching things going, 'Oh, did you see the boom was in the shot? Did you see that? Okay, rewind rewind', the days of VHS 'rewind, rewind'.

Did you see, oh, wow, hey, you remember in that scene? Why did she have a cigarette? But she doesn't have one in the next one? Yeah, I think we were already going, Oh, why is this film not working? It's not funny, this is really bad, it shouldn't be funny. You know, all of these things. And because, again, coupled with having drama school, you could practice the silly voices, the singing, doing school plays that was my training ground. That's how I, that's how I started.

And because you have that seed of curiosity, you start looking naturally, you're looking elsewhere? Naturally, you are already going I want to find out more about this? Who is that person? Where do I go to find out that was like, Oh, that how does that person do that with their body? It was in my early teens, when the light of the spirit hit hard.

When I realized actually, you know what? This is what I want to do, I don't want to do anything else. I really want to make a go of this thing because it fulfils me like nothing else. I can feel it in me, that this is what I'm supposed to be doing. And I believe that, I can see myself there. These people that I love, I can see myself there. We formed a theatre company called Over the Edge, myself and friends that I was with at school. And we were part of a Youth Theatre Company group.

So there's the Reps Theatre in Harare in Zimbabwe, which is the oldest, established, semi-professional theatre in the country. Of course, it was predominantly white. That did change over time. They had a group called Rep Teens. So they had the Preps, which was for the kids in Rep Teens, was from sort of thirteen to, I think nineteen to twenty. The great gift for Rep Teens, it was that in the main summer school holidays, I think it was August. The Rep Teens got to have a two week slot to do a play on the Reps mainstage, it seated just under 400. So I basically spent my teenage years in a theatre with all the dumb crazy things that teenagers get up to, but mine was spent in the theatre in and around the theatre, making theatre playing, you know, that was my happy place. But it is also as I got older, you know, as you started to appreciate that some of Zimbabwe's finest actors, because this is a relatively small country, even of its finest actors, we had very few who were full-time professional.

So everybody was pretty much semi-professional, or amateur. But what I loved, what I learned from it was that nobody got paid a penny. The only people who received a salary were basically the theatre staff who ran the building. Those who ran the bars, who ran the office, who ran the wardrobe, who ran the workshops, who built the sets, they were and I think the Artistic Director was also, that was their full-time job. But pretty much everyone else, no one got paid. And so, I grew up seeing dentists, lawyers, teachers, accountants, radio presenters who from nine to five would be in their day job. From six until eleven, they were in the theatre. And on Saturdays it was either you're rehearsing during the day, or you're rehearsing, and then you do the matinee. And you do the evening. So I learned my craft, watching, and working with people for whom it was really their passion. And some people were incredibly skilled. I mean, some people who you're like, wow, in another lifetime, and another way you would have been a megastar.

But I also got to learn the value of not making pressure in your art to also be your main source of income. And it's something again, which I counsel, it's when I talk about this in the book, amateur dramatics gets a bad rap. Of course, there are some extremes where it's like egos, and you know, people who don't know any better. But there are some incredibly passionate, skilled, brilliant, creative artists who love this as much as we do. And practice it with the same rigour, the same interest, the same passion and dedication, without making it their sole source of income, which means that they can do it for the pure love of it and enjoy it.

Out of the Black Box

I'm very proud to say that, I remember doing an exercise with a group of students once and I said, think of the worst thing that could ever happen to you on stage in front of a live audience.

PJ And tell me what it is.

LM And I'm going to tell you now absolutely everything that you could think of, the absolute worst, your actor's nightmare. I've experienced it in front of a paying audience. That is, that is how I learned my craft as an actor. Like missing an entrance, drying, the most extreme debilitating corpsing, everything. I've been heckled. I've been pelted on stage. That is how I've learned my craft.

You don't get anywhere by talking about it or by reading about it. And I think this is the advice I try also to give to those who haven't formally trained, and those who have formally trained, is that no actor that I know ever got a job because they read Stanislavski.

PJ What drives you? Looking at issues of employability, how do you navigate this?

LM Having grown up and worked somewhere where everybody looked like me. The first time I ever heard the term Black actor was twenty years ago, when I worked here. I didn't know what that meant. But I was an actor. I very quickly learned what it meant.

But for me, and I said this to my agent. I said, I have not come here to clean toilets. And I've not come here to be the third spear carrier on the left. I came here for the throne. That's my dream. I'm not going to be content with 'but you know, you must be this role'. Like, no, no, no. I don't care about *Othello*, I don't even like a *Othello* as a play. That's not my aspiration to play Othello. I'm much more interested in playing Juliet, actually. Because that's a challenge as an actor. And so, I suppose I'm also the beneficiary of a culture change, at a time when this country was opening up its eyes. At a time when I remember friends of mine saying, when I first moved here, the likes of Nikki Amuka-Bird – I remember the first time we ever met at a play reading, and I said that I had just come from Zimbabwe and this is what I want to do. I guess the other important thing, the important thing to say is that I arrived by professional journey in this country, I arrived already fully formed as an artist. I had a career. I had success. I was established. I wasn't, I wasn't green. I wasn't, you know, I wasn't 'Johnny just come'. I knew my stuff. I had been at festivals. I've been there. I've done, I performed. I knew my, my onions.

I came in the early noughties. So between 1998 and 2003. Over the Edge, we were at the Edinburgh Fringe Festival regularly. And London was a very convenient stopping-off point for all the international festivals. So we did festivals in Germany. We performed in the States. So we were always here. And eventually our work was spotted in Edinburgh and we were invited to The Blue Elephant Theatre in Camberwell and it was Antonio Ribeiro. I love Antonio forever. Antonio saw us in Edinburgh and said I have to bring you guys to London. Your work is brilliant. And we're a small theatre. We were buzzing, like London, London baby London. I'm very proud to say that we were part of the growth and birth of the Blue Elephant Theatre in Camberwell, off of that because the show did very well. We were invited to the Battersea Arts Centre Timeout Critics Choice Season. So, we came back and it was during that run that the late Maggie Lunn, the casting director for the Almeida Theatre, at the time, saw the play and went oh, you know we're casting a play by Antony Sher, it's his first play for the Almeida and we think there's a part that you'd be up for? Would you be willing to audition for it?

Me, I am like what, this is the dream, this is the dream, this is the dream.

Interestingly, that audition at the time. I mean, there were months between us getting the email coming back, at the time I was staying with a friend in Bristol and I went up to London early I was so nervous. I arrived very early in King's Cross. I arrived stupidly early. I sat in a park across from Almeida early in the morning, wrapped up but I didn't want to be late. I walked in, there was Maggie Lunn, the late Sir Anthony and Nancy Meckler the director. We had a great chat, a great laugh, I read they loved it. Then they said 'so you know that the character has that high-stamping Zulu dance?'

Can you do it? And I said you know, I can dance a bit haha laugh, laugh, laugh, laugh, laugh. I stopped laughing and they were literally sitting there looking at me like this, okay, all with deadpan expressions. And it was at that moment, right, bro, better get up and shake your natural arse. So I got up I turned around.

Now, we've just recently done a collaboration with a company from Bulawayo called Khaya Arts, and Feel Good Theatre in Manchester. We were part of the Commonwealth festival. Khaya are all brilliant, the dancers and actors, and we had learned all these dances. So I got up, turned around and thought, right, okay, by the time I get to the back wall of this room, I'm going to turn around and dance my arse off. So I turn around, and I dance my ass off. And I finished it, knowing in myself, you're going. I know that if the guys were sitting here watching me, they would either laugh, or they would pelt me, pelt me, because I know, but strong and wrong is better than not at all.

So, I'm thankful for those moments when that's in your toolbox. That is what craft is, it gives you a toolbox to be able to deal with the situation. So I did that. And that was that was it. That was the beginning of, you know, the near touch wood twenty-year career that I've had in this country. I have made it to the place I said I was going to make it. And I remember meeting up again with the lovely Nikki Amuka-Bird saying you did it, because I'll be honest with you when you first met we were like, eh, okay, good luck brother.

PJ Thinking in terms of how you choose to identify, what do you think are the challenges in the acting/creative industry now?

LM Am I any less or more capable than anyone else? No.

Am I more or less hardworking? No.

Talented? No.

In the end, it's about my own vision. My own dedication to the craft and the belief that I have in myself. And the thing is, belief in oneself isn't about arrogance, people get it wrong. The belief and confidence I have is because I've worked at it. Not showing up, how many auditions have I been in, how many actors have I worked with where I've gone, I can see them coming, the gift of experience is, you can see them coming. When you go you have no idea, you thought it would show up here with your frosting. And it's, come on, I hold myself to a high standard and I'm always checking in with myself. I'm always going look, have I matched my standards? And I have made sure that there's a handful of friends, a handful of people, who I know because we trust each other, love each other, know each other and believe in each other, we keep each other right. We keep each other honest.

PJ What motivates you to want to act and keep doing it?

LM I had a, I had a TV audition few years ago, and again talk about the tests. I walked in. The casting director was very happy to see me, oh great, we've wanted you for so long. I met the director. It was all great. So we literally sat there, he had my CV. He looked at it and put it down. He said, so what have you been in lately? We're literally a day or two from the end of *Amadeus* (the first time round). My ego was going, Wow! How dare you, do you know who I am?

You know, so that was literally my ego going what? Is that fully someone asking me what?

Then I was like, you know what, to myself, dude, these are film, TV people they want to know about you. He doesn't know he – the way he looked at that. He wants to know what have you done?

Are you still hungry? Yes. You still want it. You still have the fight in you. Because if you have the fight in you, come as you are. And so in that nought point nought two seconds. I was back in the room.

PJ If a young Black and Global Majority person of eighteen made the decision that they want to become an actor, what would your advice be?

LM I would say go for it. But it's a hard road. And you need to work on your craft. If you want to be famous, forget it. If you want to be famous, learn your favourite nursery rhyme backwards. Paint your face and green film yourself on YouTube or Instagram on Snapchat, put yourself on there, you'll be famous. But if you want to be an actor, it's a long road. It's a long game. And the gift is that when you get to the place you see yourself or want to be, you will have the tools to keep you there. That's what practice and craft is all about.

The traditional training that is still being taught is producing very much the same type of performer. And it is very much a type of performer who is suitable for one type of market. And who is suitable for one particular box. And so my question is, my, provocation to you is, what do you want?

What do you want? I don't, I couldn't tell you who went to which school, what I will look at and see is are you capable?

What is it that you're training people to do, to feel? I'm not saying change how you speak, change how you look, but I've got to be able to hear you. You have got to know what to do with your body. You have got to understand the words that you are saying. Training cannot keep doing this, you know, auto the auto effect? Because the effect disappears its gone. it's like, we want the cake, not the icing.

PJ Hard-dough bread, Sourdough bread, Chin Chin, Sweetbread, Roti, Sudsa, Bun and Cheese, Nai Wong Bao -奶黄包- Custard Bun or Naan?

LM Yeah, the above, all of the above.

Noma Dumezweni

Photographer: Helen Murray.

Noma Dumezweni is a two-time Olivier-Award winner for Ruth in *A Raisin in the Sun* for the Young Vic and Hermione in *Harry Potter and the Cursed Child* in the West End. Theatre includes productions at the RSC, the Royal Court, the Donmar, the Almeida, and many fringe, pub, promenade and Edinburgh festival productions across the years. Film and television work include – *ReEntry*, *The Little Mermaid*, *Retribution*, *The Watcher*, *Made For Love*, *The Undoing*, *Normal People* and *Black Earth Rising*.

Pamela Jikiemi – PJ Tell me about your journey to become an actor.

Noma Dumezweni – ND Oh my God, this is a long journey. Journey to becoming an actor, immigrant child arriving in Suffolk finding youth theatre just as a sense of play on Sunday afternoon, Mum very happy that I found somewhere to go and enjoy. And then realizing that these are kind of my people as it were this tribe of youth theatre makers, but didn't know I was going to do it.

But then going oh let me audition for drama school. So then auditioned for drama school at eighteen, didn't get in, didn't get in two years running, auditioned for RADA, LAMDA, Guildhall, Drama Centre, maybe I did Central once, those are the big ones.

And then ended up getting a job as a receptionist in a PR company called Lynne Frank's PR. Which the characters in Jennifer Saunders's BBC comedy *Absolutely Fabulous* are loosely based on, which is very funny.

Thought that was going to be my career, I was going to work myself up from reception, to newspaper cuttings person, to assistant in the post room.

And I remember kind of being asked to potentially to join an account as their assistant, their PA, I was so excited. And within a month being one of the seven people made redundant. Like my whole life changed, what the fuck?

But then it was like, okay, so what do I want to do? And this is the joy of that time because we could sign on and not feel stressed and not feel that you've got to do it in a very short time. And you also don't have to explain that you're an artist in a way. Now you have to explain that, that you're an artist in a way that's really confusing for people who don't know what we do. That's what I find with people who are artists signing on now, because it's not tangible for people.

Anyway, so it was this sense of going, what do I want to do? And is that oh, let me go back to the acting thing. And maybe trying to audition again a bit later. But just as I started working doing workshop script reading at City Lit. I did an improvisation class at Jackson's Lane that the Fletcher brothers, Dexter Fletcher and his brothers were running.

I was kind of in my mid-twenties. There were a lot of people a lot younger than me but I was having a lovely time just kind of trying to figure out what it was. And then I did this thing called the Casting Couch, run by this woman called Moira and I can't remember the last name. But that's where I ended up meeting my mentor, who is now eighty-seven years old.

Tony, he was fifty-seven, so I've known him for thirty years. And he's the one who made me believe that I could do it. I didn't necessarily have to go to drama school. But yes, I had the talent to do it. And he said, If you want to work with me, because it was Moira, she put you through to this next stage, and then if she liked you, she got Tony to work with you. And if Tony liked you then you went through to the evening. And it was an evening of directors, casting directors, agents, just seeing people doing little monologues here and there and stuff like that. And yeah, it was Tony, the most important thing I'd say, I got Tony out of that. And he was an older, ex RADA-trained actor.

Anthony Singleton, Tony Singleton, A-N-T-H-O-N-Y, with an H, I always have to say. But yeah, even now I speak to him going, oh, there's this offer of potential Shakespeare, what do you think? We go through it, we talk through it together.

I'm going to be heartbroken the day he goes, because I know that day's coming as all life is, but when someone has been so fun to be mentored by. He's also set me up in a really good way to think, to really trust my instincts and think in that way. But my mum always says, Oh, but I remember you were three years old looking at a TV, or watching a movie, and you would just you watch it and say, I want to do that. And she said, it makes sense.

PJ What drives you? Looking at issues of employability, how do you navigate this?

ND When I was young, because I think there was a differentiation now. It was about, I should be in that room, why can't they see me? How do I get into that room? Because I didn't have the drama school thing, and that used to drive me be a bit crazy.

But with Tony's help, I started doing loads of fringe work, pub theatres. The brilliant Christopher Geelan, who still runs the Young Shakespeare Company, he did this theatre in education gig where you took Shakespeare out to schools, and that was amazing.

I got to do my Titania there, my Lady M there, that show. And you're doing it to little ones, up to the age of six, seven years old, who when they're given a tiny little piece of the iambic to read, and then they read it in twos in a circle, it's the most magical sound because kids don't judge themselves. They just read what's on the page. And especially when it comes to Shakespeare, just read what's on the page, and trust that those rhythms will lead you there. So my learning has been not linear, that's the only way I can put it.

So therefore, in my later age, what I now realize about myself, it literally has to be physical body realization that I really want to play. Or if I just sit with that, and kind of go because I've made mistakes again, yeah, I must do this. I must do this. I must do this. And what that's taught me over time is that yeah, you rushed too quick into that. It was an ego thought, as opposed to what the body wanted. And then there have been other times, phenomenally and fundamentally. So I was asked to take on at the last-minute play called *Linda* at the Royal Court, and the main actress had left in the last week of rehearsals, for absolutely valid reasons.

But I got a phone call from Michael Longhurst and Vicky Featherstone saying, if you can go on with a book, you can just go on with the book. So in my head is like, oh, that's fine. I'm going on the book. I'm just, I'm not saving anything. I'm helping this play carry on. But what was extraordinary for me Pamela is like, it was my body. I will say this, my body screamed. And it was like this huge expansion of don't even think about it. It's like it was a whirring from my solar place was going Yeah! Yeah! Yeah! Yeah! And then I woke up in the morning, and then my head got in the way I went, What the fuck are you doing? What the fuck am I doing? But the body was still going? Yeah! there was no fear, and I've been kind of doing that. And I was doing that before. But that was the most visceral confirmation that I really have to listen to my body.

Now, especially, and I'd had versions of that when I was younger. And I could tell you what worked and what didn't, but I couldn't explain why. And again, my body tells me so I really try and send to that spirit space for myself, of my physical body being much more knowing than my head.

Because I do go, the more we can trust. And I've kind of said this to young actors as well, you may not know literally, but your body does something your spirit, knows to lead you to this, because it could be for a longer-term journey.

So people I've worked with, John Tiffany and Steven Hoggett. I did a workshop with them two years before at the Royal Court and they were the directors of the Harry Potter play *Cursed Child*.

So they said, Oh, can we call you in for these workshops? And all it was was just workshops.

So, all these things are possible. Yeah, it's all good, but they're not linear. And so therefore, that's what I finally absolutely understand about my career. It's not linear. And that has served me when I've started sitting into that because that young person was going 'why can't I be in that room?' I wasn't listening to what my body wanted to do. I was listening to what the expectations of this predominantly white world that we're in, saying you should be there, but you can't get in there, that's literally what my head was telling me, you should be there. But you can't get in there, because? Because? Because? But actually, the more I listen to my body, it leads you to the places that you're supposed to be, if that makes sense.

I don't mind the long gaps now. Because I feel as if I'm becoming much more discerning with the choices of those stories. So, they do feel full for whatever the learning is even like doing *A Doll's House, Part 2* last year written by Lucas Hnath and directed by James Macdonald, felt good and clear. But now I realized the bigger picture was for me to learn something about myself, not necessarily the gig itself. But to learn how I am in this world and how to hold my space in this world. And that was a big learning. Yeah.

PJ Is your preparation for a role different for theatre and screen?

ND It's different for every job (laughs). Because I used to go 'oh shit I haven't a process, everyone seems to have a process', and then I used to beat myself up about it, why haven't I got a process, because everyone seems to have a process. And then, there was the realization that my process is truly, that gut reaction, that stomach reaction, that body reaction, going, you've got to be in this room, you've got to be adjacent to this person, and the universe leading you there and then going, okay, what do you need from me? and therefore, I'll figure it out. There is usually somebody in the company who knows how to be off script within a week, and I'm going, how do you do that, how the fuck do you do that? I don't know how you do that.

But also, it's all form and play because the more I play, the much more excited I am in a room. If I'm sitting down at a table for ages, I know that's part of the process that I don't enjoy, because my body is literally twitching to get up. But again, it all falls into the bit before, your instinct, your intuition leads you to that space, something opens up you go, I'm playing, I'm playing, I get to play with these people. So that's what my process is and that, shifts, what I learn, in terms of how people do their stuff.

And another part that Tony taught me is that he was taught by somebody else. And I tried to teach younger writers. Oh, anybody, actually, anybody creative, steals from the best and makes it their own. Yeah. It's simple. It's simple. And then the other side of that another lesson of process, because then it negates how big or small the part is, and that's a head thing, is, wherever you are, is the centre of the stage.

I loved learning that one, and he'd been taught that by a teacher of his at RADA in the fifties and I thought that's a genius one, because, you're focused.

So therefore, playing Ursula in *Much Ado About Nothing* who has like two lines. I got good reviews on two lines; I absolutely loved it. I love being in the room listening, being in the space and being in the world. Yeah, which was gorgeous.

PJ The industry and your place in it?

ND Right now the industry feels very amorphous. We don't know where and how it's going. What I do know is that if the 2022 SAG-AFTRA US actors' and writers' strikes had happened twenty years ago, I'd be freaking out. Because what it would be doing is saying, there's no room for you. That's how I would read it. There's no room for you in this industry. I remember that that was a story I would tell myself. And also, we've got to be really careful of the stories we do tell ourselves. Because that shit is real. That shit is absolutely real, those mantras that we say, the world will confirm to us what we are saying inside our heads and our hearts.

So, where's my place in the industry now I have no idea. I have no idea where it's going, but I'm in America, New York right now, because I came with a job. And a year and a half later, I was supposed to go back to London. But I just flowed with the needs of my family and then ended up getting a job within couple of weeks of making that decision. That amazing TV job landed in New York, so I go, let's just flow with these jobs. And these things just kept opening.

So, what my place in the industry is, is a surprise more than anything. For me, it really is a surprise. And so therefore, I lean more into the spiritual divine game, am my feeling right in this? And the more I think can we tune into our essence? And I still don't know what that is, but the essence is, Okay, do I feel good? Is my body vibrating with joy? Well, then I have to follow that, as an elder said to my daughter recently just try and follow your bliss, just follow your bliss.

Now, my place in the industry, I will go back to that and say is to tell young people to stop worrying about what other people think because it's just deadening, its deadening. If you can make it, make the theatre, make the joy, make the bliss happen, or acknowledge that maybe it's not for you, be brave with that. Don't hold on longer than you need to and then get bitter over that and angry. And I remember I was on that cusp as well. Going should I be here, all that, when the head stuff goes because you're looking outside at what other people have or you think you should have, based on what other people have.

There is a magic in it taking a risk with yourself, if that makes sense. And that's where my place is in the industry right now. So therefore, by the time this book comes out, I have no idea where I'm going to be. I have a dream. But maybe I feel that there's something more about setting up home for myself and I don't know where that home is going to be. But my work will lead me there. I'm very lucky that I feel that way, that my work will lead me there.

PJ Thinking in terms of how you choose to identify, what do you think are the challenges in the acting/creative industry now?

ND I am a Black female, yes, I am part of the Global Majority. I remember hearing that coming out two or three years ago, when I consciously heard that phrase, Global Majority, which is coming out of Black and Minority Ethnic (BAME), and BAME never worked, that shit never worked, as somebody said it was an imposition on everybody else who was not white by whiteness.

And then here on the phrase, Global Majority, I'm going, there's such huge power in that even those two phrases, those two words coming together, energetically, there's such a power to that. I am a Black woman, I am a Black woman, I love my Blackness. I'm an African, Black, British creative. But first and foremost, I am a creative person who happens to be African and Black. And with that it informs how I move in the world. And when I was younger, it was very painful to see myself in the world because I couldn't see myself represented anywhere, but you'd had someone like Josette Simon and you would feel there's a possibility, there's a possibility when you're growing up. But now everything is pre- and post-George Floyd for me. The murder of George Floyd. And in his murder, a mirror was absolutely held up to society in all different ways around the globe. And that mirror was held up to me to choose who do I choose to be in this moment? Who do I choose to be?

And how do I choose to live my life because, fuck me, everywhere hates Black people. That's what I'm hearing. Everywhere hates Black people. And that is the biggest sadness, because I know, I know my mother's story. My story, my father's story. We are amazing. To look across the diaspora, and see what we've all acknowledged, and we've all gone through it. And as people say, with joy, with laughter, with loudness, which we've had to hide, so it's actually all those things, okay, we can't hide that shit any more. But the biggest learning lesson is I am not African American. So therefore, there's another conversation about what it is to be Black. Then, my place in the world, as a Black woman, as an actor, as a post-menopausal woman, of African heritage is complex. But it's for me to dance with and for you to make up your mind. But I can only dance with it well, if I'm not worrying about what you think, or how you think I should be dancing, if that makes sense. So that's why I see myself right now. But that's also me being the age I am now. Yeah, so if you'd asked me twenty years ago, I would have had no idea. I know it would be totally different. And it would have been related to how other people saw me. So, all I can do now twenty years later is kind of go, I have no idea, but I like this, and like this person, and I'm liking them a lot more. So whatever they say, I'm going to be a story for somebody, in another generation to kind of go well, that's a possibility. Because I realized, I really sit in this, Pamela. I'm really sitting in that in my life. Again, I am here for a story. Yeah, we all are. But I'm finally meeting my story, if that makes sense. And the thing is, yeah, I don't know what it is. But I'm, I'm yielding. I'm surrendering. I'm okay. Let's see what's going to happen tomorrow.

PJ If a young Black and Global Majority person of eighteen made the decision that they want to become an actor, what would your advice be?

ND I realize now, that drama school was not meant to be my route. But when I didn't get in, oh, for a few years, I felt really stupid. Like everyone else who'd been to drama school knew something that I didn't. And in a sense, they did. Because what they learned was formed, they learned this structure, they learned different modalities of what storytelling are, and yeah, there was an older actor I worked with on a show in Edinburgh, and his daughter was directing it. That's why I got to be on, it was like a fringe job that I auditioned for and got, and this actor who I didn't know, but apparently, he had been well known when he was younger. And he'd asked me that question. And where did you go to drama school? I remember feeling a twinge of shame as he asked me.

And I said 'I, I, I didn't'. And he went, 'Oh, darling, that's the best way – you're doing it on the job'.

So I sort of realized, oh my God, yes, I am.

Because he just said, you can go to all the schools you want. But there will be a moment where you still have to start all over again, everyone finishing drama school has to go out into the world again. And in that moment, I let go of that angst.

But there is a different thing to accessibility. So if you don't go to drama school, the route will be gnarlier, more windy, wily and winding.

I've met people who were huge when they came out of drama school or young actors. And in their thirties, forties nothing's going on. So, for young performers, creatives, anyone who's wanting to create something of themselves, and this is my story, I'm telling you, is stop looking for validation.

And it's still a part of my world even in my fifties going, what does that mean?

That's been such a trigger for me in growing up, from going Do you like me? Am I good enough? Am I good enough because I didn't go to drama school? Am I deserving to be in this place? Because I didn't 'classically train', I didn't do it the way that 'everyone else' in quotation marks was supposed to do it. So, let go of needing outside validation, lean into what you truly know. It really doesn't have to be articulated. But the problem with the world is people need things to be articulated, then why are you going from A to B? Actually, I'm not going from A to B, I'm going to go from A to F to C and then I'm going to come back to D because that's the way it makes sense to me, and then maybe double back to B. And then we move on to C. I realized for me, that's the way my world works, that's the way my head works. And I'm finally sitting in that place going, so we're going to go around the houses. I think I said this to you when we met. I'm going to go around the houses. But before I used to think I was stupid, yeah, that that's where my head was, why can't I hold on to a linear thought? But I can hold on to so many thoughts, I just do it in a different way.

So, I would say, drama school does a number on people I now realize, when young people tell me their experiences of drama school, I am like, 'Thank you universe, you protected me from that'. Because I don't believe I would be here. If I had gone to drama school. I now understand, that was not meant to be my journey, because there's a lot of mental health issues, especially with our generation, or I would have been the one Black girl in school.

And with my mum the way we were brought up, for us as immigrant kids, 'you don't shout back at me', 'you don't make me embarrassed in front of other people', 'you don't tell tales on the family, we don't air our dirty linen in public'. Because it is survival. We've arrived. We don't want to give them an excuse. Or send us back if they need the option.

So, you're in this generation now, where you look after yourselves better, you look after yourselves intentionally better. But, and yet, what I will offer you, young person, is listen to the story of your elders. Be curious about the stories of your elders, because there was a lot of learning and information in that space about how you can navigate. So when Tony tells me to steal from the best and make it your own that visually makes sense to me, as an artist, because yeah, because then the world is my oyster, to look around and decide, what do I like? What is the thing that makes me feel good when I'm in the presence of, as an art form? Or now? Can I bring that into my cells? Can I bring that into my consciousness? How will it transmute to my body in my learning and my education? Because everyone is different. Because there is only one version of this. And that's the problem. I used to think there was so many versions. Now, It's just this is it right now.

PJ Hard-dough bread, Sourdough bread, Chin Chin, Sweetbread, Roti, Sudsa, Bun and Cheese, Nai Wong Bao -奶黄包- Custard Bun or Naan?

ND I'm so bougie, Sourdough bread, sorry. What I grew up with was so eclectic. But Sourdough bread is good on the stomach. It's a fermented bread. So, I'll take that one, thank you.

Jenny Jules

Photo: Hugo Glendinning.

Jenny Jules played Hermoine in *Harry Potter and the Cursed Child* on Broadway. Other theatre credits include *The Way of the World* at the Donmar Warehouse, *The Crucible* on Broadway opposite Saoirse Ronan and Ben Whishaw and Phyllida Lloyd's all-female production of *Julius Caesar* at St Ann's Warehouse in New York. She won the Critics' Circle Best Actress Award for her performance in *Ruined* at the Almeida. Television credits include *New Amsterdam*, BBC1's *Death in Paradise*, *Law and Order*, *Skins*.

Pamela Jikiemi – PJ Tell me about your journey to become an actor.

Jenny Jules – JJ My journey starts at age five, school play. I am a Christmas baby. And the play was on my birthday. And they just were choosing students, you know. Put your hand up who wants to be in the play. They didn't pick me.

But they picked – you know from the other students in the school, they picked my brother. And my brother was in the play and my mum, out of some kind of sense of I don't know what wouldn't let me go and see it. She didn't let me see him.

So, I didn't see the play. And I'm the most fiercely competitive person. And that's when I understood that the things that drive me are ego, injustice and competition. And I was like I could do it better than him. And from about the age of five, I was just – the sense of injustice at not being chosen – I am so special on that day. That was my day to shine. Yeah. That's what made me become an actor. That's the beginning of my journey.

I joined a youth theatre when I was young – probably about twelve, actually. The Tricycle Youth Theatre. And just fell in love the first day I walked in there. I had seen plays at Moonshine, which was on the Harrow Road in north-west London, which is where I'm from. I think the first play I saw there I was about eight. And I can't remember the play, but I remember just being – just – I was in heaven. You know, I was like, what is this?

These people are just being magical. Because I have lots of siblings, and we used to just do magical things. And that was performance. And tell stories and make up songs and sing to each other. And that's what these people were actually doing. And they were grownups, it was rather marvellous.

So, The Tricycle led me to taking it seriously, led me to meeting really fantastic practitioners. Some of them told me not to go to drama school. Some of them didn't speak of drama school. And I went to – I did further education at Cassio College in Watford. And I was doing A-levels in Drama and English. And I was just surrounded by really wealthy kids, who were all just wastrels as far as I was concerned. They had no sense of what the world was like. They only knew about their entitlement. And I decided in that moment that I was never going to go and spend three years with those fuckers. So, I didn't go to drama school. I was very political. And I did lots of political things and went on marches and rallies and stuff.

PJ Training around learning 'the craft'; did you go to a conservatoire drama school? Talk about your creative career and your commitment towards pursuing it.

JJ I joined Theatre Centre, a young people's theatre company, and they were touring the country. I was also at Red Ladder. And we – I toured for about four years. The whole country. Toured schools, mostly. And with Red Ladder which was based up in Leeds. We toured working men's clubs and youth clubs up in the north, and that was an absolute eye opener.

I learnt my trade at Theatre Centre, I learned how to structure a play, how to write, what it looked like. That was – my mentor, Noel Greg, who was – who I'd met at the Tricycle Theatre. And yeah – and it's so interesting, because Roy Williams, was at Theatre Centre then. And that's who taught him how to write. I learned about racism. And I learned about our country, and I learned all kinds of things then. I was still really young. And – yeah, that's kind of my journey, really. Because then I came back to London after the four years of touring and went back to the Tricycle.

Before that I was learning my trade. I was learning how to do the lighting; I was learning how to do the sound. I could edit, tape to tape, reel to reel. I had to stage manage. We would – unload the van, put the set up, pack the van up, do a discussion after every single performance with Theatre Centre and – with Red Ladder.

With Red Ladder, it was mostly talking about racism, because that's what we discovered. I did two seasons there. We devised a play about racism. And went back to places where they threw fireworks at us when we were in performance near Newcastle. And, you know, threatened to slash the tyres of our van. Said, 'if you fuckers come back here, we will kill you'. This kind of carry on.

PJ What did you get from your experience?

JJ When I came back to London my head was wrapped. And I always say that that was because of me experiencing racism.

Because I actually really didn't experience that much racism in London growing up. I really didn't. You know, I think I heard the word wog once shouted in the street and that was by an invisible person.

It wasn't anyone shouting like, 'you wogs'. It was an invisible person – all the people on the road were like who said that. Do you know what I mean? Who could have possibly shouted out that?

I was called all kinds of things up in Yorkshire and – and that was hard to stomach, and it was hard to swallow, you know. And I met some hardcore Caribbean people up there as well. I lived in Leeds for a year.

So I came back and was literally just like 'guys, guys, guys', to all of my London people. 'It's really terrible up there, you know, don't go up there becah' – yeah. Literally just trying to say to people, London is a little oasis of – integration and a kind of collective harmony in a way.

You know of people actually living side by side and getting on with it. For the best part. But, yeah, just like two miles outside any city centre I visited. Coventry, Birmingham, Leeds, Bradford, any one of them was BNP, was NF with their signs, with their posters. It was like, wow. Wow. It was horrible.

PJ What drives you? Looking at issues of employability, how do you navigate this?

JJ Like I stated, I'm innately competitive. I believe my skillset is limitless. So, therefore, I don't put any pressure on myself to know my place or to stay in my lane.

I want to play everything if it sparks me. And so, what drives me is the spark, the seed, a part, a role. Telling some story that no one's told before or feeling something that is in my belly that I feel I want to share that piece of fire. So, that's kind of what drives me.

PJ Is your preparation for a role different for theatre and screen?

JJ Yes and no. I want to find out as much as I can about the character I'm playing. I learn the lines.

The execution is different. That's what's different. We have to start – we have to use our short-term and long-term memory strategies for theatre. And usually short-term for film.

Sometimes we can have to learn the lines the night before. If it's an historical character, i.e. Harriet Tubman, then you do the research, you read, you watch whatever there is to watch, you listen. Then you conjure up the world that they lived in, in your imagination. And find where – where you are similar. Find lampposts or signposts, find things that – structures that you can land on and keep coming back to or keep moving forward to if you get lost. Places where you feel secure.

Yeah. There should be a safe place for you, in order for you to be able to conjure up the character, i.e. a woman and I'm talking as a cis, so there's no confusion. You know, you've got a vagina, you've got blood flow, you've got hormones, pregnancy, there's a sense of duty, and until the world changes, we need to feel this strongly. Duty to our kids, to our parents, to our spouse, to our – our friends, to our community.

Repetition, repetition, repetition. You know, the words, the feelings, the movement.

It helps to cement the lines and the sense of the scene, in your – in your head and your body.

Theatre, more embedded in my soul. TV and film stay for a short time – unless it's a TV series. And the character must remain while the lines change.

So, there's just different ways of using your skillset and using your muscularity and using your intelligence. Yeah – because we can learn techniques as we go, how best to use them.

When I did *Prime Suspect* I remember Helen Mirren would learn the lines for the scene the next morning the night before, because that's how she worked.

PJ How do you decide what roles to go for?

JJ I am much more discerning. But at the moment my priority is getting paid. So, that's hard. Because I've spent most of my life being an artistic creative actor.

Just going, no, no, no. I – this is – this is how I want to be seen. This is what I want to do next. And I've not been paid. You know.

And now I'm a big crusty woman going, wow, what about pension? What about long term? What about later? You know, and I moved here to get paid and that.

Thing is, though – it's mostly through auditions and I'm sent scripts from my agent. Sometimes colleagues request that I take a role. And sometimes I'm going to say I can't do that. And there's been so much I have said no to in the UK since moving here. And some of it has burnt me, has blistered me because they're my lovers I've said no to. But I have said, I have come here to set something up for myself and I have to stick to it. Because I always crumble for the art, always. I was like 'I just got to do this' – you know, and so I've made some really stringent choices.

But I do love a challenge. And if it's a part that I can flex in, then I'm really interested. If it's a part that I can see anyone else doing, I am not interested. If anyone can play it then I don't need to do it. Go find anyone.

PJ The industry and your place in it?

JJ It is not really something I think about. Really. I still feel like, I'm an actor, looking for decent work, or well-paid work or experimental risk-taking work with brilliant creatives and collaborators.

So, I find it hard to kind of track myself. As I go. Because I'm still in it. I still feel like a youth. Because we're hungry. That's why – stay hungry. And I feel like I'm still a youth.

So, I can't map where I've been and where I'm going and where I will end up, I can't see that. I can't see an end game for myself. I can't see a retirement, you know. As Serena Williams so eloquently and beautifully put it this year, 'That's not a modern word for me'.

PJ One of the recurring issues in the creative industries is the discussion around representation. How do you see your role in relation to that conversation?

JJ I think it's well overdue. You know. Women, people of colour, people with disabilities, it's just too long picking up crumbs from the entertainment industry's one at a time policy. Oh, sorry, there's nothing for you in this coming season. Oh, so there are no parts for humans in your forthcoming TV shows?

It's like, it's been casual racist bullshit inflicted upon us by corporations and individuals who are happy with the status quo and the stories that tells.

It's long overdue. I'm really proud. I'm proud of my whole career. But there are some pinnacles in my career that I'm really, really proud of. Because I really feel that there was some kind of forward movement, or there was some kind of light that went on it that stayed on it in a positive way that other people could – do you know what I mean? It's like the light – you shine the light in the room and all the cockroaches scatter.

PJ Thinking in terms of how you choose to identify, what do you think are the challenges in the acting/creative industry now?

JJ It's kind of complicated for me because I'm not an African American. I've got a British-sounding voice; my cultural experiences are all from the UK. I walk around, looking, you know, people think I'm – I live in

Brooklyn, I walk out my house and I look like I'm from Brooklyn, like I could be African American. And that – I carry the legacy that the African Americans carry, which is the slave legacy of the 400 years of parallel existence between Black and white.

And – when I open my mouth, I'm clearly not – do you know what I mean? I find it interesting. Sometimes it's charming, that people just presume I know and that I get it, and I'd fit in. And I quite like that. Because I still feel like a foreigner, even though I'm an American citizen. But – when people do – when I do feel sexism or racism, or I do feel some kind of injustice creep in someone's eyes at me in a shop or wherever, they're getting the Queen's English spat at them.

And I literally see people check themselves and they're not quite sure what's happening. Sorry, mam, I am so sorry, mam. I beg your pardon, mam. And I am just 'that's right'. Treat every single person you meet as an individual. Stop presuming. That's why we're in so much trouble.

You know, just be open to every new person in your day.

Yeah, how do I identify? As we get older, I am a woman. I am Black. But mostly I'm me. And it's probably because I've been transplanted into a different environment than the one I was raised in.

When I lived in the UK, I was reminded that I was a Black person, when I walked out of my house, whether I was feeling particularly female or Black. Now I live in Brooklyn. I'm viewed as an African American. This subtle, yet real difference. It's a great – it's of great amusement to me. It means I can choose to speak or not. That's what will separate me from the next person who looks like me. And – you know, it's just nonsense.

PJ What pitfalls should actors emerging from drama school aim to avoid?

JJ Being pigeonholed too soon. If you don't explore your talent, your predilection and your capabilities when you're young, it gets harder as you get older.

Unless you can hit the jackpot first time and you can start your own production company.

Margot Robbie, who started her own production company with her husband and their two friends. They made *I, Tonya*. Boom. You know. That's – that's the main pitfall.

Also, representation. Your agents have to get you, like really get you. Don't just get excited because that might be the biggest agency, and they've got the shiniest colours. And, wow, they've got the big names and they've got the big – you could be getting with them so that you're standing three to the back from the person that they have at the front.

Who is the one at a time, who is the one at that moment? So, when she's not available they'll give it to the one that's behind her. And then when she's not available – then it might be you. So, you're still feeding off the scraps. You know.

You have to have a plan. You have to have a plan; you have to know why. You have to know what you're – yeah, exactly what you're reaching for, what you want to do.

PJ What motivates you to want to act and keep doing it?

JJ I'm a storyteller, gregarious communicator who feels so passionately about connecting with people through drama. Yeah. And – absolutely, actors. Yeah. Sorry, there's a question about actors, isn't there?

PJ What are your broad aims for the future of your screen acting presence?

JJ To have one …

I want to be a series regular in a popular TV show. You know, I want to appear in more movies, hopefully as a leading character. Yeah, I still have these hopes for myself.

These are things I believe I can do. I can achieve, I will achieve. Because I want to, I'm prepared to work hard for that. You know, and to use my voice as a – as a woman of … As an older woman.

PJ Who are the actors and directors that have inspired you?

JJ Viola Davis and Meryl Streep, I think that they're absolutely just goddesses. And inspirational.

The technique, the work ethic, the – with Viola it is like the steadfastness, you know, the determination and then the craft and the weird chameleon – you know what I mean? Mercurial skill of Meryl Streep just like she did that, she did that, she – that, that, that, that.

Yes, I want every actor to feel like they can be that, but be them. Be themselves because they have their capacity to just shape-shift in the way that she does. And I do love Will Smith as an actor. Just watching that man, watching him grow in his performances.

But also, every actor I've worked with. And I genuinely mean that. Well, most of them have inspired me, you know, loads of them. Their approach to the work. To watch people, make choices, how prepared they are and how focused they are. And I – and I mean that from my heart, you know, in the same way I know people have given me love, I give love. I give the love back. Because I love my community and I miss them. And I'm doing what I sometimes feel is a selfish thing every now and again. But I have to satisfy myself in a way otherwise my whole life would just – I'd just be full of regret, and I don't want to be bitter.

PJ If a young Black and Global Majority person of eighteen made the decision that they want to become an actor, what would your advice be?

JJ Don't limit yourself. Never stay in your lane. If you dream what you think is impossible make it your business to make it possible. Smash the glass ceiling for everybody. Mash up all the boxes you are put in. Unbrainwash yourself. You are more than enough.

Hard work. Hard work, grow a thick skin. And stay curious. We have the ability to change the paradigm because so much is happening. Has happened already.

Drink that in. We need to kick fear in the teeth and just run with the time at the moment because there's been a door that's been cracked open. Yeah.

PJ Hard-dough bread, Sourdough bread, Chin Chin, Sweetbread, Roti, Sudsa, Bun and Cheese, Nai Wong Bao -奶黄包- Custard Bun or Naan?

JJ Oh, Bun and Cheese. Oh, fucking hell, Bun and Cheese makes me fat. I don't know between Bun and Cheese and Hard-dough. Sourdough is nice every now and again …

Colin Salmon

Credit: Jolly Thompson.

Colin Salmon's credits include *The Lazarus Project* for Sky, *Culprits* for Disney+ and *Changing Ends* for ITV, as well as playing the role of Charles Robinson in the James Bond franchise. Other credits include Peter Jackson's futuristic Earth dystopian franchise *Mortal Engines*, two seasons of the Syfy/E4 series *Krypton*, *Master Of None* for Netflix, *24: Live Another Day*, *No Offence* and *Musketeers*. He is currently starring as George Knight in the BBC's *EastEnders*.

Pamela Jikiemi – PJ Tell me about your journey to become an actor.

Colin Salmon – CS Good. So, it's a conversation. Good. That's fine.

Well, a conversation. A conversation is quite nice, you know.

I think Baldwin did it, didn't he? James Baldwin was a master of it. And I met James Baldwin.

We did drama at school. I had one or two teachers of colour. One was a drama teacher who followed me through school and put me in plays. Mrs Christian, Celeste Christian, who was a Sri Lankan teacher. And she put me in plays, and I never thought anything of it. I just kept doing shit and being a footballer and everything else. I liked performing. I mean, I was diagnosed with ADHD three years ago. Now, that makes so much sense now.

My childhood was completely active all the time. And people would say Jack of all trades, you know. And then the problem is, master of none. But what you do is actually master yourself.

I was a good boy. My mates who were in my academic group were really sort of quite political. And they started going to punk. And then that ethos of rebellion just really, really resonated with me. So, I got into that.

And that caused a few eruptions in the house and amongst some of my Black friends. But that was closely followed by Two Tone.

And then – then I went to London – I got a job on a building site, started doing a bit of labouring and stuff, and then went and worked with some of my mates on some house in Barnet. So, I cycled to London up the A1, and that was it. We were living a squat, in Willesden Green.

And I've never returned back to Luton, where I grew up. I grew up in Luton. I left, and that was it. There was a particular girl in the squat I liked. She did this drama therapy thing. So, I sort of go, oh, I'll do that. And actually really, really enjoyed it because it was working with a lot of kids like me. Mum sort of had been through psychiatric issues. And so, I wasn't afraid of psychiatric hospitals. And yeah – our job was to create a trust environment and I was a big old lump, so therefore as an Alpha who is prepared to make a dick of himself the kids were prepared to come along with me.

PJ Training around learning 'the craft'; did you go to a conservatoire drama school? Talk about your creative career and your commitment towards pursuing it.

CS You see I didn't go to drama school, so I – bless, sidestepped that. I come out of punk. I come out of reggae. Do you know what I mean? I was like – I am that age – that age of the late 70s where you just fucking – you do it.

And I worked that out years ago. I just read all this stuff about drama school training and went, hang on. We can't do that. Firstly, I can't afford to do that. Secondly it is patronizing shit. Because I started out as a busker. So, if I played a homeless person and pretend to be a homeless person for a while, I know psychologically I'm going back to my bed.

So I started in drama therapy. I worked in the community taskforce sixteen hours a week going into psychiatric hospitals and children's homes.

And basically, that's how I started in this game. And I realized – stories were healing. I was taught, trained then, you know. Stories were a way of healing. So, before laws – there were only stories. Who feels it, knows it. You feel through a story, and it makes sense more now than ever. And it's based on the work of Augusto Boal. Who feels it, knows it.

And that's my starting point, that and church, and the Salvation Army and great orators, you know, great speakers.

So, performance came from that. That's where my performance came from. Doing drama at the sort of Salvation Army 'open airs' as we called them, we'd go out in the street and play on the council estate I lived on. In my little shorts and my cornet. And for the rest of week, I would get the piss taken out of me. But I said, you know what, fuck it.

PJ How did you book your first acting job?

CS I had been working in drama therapy and role playing and life was getting a bit tough at the time and from there I started busking outside the Tricycle Theatre. It was just tricky times. Experimenting. Messing about with, you know, self-medication and stuff. And I was busking outside Tricycle Theatre and there was a play – it was – I think it was my twenty-third birthday. I lost my girlfriend, and you know, it was just bad. And there was a poster of Jack Johnson up on the wall in Kilburn where I lived. And it was *The Great White Hope* by Howard Sackler and it's the story of Jack Johnson, the first great Black heavyweight champion of the world. So, that's a Miles Davis album. Right. So, he's one of my sorts of – I don't know how to put it, it's like a sign – it was like a sign. And I'd never busked in London, and life was pretty rough, and I just decided to go and busk. I just decided I'm going to go, it's my birthday. You know, nobody is celebrating it, just me.

So, I just said, I am going to go and busk. And I was debating whether to go back to Luton or whatever and I took my trumpet, got my cap, strapped it – lowered my head, went and stood in the hall, the corridor of the Tricycle Theatre, where there was a little doorway inside the corridor. Put the mute in, put my case on the ground and started playing. And I was nervous, nervous, nervous. And two guys came out. So, a few people passed, and then two guys came out. And it's transpired it was John Matshikiza the South African actor and Terry Mortimer who was the musical director of the place. And they listened. And so, you know – I was pretty wild, feral myself at that point. So, they said, look, you know, this is lovely, do you want to see the show? And I said, yeah, okay. So, they went and got me a ticket, they gave me a ticket to go and see the show. And, of course, I went to see it. And it was wonderful. It was such a huge cast for that time. And it was like, wow, wow. And that act of kindness meant, that Charlie the front-house manager, he said look, you know, you play anytime you like, man. Love it, love what you're doing. So, I literally would – that was it, I just kept coming back. And I saw everybody, I met Sheila Hancock. Because everybody used to go to the Tricycle Theatre.

And they didn't know me. But I recall – that I was 'the busker'. So, I'm like this mysterious character. But that was literally how I sort of entered – it sort of chose me and opened its doors to me, and I just found it – I found the conversations really interesting. I found the plays amazing. And I went and watched all the Brendan Behan because they did Irish and Caribbean plays. So, like, all the plays that I would want to see, really.

And then I bought my band and, you know, sort of crazy gig situation. Just tried to make it work for me. And then they asked me to be in a play called *All or Nothing at All* written by Caryl Phillips, about Billie Holiday. And they were casting it. And I played trumpet with all the different actresses who came in, and they sang and stuff. And Pauline Black got the part and is amazing.

And then the theatre burned down. But literally, just before that all happened. I mean, there was James. James Baldwin came with *The Amen Corner*, so I met him standing in the corridor, he shuffles past and then of course, he gave notes and then sat in the bar, and I finished playing and would go to the bar after watching the play a few times. So, we chatted.

I met my wife, Fiona, there. One night after Charlie's leaving party, she was there and we've been together for thirty-six years.

So, the Tricycle Theatre was like my – *Lion, the Witch and the Wardrobe* – it's my wardrobe. It was where Narnia – and the world of theatre revealed itself to me – I loved – I loved theatre. I'm a musician, but I love words, and I love ideas. So, it was really useful to sit, and watch plays again and again and again. You know, I saw so many great performances, and some not so great. And I could also see what works and didn't work. And you could see actors who were doing it with ego and some who were just fucking amazing, and you were being transported, it was an intense period.

Then the Tricycle burned down. And it was rebuilt obviously, and we had to generate money and there was raise the roof and all this stuff at the Royal Court. And Fiona and I were together by then. So, she sort of focused my mind. So, I started running a jazz quartet and I got into all sorts of things, productive, positive things, and then it reopened. And I play – and we did it. And of course, because it was the reopening of the Tricycle everybody came, including Doreen Jones, who three years later – after – then cast me in *Prime Suspect*. And I'd never been on television in my life. So, I'd never been in front of a camera. So, that was my debut.

But again, because of the drama therapy when I got the role at the Tricycle, it was like a tech musician's union contract or an Equity contract. And I remember at the time everybody's talking Equity cards. So, I got an Equity card. I don't know why, but I got one. And that meant I could do a few – let's say a few lines. But I knew one thing, through drama therapy, that was just be absolutely honest, just stay absolutely focused on the client, or the person speaking, you know. It's the rule. It's the rule and I just applied that to it, and clearly it worked. So, that was it. That's how I got into the mainstream, really.

PJ What drives you? Looking at issues of employability, how do you navigate this?

CS Well, I'm a father. We have four beautiful children, so you have to eat. And that has meant for me – it's made theatre slightly more difficult, if I am honest.

I'd love to do more. I have done interesting things. But the success of *Prime Suspect* was great. But again, it's a very difficult place to start because it's a high benchmark. So, everything after that could feel like a sort of an anti-climax almost. But for a while there – I think one of the things I realized quite quickly, and I raised it in interviews straight away, because of my knowledge of *The Great White Hope* and certain actors around me. I would often talk about other Black actors, actually, that I knew. Black British actors. And people would sort of say to me, why are you talking about them, they are your competition. I said, hang on a minute, this isn't a sport, come on. This is an art form. These are my friends, and I knew Lenny James and I knew Cyril Nri. And I knew some great people who were really generous people. And I cared about them and felt that we should all be there and go up together.

I think, with my reggae background, it's that consciousness, I was always very aware of unity, that was important.

And I've often realized – you're on your own – when you are on your own, you're easily picked off or you can be, if you psychologically – if you allow yourself. I'm a team player, and I've worked – and I love ensembles. I am somebody who tries to be present 100 per cent wherever I am. So, I do a lot of charity work. I always did, I always went into schools. I am an activist. So, it's sort of a strange one because it sort of doesn't play against being an actor. But it's really interesting the word itself is an act, to act – to do deeds. Do stuff, yeah. Well, to act, you know, action.

So, I just keep doing stuff. So, Fiona and I, we've run a sort of ska band for like twenty-seven years. We used to take all the kids out and masquerade at Notting Hill Carnival. So, I've been very involved with that. I was involved with the Portobello Panto. And just kept bringing in people who weren't actors who worked on the market. You know, we would act alongside them. So, I just got involved in my life. 100 per cent. And that's how I did it. So, employability and things like that.

I read to my children out loud, I read in nursery schools out loud and learnt how to do voice-overs. I worked on my voice. I got blessed with a short tenure at the Royal Shakespeare Company (RSC), because I couldn't spend sixteen weeks away because that would have been my marriage and everything. So, I did The White Cube and got to work with Cecily Berry, who got my voice out. Muscularized it, she gave me my voice back so I can speak with my tone now. And I continued to play music, played trumpet. And I think that's probably been my mindfulness. That's why I love my trumpet. Because it's a similar thing, you sit, and you play. And I have just kept busy really. And I don't look back, and I don't look down.

Yeah, I don't know what the future holds. I mean, with my wife's illness, we've had to go through some stuff. I am looking at trauma and grief and studying it, actually, really, really deeply. And it's really illuminating that I come from a punk background because that was all about decay, which can seem very negative. But actually, now, it's not. It's the *realization* that you will die, it is understanding that. And it's like, one of the biggest books probably of my life now is a book called *Entangled Life* and that's how fungi – created our world, it's by Melvin Sheldrake, it is amazing.

PJ Is your preparation for a role different for theatre and screen?

CS Well, obviously, with the theatre you have that wonderful rehearsal period, which I adore, and that's the thing I miss. Not doing as much theatre as I'd like. And I will do more as I get older, I think. The economic demands on me are different.

So, hopefully, I'll stay fit enough and strong enough to do it. But I think at the end of the day, I think with anything – because again, I have no method, that's the wrong word, I think in this life, you realize, there's that spiritual thing of there but for the grace of God. Now, as an actor, there but for the grace of a deflection go I, you can be you. That's the thing I realized very quickly, when I met people.

So you just read it and study. I read about the character if I can or around the history and – literally from the origin of the name. You know, it can be what does the name mean. Start there. And then just go, what did you do, go with the position of that profession and that's taken me off and down so many wonderful, wonderful rabbit holes and just absolute joyful knowledge, searching for knowledge.

It's like, you have a soul of acting, to have that – it has to be authentic and have integrity. And I watch roles, and it can be small roles, it doesn't have to be big roles, and I see things that make me smile. Because I just know that that actor is making choices. I think that's all we can do in life, is leave behind a legacy of choices.

And when you said *Some Girls* (television series 2012 to 2014, written by Bernadette Davis), I smiled because I know – I grew up with girls like that. And everybody loved it because it was real, It's like being paid to do professional development all the time.

PJ One of the recurring issues in the creative industries is the discussion around representation. How do you see your role in relation to that conversation?

CS So, yeah, you mentioned the James Bond rumours, that was wonderful because then I took that – took that left turn and went and played.

So, I just get nourished by that. I get nourished by it. And that is how I keep going too. So, it's – as much as it's about 'Bond', or whatever. I think the Bond thing that I love – and I've said this people and they have thought I was being a bit disingenuous.

But there was that thing of I've already been in it as a character to be honest. But I just thought the debate was so important to be had. So, I kept it going, I just kept it going and kept sort of flirting with the idea and going, yeah … And I can say it to you now, there's only one guy I think who can do it. It's Paapa, Paapa Essiedu.

Absolutely. He is Bond. I saw a glimpse of this in *The Lazarus Project*. I saw him on a bike with a gun and I went, of course it is him. Nobody's talking about him. But he is without a doubt – he has the danger, the charm, and the chops. I think Daniel Craig bought it to a level, and Pierce was brilliant acting – actually, you know, short of Roger Moore, I think they're all pretty good. But Roger delivered the one-liner better than anybody else. But ultimately, it's an acting job. And it's fucking serious one. So, I think if it's going to be anybody, it would be Paapa. And I think that would actually take it to another level.

I have just been slightly avant garde. And I know that. I've taken it with joy, I have loved being part of the avant garde. Going in first, breaking down, playing men, not Black men but equals they are. And just playing men.

I am what I am. I look out of these eyes, and I get on with my life. And, you know, people remind me … I don't consider it – you don't consider it all the time, every day, every minute of the day, do you? No. Of course. No, you don't. It's not extraordinary for you. It's like diversity in my band or whatever. You were talking about representation. I live it. And people remind you about it and then you go – wow, people still actually have to fucking be told. Okay. Wow.

Okay, well, if I can help, I'll help but for me it's life. It's living it, and it's not being patronizing or smug. And I can still be a dick. I can still get things wrong. But I'll be getting it wrong because I get things wrong, not because I'm picking on someone or trying to exclude. But when I give out prizes, I also put it through the sort of prism of, where you're starting from and how – what it means to you. So, if I see a child who gets to Oxford, and they started on tin town estate, like my mate, I just – I go, wow. And that's not because I am going, they're better than anybody else. It's just like, wow, you started there, Jesus, that's a great – and what is that story, I'm celebrating the story. Because it's not because it's less or more important, it's just rarer. And I'm really interested. Because I've heard the other one. I know the one man who nanny picked up and dropped off at school and everything's done for you and blah, blah, blah. I get it. That doesn't negate their intellect. But what about the emotional IQ of getting to Oxford from the tin town estate, what's happened?

PJ Thinking in terms of how you choose to identify, what do you think are the challenges in the acting/creative industry now?

CS We just need to embolden the next generation. That's my philosophy. And then see where it takes them. And tell them, what to watch out for. It's about the work. And in one generation, I think, they have come a long way, actors. I remember, with respect the generation before me, and I'm not going to be derogatory to them, but you know, the carnage, the drinking, and we got caught up in it and had to straighten up. We started out that way. And then we had to straighten up. And now this generation have just gone, boom. Don't do that. It's the notion of self-care in a sense that – that we didn't sort of have because, well, we, we were trying to fit in, and you don't want to fit in, actually. Because, what you are fitting into, is something that's actually mediocre.

PJ What motivates you to want to act and keep doing it?

CS How do we get hard outcomes and teach them how to develop the skills for work? So, you can do that through play, you can do that through so many things. So, that's how I can keep going – it's not just the acting for me, it never has been.

I play in a steel band, we had a steel band. Fiona, my wife and I, we've got a lot of women – women around fifty to sixty who never thought they'd be in a band and all of a sudden, they're in the band, and they're playing.

And I play trumpet, and, it's perfect for me because I can jam, have fun. But they love it, they're in a band. And it's not because they're in a band with me, it's just – they're in a band.

It's like, how many people dream they want to be in a band.

And then you go – at sixty, you can be in our band. And they are like, what? Yeah. We will teach you. And they learn. And their commitment is amazing.

So, I just get nourished by that. I get nourished by it. And that is how I keep going. I am now chair of Green Park Foundation, trying to help kids – make sure that they have a great life, but also help them into work.

PJ Who are the actors and directors that have inspired you?

CS Sidney Poitier without question. You know that story you alluded to with your dad with his shirts. You know when I saw *To Sir, with Love*, and it's the one shirt he has, he washes it every night.

Which brings me on to Michael Caine as Harry Palmer. They were both working-class men. But then I would go to, *Carmen Jones* was an extraordinary film. I loved that film. I loved – Gregory Peck. You know.

Akala does – he just digs deep. We dig deep together. You know we just come and meet and talk about books and things and – I've got to say Michaela Cole's performances, her honesty and integrity, Paapa Essiedu's work has been fucking exemplary. Lennie James, Hugh Quarshie back in the day and just his generosity at that point and to this day, I feel – I just find him incredible – I just loved – I just really loved Hugh's presence. He has just got a presence. I have just watched everybody. Everybody's given me so much.

PJ If a young Black and Global Majority person of eighteen made the decision that they want to become an actor, what would your advice be?

CS I think, you can talk about alcohol, you could talk about this and that and the other. But I would always say – I call those things self-medication. Watch out for self-medicating. Because your body's not wrong. But it's not what you need. So, either you hit the gym, you start running. Go see a psychiatrist. There's a chemical missing in your brain, go find out what it is. Don't just do the old – same old, same old. Because you've got to be a safe bet, really.

And also, with the digital camera's, screen and things – now you can't hide it, your skin will show it. You are not in good shape. The game's changed, you've got to be healthy. So, it's almost like the Greek times of gymnasia and academia, the balance of both. Because I think they get it – I think the young sort of understand. And also, I'm sort of exec producing a documentary and starting to produce a few things and – or create a few things, but I work with writers – I am quite Socratic, I like chatting. But some of the people have got their notebook or the recorder on. They all get the juice. But I am converting a couple of things. And I just say to people now, you know, that punk element again – in music, I would make my own music. And I decided produce stuff, make stuff, tell your story, create it, whatever way whether it be radio, blog, whatever. Keep a diary. Because ideas are what the world needs.

And you'd be amazed you have them, and they come, and they go. So, don't underestimate what you already know and what you already have.

Because they can dry up. So, don't underestimate – yeah, the biggest one is don't underestimate who you are. And write your backstory. Write a backstory, to your character, because it will be unique to you. And that's a fucking story that you can take and use somewhere else.

Actually, just by doing that you're creating a library. I did the Woody Allen's (2005) film, *Matchpoint*. What I did do was – I knew I had to work. I really wanted to do it well. I wanted to do well. So, I did what I always do, I just wrote this incredible backstory, and in the film my character just comes down a flight of stairs, right, and I meet the character Scarlett Johansson plays, Nola Rice a couple of times. And then he goes off and then the police arrive, and there's been a murder. But I wrote this whole thing about why did I knock on the door and … about the fact it was based on the Monday, it's my favourite day of the week, she bakes cakes and I can smell it around the flat – around the house. And that day, I woke up and there was no smell. I was like, do you need anything? I was going to shop, so I asked if she wanted anything. And she didn't answer. And I was a bit puzzled. But anyway. And I wrote this whole thing about my daughter. And then when – Woody Allen said, right, well, we've got it, now just play. And I just recounted the backstory as the statement to the police. And it's in the film.

It's not just an improvisation, it's literally what I wrote.

And I cannot stress this enough to young people coming up. Whatever it is you're doing, do understand you will be inspiring people. We stand alone together and seeing each other up there doing it pulls us all up. We all go higher. So, that's probably it, really. Seek beauty. Always walk with dignity. That's what I say. Seek beauty, speak truth, and always walk with dignity.

And don't just wait for your agent to do stuff.

PJ Hard-dough bread, Sourdough bread, Chin Chin, Sweetbread, Roti, Sudsa, Bun and Cheese, Nai Wong Bao -奶黄包- Custard Bun or Naan?

CS Sourdough, I have got three bits looking at me right now.

CHAPTER 3
ALIYAH ODOFFIN, PHOEBE CAMPBELL, JAMAEL WESTMAN, CALEB OBEDIAH AND SHAKEEL HAAKIM

Keywords/concepts: Training → acting → opportunity → people → race → opportunity

Good training at its best will provide you with the ways and means (tools) that will allow you to have a conscious approach to finding the natural ingredients that go into creatively interpreting a character for public presentation and scrutiny. Acting at its highest level, is not a skill or a craft that one can do to the ultimate extent unless it's something you absolutely need to do. Something that you need for self-expression in some way that is going to allow you to put in the effort to do it well. And to also be able to stay with it in the face of all the negative frustrations that you might have to face in just trying to be meaningfully employed in your profession. Especially when you're Black and have to deal with discouragement coming from so many areas of society. You cannot allow this to stop you. But resisting or trying to be immune from it takes a lot of power and will. And that's why I say it must be something you really need to do.

Advice to a Young Black Actor (and Others): Conversations with Douglas Turner Ward, by Gus Edwards (2004), p. 103.

Aliyah Odoffin

Photo by Andy McCredie.

Upon graduating from RADA in 2021, **Aliyah Odoffin** worked with Working Title to play one of the leads in *Everything I Know About Love*, which landed her an RTS North West nomination 2022 and Best Breakthrough Talent nomination at the Edinburgh TV Awards 2023. *Sleepova* at The Bush won an Olivier Award for Outstanding Achievement in Affiliate Theatre. This was followed by *Suffrajitsu*, a short film produced by Lammas Park, Steve McQueen's production company, and she has just completed filming two series of *A Thousand Blows* for Disney+.

Pamela Jikiemi – PJ Tell me about your journey to become an actor.

Aliyah Odoffin – AO Well, I have been acting, singing and dancing since I was a tiny, tiny child. And I did all the school plays at primary school, and stuff like that. And I would always ask my mum to send me to any and all classes that we could afford.

I remember my first experience of a school play. And it was all of us in the room reading the script together. And I'd kind of seen that script, the table read on YouTube and things like that, even at that young. So, I knew what it was. And I remember feeling so excited in the room. I think I had my bottle of water. And we were all around the table. And I was like this is it. This is what makes you the actor, this is the table read time. And I was giving it ten out of ten in that table read, and it was just the most exciting thing.

Every time we had a rehearsal, I'd run into the assembly hall, I'd learnt my lines – I was just ready to go. I was so, so excited by it. And then the costume came in and the lighting came in. And everything came together. And I was just, I want to do this over and over and over and over and over again. I was obsessed with it and I continued doing that.

When I then went into secondary school, I would do all the school plays. But then you start at the bottom of the food chain because you're in year seven. So, you go from the lead in your Year Six school play and then you're playing one of the chorus. But I loved it so much.

But then also, I was begging my Mum to send me to classes outside of school where I was dancing, singing and acting. So, I was also doing those kinds of end of term shows and outside of school stuff. And so, I just carried on doing that throughout the whole of that secondary school period of time. And then had college because my school had a sixth form college attached.

Then after college, everyone was applying for unis. And I was well, I knew from the beginning I wanted to act, and I wanted to do that professionally. So, I was ready to audition for drama schools, but I didn't know anything about how to go about doing that.

There was so much research I remember that was happening at that time. I'd be searching the number one schools, people who inspired me, where did they go. Me and my Mum would be there all the time. And we would just collate lists. And then we'd be looking at the factors and what did I want. Maybe not that, or this, because this is more Musical Theatre (MT) focused. And even though I want to do musicals, I wanted my base to be classical acting. And I was kind of figuring all this stuff out as I was looking through all my options about what I wanted. And then I applied for some drama schools, I auditioned at ArtsEd, I also auditioned at Guildhall. Yeah, I auditioned for them, and I got into all the ones I auditioned for. And chose RADA.

PJ Training around learning 'the craft'; did you go to a conservatoire drama school? Talk about your creative career and your commitment towards pursuing it.

AO I actually started auditioning at some other schools. But as the process went along it was kind of like the story you were saying about Viola Davis, it was, I'm doing all these things. But as time is going on, I'm realizing I'm having to split myself into so many different pieces and to start to do some of these things on the same day. And it was causing overproduction, almost. So, then I had to be – out of the processes that I'm going through right now, what is actually speaking to me? And the ones that weren't I decided, I'm really grateful but I know in my soul that this isn't for me. So, I'm going to leave it and I'm going to continue giving myself to the ones which I feel are for me – I mean Guildhall, ArtsEd and RADA having auditioned for all of them, were so different. But there was stuff at each of them that was still kind of keeping me going and my interest was piqued. And, I wanted to go deeper into there. So, I kind of let the other ones go. And focused on those. I was offered a place at Arts Ed, but I was still doing my Guildhall and RADA next rounds. And then I found out I got RADA, and then Guildhall I was still doing. And then I found out I got Guildhall. And then it was suddenly, oh, I am in this position. At first you are like, I'm just really happy to get anything, and then you are at the position where you've got more than you wanted.

And you're, okay, but now it's about choosing really wisely. And then that was a whole other journey, in and of itself. But you have that moment where you go, I know I can do it, I have the power. So, let me take my time with this. And that's something if I look across my acting journey so far, that I'm really proud that I have always done is, not rush because I think I have to, and take my time with decisions. Because I feel that when you're starting out, it can feel like you need to do things quickly. And not bother anyone and kind of get it over and done with and keep moving. But I was so serious about making it my profession and making it my career that I knew, I really want to be careful about this next junction, because it felt almost the most serious one. It was now I'm studying it for a vocation, to make it my profession. I really want to make the right decision.

When I started to apply for drama schools, that was a whole world that I had never experienced before, auditioning on that scale. So, that was all new. And once I'd kind of gotten used to that next level of newness, and I was like, okay, so this is auditioning, and I have to do my speech like this. And usually in the rooms, they're going to make me stand really far back. And I have to get comfortable with that. And take your time before you do your speeches. And I learnt all of that. Once I had checked that off, the next thing was, what is the difference I'm feeling between these things? With Arts Ed and Guildhall, there was a certain level of comfort that I had felt previously. There was a certain level of familiarity and easiness. Not in terms of what the process would be, but ease kind of being in that space, which I had experienced before.

And then when it came to RADA, there wasn't that. I had no clue what to expect. Everything felt so new and different in terms of what I'd experienced when it came to acting and teachers, that I was so intrigued. There was a level of I don't know what I would experience when I'm here, that I wanted, because I didn't want to be comfortable. I really wanted to be challenged when it came to the next level of where I was going to go with acting. And I was, I can stay somewhere, and I can choose somewhere where I know kind of how I'd sit and how I'd feel. Or I can go somewhere where it's literally the vastest kind of pool of 'anything could happen'. And that really excited me, and I remember doing my auditions for RADA and feeling like I was learning so much through the audition process. And I would go home, and I would be, oh, my gosh. And then, Mum, they gave me this note and then this happened. And it just – I completely changed and it was opening my eyes. And it was so different to anything I'd experienced. And it was actually probably the scariest out of all the auditions. It felt really big and far away and I was like, gosh, I don't know what I expect I will get if I come here. Do I need to go there because I don't want to know what's going to happen next. I want to be challenged. I want to feel like I'm on the tip of my toes. Because this is what I want to do. I'm like at RADA it looks like I'm going to start to find out things that I haven't yet known. And that's what I want. And that was RADA. And that's why I chose it.

Yeah, I always say that I feel like RADA – my experience in training, the word would be growth. Because what I expected, which was – I didn't have a lot of expectations, because I had no clue what I was getting myself into. But what I did expect was to grow and to learn so much more than I had known before. And I did.

But the lessons weren't kind of this thing that was so far away from me that it was, oh, my gosh, this is amazing. It was more a kind of unpicking, unlearning, opening yourself up, and realizing that those answers are kind of already here. And it's more just like a reawakening to lots of things that you already have innately within you. That's kind of what the actor training felt like. And it was a growth almost, in the opposite way.

It's like a growth into the truth of who you are, that self when you're really young, and the girl who was doing plays for her family in her living room and stuff like that. That's the actor, that's the truth of the matter. It was kind of a reversal to find who you are and grow in that way. And then you become a stronger person. That's kind of how I feel my process was.

PJ What did you get from your actor training?

AO In a positive way, what I got from that was, I realized that the power is completely within me, there's no shapeshifting that is required to be something that you think works. The artistry, the power, or the truth is within you. And that's kind of where the performance will come from. It's all the tools – otherwise, I always say, I don't think there'd be so many actors that exist, if we didn't all have something innately uniquely that works for all these different roles. That's why the same role can be played again and again and again, because no matter who you are, you're going to bring who you are to it. And that's going to make it different. And I kind of learned that along the process. It was, oh, wait, it's here. It's not there. I'm not trying to run to it. It is in here that I need to open up to. And that was the positive I got through training.

And I think the negative wasn't so much an impact, but a lesson I was thankful to learn when I was there, which is you're inspired by so many people, and it can feel like the answers come from them and their approval.

And I think drama school runs the risk, if you're not careful, of you becoming dependent on the approval of those tutors, or people like that. Because you rely on them so much when you enter the institution, you're so open to learn and absorb. And it's completely understandable. But there's a moment when I think that lesson has to be learnt for the benefit of yourself. Because in this profession, everyone only knows so much. And the rest, and really most of it, if not all of it is up to you to kind of figure out yourself. And you have to constantly learn those lessons and stay open. And the answer is there's no kind of acting Bible as people say. It's kind of you, figuring it out. And the next best thing that somebody thinks is amazing that they see on screen, it can be something that we've never seen before. But it's not because I think that thing is really distilled. And that person is doing something specific. I think it roots itself in truth of who you are. And I think drama school can, if you let it, make you feel like everybody else are the experts. And you're beholden to that. And you have to unlearn that lesson, I think pretty soon otherwise …

PJ What drives you? Looking at issues of employability, how do you navigate this?

AO I always say to everyone, no matter what you do, something's going to be hard. Whatever job that is, if it's doctor, lawyer, etc., writer, whatever it is. And you just have to choose where you want your hard. And I choose the thing – I'd rather find things hard in the thing I love than find things hard in another thing that doesn't bring me that much joy.

I think as an actor, you have to come to terms with the reality of your job. Otherwise, you'll just keep kidding yourself to what you think it should look like. And you'll keep thinking that you're doing something wrong, because it's not looking a certain way.

Once you become honest with yourself about what it looks like, you can kind of start being honest about what you can do in those moments where you're not working. Because unemployment is a factor of an actor's journey at some point.

PJ Is your preparation for a role different for theatre and screen?

AO Yeah, it's definitely different. And it's different depending on the project, never mind just theatre and screen. If I look back on my process, I don't find that I go to something specific constantly.

It really is a dance with whichever character I have in front of me at that moment. But the factors that I think always reappear in my process, no matter what it is, is music, visual images, and writing words for my character's POV. If I look at all my processes, no matter how much they change, those things are always present in some way, at some point.

PJ How do you decide what roles to go for?

AO I have to be super honest with myself when answering the questions about what I could be embarking on at that time. And if it aligns with what I want in that moment, and what will be great for me and how it will feed me creatively.

I definitely think auditioning for things that come your way is important because you kind of get the practice of doing the auditions. You get to be seen. But then saying yes to something if it comes away as a whole other thing. And I think people have to be honest with themselves, because no matter what you say yes to it's you who's going to have to commit to that time period. And that work. So, if you want that for yourself, or if you're doing it because you think everybody else is telling you, this needs to happen …

You're not going to do it justice or do yourself justice. So, I think you have to be honest with yourself when asking questions of yourself when taking things on. But I feel experiencing things, whether that be auditioning whatever, that's important as an actor.

PJ The industry and your place in it?

AO I see myself at the top. You know, I see, this industry is yours for the taking. And everything is a stepping stone. And the industry is just growth to getting where you want to go at every opportunity.

Like every credit is another opportunity to learn and grow and then reach other things that make you excited and things like that. But I see myself very much in the midst of it, doing amazing work, working with amazing people, honestly.

PJ One of the recurring issues in the creative industries is the discussion around representation. How do you see your role in relation to that conversation?

AO When it comes to representation. That's one thing, you know, just having different people in a space being there. But for me, inclusion is the important thing, is the care to actively include people in their stories, and the chance to tell their stories. And then have representation within those stories those people are telling. Every story is going to have the diversity of experience within that. And to know that one community doesn't have one kind of story arc or one way forward, that there's a diversification within those stories. And if you give people the chance to tell those stories, then you have the opportunity for other people to see themselves in twenty or more different lights and know that there's not one thing that they have to follow in order to be successful. And that's what's important, in my opinion.

But also, for me, my job is to tell stories, and that's how I see my role in the industry. I see myself in a diverse number of stories as a storyteller. There isn't one thing or one rhyme that I think I just have to follow, even though other people will put stuff on you. I think it's important to remember labels come because people want to box things, to make it make sense in their mind. But if you know you can exist, because you can, in many different spaces, you kind of create that for yourself, you open yourself up to that. And people will try to – I think, whoever you are, if there's some sort of success – to box you and make it make sense for them. And you have to, at every opportunity, go with what feels right for you and just ignore the labels or the boxes. Otherwise, you start to label yourself and you start to get stuck. But labels are created by people, other people who are insecure about, holding onto what you are, like greatness is incredibly intimidating, I think. And success, you can let yourself shrink or you can just stand in your light. I think – there was a quote, I can't remember who said it, but it's like one of the scariest things for other people is somebody standing fully in their light, in their brilliance. It's absolutely terrifying.

PJ It was Marianne Williamson 'Our deepest fear is that we are powerful beyond measure. It is our light, not our darkness that most frightens us … And as we let our own light shine, we unconsciously give other people permission to do the same.'

AO And I think, just like what we were saying about leaving drama school and having that hang up, you kind of have to let go of, I'm a student, I'm this. Asking questions is even a point of standing in your light. Being front footed about wanting to figure things out. I feel like you think that you kind of can't and you kind of don't want to make a noise. But that's just as important and doing justice to something that you're stepping into. With the job that I just did (2022 screen adaptation of Dolly Alderton's *Everything I Know about Love*, Aliyah's played Amara) I remember there were all these questions that I had, I was like, I need to ask this. And I want to see why this is happening. And because that happened. There was so much I was then proud of when I left the job, and I could watch back and I was, no, I fought for that. And I really wanted that. And I – and that actually happened and now it's on – like there's a scene, it's so tiny. But I spoke about it in an interview.

It was my character, 'Amara', being seen undoing her braids.

We had worked out throughout the storyline with the hair and make-up crew that we wanted lots of different hairstyles for Amara. I offered that, that's very natural and real for Black girls, I'm always changing my hair. But I said I really think it'd be cool to see a scene of her undoing her hair. Because I haven't seen that before. And the lead of hair and make-up was incredible. And she was kind of like we're going to get somebody to come on. And she got this hairstylist called Nicole Ruby Rose. And she created this thing where it actually looked like I was taking out my hair. And it's like a split second.

But one of my best friends growing up, we went out for lunch. And she was, oh my gosh, I love that scene where she's undoing her hair. And I was like, stop. I was, that is something it's so important because it's so normal. And I wanted to see it on TV. And the fact that you have noticed that, and I haven't even told you the whole story behind it was massive to me. And I was like that can seem little and some people kind of didn't understand it. But I was, I know what this is. I know what this is. And you kind of don't have to understand it. You kind of just have to trust. And it's hard to be that young at that stage and be, hey, big, big departments and people just trust that what I'm putting out is going to work. But then they did and the response that I got was just ah, so worth it. And even if I didn't get a response, it was so worth it because I knew what that meant.

PJ Thinking in terms of how you choose to identify, what do you think are the challenges in the acting/creative industry now?

AO Yeah, yeah. It's definitely not the same for everyone. Especially if we're going to go off the thing of, where you come from, like an upbringing in London to somewhere else, it's going to be so so different. And if I'm honest, I don't look at my profession in that light.

I've never searched out for the hurdles or the pitfalls or focused on them. It's just something I've honestly never had an interest in doing. It's never how I've seen things. But what I do do is know what I want and I'll get. And the opportunities, like plural for – it's for others to see me the way I see myself, which is in a number of stories, and a number of world accent scenarios, mediums, whether it be theatre, film, TV, radio, etc. And often not just the drop in the ocean kind of splash of something different that captures everyone's attention in that moment, and everyone talks about and then we don't get again for a while.

I think the frequency at which we get those opportunities is something that's not so present. But I fully plan to indulge in the frequency of those things. Because I didn't know I've – I feel like if you can't, you're heard or sometimes that's all you see. And it doesn't mean that you're naive, or I'm naive to the industry. It's just when hard moments come you deal with them as they come up. And hopefully what was once hard becomes easier.

But as for me I choose to kind of live it in the way I'm going to experience it, which is kind of fully and openly and powerfully.

PJ What pitfalls should actors emerging from drama school aim to avoid?

AO I feel like that's almost impossible to answer. Because you'll never know that they're there sometimes, unless you fall. And I feel like that's not really a bad thing, because you kind of just get back up and dust yourself off and carry on stepping.

But it is a whole new landscape once you leave drama school and enter the industry. It's something that you just have not been a part of for three years. And three years is a long time. Because in that three years you're doing so much.

But I will say is when you're at drama school, it feels like you are going at 100 miles per hour. Because you are, you're doing classes and projects and this and that and everything's happening. And then when you leave drama school, it feels like you're doing ten miles per hour in like a seventy-mile per hour zone. And that can feel difficult.

I feel like you have to then again, be honest with your situation and know that that's okay. Because it's just a feeling. It's not the reality of the situation because you're moving in your lane. And that is the speed limit at that time. And again, your path isn't like anyone else's. So, you have to stop looking in other people's zone.

So, in that sense, I think it's just about being honest with the race that you're running. And coming to terms with the honesty of the actor's profession, and not trying to paint it as something that it's not. And thinking that if it doesn't look like something, it's not working.

Because I could have a career that nobody else has had and then suddenly, I'm this really unique story that's like, oh, my gosh. And when really, it's just my path and my journey, and it looks the way it looks. And then the other person who also has great success looks the way they look. And I don't know, don't get bogged down with what other people are doing. I feel like that's a pitfall to avoid, that's probably the thing you can start helping yourself with the earliest – early on once you leave drama school is like, being happy for people and doing the work for yourself. Yeah.

PJ What motivates you to want to act and keep doing it?

AO My joy for it, honestly, there is so so so much joy that I find in doing this profession. There has been since I was really, really young. And the things that I encounter in the world every day, keep me going. Books, plays music, musicals, other people, those things kind of get me creatively like, oh. And I can't help but see myself living truthfully in somebody's shoes or in a world or in a lifestyle and something.

My brain just keeps going both hard times and great time, and motivates me. I don't know, it's just, I – I feel like we live in a world that kind of screams art at every opportunity, whatever that is. And that just makes me think – it makes me go, oh, gosh, I'd love to – I'd love to do that. I'd love to do this.

And I feel my love to do that in this series. Kind of opening yourself up to the world. That stuff just gets my heart going. I love it. Honestly there is so much joy.

PJ What are your broad aims for the future of your screen acting presences?

AO To inhabit many worlds and characters that I creatively love. And to do it in many different mediums.

To also work with other incredible creatives who inspire me and welcome me to the other faces of this complicated and simple and brilliant craft and make me feel again like the kid doing the performances to her family in the living room. Yeah.

PJ Who are the actors and directors that have inspired you?

AO Oh, it's honestly – gosh, there's countless. I'm hesitant to name them all because I want to – the list is very long. And I keep going – but I'll – I'll like talk about an experience that I had. Because they're always – they're kind of like distilled in moments.

I remember being blown away when I saw Barry Jenkins's (2018) *If Beale Street Could Talk* at the BFI. There was the sensitivity and the warmth and the beauty of not only the performances, but the direction, the music and the cinematography. I remember it just blowing me away. And I remember my mouth just being open for most of the film. Because I'd just never seen my skin portrayed like that on screen. It was just so beautiful and stunning to look at. And I remember reading the interviews with Barry Jenkins about his process to doing that. And it was one of the most inspiring things that I read. And I was like, I'd love to work with a director like that. I can't help but become and fall like deeply in love with the craft of people who are so passionate about what they do. And it's so intricate and I loved reading that.

But I mean as an actor and director Regina King is amazing. As an actor Brian Tyree Henry, who was also in *If Beale Street Could Talk* is amazing. Mark Ruffalo is amazing. I remember falling in love with him when I was like thirteen. Watching *13 Going on 30*. It was one of my favourite movies.

Same with Jennifer Garner. Taika Waititi as a director just seems so cool. Greta Gerwig, Ava DuVernay, I mean her movies do just make me cry all the time on – on like a real deep level.

But there's something about the passion. Again, like I was saying about the craft, being around somebody like that, being directed by somebody like that must feel amazing. And then you have Gina Prince-Bythewood, who like did *Love and Basketball* and *The Woman King*.

PJ If a young Black and Global Majority person of eighteen made the decision that they want to become an actor, what would your advice be?

AO I'd say go for it, nothing is stopping you, there's no time like the present.

Everything is just noise, and nothing is impossible. And if it hasn't been done, you can be the one to do it. And again, other people may project their fear onto you in the guise of, well, warnings and it's just noise because you set your path.

And you just have to go and do the thing that brings you joy and not lose your faith. Because you're born from something bigger than all of us. So, you have to hold on to that. Yeah.

PJ Hard-dough bread, Sourdough bread, Chin Chin, Sweetbread, Roti, Sudsa, Bun and Cheese, Nai Wong Bao -奶黄包- Custard Bun or Naan?

AO Okay, Chin Chin. That is – that's my home. That's my heart. Take it on a plane. Take it to set. Have it in between takes. Like that is the place to be.

Phoebe Campbell

Photo credit: Clare Park.

Phoebe Campbell graduated from RADA in 2022 and is currently playing Rhaena Targaryen in *House of the Dragon*. Since graduating Phoebe has also performed in ETT's production of *The Importance of Being Earnest* where they played Cecily.

Pamela Jikiemi – PJ Tell me about your journey to become an actor.

Phoebe Campbell – PC I started doing acting when I was really young. And then I had some incredible teachers at my school when I went to secondary school. And my drama teacher worked also for Pleasance. So, then she made it easier for us to audition for Young Pleasance.

And that's when it all started. I did my first Young Pleasance show when I was thirteen or fourteen. I did *Teachers*. And then the next one that I did, we went to Edinburgh. And then it all snowballed from that, and I was like, yeah, for sure this is what I want to do. And then in my first production that went to Edinburgh, which was *Rights* – a children's tragedy, which is based on Frank Wedekind's *Spring Awakening*, that's when I had agent interest, and that's when I got signed.

My parents were very firm. No, you need to get your grades first, and then you can work. So, then I started to work in my final year of school. And then I went to uni because they were also very much like drama school is not a thing we want you to do.

You need to widen your horizons. And so, I did uni, I hated Bristol. I loved Bristol for a lot of reasons. But the actual course was useless.

I studied theatre and performance but it was purely theory and that is – the joke is on me because I just didn't read about it. I was like, ha ha, you said I couldn't go to drama school. I'll study drama.

PJ Training around learning 'the craft'; did you go to a conservatoire drama school? Talk about your creative career and your commitment towards pursuing it.

PC Okay. Oh, goodness. So, I was convinced that the place I wanted to go was Guildhall. I was like, this is it. Great, my Guildhall auditions were so much fun. I had the best time in the world. I knew loads of people already there. And then I got offered it and I was, right, this is sorted.

But I was still doing RADA audition rounds and RADA was frightening. It was so frightening, I remember because I only wanted to go to Guildhall, I looked only at what Guildhall required. And they said two contemporary speeches and one classical. But RADA was the opposite. It was two classical and one contemporary. And I saw this on the sheet of paper, and I just thought I'll just write down something. I'll just write down *Romeo and Juliet*.

I hadn't learned it, didn't care. Got in and it was Nona Shepphard. And Nona was like, yeah, *Romeo and Juliet*. And I was like, oh, my God. Okay. Sure. And Pamela, I kid you not. I just made it up – I just started talking. I had no idea. And she stopped me. And she said, yeah, love, you have a tendency to paraphrase. And I was like, oh, that's – that's so mad. That's so crazy. So, I had only said about three lines of nonsense, and thought it was over.

And I called my friend, I was, I'm never setting a foot in this building.

This was manic. But I found it really funny. But it was also – RADA was so direct with me about all the things that I needed to improve on immediately. And I hadn't had that anywhere else.

Like everywhere else had just been, yeah, great, fine, sure. And that was really inspiring. And also, this sounds like a lie, but it's not. I met Deborah Dada, now Deborah Alli. I met Deborah at a Guildhall audition, and she said one line and I thought this is the best actress I've ever seen. And then before the final round of Guildhall, she messaged me saying she got into RADA, she was going to RADA. And I was like, wicked, I'll go where you go, that's great; I want to be alongside you. You are phenomenal. So, yeah, I chose RADA.

Overall, I wouldn't change it for the world. I really wouldn't. I'm – yeah, I'm so thankful and grateful that I went to RADA.

PJ What did you get from your actor training?

PC It's obviously had its ups and downs as every place has. And I think especially with our year and Covid and having years above wanting to set fire to the school. And then, finding out everything that happened, and then reflecting on your own experience, there was a lot of stuff that wasn't great.

But it's not anything I hadn't already experienced throughout my education. Of teachers saying things to me and students and whatever, whatever. So, it was helpful.

Just in terms of racially, it was very insensitive when I first got here, and there were a lot of conversations, I had teachers calling me angry, and I couldn't understand it. And a lot of comments when I had braids in about they're too heavy, it will affect your movement, you need to take them out. All this stuff.

But then there were all these people next to me, with long-ass hair and I was like, right, okay. And a sort of lack of awareness, I guess, in when you're given all these texts and scripts that are historical or just further back in time, it's like, okay, but so then, do I also, on top of doing what everyone else does have to research how people were to address me racially in that time? Because that adds certain – it contextualizes so much of what you do. Because there's been so much racial prejudice throughout all of history. It's such an added thing. And it does completely affect how I would play a role. And there was a huge lack of awareness of that when I was first here, and a massive confusion as to why I would ask okay, and so do I – am I from the same place?

This is actually – it was a positive and a negative. So, in first year, I think when I came in, I didn't realize that so much of it was about you as an individual.

And they really interrogate you as a person which can feel so confronting if you feel like you've – you've built yourself finally into a human that can function in the world, to have all of that be pointed out and picked apart and – it's just so difficult for such a young adult. But then you realize you bring all those things to each character. If you don't address that, you will never realize why – I don't know – you might always wink on stage by accident or have a twitch in your hand. And then isolating those things and being, oh my God, Phoebe doesn't have to be present in everything I do, was a huge learning lesson for me. So, it was horrible at the time. But then, as I progressed on with my training, I realized how important it was and how thankful I was that I'd had that.

What didn't work for me. I think, I struggled with sometimes the dynamic, I have a bit of an authority complex as it is. And I felt immediately, we were sort of made to feel that we had to be so thankful for being there and being in that building. And it was, well, but I've come here to learn, I don't want to praise you and idolize you, I want to keep my sense of self. And I want to always know how I feel in situations and not just sit there and take everything and think it's all okay when some things aren't okay. And that's no one else's responsibility but mine. So, I did find that – that was tough. But it eases, that's just first year. And then the teachers get to know you. And they know you're a real human and they're like, great, you can navigate your own training. But at the beginning, it was like it has to be done this way. And I don't think that works as a collective statement.

A lot of people, their identity is celebrated. So – I hate to say it but say, if you're a straight white cis man in the building, you're not really challenged on that. It's like, great, this is what we'd like you to play with because this is so strong and whatever. But if you're anything other, it's like now let's try different routes. Let's try you doing something else. Which again, felt at the time quite attacking. But now it's so great, because I can do so many different things. I don't have to be myself; I don't feel a need that that's my comfort zone. I feel able to – to jump into different things. So, a blessing, really, but it was tough.

PJ What drives you? Looking at issues of employability, how do you navigate this?

PC What drives me? I just really love what I do. I love it. It's something that makes me so happy. And I think I learned so much about humans in general. And I can't understand why people wouldn't want to do that all the time.

Because not only do you get to meet such an amazing scope of people from different life experiences, but you also get to be those people. And that's amazing. And then also hustle – you need money too. I mean, that drives me, I need to survive massively and provide – return to my family and give what they've given me.

Do you know what I mean? There's a load of things. But I don't think I could do it if I wasn't as obsessed with it as I am.

PJ Is your preparation for a role different for theatre and screen?

PC Yes, yes, because I feel like the preparation for theatre happens in the room. It's nurtured in the space where you're also all preparing together. And you all do all the context of whatever play you're doing.

Well, it depends on your director but usually – and character work, that's a constant process. Whereas in screen, you sort of just have to turn up with it all there. And that's what I'm so thankful for training for as well.

Because it means that that doesn't stress me, I know how to do that. I have a set of questions I need to be able to answer for myself as this character. And if I can't answer them, I've got no idea what I'm doing. So, that's such an important process for me before I do anything.

PJ How do you decide what roles to go for?

PC I sort of just take anything at this point. But hopefully that is going to change. I don't know when that's going to happen. But – but maybe when I'm a bit more settled in the industry, and it feels like, I've worked hard enough and got enough exposure as such to make those choices. Yeah, I don't know.

PJ The industry and your place in it?

PC Oh, I think the industry hasn't changed as much as everyone thinks it has at all actually. I think that's why I'm also glad that RADA wasn't smooth sailing and there was a load of things I had to deal with, in terms of how people perceived me and projected that onto me. Because it's exactly what the industry still is. So, I'm a little bit sceptical about it.

But I do think that there are so many amazing things coming out at the moment and being written, to be honest with you, that the industry is a really exciting place.

And luckily, it seems for now anyway, that I have things lined up.

So, there isn't that immediate stress of I don't know what to do with my life. For the foreseeable, I'm okay. So, yeah, it feels alright.

PJ One of the recurring issues in the creative industries is the discussion around representation. How do you see your role in relation to that conversation?

PC Yeah, so doing a job recently, that was a huge – oh, I don't even know if I can talk about this. Let me rephrase it as a general thing.

Working in a space that was celebrating having people of colour being in these spaces, it was a new choice that they made for the show that they would put people of colour in, also meant that we had to face some backlash from the internet of people being really mad that that was happening. And it also meant that – it wasn't necessarily – but it sometimes could feel like it was just shoe-horned in.

This was just because they had to and it wasn't actually thought out to the extent that it should have been. And being very gender queer and not – not defining by anything is also nonsensical in the industry, because no one acknowledges it really.

It's like a huge discussion where they are, oh; it's all happening and working with people who are the same which has been incredible. But I know that they also get misgendered all the time and yeah, it's tough. It's really, really tough. So, I hope that in my lifetime, I will be able to change this, Pamela, I'm so determined.

I promise you; I'm going to fix it. Yeah, and I'm excited for that. I am excited, but it's – yeah, it takes its toll. Sometimes it really does.

PJ Thinking in terms of how you choose to identify, what do you think are the challenges in the acting/creative industry now?

PC I think being mixed – how people would perceive me as a mixed female presenting is such a gift in the industry at the moment because I don't think enough Black women are getting into the spaces that they need to.

We're at the stage where it's, if you're mixed, you will count as Black. And that's what we'll see. And despite that being obviously very beneficial for me that's – that's heart-breaking, I think, and I can't wait for the industry to change.

I think the Black man is getting his time massively, which I think is gorgeous and beautiful, but I can't wait for it to be the Black woman. And in terms of what's hard about it, is when you're working in a majority typically white space and they've got POCs in being called the wrong name for months, because they cannot distinguish you.

What do you mean? We don't look alike, we are not even the same skin tone. This is silly. This is just like, silly. And so, that's when you start to feel like, did they ever – was this just shoehorned in? Was this just for the sake of doing it, because it's so topical? Which I don't think it is.

But these little, small things that happen make you feel so much smaller than everyone else. And like you don't matter in a space. And you're all just seen as a collective. It's not you, as an individual bring so much to this project. Which is hard. It's hard, but it's never intentional. I know it's not intentional. There's no malice behind it. It's just where the world is at right now.

PJ What pitfalls should actors emerging from drama school aim to avoid?

PC I think – I mean, I speak from a really privileged position of – of having work and – and being signed. But I can only imagine the stress and anxiety you would feel if that wasn't the case. And feeling like it's a 'you' problem.

Instead of it's actually just the industry. It's not that you're not good enough. Because I know people are struggling with being signed. And it's so hard to watch, because they feel like it's a judgement on their abilities, when actually, they're amazing and what they've done has been fantastic.

So, I think a pitfall would be, telling yourself that it's not for you, when that's not the case, or relying on external validation, when there is so much work you can create yourself and then – and do brilliant things with. And we've seen that. You know, we've seen that on TV so much.

PJ What motivates you to want to act and keep doing it?

PC I think it's a lot of what I've said. I just think being empathetic to everyone's stories in the world is so important.

I think the world would be such a better place if people would just put themselves in other people's shoes. And we literally do that. And I just – I feel so blessed by the people I've been able to meet through acting, and being able to watch incredible, incredible performances.

And see what humans are capable of – the emotions we store inside of ourselves. And – oh, I just think it's – everything else sounds boring. It is so great.

PJ What are your broad aims for the future of your screen acting presence?

PC The broad aims. Well, I hope what I'm doing at the moment continues. And then that to me is just like such an exciting prospect to work on a character for potentially years. Like, wow!

PJ Who are the actors and directors that have inspired you?

PC Deborah Alli. Directors are harder to say, because I haven't been in the industry for that long in terms of working in that way.

I could probably answer actors better than that. Because I'm terrible with directors' names. But actors, I've had the privilege of working along someone called Emma D'Arcy. And they are the most talented – oh, my goodness – oh, wow. And Eve Best, as well, and she's an ex-RADA grad. Steve Toussaint – on – the cast of *House of Dragons* is unbelievable. And that has been so, so inspiring. And Bethany Antonia she's my age, and she's just incredible. And then in a wider sense, Naomie Harris. And Viola Davis.

PJ If a young Black and Global Majority person of eighteen made the decision that they want to become an actor, what would your advice be?

PC I'd say go get it. We need more of you. Come, come shed your light, shed your stories. Bring your authentic, beautiful selves.

I can't wait until the industry is oversaturated in fact, with us, because I think it would be better. I just think it would be great.

Yeah, and just know yourself and know that no matter what anyone says to you, you just have the most beautiful story to tell. And that story just lives inside of you, I think. Yeah, I would only encourage.

PJ Hard-dough bread, Sourdough bread, Chin Chin, Sweetbread, Roti, Sudsa, Bun and Cheese, Nai Wong Bao -奶黄包- Custard Bun or Naan?

PC Sourdough. For sure. For sure, for sure, for sure. For sure. Sourdough.

Jamael Westman

Photographer: Ruth Crafer.

Born in London, **Jamael Westman** attended RADA. His titular role in the West End production of Lin-Manuel Miranda's musical *Hamilton* earned him an Olivier Award nomination and the Evening Standard Theatre Award's Emerging Talent Honour. Other theatre credits include *Imposter 22* (Royal Court), *Torn* (Royal Court), *Patriots* (Almeida), *The Lorax* (Old Vic) and *The White Devil* (Globe). Television credits include *Get Millie Black*, *The Essex Serpent*, *Anne Boleyn* and *BBW*. Film credits include *Good Grief, Munch, Animals*.

Pamela Jikiemi – PJ Tell me about your journey to become an actor.

Jamael Westman – JW I used to sing a bit when I was younger. Not like sing, sing. Like I'm always going to play it down.

Someone might say, no, you ain't singing. But I used to be in like choirs at school. And my mom was into music and my dad as well, not necessarily artists or anything, attached to the industry. But they had a thing for music and definitely introduced me to that. And, yes, so I started singing. I did a lot of football, a lot of performing things.

I guess, I was a bit of a performer. You know, there's old VHS of me singing at home; Seal or something 'Kissed by a Rose', I remember that song quite vividly. And yes, so I used to do that.

I felt like a lot of kids – my cousins, everyone, and we all used to do that. Yeah. Sing to MTV videos and make up dance moves, or what's the next move that's on at the moment, I definitely had that at the beginning.

PJ Training around learning 'the craft'; did you go to a conservatoire drama school? Talk about your creative career and your commitment towards pursuing it.

JW I kind of got introduced to theatre when I was in secondary school. There wasn't a drama department. But we had numerous teachers who liked to put on plays or started putting on plays. [One of which was] *Stand by Me*, based on Stephen King's *The Body*. And so, they did like a staged version of that.

I did that, I had a great time. I was outside of the confinement of formal education, and then another world if that made sense, in the institution. So, there was something kind of cool about that. I got to sit among people in different year groups – I could call them my peers. It wasn't like some kind of stratification or a feeling of being less than, it was like no we're all here to try and create something together.

So, I got the bug that was it. I kind of got the bug. My teacher did a couple more plays there. And then, yeah, I didn't really know what to do education wise, I guess it was that or football. But football just wasn't an avenue. I always played that, and then I did A-level Drama. I had a great time.

Then my teacher there suggested, the next thing is drama school. And I thought, oh, okay, that's what I need to go and do then.

So, I was in New Fitters, Oval House, Lyric, Hammersmith and South London theatres, and amateur theatre. I joined Weekend Arts College (WAC) as well. Anywhere I could get my teeth into some relatively inexpensive/free theatre training clubs..

But it just costs money. It's money that I, we, didn't have, we just could not afford that. Because I am there looking up courses and summer camps and things like that. And all that was mad expensive. One thing I did do that cost money, but it felt worth it maybe because of the prestigious nature of it all was National Youth Theatre (NYT). So, I definitely – I did that. Did the summer course for two weeks, but that was my own money. So, I just put together money from Sainsbury's – because I was working at Sainsbury's at a time. And then I put that towards it.

And then, yeah, I was just trying to get in – I remember actually getting the letter of acceptance into NYT for that summer camp. That was a really good feeling. It was nice to kind of go right actually, someone's thought, yeah, you got something. Let's see what we can do with it. During that time I was also auditioning for drama school, but I was also trying to figure out why I wanted to go to drama school in a way. I just knew I was meant to go, that that was the thing to do.

But then somewhere along the way, I think after having maybe done NYT and the time that I got into drama school, I was in a show. It started off at my youth theatre in Oval House, and then it kind of got picked up by CLT Theatre in Peckham. So, we did a play there, and I was auditioning at the same time. So, I think in that moment, I felt when I went to audition, I'm already acting. I'm an actor. I'm already in the process of working and exploring my art. And so, I realized actually, I want to train. And I guess after a few years of training on the job, I was like I actually want to go to drama school to refine this work, and to develop more. As opposed to I want to get in because I want to be an actor, or I want to get in because that's where everything starts working out. I was like no, I'm already working things out. But I would love some rigorous training to add strings to my bow. I walked into those audition spaces knowing a bit more about myself. Also, I had a piece that really spoke to me. I did some pieces in the years prior to that that didn't really speak to me. I liked the idea of them, but I don't think they really touched me in the same way as the piece I did from *God's Property* by Arinzé Kene. That play really set it off for me to be honest. I saw that play and I was just like, wow, I felt seen. I felt – it was probably the first time I had ever cried watching theatre before. And so, I was reminded through the power of theatre of my humanity, I felt seen, and I felt connected, and I felt the power of it.

I recognized it, maybe in an outward sense coming from me, but I never really experienced it coming at me. And so, yeah, that play, *God's Property* by Arinzé Kene was major, major influence on my sense of self and – and the power of theatre. Took that play – took that speech to – to drama schools. And I got into RADA with that speech, as well as a I don't know – a classical piece, I don't know which one that was.

I didn't really want to leave London. I was like, yeah, I'm a Londoner so I'm going to probably stay in London for this. I remember auditioning for Manchester Met; I went there, had a great time in Manchester. I auditioned and I was like, this is my event and I got in. But I was like, I'm not living in Manchester.

I'm a Londoner. I don't think I'm going to leave like that, and then I auditioned at Guildhall, LAMDA and RADA and over the course of four years maybe I got a recall here and there. So, I started to get a sense of not only what it is they were looking for, but also how to refine the work and speak more truthfully, at least in the eyes of the people that were judging it.

Then I went to RADA and was almost – in the way of white world spoilt with the diversity of our year group. I felt there were people that I mixed with that were like, oh, you are from where I'm from. Which, having seen the history of RADA and looked at it more in depth, that was not always the case. I mean in terms of who I was surrounded by and where I could feel a sense of belonging. But, yeah, and obviously, regardless of race, we all found a tribe amongst each other, and all really got close as a year group.

We had a good year group, not that all your groups get on so well. Didn't mean we didn't have our moments. For sure. I know that one member of our year group, Abraham Popoola, yeah, an absolute beacon of hope and progress and real change agent and just a great human all round. We kind of pushed forward the idea of actually putting on a play, a Black play, but it wasn't really as such like a Black play. It was more like let's put on a play that has just got back. We had enough people in our year for that to be the case. But it is – and the line was if you will, was like every other play that's on, we don't call it a white play. There were moments where it's like we're going to put on a Black play, we are going to have a little meeting with other Black students just to discuss that, where we're at and how we saw the current kind of system of RADA as being run. And if we feel heard and seen.

And yeah, some people in our year group – people that we called friends took umbrage with that, you know, they felt a way about us doing that, 'oh, I'm not invited then?' Or, 'is that not like racist?'

It felt like how – not so much now I guess you kind of get used to it. But people who you thought were level-headed, or empathetic or open-hearted people suddenly turned ignorant and very closed-minded, especially the more you read into the Black experience, or Black thought around race, racism and the current state of affairs.

So, yeah, RADA had a lot to offer. But had a lot to say for itself in terms of a really outdated way of educating its students, particularly with the ever-changing representation of the students, even to women. So, to add some more on that when it came to people of colour who, you know, they had never seen, or only seen in the past, however many years, had an incredible education there. But I guess it was like a microcosm of Britain all the wealth, all the things you could need, but just completely mired in racism and – and really problematic viewpoints on people, and the people that exist in the country. As well as its history. So, that's what it was. It is just an institution, which upheld and perpetuated the same issues in terms of its denial and ignorance. So, yeah, lots to benefit from, but lots to answer for and work on. So, we faced that then. But I was very lucky to be surrounded by – and we actually managed to – we did put on a play as well in the end. It was called *Bricks and Pieces*, and it was directed by Natalie Ibu. And – it was new writing as well, so it was written around us as – the students. So, we came in with the writer, and from who we kind of were and the conversations we had, maybe a workshop, came up with a play. Charlene James, yeah, man, I miss her. Where is she at? She did *Cutting It* as well which was on at the Young Vic, which is where I saw it. But yeah, I need to contact her still. That's another thing as well, there's nothing like community when it comes to being a Black actor. Nothing like it. Nothing like having a community – and so even this kind of collating that community and putting it into a generational historical document. Yeah, man. That's cool. That's really cool. Because, you know, sometimes it's fleeting, when you find moments with fellow actors just on the road and you're like, yo, you know, you might not even have time to have that conversation. But you both know. It's almost like the nod that you get from our fellow people, just other people – on the road. There's an acknowledgement there. And if you have more time, you can talk about.

PJ What did you get from your actor training?

JW Feels lonely, man. It's a lonely enough thing in itself especially – especially as a Black artist, I think. Because you know, proportionally, or whatever it is, or just, categorically there are less of us within this industry. And it's very white dominated. So, in terms of the people that you – on your everyday interact with the more time, they're going to be white. Those are the gatekeepers. Those are the people that are our agents more time. So, those are the people you're more in contact with. And then – so, it's isolating, it's just isolating in and of itself. And then obviously, even just as an artist, like – obviously, you know, you've got a community but not – in terms of – where I come from understands the experience. Obviously, we all share an experience of just being human beings. But I think on a creative level, there's an isolation there, because I definitely feel that, I'm on my own – people are like, oh, you're doing that acting thing, they kind of get it, but they don't really get it.

And it's not a job in like nine to five – yeah, the weekends aren't the same. It's a bit sporadic. So those kinds of relationships are even more so kind of essential, but also, the most deprived as well.

And there's also a level of – and I even felt this – it was funny – I mean, I guess I had this in my third year. And you know, you hear about it from third years, the years above you, of competition. It is like everyone feels like they're competing for an agent. But we're all different. I'm not you, you're not me. I get it to a degree in terms of grabbing someone's attention, if there is a comparative element, you're just trying to get an agent. So, there is an element of competition there. But, I guess, my thoughts on that have never gone further than, why – how can there be a competition when we're so different? Competition always suggests there's something comparative between us and there isn't. We're just different. Whatever I offer is not going to be what you are offering to a degree.

We are drama school students. And so, we're all trying to be the best drama school student. And I guess the parallel of that was, oh, we're all Black actors. We're all just seen as Black actors. So, we're all brushed with the same kind of generalization. But actually – I found anyway that it's all love, it's all love between Black actors. Even if – we are in the same room, I will not feel like – kind of part of this is, I'm just glad you're in the room. I'm glad that we're here. But I always feel very acutely celebratory of whatever Black actors are doing. I guess – yeah.

When I left drama school, I knew that people that were put on a pedestal, people that were yeah, you're the one. You're the student that RADA wants here. You are the student that RADA wants to promote. And, you know, Black students we were getting older roles in third year. I couldn't help but feel like they were the golden children. Like they were the ones.

Out of the Black Box

And I knew I wasn't one of those in third year. So, I was like, okay, cool. I had a bit of a run in with drama school. They were on a bit of a kind of – I don't know how to put it – like it was a bit sick to a degree, in my opinion, in terms of how I had to conform – well, not even conform. Yeah, conform initially, but actually it was things were just – I just became the kid that was a bit of – the – the tearaway kid. So, I kind of – in my third year I was like, look, this – this place ain't going to give me no handouts. I was very acutely aware of that, as we became more exposed to the industry and kind of leaving. But yeah, like there was no preparation for when we left. So, I was already on my thing, like look I'm going to have to do this for myself, nobody here is going to do anything for me. I became aware of that in second year. Obviously, some people were still, no, RADA has got me, they've got my back, they're going to put me forward for things, they're going to support them the whole way through, dah, dah, dah, dah. I'm going to make it. And then we all leave now.

You know, I left without an agent. Some people left with agents. Some people thought they were going to blow up big.

And yeah, it's funny how, out of that the people that I've seen anyway in my year, the year before me, the year after me – obviously, there's been – you know, a diverse level of success. But I feel a very acutely aware of the people that they weren't rating, or the people that – basically people of colour, Black people, have all been killing the game. And so, yeah, I'm just, right, well, it goes to show. And then the people that they were putting on top. Boy, they went through some shit. They went from an institution that really gassed them up. And then an industry that did not – the level of disappointment, depression etc. So, it's just kind of mad that you're seeing this happen. And you think, this is the fallacy of an institution like that. The delusion, which exists in the industry as well. But the industry is more cutthroat than that. And the industry – it's not really there for you like that in the same way an institution purports to be.

At drama school, people were gassed up. They were, yeah, this place loves me. I was like, they're gassing you up. But when like now what? Like you are out in the industry, and they are not there for you no more, you're kind of out on your own. And some people acutely get that from early on. They understand that they are there for you to a point. Do you know what I mean?

It's more nuanced than just being wholly positive or wholly negative. But again, yeah, it just feels like a microcosm of what happens outside. I guess what I did feel in my naivety in my – in my young hopefulness in a way and my feeling towards acting and my passion and in and around my passion to create and be creative, which is obviously, in my belief is like every kind of person's spiritual kind of destiny is to be creative in some way or other. Every day is a day, an opportunity, and a moment to be creative. What you decide to have for breakfast in the morning, whatever it is, it could be the most mundane thing. But in a way of, choosing that to be a career path and to choose that to be the way in which I identify in terms of my work. I felt betrayed, really. But that was – in my head that's a naivety.

Obviously, drama school purports to be progressive and a place for radical change. And all the shifting thoughts of how people are and how people can be and getting into the nitty gritty of what it is to be a human being, and to be a place of social commentary. And even in the first conversation I remember having in drama school was – I remember our teacher said to be an actor is political in itself. It is a political act to be an artist. It's a political act to step on stage. So, okay, cool, it sounds like you're challenging the status quo on what is possible, and how people can be.

Incrementally it wasn't long after that in my first year, I was just let down. I was like, okay, I see, I see what this is – despite your proposals of infinite possibility in what it is to be a person, and how it is to act, you have a very limited and traditional – and I guess, oppressive way of seeing things, which doesn't allow me to flourish in the way I want to flourish. It doesn't allow me to flourish in ways that I don't even know are possible, but should be, you know, like provoked in a way, and not just me as a Black student.

But when you go through drama school, I felt oh, I see, you know, like, there's a filter. Some of us can pass through that filter and some of us can't pass through that filter. Because – and that's the filter of perception, the filter of what is a good actor, what is creative and what's good art. I'm like, oh, I get it.

But in terms of where it can go. Yeah, they weren't giving us the future. They were giving us the past and in there lies hella problems. Because in terms of the student body and institution it was like the future meeting the past, or the future coming into contact and in conflict with the past. A past that is, completely ignorant of its position and how it's consistently like pulling down on the present moment and just reducing possibilities and saying … samey, samey. But then the unwillingness – well, I guess it's starting to change now maybe with some people who led whole departments and one to ones but didn't actually teach and some who have been there over forty years, we'll see. But the willingness to listen, and the willingness to adapt and change and evolve, at that time was not enough. And when you're hearing from other people that went to the drama school back in the 90s, they were asking for the same things. You are like that's wrong, that's wrong, from the off that's wrong.

But yeah, for places like that, with the things that you're responsible for, for the amount of investment that the students are putting in, the hours, the way in which this is such an intimate means of work, in terms of how we relate it to ourselves, our own personal journeys, acting is such a radical thing, personally, it can be anyway. And also, in terms of how it affects us to go to these places, to explore these people, to tell these stories. Yeah, man, I don't care what's going on outside, I don't care what country we're living in. Always, it's got to be better than that, man. It has got to meet where the students are at. And I think that it didn't in that respect.

So, it's quite long story short. It's nuanced. And it holds such a high responsibility and sets such a high bar that, you know, it – instantly it is going to be held to account more so than – you know.

I do appreciate that progressive is never progressive enough. But I think if you are in that progressive space, you have to hold space for the fact that there's stuff that you just don't know, and you need to do more. You need to do better, so it's a constant working thing.

PJ What drives you? Looking at issues of employability, how do you navigate this?

JW Stories. People, life. The little things …

I am driven by a curiosity really, in the way of developing – and continuing on a path of some kind of spiritual enlightenment or some kind of enlightenment. Art is an education, and I find education in shows that I see, music I listen to, art galleries that I visit, people that I interact with. It's all education; it's all about learning things that you never knew about yourself about the world that you live in.

Also, I'm after peace, happiness and stuff can be found in just little pockets and moments. I think the art kind of shifts me. But also – yeah, and where the art lives. Like art doesn't just live in the next job, or the next tape that comes in, or audition.

PJ Is your preparation for a role different for theatre and screen?

JW Yeah, it has to be different. Because if I'm taping for both things, one is going to be different to the other, It's going to be a bit different, just because film is smaller. And I always feel like at least it's my own kind of – I don't know – no, it's not a paranoia, it's a reality – that, directors, casting directors, whoever, producers, whoever's looking at this, are also looking at your technical ability on screen.

I think they're looking at how you hold – like how you convey a story, knowing that if it's a film or if it's TV, there's only so much you can play with and it's hitting the beats and creating images.

In a way that theatre is not – the images are more kind of – proximity, like where you're standing in a space – beyond that, yeah, act the hell out. Do what you need to do, but yeah, the kind of specificity I feel that exists in film and TV is kind of instantly picked up on.

PJ How do you decide what roles to go for?

JW Oh, I don't know if I do. I don't know if I am in that place yet. I remember, someone came one time to drama school. Maybe in the second year or so. I remember. And they came with like a sheet, and it had like, different type of actors. A, B, C, D, it was just like A, B, C, D, and some actors who just didn't get any jobs. And then it kind of distinguished between the actors that choose the type of work that they wanted to do and then the actors for whom it didn't matter what job it is, just as long as they are working. Yeah, I'm not there yet.

I mean, maybe I can say pass to a couple things. But those are less to do with the quality of the work. Because frankly, when it comes to this I am not going to start to turn my nose up.

Well, I don't know if it is just something that's not up my street that doesn't really bother me, I'll still do it.

But then I guess more for me, it's more about where I'm at in my actual life. If I can afford to take time away or leave the country or invest in that thing over there, but otherwise, I'm here for it.

PJ The industry and your place in it?

JW I think initially, maybe those feelings of like yeah, you want to be doing great work and we'll be doing all whack scripts. And when it comes down to it, when you're out on a hustle it's like, yeah, I will take anything at this point, I don't even mind.

If you were to take the kind of viewpoint of all I want to do is acting. That's my whole thing. That's it. I don't want to do anything else. Or I want to be in theatre or whatever it's hard to become anything else.

Everything feeds that. So, even, you know, the wackiest script, no scripts, just being at home, the relationships that you have with people, nurturing those relationships, they all fulfil that. It's almost sociopathic to go down that road and go like, oh, I'm just doing this to be a better actor. But it is also useful to think that everything in your life can nurture and nourish your acting.

And so, therefore kind of cherishing everything, maybe not through the lens of, oh, this will make me a better actor, but it's helpful to know actually a by-product of really enjoying the moments that are fleeting, and you know, might not in those moments feel like the most amazing thing in the world, will in some way kind of nurture and nourish whatever that is.

PJ One of the recurring issues in the creative industries is the discussion around representation. How do you see your role in relation to that conversation?

JW Being attached to a show that was really promoting diversity is necessary – you know, representation is necessary. And it's so fascinating how once upon a time it felt like a radical thing. And it still is to some degree for certain people.

It comes down to that thing, the future and the past. Like representation. It's not the past it's very much a present thing – it's like a norm, it should be normalized, we shouldn't be talking about it.

It feels like we shouldn't be talking about it, but we have to talk about things like rights, it's about the ability to protest or discrimination in the workplace, we shouldn't be talking about these things, but we are talking about these things. Diversity as positive as it sounds, also feels a bit dated. But then I also appreciate that for some people it is not. And also, I appreciate that it will never be as long as the systems of power are in place, the status quo still exists.

PJ Thinking in terms of how you choose to identify, what do you think are the challenges in the acting/creative industry now?

JW All the children of racism exist. It's about whether we're willing to acknowledge them, or whether we're willing to say, oh, we've got representation now, so we beat racism, or what have you, like little performative things.

And I realize we live in a performative industry. But yeah, I find it fascinating, worrying, frustrating. And at the same time expected that conversations around race are still slow – they are happening, obviously, after George Floyd, Breonna Taylor and Black Lives Matter movement.

That change has happened a bit more, definitely – the institutions are definitely seeing themselves in a different light. But, you know, as with anything, as with any change that is needed, it happens incrementally, it happens slowly.

There's just so much work to do. And I think people are a little bit more receptive than they ever have been. But yeah, so as a Black Mixed race person in this industry, I just recognize both the privilege. I recognize the work needed to be done. I recognize and see the systems – oppressive systems that are still in place.

And yeah, my responsibility whether it's, you know, in this case I'm talking to yourself, or in any place that I work in talking to that particular institution or production and saying, actually, what else has been done here whilst I'm contracted to this job. Like I realized that I don't really have a say if I'm not working there. But if I'm working there, I'm like, okay, what's the deal?

PJ What pitfalls should actors emerging from drama school aim to avoid?

JW My passion for this thing came before I went to drama school. So, don't forget that. Like my passion, my desire, my love of the craft, or my love of acting, of meeting people, of being in spaces, you know, would never leave.

And also just have faith, you were in those spaces before you got in. And hey, your journey at the end of the day is always – never going to be how you imagined it.

Some might work out that way, but more times it's not going to be the way you imagined. Do you know what I mean?

You are like, oh, I want to get this by this time. You do get that thing by that time. But how you got it and the feeling of when you've got it isn't going to be the same thing as how you imagined it.

Obviously. Undoubtedly, you know, none of us are God. So, let go, and be positive. And have faith, stay in contact with people, be in touch with people. To be fair, that's what you see all the time. I see people going through all sorts of things. Some people are in places like, yeah, that's not working out. And, you know – but keep the faith. And just – enjoy the journey, man.

Be honest with yourself in any given moment. Yeah, a bit of honesty always helps.

PJ Who are the actors and directors that have inspired you?

JW Well, directly one actor that inspired me was – at least in terms of my director, a guy called Toby Clark, who was the head of youth theatre at Oval House back in the day.

He's now doing acting coaching. And I think he's doing a bit of writing and directing – he ran a free youth group, at youth theatres and that has been hella good for people in the community. An actor that inspired me was an actor called Kingsley Ben-Adir. And that kind of inspiration wasn't necessarily like his body of work or like all the things that he's done as an actor, writer or any of that, it was just the story that I saw him in.

I saw Kingsley Ben-Adir in a play by Arinzé Kene that blew my socks off. It blew my head off, blew my whole spiritual cage open. I knew then that I wanted to be an actor.

This is it, whatever that – whatever, I was crying, you know, it hit me in that way. The story was amazing. The relationship between him and Ash Hunter who's playing his brother who I've worked with on *Hamilton*. And so, I was a bit like … seeing men that are on stage that I kind of put on a pedestal. I'm standing beside you right now. Yeah, man.

But any actor that just does work, usually tied to a show. I'm inspired by my friends, man. I'm inspired by people that I work with, my peers. Yeah, I think I'm a bit of a recluse on my socials. When I'm in person with people I'm fully – I'm there. I'm like, yes, what's going on, like I'm here. On my socials, I'm just kind of like sitting on it. But I feel a bit inhibited by social media.

PJ If a young Black and Global Majority person of eighteen made the decision that they want to become an actor, what would your advice be?

JW Be yourself …

I'll put good money down that the majority of people – I will say that. Just be yourself. There's nothing like you and there never will be. That's amazing. For me, I need to tell myself that. But that's amazing, in the infiniteness of life, reality, that there's only one you.

Even if you've got a twin. That's crazy. So, yeah, be and celebrate love. And be kind to you, yourself and all those that are around you, man. Yeah, 100 per cent.

PJ Hard-dough bread, Sourdough bread, Chin Chin, Sweetbread, Roti, Sudsa, Bun and Cheese, Nai Wong Bao -奶黄包- Custard Bun or Naan?

JW Bun and Cheese. There you go.

Caleb Obediah

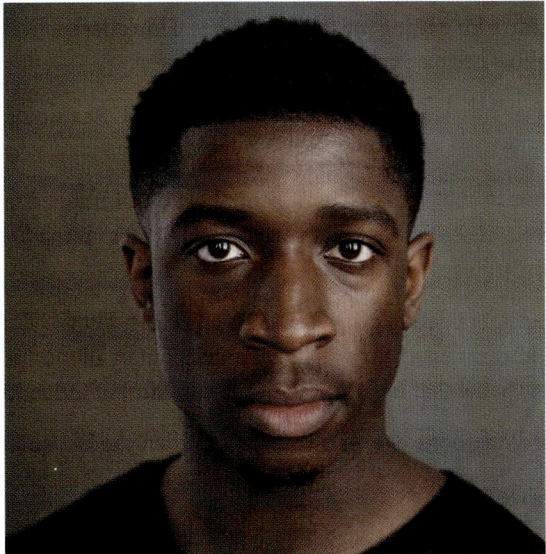

Photo by Clare Park.

Caleb Obediah, a RADA-trained actor, is a versatile artist who navigates the worlds of acting, music and creative production. Theatre includes Albany in Kenneth Branagh's West End production of *King Lear*. His screen roles include portraying Lord Cho in Netflix's *Bridgerton*, a role he is set to reprise in the upcoming seasons. Caleb contributes to humanitarian music-theatre company Wind-Up Penguin. He delves into podcasting, singing, and music production, currently crafting his own EP.

Pamela Jikiemi – PJ Tell me about your journey to become an actor.

Caleb Obediah – CO I'll start by saying that I wasn't like coming out of the womb, saying that I wanted to be an actor. I wasn't four years old or anything like that.

I was around like fourteen, fifteen, sixteen and I just loved the way I could watch something and laugh, fully laugh and leave happier or watch something sad and be really moved.

I couldn't believe the power of watching something and that happening. And I've always had some funny bones in me and I said, alright, let's actually make this happen. I remember watching *Tracy Beaker* and seeing all these people that kind of sound like we're from the UK, as opposed to America. This was local and I searched up where one of them went and they went to Identity.

So, I started going there, then from Identity, I went to another place and another place, and I literally ransacked all the youth theatres in London.

I was from Reading and so some of these places, they didn't have any spaces left. But I would literally lie and say no, no, I'm from around the corner, or – or – I had to be there. Yes, and now when I think back, I'm like,

Pamela, did I really come from Reading to all these places? How did I afford it? I just made it happen. I got a job at Nando's.

And I have to thank youth theatre for getting me to where I was. I look back and think how the hell did I afford that. But you just did it somehow because you needed to.

I think it's that, that has what has kept me going. I loved what I was doing. So yeah, that's how I got into it.

And then, obviously, it was time to audition for drama school. And I auditioned for ten places. And I was lucky enough to get into nine of them. That's where I met you, Pamela. It was on the CDT (BA Acting Collaborative and Devised Theatre) audition at Royal Central.

That was the one that I was most terrified to do. Because it's all acting, but CDT, it was different. So, I was like, oh, no, I need to bring something different. And in fact, Pamela, out of all the auditions I did, it was the Royal Central Acting CDT interview panel that has stuck with me and kind of influenced everything else.

They asked me all the standard questions like who you are and then the last question was, so what makes you angry?

Which is a simple question …

But then I was like, oh, no, they've asked me that kind of deep question and I didn't want to lie. I didn't want to be like, oh, just because for example, I'm Black. And I remember, it felt like, an hour of me just being silent and stuttering and then they looked at me and said, no, listen, don't worry, like you don't have to – but just know that it's your point of view that is the work.

And that has been like branded onto my forehead from there on, anyway, just to answer your question. That's how I got into acting and the drama school process, but it was because of all the youth theatre, that when it came to the rounds, it was like, oh, this is not so foreign to me.

We have to walk around in a room, we have to connect. Walk through the space, commit, have fun. And that's what I just brought into the audition rooms.

PJ Training around learning 'the craft'; did you go to a conservatoire drama school? Talk about your creative career and your commitment towards pursuing it.

CO I will start with the RADA Youth Company. So, when it came to, you know, these final decisions between this school and this school, I just felt coming to the Youth Company at RADA completely demystified any thoughts I had about RADA.

And again, it's about the people. And do you know what? I'm going to go to RADA. Because of the people that I've met and also just the year that I'd had before on the Foundation course with Joan Oliver, which was incredible. So, that was my sort of – the reason why I chose RADA.

PJ What did you get from your actor training?

CO Well, I'll start with the positives. Imagine it's second year, you're knackered. It's 5.30 pm, we finish maybe at 8 o'clock and we're in the middle of scene work, and you're tired.

But then two people get up and do a scene that kind of like – it's like a pinch me moment. It blows you away. It's like, where am I? These people are so, so good. And I'd done lots of youth theatre and I'd met lots of people. And so, it was like, yeah, everyone's good. But the people in my year were so good.

During the times at RADA, there might be times – luckily, we're in Central London, so there might be time to go see a show. But it's like, man, this show isn't better than the stuff that we're doing at 5.30 pm. On this tired evening at RADA. That was like a pinch me moment. So, I say all of that to say that the people in my year were incredible and I got to learn lots from them.

So, that's a huge positive for me.

I'd say another positive thing for me is, I remember in first year – I would not necessarily try to hide. I would just sort of come in, do my work, and then leave and I think they spotted that. And I think they could see the potential and they would put me in the front. And they would make me do like – especially in first year and second year, like kind of – I guess, the lead stuff to get me out of – I remember we had Chekhov, and it was with Beru Tessema. And I remember it was, I think the power of having Beru, a teacher that I trusted. Who I felt was similar to me, a Black man, a Black tutor, direct us. And just the way he spoke. I would do something like some sort of movement thing because I couldn't find the right word. And he understood exactly what it was.

And usually with other tutors I might get a frown and, of course, use the right words. Of course, use words. But it was something about working with him, him understanding me and the process that allowed me to trust the space and just step into it. And I remember from that day on – from that performance, and – because we went to Hampstead Heath and because the play, Chekhov's, *The Seagull* is out in the open, we did it – the play out in the open.

To this day, I can't forget how beautiful it was seeing it in the open space. And it was all through him, gently pushing and understanding me as actor. And from there, I think I didn't stop daring to be in the space. And that's all because of that. So, I'm really grateful that happened in first year.

Because the way I look is quite positive, it's quite hard to find a negative that I haven't already changed the perspective to. But I guess a negative would be, you know, obviously in 2020 there was the massive Zoom, and the Black Lives Matter movement.

It was post that, because I felt it was – I felt because I was Black, I had to say something all the time which was really interesting for me. That was quite a lot for me. So, that and also realizing that the training is supposed to make you neutral. But what is neutral, it is definitely not me. Neutral is, you know some of the other colleagues in my class.

I'm also saying that I was trying to be the best neutral, I'm trying to be the best representation of neutrality in a Black body. I was trying to do that and so, do you know, how messed up that is?

And so, it was not – it was it's like, oh gosh, I've been tricked in the past – it felt like I had been tricked or I tricked myself not realizing the past two years of my training time at drama school that I've – that I've been discarding, all the stuff that made me, me.

But and also, there was grace given because I was like, Caleb, you come in every day to absorb. You can't be too angry at yourself that if the things that you're absorbing – I just feel like you can't be too mad on yourself if what you were 'eating' at school every single day – in the hopes that you would learn something, it wasn't necessarily your culture or who you are. I can't be too mad. Like, does that make sense?

PJ What drives you? Looking at issues of employability, how do you navigate this?

CO So, everything about me is all about widening how we see ourselves as a community. Yes, we're not all one people. But I think for me, that's what drives me. And if I don't see anything that widens – a different perspective, then it puts me off and I'm not going to be happy. I just know it.

So, now it's like, no, I'm going to pass on that one. Or I'm going to pass on this one. So, it's all about widening the imagination, of how we see ourselves.

It doesn't matter what way we get there, but my work needs to widen the imagination of how I see myself and people like me. That's what drives me. It is like a calling.

PJ Is your preparation for a role different for theatre and screen?

CO I think it is the same.

The way I get into learning the lines, doing the work. But I think just before getting onto set or to fit, it is different. Definitely for theatre, I have to be in the space and breathing it all in and I have to take a moment in there to absorb it, see the stuff, but also let the chair see me, let the top of the thing see me.

I have to be in a space. Whereas on set, I have to – I notice that especially with the stuff that I've done; it's not about everything seeing you, it's about literally just getting the words fluently and with ease – ease, there we go. Not to say there isn't ease on stage.

I watched this cartoon where the chakra was flowing all around the body, and this guy, this character, he could send the chakra to a certain place. For theatre, I feel like the chakras are flowing all around your body.

But with set I feel like it kind of flows – you can send the energy to all your body. But there's a focus, it kind of intensifies.

PJ The industry and your place in it?

CO I had a conversation with my mates recently, and we talked about are actors activists? One of them said, well, no, they're not, they're just not, they don't do anything. They don't go on the marches. They don't do all of that. But my other friend was like, no, hang on. They're using what they're good at, to tell stories and stories change the world. Right?

So, it's that kind of 50/50. I think I agree with my friend in that, I think stories – the very fact that I could be on a stage is – just me being on a stage is political. The very fact that you can see me in something does a lot. So, in terms of where I stand with diversity, I feel like it's always going to be in the works for me.

It's funny my sister always says 'Caleb, you better not be one of them people that don't say nothing at all and just kind of like smiles'. And I'm finding you have to be smart with it though, I think. But it's always – definitely, definitely going to be in the work and the fact that I'm trying to imagine ourselves more.

Because I feel like if – the more we – we do need to make a ruckus, we do need to put a voice there, put our foot down. We do need to say something. But we also need to make sure that we have – I'm going to – I promise you I'm going to have that same energy when it – when it comes to getting those roles.

That same energy we have outside, I promise you I'm going to have it when I need to get the role or the role that I know will widen our imagination.

PJ One of the recurring issues in the creative industries is the discussion around representation. How do you see your role in relation to that conversation?

CO It's difficult because it feels to me that I'm trying to see the positive, but I'm trying to be real with it. For me right now, I would say the difficulty that I'm finding, and I'll just be very honest, is that I feel sometimes the industry isn't sure what type of person I am.

Because I'm not quite like London, London. And I also am not like I don't know, posh posh boss. I don't know – I'm somewhere in between and sometimes I feel like – also when they look for Black actors, they're looking for this kind of rawness.

PJ What pitfalls should actors emerging from drama school aim to avoid?

CO You've been a student. You've been open, but now it's about taking up space.

Don't feel that you have to be like, yes. Yes, sir. Yes, madam. And I say this particularly to like the Black and Global Majority students. Because I don't know – yeah, I just say it's for my – yeah, for my young Black men, if I just talked to them, it's like don't ever – don't compare. Don't compare, that will kill you. Trust in your source. The fact that you've got here so far, don't feel like you have to change anything. So, open your mind up to that. You opened your mind here in the middle of class.

Great, now open it up even more, reach higher. It's a different world. It's asking for a bit more of you. And know that. Go there.

PJ What motivates you to want to act and keep doing it?

CO So, recently, I've been doing a facilitation course I've been facilitating. In a producing course, I've been producing. And what's funny about all of that. Because I like to keep busy and make sure I'm learning stuff. It is like that I know for certain that I actually want to be performing.

Like that's what's really beautiful about doing all these things. Sometimes you need to know and taste and get your feet wet. And I've realized that's what I – even if I tried to run away from acting. If I'm getting a bad month, I'm like thinking – it's still there the idea of connecting with people. I also see it as a calling.

I see it as – that helps not make it about me, but about the person who might read this book or the person who might see this in ten years.

If that really helps about why I want to act and I just think stories are the way to do that.

PJ What are your broad aims for the future of your screen acting presences?

CO It's so weird what I'm about to say. I need to see me but as the lead.

I need to take up that space. I need to be there. And then I feel like – you know, part of me is like, oh no, I'm scared, but no, I can't be scared. It's not about me. It's about my community – widening that imagination.

Out of the Black Box

So, I need to see me in more beautiful projects, not Black projects, not white projects, but fantastic projects, fantastic writing, fantastic team. But also, I – we need to see people that look like me as the leads. It has to be. And it's happening. So, I'm exciting – I'm excited.

PJ Who are the actors and directors that have inspired you?

CO Oh, there's so many. I'll just – I'll list them. And I'll tell you what I find about all of them. So, there's Riz Ahmed, who is incredible. Dev Patel. I'm a fan of Andrew Garfield, Robert Pattinson, Jonathan Majors, Will Smith, yeah.

I've read Reggie Yates – he's not an actor. He's a director. But he's – you know, we know him as a presenter, Reggie Yates is huge. And you know, A24 production company.

PJ If a young Black and Global Majority person of eighteen made the decision that they want to become an actor, what would your advice be?

Listen to your heart's whispers, be curious about that urge. About that feeling, that point of view.

Like, what do you like? What don't you like? Now that you know what you do and you don't like, express that.

Like, that might be in the hair, that might be the fact that I wrote it. Express that. Yeah, express that in your clothes, express that in the food you eat, in the films you watch. Like have an opinion.

And then how do you see yourself in the world – your world? How do you see yourself in your world?

Get to know yourself. Once you do this, and once you're on that journey of really being curious about who you are. Because the more you know thyself, the more you can get to know others.

Do you want to do it? Great, now make it happen.

PJ Hard-dough bread, Sourdough bread, Chin Chin, Sweetbread, Roti, Sudsa, Bun and Cheese, Nai Wong Bao -奶黄包- Custard Bun or Naan?

CO Chin Chin is actually the one I choose. Chin Chin.

Shakeel Haakim

Photographer: AKTA.

Shakeel Haakim is an actor based in London who graduated from RADA in 2024. Before graduating, he made his professional and West End debut in the Olivier-Award nominated and multi-award winning *For Black Boys Who Have Considered Suicide When the Hue Gets Too Heavy*. In 2025, Shakeel started touring with the RSC.

Pamela Jikiemi – PJ Tell me about your journey to becoming an actor.

Shakeel Haakim – SH It's been an interesting journey. With acting, I feel like there are so many moments where you say, okay, this is a career that I want to do. But there isn't really a streamlined path of how to get into it. My first realization that this was something I definitely wanted to do, was when I did my A-levels. I remember doing my A-levels, I did Drama, Theatre Studies, Media Studies, English Literature and Music, so very creative topics. And I remember getting into like the second part of A-levels, and thinking, okay, cool, interesting, I'm getting pretty good grades in these things. I feel like this is the right thing to do. I've been grateful that I've had supportive parents who have been, if this is what you want to do go for it, which I suppose in a Caribbean kind of household, is sometimes a rarity, but I kind of always felt that support. And it just so happened that my A-level teacher, she kept it from us for a very, very long time, but it turned out that her husband was the head of East 15 at the time. And, a lot of us had no clue about drama schools, we were like 'what's drama school?' We didn't really know what it was, we had heard about some drama school things, but it wasn't on our radar.

For me, that wasn't even an idea of something that I could do. And I respect the fact that she didn't tell us who her husband was, because that actually allowed us to really have that inquisitiveness without having that kind of, oh, well, we'll be fine, because we know someone, who knows someone.

So then towards the end of the A-level second year, we all started applying for drama schools, with some people applying to uni. I think I applied to four schools back then, Guildhall, East 15 and Central. And somewhere else I can't remember, but it wasn't RADA. Funny enough, because at the time, I looked at RADA's books and I thought, yeah, okay, this isn't for me. There are no Black people, there's no one that I know that will look like me that I'll feel comfortable with.

So, I just thought I'm going to apply for the places that I've seen, have people that I know and are doing really well.

And I think that at the time that I applied to Guildhall, that was Kingsley Ben-Adir, Michaela Cole, those were the people that I knew of their work and those are the people that I want to aspire to.

Did a bunch of auditions didn't get anywhere, and I was kind of oh, okay, I don't know what to do now, all of my other friends got into East 15, ironically, and did courses there.

And I just had no clue what I was going to do. I had left school by this time and what's the next stage? I almost went to university to study journalism because I thought that was something I was going do well in because I had done really well in media studies, and I'd loved that side of the world. And honestly, it was like the day of almost going into uni, and I was like, no, this isn't for me.

Then a couple of months later got into National Youth Theatre (NYT) and I think from there onwards, it, it kind of just made sense, to be in that world, I realized that there was nothing else that I could be and that would actually fulfil me in that way, than acting and doing National Youth Theatre and meeting people from all over the country and meeting people that are Black people from Scotland, and I'm looking at and thinking, I didn't even know, there were Black people in Scotland and all of these kind of things. And all of that was like such an exciting time because it made me understand so much about myself, like I was only eighteen at the time. So, discovering who I am as a person and, and spending two weeks on a campus with all these people. At the time the National Youth Theatre was like the biggest thing for me that was wow, hearing about all the people like Helen Mirren and Daniel Craig, and all these people that had gone to NYT. Oh, wow.

I did that in 2014. In 2015 I came back, and I did some projects.

And then that was a bit of a rocky road because I was part of a project at the time, which was called Homegrown, and it was this big, like 100-plus cast of actors. And it was based at the time around the story of those two girls that went to join ISIS from East London. But they were trying to do a site-specific promenade kind of thing in a school, that was showing the journey of what would have happened and what would happen in this school.

It was a massive thing for NYT, it was on the news, it was everywhere. Then we got maybe five weeks into rehearsal, and the play got cancelled, and we didn't know what happened, we were asking what's going on, why has the show been cancelled? Then we were all called in, and Paul Roseby, who was the Artistic Director of the NYT, he came in and basically said, yeah, the play been cancelled, we don't feel comfortable enough to do it.

And then it just turned into this massive whirlwind, because the news got whiff of it and it was this big thing about censorship, why we didn't put it on, and it was a huge thing. But for me, it really ruffled me up in terms of, do I want to do this acting thing, actually? Because all of these people that I had placed in high regard, in so much as, oh, they are the people that are going to help me get into this next stage of my career. And I'm in an NYT, and suddenly, people have done some amazing things. I think of people like Sope Dìrísù who's like, amazing, and he was in one of the first National Youth Theatre rep companies. And I just remember looking up to him and being like, that's someone who I want to be. And then for all of this to happen, and to watch it on the news going, 'NYT are withholding stuff from their members', and all of this, I was like, I don't know who to trust?

And I remember, after all of that kind of died down, I just stopped acting. I went and got a part-time job, which turned into a full-time job, working at Waitrose for a couple of years, ended up becoming a manager and then just stopped doing it.

Because I was just like, I don't know if acting for me? I don't know if this place is made for me if I'm not going to feel safe and held. Which, ironically, I look back, there is never going to be a time where you'll feel safe and held. You have to do that for yourself. But the naivety of me back then was, I've put these organizations and these institutions on such a high pedestal that now they need to be the ones that helped me get through this. So, I stopped doing for a while.

Then ended up doing a youth company, I saw auditions for it with a young company at the Lyric Hammersmith. I ended up doing like a nine-month course, worked with Simon Stephens and really great directors and stuff. Ended up getting my agent from that. And then yeah, last couple of years just was working pandemic happened, decided I wanted to go back and train actually because during the pandemic, I was a bit, I don't know where I am now. And it felt like for the last couple of years of having an agent, I felt like I was just working off of flukes. I felt like I was just kind of going, oh yeah, this thing works. But I didn't really have any tangible training to figure that out. And I had an epiphany in 2020. And I was like, you know what, if there's any time to go and get training, think it's now. I applied for RADA and Guildhall. I got into both, but ultimately chose RADA, which is so ironic, because I just felt so supported. I mean, you were there, Pamela, there were so many amazing people in my audition process that I was like, actually, I feel so held. And it feels like the right time. Being slightly older, I got in when I was twenty-four, it just felt like the right time. I'm really grateful for that, because I think I got to understand exactly who I am, and what I want. Now I am so grateful to be in *For Black Boys Who Have Considered Suicide When the Hue Gets too Heavy* by Ryan Calais Cameron, and to have this amazing journey, it just feels like all the cards aligned at the right time, and I needed to go through those things to discover what works well for me. So yeah, here we are now at the Garrick Theatre, doing my West End and professional debut. So yeah, very, very grateful.

PJ Training around learning 'the craft'; did you go to a conservatoire drama school? Talk about your creative career and your commitment towards pursuing it.

SH The audition process was tough, it was very tough. Yeah, it was mainly tough because we were just coming out of the pandemic. So, there was still a lot of things that I think we were all trying to refigure out. All of RADA's audition process was online, and it was all virtual online via Zoom. So, the idea of being on Zoom wasn't you know, out of the ordinary because we'd spent the last two years having that.

I think for me a big telltale sign was that as much as all rounds of all in-person auditions were so rigorous, I ultimately felt more supported by RADA, and I felt like that came across mainly because I felt it more online than I did in person so yeah, that was a big thing for me.

I definitely had a mixture of experiences at drama school. I think coming in having not only a lot of acting experience but life experience, I kind of approached the training in a different way. Because I came into it attached to an agency. So, my main point of focus was, I need to be here to get an understanding of my craft. And the training. I actually wasn't necessarily arriving there, like everyone else does to focus on the showcase and get all the agents and all that stuff, to me at that time it was a byproduct. But at the time I arrived in the moment I needed to focus on the training and recognize that the training will support that.

It's hard though, because you're in an environment with people that are at different stages of their life and at different stages of their understanding of the craft, and at different stages of understanding emotional intelligence, and all of that sort of stuff. That there comes a point where you have to go, okay, cool, blur out the noise, but stay focused on myself.

But the one thing that I think I've been so grateful for, from the training is RADA, in comparison to other schools, it feels like, in terms of group sizes, of how many people you have in classes, or how many people you have in any sort of sessions or workshops you do, because they really have the opportunity to have smaller groups, you don't feel as if you're just sort of one number in this massive, heap of a class of thirty plus, and you're all trying to get the information. Actually, at RADA you get split into smaller groups. And those are groups of around five to six people in classes that actually make it really easy to feel like you're getting your own tailored training, as opposed to just here's our one for all kind of opportunity for everyone to pick up something. Actually, especially for the first year, I felt like there was such a good opportunity for me to really feel seen and not feel lost in the crowd. Which is, I suppose something that is quite a privilege that you don't get not only in an acting training space, but in the industry as well. So yeah, I'm very grateful for that part of the training.

PJ What drives you? Looking at issues of employability, how do you navigate this?

SH I think it's a mixture actually because now I feel that I know myself more. I think that links to me an understanding the authentic work that I want to do more of, things that align with stories that I want to tell. And I know sometimes in this industry, you've got to make money, you've got to do those jobs that sometimes aren't going to be the ones that are fulfilling, saving the world, or creating world peace and all of that sort of stuff. But I do think now that I'm aware of things that I don't want to do more.

I remember when I first got signed to an agency, that I got a question along the lines of, so what would be the things that you wouldn't want to do?

When you first meet an agent, they're having conversations with you, and you're meeting them and they're kind of figuring out who you are as a person and your dynamic. Anyway, this agent she said, so what are the kinds of things you don't want to do? And in the back of my head, I was like, 'I don't want to do?' I want to work; I can't tell her what I don't want to do? But actually, ironically, through the three years of training, through the years, before of auditioning, and having this job, now, I'm so clear about things that I don't want to do. Because I'm so aware now and even more being in this play, because how much of a message this play brings. And, you know, even though this stands alone, as a piece of art that I would never really compare, I don't think I'm ever going to be able, would want to compare this to anything I do in the future.

I'm so hyper aware of the power of theatre, not only just theatre, TV and film, whatever sort of medium, you know, motion capture anything I want to do work that resonates, work that inspires work that engages, work that is provocative, work that actually has a story versus doing things that will just bring the money in. And that's not me saying I'm going to turn my nose up at something that necessarily might not cover all of those. But at least I know, it's that integrity that I want to keep in the work that I do. Because it's a reflection of who I am, in a sense as well. So yeah, keeping that understanding now. I'm very hyper aware of the work that I don't want to do. And the work that I know will speak volumes for.

PJ When I graduated from drama school students were advised not to take the spear-carrier roles, in the belief that after a time it would lead to a mainstage role. But as a Black and Global Majority female actor, those were the roles that were generally if ever only offered, Josette Simon was a huge idol of mine at the time and she created some outstanding roles for the RSC and then they stopped asking her back, it was a fight to get a mainstage role. In fact, it was not until 2001 when David Oyelowo played Henry VI for the Royal Shakespeare Company that a change in the quality of the roles that Black and Global Majority actors were offered in an ongoing way, signalled another subtle shift in the glacial rate of change.

SH It's interesting, actually, because I had a taster of saying quote unquote, 'no' at RADA. Because we were quite lucky that as we were in our second year, and we were able to discuss the plays that we wanted to do, and this was in second year. And then we were able to form a list of plays we wanted to be in, directors we want to work with, which I mean, it's such a rarity to be in drama school and have the opportunity to choose the things that you want to be in, the plays you want and the directors you want. But one of the plays that was the selected was a play about slavery, it was based around the idea of a group of abolitionists during Britain's involvement in the transatlantic slave trade. It was an interesting play.

I think it had been on the at the RSC. But I was, really? I don't want to be in a play around slavery at drama school where they will cast traditionally, and the only roles for Black students are roles as 'slaves' whether runaway or otherwise, the character description for this play had 'slave' as part of that description. I just didn't want to be in a play around slavery, with the slave-'white saviour' narrative, it just did not and doesn't appeal to me. And it's interesting, because if anything that's more nerve-racking, telling the Director of Acting, I don't want to do this play, but don't kick me out. But I was like, 'no', actually, I have the right to say that I don't want to be in this play. And it was funny how much of a catalyst that was for other people in the year group to actually also admit and say, I don't think I – we, were like, no, we want this opportunity to put forward a list of things that we all wanted to be part of. And everyone put in a suggestion, and it was a very long process of trying to get a year group of twenty-seven people on board and try to agree on all of its varying aspects. I could not see a world where I would be in my third showcase year at drama school, and it's, oh look at the credits, Shakeel Haakim, slave number two to the left, or whatever the name was. I just didn't want to do that. So, I'm glad that I think that it has also sharpened my like headspace of knowing what I want to be in.

PJ Is your preparation for a role different for theatre and screen?

SH I think it's, it's fine sometimes to be like, oh, you know, classical training. But I think there's a difference between classical training and actually intuitive training for the career that I'm going to go into. And I'm really grateful from a theatre standpoint of, especially I noticed that coming into this rehearsal process, that I was actually like, oh, wow, it's interesting watching people who hadn't trained, and like what their processes and without judgement just going, I'm grateful that I have a range of things that I can pick from. Whereas like you, sometimes when you see people who haven't trained, and it's not that they don't have the same amount of knowledge, it's just maybe they've been so used to one way for the longest time that they're just in that sort of loop. Where I go, okay, cool, I can pick on this movement technique, or this, or this technique, and, and figure out what works until something lands. When it comes to screen stuff and self-tapes I've done and all of those kinds of things, I've ironically done the same thing as those people who haven't been trained, and just been used to my set-up. This is how I get my lighting, right. This is how I prepare. And, you know, over time, it is actually the best way, I suppose, is that you discover what works for you. And I think it's also just understanding these other mediums that the industry wants actors to understand how to work in, it makes more sense to have more of those tools in our arsenal. So yeah, definitely more exposure to digital work can be done.

PJ Thinking in terms of how you choose to identify, what do you think are the challenges in the acting/creative industry now?

SH I identify as Black British, and the biggest challenges, and it's something that I didn't realize would catch me off guard being in this process of being a cast member in the *For Black Boys* ... production at the Garrick Theatre London, is having Black creatives outside of being on stage, like having a Black stage manager, we have a Black theatre therapist, all of these things. I think there's the representation that we see visually, and it's what we see when we turn on Netflix and we go, okay, what shows have Black people? What shows have people of colour, etc.? But actually, the behind-the-scenes team and the creative team? That's where the conversation still needs to be going. And if anything, being pushed further. Because a lot of this show that I'm in now, which is, you know, a predominantly 'Black', show, which isn't necessarily saying the show is only for Black people's consumption. But we're talking about topics that are inherently faced by Black people. Having a Black creative team, almost 99 per cent of our team is, it does something that I've never experienced, because I've had to, you know, maybe be on a set or on a project with other Black people. But then behind the closed doors, the people who are running it, are not Black, and they don't understand the same things. And if anything, they have a higher position power on the project, which actually navigates the dynamic of the overall outlook to completion.

There are certain cultural things that come with this understanding and having a Black producer and all of this sort of stuff, I think, is where that the conversation needs to continue to go. Because actually, it just means that you don't have to hold up this tension of going, oh, yeah, on stage, I can be free. But behind stage, I have to kind of code switch and figure out who I am, in order to make sure the production goes well, or you don't want to ruffle any feathers or don't want to be misconstrued as this or misconstrued as that. So yeah, I think there still is a lot of work to be done.

PJ What pitfalls should actors emerging from drama school aim to avoid?

SH The biggest one that I would say is, I have a lot of mates and a lot of mates of mates who have left drama school. And sometimes there can be this very sort of pessimistic 'woe is me' attitude about going into the industry. And the industry is hard, and the jobs are hard, and people aren't getting enough self-tapes. And I would say the biggest pitfall is getting lost into that frame of mind.

Because that will completely debilitate you. And, you know, I'm really grateful that I have strong support systems. I have a great therapist, because I have moments where I feel like that, just the other week, I was like, oh, my God, when this run ends, what will I be doing next? I've got to worry about this and that. I had to have a conversation with a therapist. And she just said, 'Why do you feel like you need to be in that position?' And, and I was like, I don't know, it just feels like that's the norm of an actor. And it was like, but where does that norm come from? And I think it comes from this perpetuating feeling that so many actors and drama school students get into once they've left of going, 'well, I need to be doing something', 'I need to be busy', 'I need to be here', 'I need to be proactive'. And to an extent, yeah, it's a muscle, you need to keep it working.

But the pitfall that you can fall into is thinking, someone needs to be doing things for me why? Why hasn't this happened? Why isn't that happened?

And actually, the question is, why aren't you taking things into your own hands? My best mate, he's a writer. He also takes acting classes, he does all of these things that allows him not to be able to say, someone isn't doing it for me, he can say I'm putting it in my own hands. And I'm deciding to. Not everyone is a writer, some people might think yeah only acting is for me. But it doesn't mean that you need to get into this mindset of now that the training is over, and I've been used to three years of people holding my hand and going, here we go, we're going to this class, and here we go, we're going do this. When actually what the training should be doing is preparing you to be self-sufficient, to realize this is what I need to do for myself.

You can't really train people in emotional intelligence and emotional maturity. I'm only still just figuring out a lot of it, but I think it's very easy to get lost in the echo chamber of what other people think. I think that's an area where the 'I'll just wait for something to happen' approach, comes from. I think there's a lot of inherent things in this industry that sadly, we're still trying to unlearn, and unpick.

But I also think it just comes from the fact that some people like to be led and be taught and don't really know how to stand on their own two feet, sometimes. And, yeah, it's interesting because I can't really pinpoint where that comes from. But I just know that it's a rhetoric that gets used to so often. And it's interesting, because I think about all the people that really inspired me, and they're so multifaceted because, you know, no, one's one thing. We can't just be one sole thing, on this earth, we've got so many opportunities to do other things. And I'm grateful because, you know, I've worked so many jobs, both acting wise and non-acting. That's just been something inherent to me. But I can see from the people around me that it's very much like, well, if I don't get this, then I'm not going to be able to do that, and I'm not going to do this. I'm like, but what are you doing proactively? That proactive nature is I think what needs to be a new graduate's driving force. The pitfall is when you go, well, I'm just going to wait until something happens for me. Then you'll be waiting forever.

PJ What motivates you to want to act and keep doing it?

SH You have to have lived life. The thing that keeps me motivated is remembering who I am outside of being an actor. Because actually, that's the thing that I need to ground myself back to when, when things don't go right. And remembering the things that make me happy as a person. Because, actually, this is something I want to do indefinitely for the long run. And if I'm going to do that, then I have to be able to have things outside of this that equally support me at the same time. And, you know, my friends, the people around me, inspire me. Just watching people really go for what they want inspires me and being unapologetic about that. And that's where I want to try and be for the things that I do in my life. If I want to do this for the long run, I have to be able to know myself so well that I know when to say no, I know when to say yes to the right things, know when it's time to take a break and completely just shut off for a bit and reset, and refresh. And I think there is a kind of toxic positivity to like, everything's going be okay, and just keep working and everything's going to be fine. Well, the reality is, is like, no, things aren't going to be fine. And that's fine. Like, that is okay in itself, and actually just allowing those moments to go, okay, things aren't going the way I'd planned right now. Why is that? What can I do? And how can I inspire myself to keep going, as opposed to being resigned to just going, it's not working, oh, well, I've tried. Doing something completely different, like, travelling somewhere else, taking up different classes in something else, I just really feel as creatives and as artists, we have to keep our interests just open all the time. Otherwise, we get so complacent because the one thing that we think we should be doing isn't happening. And it's actually, I could go off and do teaching for a year, and come back and realize, I'm even stronger as an actor. And I'm really hyper aware of that now. And it's quite exciting, actually. I go back to what I was saying before about being really like, anxious and nervous about oh my God, what am I going to do next? And what's my next job going to be? And how am I ever going to prepare to do this? And I went, actually something really exciting about not knowing, there's something really exciting about going when I've done this though, and I'm in this so let's enjoy this. So that I can look back, I can go I did this, what's next? That will come when it comes. So yeah, keeping myself grounded in that is really helpful.

I really want to subvert the norm. I think we do it in elements in this play, and it really brings me joy to go, oh, wow, I've never seen something from that point of view, or having audience members go, oh, this is really interesting. I didn't know that, you know, there are so many elements and minutiae to the detail. For me, I love characters that are flawed, and you are able to see why they're flawed, and you really go on a journey for them. And I love seeing that because I think what it does, and what a beautiful thing that we have, as a gift, as actors and creatives is to really make people like, think and see things from different perspectives. And I really want to be in roles that continue to challenge and drive that and actually show elements that have never been shown before. Sometimes I get a bit frustrated, because it means that you know, you got to be the first you've got to be the first person to do this. And you got to be the first person to do that. And sometimes that feels like a pressure to be like, I don't want this to be the first production. But someone has to do that. I went to see Tyrell Williams's *Red Pitch* the other day also in the West End at Soho Place Theatre with the rest of the cast from *For Black Boys* … And we all caught up yesterday, and we were like, I don't think this has ever happened in London's West End when we've got two massive, sold-out Black plays, how many metres away from each other, taking over the West End. That's the kind of energy of where I want to be just inspired by the people around me. But also creating work that's meaningful, and people are talking about. So, we took a picture like all of us, so the *Black Boys* cast and the *Red Pitch* cast, we came together and took a picture, and this Black lady came over and she said, I've just seen both of your shows, and it's so amazing to be able to see this and, have this space. And as she's talking, I'm like, I know this voice. It turns out she taught me in high school. She was my high school teacher. It was a really out-of-body experience. I was like, you taught me when I was in like year nine. Do you remember? She was blown away that I remembered her voice and so, so proud.

I want the next generation, to be able to see and say, okay, cool. Shakeel Haakim has done that, I'm going do that when I do my next thing, even if it's not acting, it's just being able to take up space in spaces that haven't been for us as Black people especially for our creativity. This is the time now and okay, we can do Shakespeare for years and years to come, that's exciting. But actually, let's do some new work that actually shakes up what this convention is and, the plays that we see, that are not just tick-box exercises, but are actually thought through by a team of Black creatives. Like I said before, producing, writing, directing, those who are creating to make something work, and that's the energy of the environment of projects I want to be in moving forward.

PJ If a young Black and Global Majority person of eighteen made the decision that they want to become an actor, what would your advice be?

SH Just try, just and not even try, just go for it, and go for it with open arms. Because actually, it's so easy to think of all the reasons why something couldn't work. And again, it goes back into this, you can get into this catastrophizing spiral of 'there's no people that look like me who do it' and I think back to the me applying when I was eighteen, and yeah, there was some valid reasons of why I didn't want to do it. But I think a lot of it just came from, oh, well, it's probably just not for me, or it's just probably just not something I can do. And it's actually like, no, do it. Take the risk. Take the opportunity to actually know that, even if you try and do everything, and nothing works, and you fall flat on your face. You tried and you were there. It gives you the resilience and the drive that I feel like I've garnered over these years to go, well, the worst that can happen is I fall, but guess what, I'll get back up again. And that's all I can ask for.

We had this conversation, a bit of tangent here, we had this conversation in our first week of the table read, and we were talking about, you know, there's always this thing about Black excellence and like, you know, let's be the best that we can do, yeah, Black excellence! And I'm like, oh, Black excellence is tiring. In the reality, right, all of these other cultures and stuff who aren't doing, concerning themselves with excellence in the same way we have to be. Because actually what it does is, it means that we are working from such tension. Like even in these first couple of weeks of this, I think we were all so hyper aware of, oh, my God is this show for Black boys. It's Black excellence! I remember having this conversation with my therapist, of which I'm so grateful, because she's a Black woman, and she offered that we have spent years doing that, going we need to be the best of what we can do, having to work twice as hard to get half as far. And I'm like, yeah, but I hope we get to a world where we don't – I hope we get to a world where I can watch a play, and I go, yeah, that wasn't too good. But well done for just trying, it does not always have to be the best of the best. I've seen recently productions that haven't blown my mind, but I've gone, at least we're there, because we're in the spaces making this work. Yeah, that's what I look for, the day where it's not Black excellence is the only thing we can do. It's actually we can just exist, let's just be people that are existing in spaces, let's nurture our mental health.

PJ Hard-dough bread, Sourdough bread, Chin Chin, Sweetbread, Roti, Sudsa, Bun and Cheese, Nai Wong Bao -奶黄包- Custard Bun or Naan?

SH Oh, oh, only one, only one?

I'm going to go with my immediate gut reaction and that's Roti. Yeah.

Hard-dough bread was close, but I am a Roti fan, give me that and some curry chickpeas and I'm good.

CHAPTER 4
RONKẸ ADÉKỌLUẸ́JỌ́, FISAYO AKINADE, FRANCESCA AMEWUDAH-RIVERS AND MARTINS IMHANGBE

Keywords/concepts: Work → industry → race → character → theatre → change

ilé l'a nwò k'á tó so omo l'órúko – Yoruba Proverb
[We look at the household before we give a child a name]

My father Chief Olugbenga Jikiemi (Jekámi) arrived in the UK in 1955. For all of his children he adopted the West European system with surnames and a limited number of forenames occurring in a fixed order. He felt the increasing necessity of modern conditions (colonialism/imperialism) requiring the names of his children being registered for all sorts of purposes, births, marriage, deaths, electoral roll, school lists etc. and he intuited what was to become, at that time, an increasing move away from Yoruba personal names. Whenever my siblings and I asked why we did not have Yoruba first names, like our cousins and close family friends, only Yoruba second or middle names he would say 'when in Rome do as the Romans do'.

When I had my children, according to my father in Yoruba culture all individuals will have one or more àbíso names, i.e. names given at birth. These names are given by senior members of the parents' families when the child is first 'brought out'. The àbíso names reflect the circumstances of feelings of the family, or they may contain references to a particular belief system which is practised in the family.
My Yoruba name is Oláyínká – which means surrounded by wealth, justice and wisdom.

Ronkẹ Adékọluẹ́jọ́

Photo: Full Frame Atelier.

Ronkẹ Adékọluẹ́jọ́'s theatre credits include *Clydes* (Donmar); *The Importance of Being Earnest*, *Blues for an Alabama Sky*, *Three Sisters* (National Theatre); *Lava* (Bush Theatre); *Cyprus Avenue* (Royal Court/Abbey Theatre Dublin/Public Theatre New York); *Bad Roads* (Royal Court); *The Mountain Top* (Young Vic). Television credits include *Rain Dogs*; *Alex Rider*; *Big Age*; *Soul Mates*; *Black Earth Rising*; *Cuckoo*; *Cold Feet*; *Dr Who*; *Josh*; *NW*; *Sick Note*; *Chewing Gum* and *Suspects*. Feature film credits include *Dreamers*; *Chevalier*; *Ear For Eye*; *The Big Other*; *Been So Long*; *Christopher Robin*; *Ready Player One* and *One Crazy Thing*. Ronkẹ was awarded Bafta Elevate cohort in 2021 and Screen International Star of Tomorrow 2023.

Pamela Jikiemi – PJ Tell me about your journey to become an actor.

Ronkẹ Adékọluẹ́jọ́'s – RA I had a lot of energy to the extent that they used to nickname me 'Activity Po'. The Po is Yoruba for 'a lot of, or plenty'. My nickname was 'A lot of Activity'. And my mum needed engaging pastimes to keep me occupied. So, she put me and my older brother into a stage school.

Anna Scher Theatre School before their name changed, it was great from what I remember because I was very, very young. And my older brother was excelling. Of course that made me jealous. I wanted to be independent, but we would have to go together because he is only two years older than me.

My brother did it all, which didn't help my jealousy monster. I was like, I want that. I want that. I also saw how my brother wasn't enjoying it. And I was like, I want to enjoy it for you.

It became my passion, excelling past my brother in this thing called theatre and acting. It was everything to me so, at Anna Scher, I was constantly trying to be the person up front and centre. See me. I'll do it. I can do it. I can do it THE BEST!

Secondary school, I just focused on drama. That's it. Everything else was fine, because naturally, I wasn't like an A* student but I wasn't a D student either. I would always get Bs or As, so I didn't worry about that. I was focusing on my art. I didn't want my passion to be quantified in grade form, I wanted my art to be felt. I got up to a lot of extracurricular stuff.

London Talent 2005, which unfortunately I don't believe is around any more, we got to perform at the Haymarket Theatre, in central London.

I did the Jack Petchey Foundation performing arts course. And then I went to this place called John Robert Powers, that I heard on the radio. And let me just shout out my Mum. Once I told her I wanted to be an actress. She was at first afraid. But then so supportive beyond belief. She was like, okay, let's do it. Let's see where this goes. And I heard about Jonathan Powers on the radio, and they were promising Hollywood fame and fortune. If you go to the school. And the school was only in Leicester Square. My mum took me, and they were like, yeah, for the year it's ten grand. And I think I was sixteen, seventeen. So, ten grand to me at that time doesn't actually mean anything. It's just like, please, mummy, pay, please, please, please. And my mother paid. She found the money and sent me to the school.

My older brother had gone to the Navy, so he didn't want to act any more. So it was just me left, in the artist world. As I got older, I realized what my mother did for me at that time. And it was so shocking, that I was like 10K, that's a lot of money. That is a huge amount of money. What? And also that school wasn't to the standard of which I hold my art to now. But I did meet some of my current peers in the industry there. Two – three of them. And an incredible director, called Anna Osterberg, who was so passionate about the work and really honing and cultivating, and unearthing talent that she gave us sessions outside of class. But the sessions were surreal, we'd have to perform our speeches in Regent's Park or different parks. And the aim was to captivate people. We had to stop people in the street with our work. We had to make people want to watch us. Obviously, it's terrifying. But at the same time, it allowed us to connect with the people. I definitely looked like a mad woman, all the speeches I ever chose were high drama, high stakes. My desire was always to grab the attention of passers-by, connect with the story enough for people to go, what is she talking about. I want to know, what happened. And in hindsight, that did other things to my brain in terms of my storytelling.

And then I did Performing Arts at Sixth Form. I didn't go to college. I stayed at my secondary school because I loved everyone. And then my drama teacher was like, do you think you want to go to drama school? And I was like, yeah. And she was like, okay, here's Arts Ed, and here's Mountview, and here's Liverpool Institute for Performing Arts (LIPA). And I was like – I had no idea about drama school. I didn't understand. I was working at Abercrombie and Fitch. Like it was a world away because I live in Barking and Dagenham.

So, I was like, okay, I'm going to Google what a drama school is. And I was Googling drama schools. I was like, oh, great, I can get a degree. Because I know I want a degree for my mum and dad.

I also met Che Walker (during the second round of my RADA auditions), and he started asking me to do like, WAC Arts stuff.

There was also Dalston Revolution, and I used to do poems and music with Sheila Atim, Michaela Coel and Arinzé Kene. We all used to do this thing. Sheila was actually studying science. She literally was a scientist. But she has the voice of a god and is talented beyond belief. And just – and that's what I mean about knowing your talent, or knowing you have a gift and allowing – just being open in the space. Going, okay, what happens happens. From performing in church, and I'm watching her on the big, big screen. And I'm like, yes, yes, absolutely. That's work. That's work ethic. Because you said, no, I ain't backing down now.

PJ Training around learning 'the craft'; did you go to a conservatoire drama school? Talk about your creative career and your commitment towards pursuing it.

RA So, after my online research, I decided I should go to RADA. So, I got on the bus one day, I think I had some free periods from sixth form. And I went up to where RADA was and I couldn't believe it was practically in Tottenham Court Road.

I thought it was on a hill somewhere in London, or God knows the countryside, this building. And I was like I'm just going to go in, fuck it. And I walked in, and it wasn't as secure as it is now. I walked all around. And I was looking in the rooms and I was like, hurrah, these people are doing crazy things. I went to the Gower Street building. I didn't go to the Chenies Street building. And I walked around, and I was looking around and I was like, it feels like home. I want to go here.

And then I came back to school, and I told my – my drama teacher. I was like, oh, this is what I did. And she was like, that's very bad. And I was like, I don't care. Why didn't you tell me about RADA? She was like, oh, you are not going to get in. I was taken aback a little, oh, why? She goes, you're Black. You are not eighteen. You're seventeen, and you're a girl, you're from Dagenham. My eighteenth birthday was the day I started drama school.

And then I just thought, you know what, I'll tell my mum about it. And my mum also was like, no, if that is yours – the God that we serve, you're going to that school. So, get prepared. I was like, okay. Preparing, auditioning, doing all of the stuff. Each round – I remember I wrote – I wrote the dates of my first round. And then when I got my second round – on my wall, because I used to write on my wall of my bedroom. I wrote the date, the first – my first round was at the 12th of April, and then my second round – and I had all the dates on the wall. And then when I got the letter for the final round, I circled it. And I went to my mum, I said, Mummy? – she goes, let's do it. Let's do it. We're good. We prayed. She told me, it's already done. You don't have to worry. You just have to go in there. Do your work.

My LIPA audition was awful. And, of course, I didn't get in because I was terrible.

And then I did my LAMDA audition. I auditioned at LAMDA, Drama Centre, Guildhall, RADA, Bristol Old Vic, which I love, Bristol. But that audition was also pants. It's crazy, because it's going back to the desperation thing I was talking about when we graduated from drama school. I wasn't desperate to go to a drama school. I just wanted to show these people I could act. So, a lot of places said, no. I didn't get into Guildhall, Guildhall said, no. I got a recall at LAMDA, but I remember flopping that audition completely.

I tried to place my RADA audition towards the end of my first rounds of auditions, so that I knew kind of what I was going into. Because, maybe it's my control freakism, or whatever. That I'm like, if I have an idea of what it might be like, I know how to move in that space.

And I went into the first round of my RADA audition. And I saw Alan David and Adjoa Andoh, and my heart relaxed. Because I was like, there's a Black woman here. Oh, my God. Thank goodness. And there's this really old white man that is smiling so hard at me. And I haven't even said anything yet. I was like I can breathe. And we had the loveliest chat. And they were like do you want to do your speeches. I said, yeah. They were like, okay, take your time. Go for it. I did my speeches, and they just was like, thank you. And I was like, thank you. And I left feeling – I didn't have fear. Nerves. I wasn't like, yeah, I'm in or anything. I was just like, okay, that's what that's supposed to feel like. Yeah, I like that.

And then my second round came, and I was like, yes, I'm ready. And I remember on that panel – Che Walker was on that panel. Joan was on that panel. Ed Kemp was on that panel. And one person – Sebastian Harcombe, who was head of acting at the time. So, it was four people. I had known Che Walker's work. So I was like, wow, there's – and then I saw another Black woman. So, I said, yes. I was like, okay.

And in my third round, we did the workshop day. That was wicked. I also met one of my best friends at the second round. And she didn't go to RADA. But she's still one of my best friends from then, Leone, and she is having a beautiful career.

And then fourth round, the whole day taster sessions. That's when I was like, okay, the different classes – oh my gosh, it was one of the best days. I can't believe I'm saying it. But my fourth-round audition was one of the best days of my life. I had so much fun. And then we all got to watch each other's pieces at the end.

And that's probably where the work ethic started in the sense of do the work and leave it alone, do the work and leave it alone. And I remember, I think – I think I heard back in a week. And it was a phone call. You know, there's certain types of joy that you will never forget in your life.

Really – the only place I got into – am I remembering this correctly? I think was RADA. And that's because I made all the mistakes I could have made everywhere else.

And it wasn't until I got into RADA that Joan Oliver (RADA Graduate) incredible, incredible teacher, actor, director, then Director of the RADA Foundation Course, now RADA Director of Equity. And it was Joan, who I'd run to whenever, you know, the shit was hitting the fan. Because I was like, what's going on? This place is mad. All of these people are mad. What's going on? It was crazy. And you know, Mama Joan, just used to be like, just focus. And then in third year, when I got shit casting Mama Joan said, this isn't the end, do you want to do a play? And I was like, with you? She goes, I'll direct you. I was like, what the fuck, yes, of course. And we did Debbie Tucker Green's play *Random*. Joan Oliver directed me for *Random*. And it went amazing. And it was insane. And I had the best time. And the scariest time and everything. So, that was my showcase.

I remember though that it wasn't until I got to drama school that I realized I was a Black actress, which is weird. Because I read the Debbie Tucker Green's work, that woman changed my life and everything. But I was reading April De Angelis, that was my audition monologue. So, it wasn't until I got into drama school that people were like, oh, you can only play certain parts because you're Black. And I was like, but that's not true. Because I've not been doing that so far. I played an animal. At secondary school, when we were playing Dr Seuss, the musical. I was Mrs Who, like what are you talking about. I wasn't Black then.

And that became quite challenging, because I wanted to fit into a box that did not suit me. In the sense that because I acknowledged being a Black actress, I tried to portray whiteness. So, I would have – you know, my weaves – my long, long, beautiful fluid weave coming to school, you know. I was trying to emulate what I thought these actresses were, which was timid, demure that's the word I wanted and very thoughtful, and not loud. And, you know, I tried to fit something that would have never worked for me. For me especially, it would never have worked.

And then I graduated and real world hits you. And you're back at square zero, not even one, you have no squares. There are no squares. You don't even have a piece on the – on the Monopoly board. Like you're literally – begging people to hire you.

And I was auditioning a lot, but not booking anything. And it dawned on me that my desperation was getting in the way of my storytelling. I was so desperate to work, because I thought that's what validated me. I would do the work for the audition, but not allow the work to show because I really wanted to please. I wasn't telling any story apart from I want this. And nobody – what? Like nobody cared. There was nothing – there was no story coming from that. You're making everyone feel awkward. The director is probably going, okay, how do I get her to relax?

I remember this one time I auditioned for Josie Rourke for *Coriolanus*. Tom Hiddleston's *Coriolanus* at The Donmar. And I had met Josie Rourke briefly before. And she was like, I really like your energy. I think there might be a part for you in this play I'm directing. And then a couple of weeks later, I got the audition. And I was like, oh, great. And I did the work, I did the work. But I went in there desperate. And I fumbled my lines. And it's Shakespeare, you can't make shit up.

I fumbled my lines. I had to start again. My hands were sweating. My top lip was sweating. I was just like, incapable of performing. And I remember Josie looking at me. Like, well, I thought she was looking at me going that's weird, what she's doing? And I left and I said I need to fix this. I need to fix this. Something is going down. And my release from the desperation was investing in myself. I found stuff that I like to do. I was like, oh, I love going to cinema. I love going gym. I love cooking. I love knitting. I love doing loads of random other things. And the more I became desperate to be good at me, it took the desperation to be good at acting away.

I was like, I'll do my work. Oh, I've got an audition. Great. I'll do my audition … okay, I've done that. I need to knit, or I need to go to the gym, I need to do something else. At one point I was like, maybe I should learn how to cut hair. Like, there's so much out there that you can do outside of your core passion, that is just as fulfilling that. I didn't know I could do that.

And that's one of the things I wish we had been encouraged to explore at drama school. Hey, here's an hour, find something that you like to do. If it's sleeping, go and sleep. If it's screen go and watch something – I used to go down into the library and put in all them old DVDs, because there was some lessons that I was like, listen – at the time, I was quite stubborn. I was finding it very difficult to be a camel for two hours. Because I'm not actually sure why. And nobody's telling me why. So, I'm going to go and watch films in the library.

And I think because I had this angry Black girl stereotype, they kind of let me do what I want. So, I was down there watching films. And I was like, oh, wow, that's – oh, that's interesting. Oh, wow, look Marlon Brando did that.

PJ What did you get from your actor training?

RA Well, the RADA singing tutor back then, she's not there now, bless her, when I did my first lesson, she was like your voice is very R&B. And I was like, oh, my God, does that mean I sound like Usher or something? What does that mean? She was like, you know, this is a 'classical training'. And I was like, yeah. She was like we are kind of – we need to try and get your voice to sound more classical. Which now I realize in hindsight, meant white. They want me to sound white. And it wrecks my voice because I was trying to do things to it that I didn't know how to.

My voice didn't fit that. And every time I tried to emulate that, it was causing trauma and fear for me. So, singing became scary. Whereas I used to enjoy it before. I never thought I was the best singer. But I knew I could move people. That was nice.

But RADA, it changed singing for me. I didn't like singing. I didn't want to sing. I was terrified of singing. And then I graduated, and I ended up doing a musical that's a film with Che Walker. I was like, no, Che, no, you know I can't sing. But he was like, I don't care, Ronkẹ, you are doing it. It is crazy.

So, after Che Walker was in my second round, I saw him around a few times, and we became friends. And he was like, can you do a reading for me? And I said, yes, sure, and it was at RADA. It was me and Arinzé Kene, it was called 'Cloot's Last Stand'. I'm never going to forget it. It was like, those Western-type films – you know, *The Harder They Fall*.

It was like that but about two people, two lovers in a saloon – who have travelled across deserts to get to each other. It was beautiful. And then we're reading it, me and Arinzé. And my heart is falling in love because this man is like, wow, gorgeous. And we get to a part in the script and Che stops us, he is like this part needs to be sung. And I'm like, 'sung?' And he's like, can you improv? I was like, no, I can't believe this is happening. Because I know Arinzé can sing. Of course, I know Arinzé can sing. We do, you know, workshops and stuff. I was like, shit. Okay. So, I sung my little bit, whatever. I tried to improv a bit and it was terrible. Arinzé opens his throat and Jesus comes out. And my hands – I start sweating. My hands are sweating. My armpits are sweating. And I'm just looking at him, and I'm looking at Che. And I'm like, this is a set-up. And after he stops, I said that was unfair. I'm going to the bathroom to comport myself. I was in the bathroom, and I said, what the fuck. I was like this is painful. Oh gosh, but it was so much fun. And then Che was like he's written this for Omar Sy and Erykah Badu. And I was like, and you want to tell me that after you asked me to read it.

Also, with my particular year group, yeah, we created a family. I called it blissful prison. Because for those three years you don't go anywhere. You're there pretty much the whole time, from morning to night. And then you go to the pub with your friends. Because that's a way to connect and make sure everyone's still a bit human.

Because we're walking around being animals all morning and stuff, you know. One of the biggest positives for me was the way my year loved each other. We really held each other down. Because the two years above us, they didn't get on too great and everybody knew. And the year above us, they were fine. But we – we loved each other.

We were so close. Everybody was in everybody's pockets. And they called us the champagne year. We just wanted to celebrate each other all the time. Or the like verses, songs. I'll never forget, you know, everyone's doing such a shit job and bursting into tears because it was terrible. But everyone loving on each other going, no, it's fine. It's fine. You're great. You're amazing. It's fine. It's fine.

Like being there for each other. Oh, wow. It was a – it was a family. And you know, life goes on and everyone moves away from each other, and you have your – your friends that you're still best friends with. The people that you see once a year type thing. But that was – it – that was beautiful beyond belief. How much my year loved each other. I'll never forget that.

And, you know, going back to the whole, trying to fit into the whiteness. It wasn't until – once I graduated – so, my headshots, I had my afro out. Because I thought to myself, well, I was told I'm going to need ones with my weave. I was told that's probably my best option in terms of casting. And I was like, okay, I know, this shit is expensive. If I want the expensive photos with my weave. Let me get cheaper photos with my iPhone, so that I can save my money for my weave photos. I find this man, honestly, it was the cheapest photo shoot I've ever done. I think it cost me £80. I found this man called Matt. I saw his shots. And I really liked them. And once I saw the picture of me with my afro out, I said, that's me.

Why am I trying to save £500 to go take a picture of someone that isn't me?

I tell young people – I tell them all the time, actually. My career started to take off – or should I say, my life officially changed when I locked my hair, and I dyed it red.

PJ What drives you? Looking at issues of employability, how do you navigate this?

RA It was my second theatre job out of drama school, *The Colby Sisters of Pittsburgh, Pennsylvania.* And it was about these really, really, really stinkingly rich, white sisters. Five of them. And me, who was the richest one's assistant. So, I wasn't married to the idea that I was going to be playing leads straight away. I wanted to to earn my stripes. I'm like, yeah, yeah, yeah, I know, I need to take these parts. I need to learn.

And in the meeting for this, the director told me, yes, there's not a lot on the page, but the character is going to be onstage all the time. And I thought, great, I can tell stories.

Boom! Let's take the part. As the play goes on, as we're in rehearsals my stage time has been cut because – he didn't say distracting or focus pulling, but he was like, you know, we just want to watch you. So, you can't be there. Got to go somewhere else. And I'm like, okay.

So, basically, I ended up becoming a glorified stagehand. I was moving furniture, changing the set. At one point, they asked me to hide on the stage for a whole scene, so that I don't have to come on and off to move a bench. And I said, no. I was like, come on, guys. Like, I can't hide here in this corner. Let's be real. And this one day, I was walking along the corridor, just minding my business. And I bust a corner, and the set designer was there, and I must have startled him. And he takes his headphones out. And he's like, oh, my God, Ronkẹ I thought you were the cleaner! And I was like, why would he think that? And I was like because I'm Black. He doesn't see cleaners. He doesn't see them. He sees their colour. But he saw me – or he has to have seen me because of work. But he saw a Black person was like – oh … you thought I was the cleaner. And I was like, what? What's happening? What's going on? And my heart was broken. I felt like I had let the Black people in the audience down.

But then that being said, Indhu Rubasingham, who is a teacher, she teaches you, she doesn't 'direct' shows, she teaches you everything and anything. Indhu saw me, and she told me, she was like, I saw how you carried yourself in that situation. And I thought I like this girl. I want to work with her. And immediately there was another play called, *The House That Will Not Stand* at the Kiln Theatre, that changed my life. Changed my life. Written by Marcus Gardley, who is the king. He is everything. It was crazy, it was crazy.

There was such good energy. It was hugely spiritual for me. And actually, the spirituality of that show taught me about the alchemy of what we do. And how important it is to honour it. The storytelling, the magic of story. Otherwise, you're liable to hurt yourself in some way. And what we do is so – it's so demanding that you have to ask for help from yourself and from the theatre building sometimes. You've got to say, guys, I need you to hold me, to survive the run. Because we're calling on spirits. But it was – it was special. And it – it changed my life, it changed my career.

PJ Is your preparation for a role different for theatre and screen?

RA *Ready Player One* was my first big Hollywood film. It was overwhelming. I don't think I was mentally or spiritually prepared. I ended up playing Ben Mendelsohn's assistant. So, another glorified – glorified furniture part. But I learned how – I just learned how the machine worked. I was like, oh, so, this is what this part is. This is what Hollywood is.

But the confidence of being on a Steven Spielberg set allowed me to approach Roy Alexander Weise. Because Roy was having meetings – audition meetings for Katori Hall's *Mountaintop* on the day that I was filming. And I asked if there was another day and they said, no. So, I messaged him on Twitter. I sent him a DM and I was like, I'm so sorry if this is unprofessional. But, you know, I'm filming right now. And I really want to meet and do – I want to come in for the part of the maid Camae. Is it possible? And he was like, yeah, your agent told me you're busy. Yeah, we'll work out. We'll work it out. And that day, I've managed to finish early. So, I just went straight there, and I was wearing this yellow like – I was wearing this yellow playsuit that was a little bit too short and a little bit too low cut, risky. And I bundled into the room because I knew that they were waiting for me. And I was like, okay, cool. Let's chat. And we were chatting, chatting, chatting, and I knew my work was ready. I couldn't wait to perform that speech.

But, you know, sometimes – this is something Mama Joan Oliver taught me as well. If you cry, your audience don't cry. You've got to get to the point, hold on, let them cry for you, land it. And then you can cry. Because obviously all the energy is there. So, I did the speech. I am ready and then once I knew that – I was like, okay, cool. And I let go. And I was like, thanks, guys. And Roy was just like, okay. Okay. Like, he didn't let me know anything. He was just chilling. I left there knowing I did my job. I did my work. And the next day my agent called, and they were like, Ronkẹ, I was like, yeah. So, I put my everything into *Mountaintop*. Oh, my God. I said, I'm not messing around with these guys. This is it. I'm putting my all into this show. I – honestly, I called on the ancestors. I called on Dr King. And I said, this is your story. It might be fictional, but we're honouring you. Give us the strength. Give us the – the humility, you know, give us the actual power to honour and uplift you – Roy, he tore it out. And me, and Gbolahan Obisesan gave – we gave and gave, we gave. And the people that came. That's when I knew. I was like, okay, yeah. As long as the work is done, and this is – the thing, there's celebrating yourself, and then there's celebrating the work. I celebrate the fact that I like to work hard and thoroughly, because I don't want there to be any holes. I just don't want there to be any holes. So, I work hard, I work thorough. And then I play and that's what I celebrate, the work.

PJ I've got a thing that I say to my daughters all the time, I wrote it on the blackboard in the kitchen, it says, 'practice it until you know you can't get it wrong, not until you get it right'.

RA And I also do this thing – I create character books, based off a gift from my friend Harry Jardine. So, me, Harry Jardine and Michael Balogun, once we graduated, started working on a production. What did we call our play? *Quandary*. It was a wicked play actually. *Quandary*. Myself, Michael Balogun, Joe Blakemore and Harry's mum, Wendy Jardine. And Harry is incredible. And he gave me this thing called, 100 Questions, that has changed my life. And I answer on every part, even the part in *Colby Sisters*. I answer 100 questions about my character. I find out everything. Because the question goes from what – what's your name? Where and when were you born? Who's your mother and father? I describe them. And then you have all of these questions about your childhood. Where was your first kiss? Who – are you a virgin? Are you not? You have all of these questions about your wants and needs, your likes and dislikes. Are you an introvert? Are you a – ? All of these questions. And as I start, I plan. I'm like, okay, I'd like to answer maybe two or three questions a day. This is when rehearsal starts. Because I want to know everything. The wants and needs of the characters, like, what is their drive, it's not enough to go, my objective is – I am a woman in her early thirties, and all of my life experiences has made me who I am today. So, if I'm creating characters that are big, forty years old, or twenty-five years old, I need to know who – how they became who they are.

What they're doing, because this is how we play. Because there are certain things that your actors, your classmates, your fellow players might give you, that cause your character to react in a different way, because of something you know from their childhood.

Someone says something differently. And you think of that memory. That's real, that's what's happening. Because you can't be up on that stage thinking about chicken, you can see it, I think people can see it. If your thoughts are not in the thoughts of the play, it can be read.

PJ How do you decide what roles to go for?

RA I did a telly job as soon as I graduated. And it was awful. It was really bad. It was called *Suspects*. I was doing a very strange accent. It was bad, it was so bad. And I watched that, and I was like, I'm never doing telly again. And I said to my agents, I said, guys, I never want to do that again. Can we please just do theatre? And they said, okay.

And for the next three years, all I did was plays. And I had a great time. And I travelled the world. I got to go to India and America. I fell in love in – in Chicago, like so much happened. I met Mark Rylance in Boston, and he ended up becoming one of the most incredible people in my life. Literally put me in a Steven Spielberg film.

PJ One of the recurring issues in the creative industries is the discussion around representation. How do you see your role in relation to that conversation?

RA At this point, my work is always going to be solid. That's one thing I will never flop on. So, I'm going to look like however I want to look like, because this is who I am. And if this part doesn't feel safe, I can't go and give myself to these characters. And let me tell you, how many of these jobs – can we use your locks? Can we use your locks? Can we use our natural hair? And I said, no, that's me. That's mine. Like you're putting a wig on it. You have to.

I did a screen job where the character a Black female needed more dimensions than what existed on the page and I worked with them towards giving the character more meaning and context in her choices. The people on it were like, we really want to use your locks, we really want to use your locks. And I said my locks not only mean something – it's a commitment to me, I've locked myself in a type thing. But they represent something that this character definitely doesn't have. If you want me to portray her. There's – there's an awareness around my hair. And the reason the way my hair is the way it is. There's a huge awareness around it. For the character to have my hair there would have to be more awareness than what is written in the script. I said, you have got to get me a wig. But I don't want no Naomi Campbell bone-straight wig. I don't believe in that stuff. So, let's look for stuff together. Let's create work together.

And we did, and the character became beautiful. And I fell in love. And I was just like, this is what it means when we speak up and we speak to each other, and not be afraid to tell, the production companies, the people who are making the work that are paying us, this is not up to scratch. Because we can all do better. Nobody's perfect. There's always room for improvement. We have to be able to say to each other, we got to do better. We got to raise the bar; we have to raise the bar.

I think it's great that the conversation is being had with white counterparts, because this is stuff they generally don't have to think about.

Think about it now. It's weird, because I ran into someone from RADA – we were in the same year – a while back. And his comment was like, it's – it's interesting that the most successful people from our year so far are those that are of colour. And I was like, but why do you think that is?

We honestly can't take no for an answer. We have to keep pushing.

PJ What pitfalls should actors emerging from drama school aim to avoid?

Honestly, I think getting involved in people's drama. There is a lot of – I wouldn't say – yeah, maybe it is gossip. There's a lot of that. Because we're so small. As in we will know each other. The Black actors and Black people in our industry, pretty much. We all know of each other at least, for sure. So, it's important to honestly just face your front. And try not get involved people's drama. Because you don't want that to hinder the work.

You don't want anything to hinder the work. That would be my biggest advice against pitfalls. Don't engage, walk away. Stay in your lane and just focus on the work, the work alone.

Just focus on the work. Yeah, that's my advice. And always do the work. No blagging. Don't think you can blag it because you can't. You can't, you can't, that's my biggest advice.

Do the work, please, because people can tell. They can tell. And they, unfortunately, hold us and our work and our art to a higher standard because we're not allowed to fail, really. So, do the work. And if you need help, ask for help because that's what we're here for.

But people have this massive fear. So, Jamael, he left RADA with no agent.

And then the first play, he did at the Royal Court he did that without an agent. And then *Hamilton*. And I was like bro, you're setting the standard. And I like it. Because you're telling people don't let them tell you – don't let them dictate how you do your thing.

We're family. We have to be. That'd be my advice.

PJ What motivates you to want to act and keep doing it?

RA It's bigger than me. I feel like I learnt quite early on that I had – I still have a job, which is to tell stories, because that's how we kept our ancestors alive.

That's how – when, you know, the biggest disaster, in my opinion, in history happened where they stole Africans, and you know, did atrocities unknown to them, they told stories to each other.

You know, they sang songs for each other. This is how we kept our architecture, our art, our music, this how we kept it alive. The vessel. And I am blessed and honoured and humbled that the gift I was given from the universe, or God was to be a vessel. So, I write for that. I'm like we have got to keep doing it. No matter what it does to me. We got to keep pushing.

PJ Who are the actors and directors that have inspired you?

RA Mark Rylance met me once, and then I got back from America, in London, my agents like we've got a call for *Ready Player One*. They want to meet you. I was like, okay. And I went to meet them, I trekked to West London. I'm there. I'm nervous.

They give me a can of Coke. And I am thinking, what? This is nice. And they are like, so you met Mark. And I am like Mark who? She said, Mark Rylance. I was like, oh, yeah, I met him in America. What a sweet man, he was lovely, blah, blah. She was like, he spoke to Steven about you. And I was like, Steven who? I was like these people are pranking me.

I was like, 'where's the camera?' I said, 'this is a joke innit?'. She was like, no. They just want to know if you're available. They want to know, you know, can you do an American accent?

And it's like, what's going on? So, I leave, and I call my agent. And I'm like, I don't know what to do. And I don't know what's happening. And somehow, I can't quite remember, I managed to get Mark's email. And I sent him a message and was like, I don't know what's happening but thank you, I guess. This is so incredible. And he was, like, you're special.

All he wrote back was 'you're special'. That's it.

And this was my first big Hollywood film. It was overwhelming.

PJ If a young Black and Global Majority person of eighteen made the decision that they want to become an actor, what would your advice be?

RA Enjoy the ride. Stay present. Stay protected. Like your whole – your heart, spirit is resilient and fluid.

Find things that you love doing outside of the acting, because that will fuel your acting. And ask for help if you ever need it.

Because if you don't – if it is your be all and end all and you don't get the part it will crush you. And there are so many parts that you just won't get. Which is the truth, even parts that you fundamentally believe not only are you right for, you're the only person that can play them. You won't get that part sometimes, and you have to be able to go, okay, it's not the end of me, it's not the beginning of me, I've got other stuff. I'm going to go and knit now. Stuff like that. Otherwise, this industry is very cutthroat. It can really, really – it can really, really rock you if you don't have a solid core. Which isn't necessarily true, because you don't have to have a solid core all the time. Part of storytelling is about melting before your audience.

You need to have like a core strength. You need to have something to keep you standing up straight.

Even when you don't get the role, or it doesn't happen. And you knew it has got your name written all over it. And then when you see who got it and you think, oh, okay. You have got to be able to bounce back and – and it is hard to say, you know, it was somebody else's turn this time. It wasn't for me. I still feel it. You know, I just think why – I can't even articulate it. But you just have to let it go.

There was a wonderful understudy for a big production at the National Theatre, that I was part of and she went on twice. But she once came to me and was like 'Ronkẹ, I didn't get the part that I really wanted. It's been making me so sad.' And I was like I can understand why. You're brilliant. And you need to remember you're brilliant. And even if they don't recognize the way that the journey works out, if you keep at it, babe, they will know you're brilliant.

And she was like, yeah, I did five tapes that day. I should have just made a choice … I said, now you know what to do next time. You say agent, I'm going to focus on this tape because I want it. And I am going to focus on this one. And the other ones when I have time I will get to. And you take your time, because that's where the currency is. Take your time. Take your time. Because there was one gig that they gave me overnight. It was a film, a Hollywood film, and we got it from LA overnight. And they were like, we need it for tomorrow, basically, but LA time. But I was working. So, I had to do it when I got home which was midnight. And I said, okay, I could either rush this get into bed early, or I'm going to take my time, because this is what I have right now. I said, okay, cool. I was up until 2 am. I sent my tape; I was proud of my tape. I didn't get the part. I stayed calm, because I did what I needed to do.

If I was like, oh, I am going to rush it and go to bed, my brain will be going I shouldn't have rushed. I shouldn't have rushed it. I would have had – oh, my God, maybe, I will be doing this with my life right now. No, no, I did everything that I would have done. And I didn't get it. It's okay.

Anyone can turn up, anyone could turn up, put on a costume and jump on that stage. I honestly don't think what we do is brain surgery at all. I think it takes commitment. I think it takes discipline. I think it takes a lot of heart and passion. And honestly, resilience, consistency, all of these words. And that's what separates us from someone who just rocks up one day and says, I'm going to get on a stage. You have to be able to do all of these things. And if you're not disciplined, if you're not resilient, if you're not committed to the work, what happens? It's lovely. It's lovely, but it doesn't move people. And that's the most important thing. They can hear us. Yeah. But do they feel us? Do they feel the story? Are they hearing the story or are they feeling the story? And that's what – that's where the difference is.

That's the most important. You're not alone. Honestly, nobody is too busy or big – if you need help you ask for help. That's it, for sure. And enjoy the ride, enjoy it. Because it's unlike any other, it really is. It really is.

PJ Hard-dough bread, Sourdough bread, Chin Chin, Sweetbread, Roti, Sudsa, Bun and Cheese, Nai Wong Bao -奶黄包- Custard Bun or Naan?

RA Chin Chin, yes. But you know, I had one bad experience, and I haven't eaten Chin Chin since.

Because, you know, one of my mum's like, big aunties, I call her Nana, she was – well, she's passed now; she used to make them in the big celebrations box for me.

So, I'd be chopping it nonstop, nonstop, nonstop. And then she passed away. And I went and bought one from the off licence not long ago. Ah! No!

But yes to Naan, Bun and Cheese, Roti, all breads. Because bread is life. I've even started baking these days. Made an incredible focaccia.

Fisayo Akinade

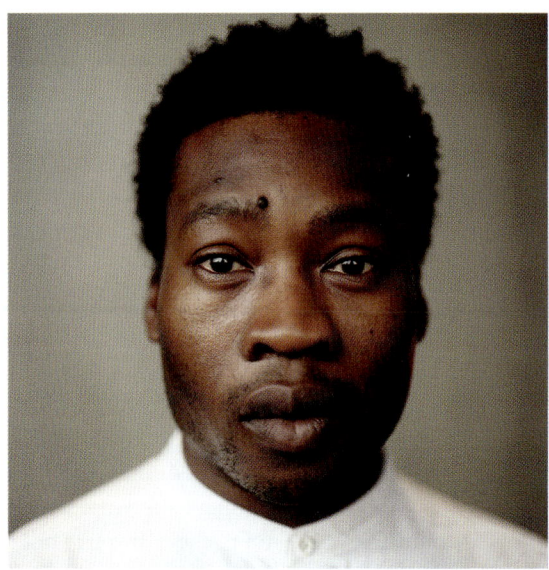

Photographer: Phil Sharp.

Fisayo Akinade starred opposite Kit Harington in Jeremy O. Harris's *Slave Play* in London's West End in 2024, and reprised his role as Reverend Hale in *The Crucible* at the Gielgud Theatre, following its transfer from the National Theatre. On screen, Fisayo can be seen in *Showtrial* for the BBC and on the Amazon/MGM Studios pilot for *Charlie Bone* opposite Joseph Fiennes. His other recent credits include *Dangerous Liaisons* for Starz, *Atlanta* for FX, *The Girl with All the Gifts*, and the critically acclaimed *Heartstopper* for Netflix.

Pamela Jikiemi – PJ Tell me about your journey to become an actor.

Fisayo Akinade – FA I grew up in Manchester happily doing gymnastics and I really enjoyed it on a Monday evening. Then I injured myself and sort of stopped for a bit, when I thought about going back, the gym had closed down. So, I couldn't do it any longer …

Acting at that point wasn't really a thing. It was something maybe I'd enjoyed, but not really a true consideration. Like I'd do things with Contact Theatre and stuff like that. I did youth groups at the Royal Exchange in Manchester. I joined the Contact Theatre Young Actors Company and spent a year with them. And so, then it was like a fun hobby that I enjoyed, but never really thought of as a career.

So, I'm doing all that and then I get to college. And I do one of the college plays. And because I failed most of my GCSEs, I was redoing them in my first year of college. So, then I was essentially a year behind.

Our drama tutor said, have you ever heard of drama school? And I was like, I don't know what that is. And they went, well, Wunmi Mosaku, who was at your high school and has also just left this college, has just got into RADA. And I go, oh, okay, amazing. What is it? And she told me because I had no clue.

So, then they explained what drama school was. And they said, we really think you should pursue this as a career.

There was a trip to see *Ma Rainey's Black Bottom* at the Royal Exchange, and Kobna Holdbrook-Smith was in it. And I remember being sat in that audience, mesmerized by him. Him specifically …

The play was excellent but him specifically. It was just this roaring, brilliant, bold thing, right. And I ran home to my mum and dad and was like I've just seen a stage full of Black people. And they were all great. And there was this guy called Kobna and he was just amazing. And I want to do that. I want to do it.

Now, at these times, I was obviously, you know, watching films, so there was like the Kobna experience, also at the time, Denzel Washington in the Jonathan Demme (1993) film *Philadelphia*. And I was just again, mesmerized by him. Like his power and his poise and his stature. The idea that you could argue against him was inconceivable, because he was so certain. It was amazing. So, those two things were very formative so, those two things combined were like – I'm going to try and do it.

So, I audition for drama school, and I do my speeches and I fuck it all up …

I don't work hard enough, and I don't get in.

PJ Training around learning 'the craft'; did you go to a conservatoire drama school? Talk about your creative career and your commitment towards pursuing it.

FA So, then I assistant teach at my college for a year. I then audition again, and only get a recall for Central. And the course was something that I was really intrigued by because it was a BA Acting Collaborative and Devised Theatre course (CDT), but they worked in a really physical way. And so, I got in.

I did my three years. I had an okay time. I think I was treated fairly well. The plays that we were in were – in third year were I think fairly suited. Some weren't. But in general, like it was kind of okay. The first play we did was a devised piece. So, we could all really, you know, pick things that we wouldn't potentially play outside. The second play was another devised piece. And then our third play was really probably now politically incorrect a Spanish farce by Ramón María del Valle-Inclán, called *Divine Words*, that was just a bit insane, but really funny.

I just thought it was a great course. Naomi Ackie, Cherrelle Skeete, Miles Yekinni, Martins Imhangbe. Sarah Wiener the Head of Library, she was brill, yeah, we would – we would always go in there and we'd be like cackling. Sarah, she was lovely, she was wicked, man. So, yeah, Sarah was lovely. And Jules on the front desk was great. And you know, I miss certain aspects of it. But in general, you know, there's not a deep connection.

There is just a lot of people who are doing very well, who that course has just benefited. And it's weird because you feel like you don't use it. Once you leave you feel like you're not using it. But then if you really think about it, the training is just sort of in you. And there's always things to learn, you learn forever, hopefully. But it's sort of you – you'll innately be like, oh, God, I was like being an iceberg melting in that moment and I didn't even realize, you know.

So, I chose to go there because it's the only one I got into. But also, the first time around, I was like, oh, I've never experienced anything like this. And a lot of things I've done before – so, when I did National Youth Theatre, we worked with a lady called Georgina Lamb and she was all – oh, God, what are they called? Frantic Assembly's sort of trained. And so I loved it. And anytime we got to do anything physical, I really enjoyed it. And when this audition happened, and I was asked to be a droplet of water on a leaf and physicalize that. I was like, this is crazy. Or when I was asked to do my speech as if I were the element, wind. I was this is amazing. And it unlocked certain things for me. This is unlike anything I've experienced before. So, even if I had had other offers, I think – because I had my heart set on Guildhall, and my experience there the second time around was really unpleasant. So, I was like, well, no. It was just, oh, it was horrible. It was really horrible. So, then Guildhall was like off the list.

And then when I went to Central, I just loved it. And what Central do brilliantly is they split the day. So, you – you do your speeches in front of everybody. And then you have a movement session with either CDT or the actor movement person. And I had mine with the CDT and it was wonderful. People were just doing like such creative things. And this was an audition, and people were coming with like, really concrete, brilliant pieces. And then I got in.

PJ What did you get from your actor training?

FA The positive aspects were, I found – I found a kind of training and a kind of acting that suited me down to a tee. I found a way of working that didn't make me feel stupid. That I found a way of working that meant that I could excel. A way of understanding my body, my brain, character analysis, projection, all of that stuff in a language that felt fluent to me. I learnt a lot about myself. I had three years in a little bubble to grow a little bit. And you do grow.

And I remember one of our directors, he said, the thing about drama school is you're not going to come in, and then leave the greatest actor ever. All you do is you go in and you like kind of just live for three years, and you leave kind of the same actor you came in, but just three years older, with some tools. And I thought that's it though, isn't it? It's a concentrated amount of time, where if you do it properly, you grow, you learn. And that just adds to your life experience. And then every job you do, every audition, every workshop, every read through, whatever it may be, just adds. And you just get filled with experience. And so, drama school is like a little bubble where you get to experience some stuff in a dramatic creative environment for three years.

I guess the negatives – it's actually more to do with like the grading system. Because how do you grade something that is predominantly based on taste?

How do you grade one actor's performance whose style you just happen to prefer to another's? And they may technically be doing the same thing, because you've got your criteria list. You know, we all get given them at the start of our assessments.

It's this thing; show that you've used your voice correctly, show that you've done this, or you can connect the text or … but then the people determining it are like four people.

It's like – it's like, reviewers for plays; you do a play, and five people go and see it and they write up their reviews. One gives you five stars; one gives you three and one gives you one. Like, which one do you believe?

So, how are you going to determine a sort of – a standardized way of critiquing something that is artistic? Like, I don't know – that always bothered me. People would get firsts for just speaking loudly, because they normally speak quietly. And you go, well, that's not right. And then other people would be penalized 'because you're normally much better than this'.

Okay, but did I hit the criteria that you laid out – do you know what I mean? So, then personal stuff gets involved and that shit really irked me. That got annoying …

But like when you start working, you realize how much of a middle-class profession it is. And so, I guess, yeah, I was tussling between like am I actually ready for this? Like, can I do it? And then it got to third year. And my final sort of critique was that someone said, there are intellectual actors and instinctual actors, and you are an instinctual actor and it is just as valid, as the people who are well-versed and well-studied and well-read. It's absolutely fine. It's not a lesser thing to be. And that's been really wonderful. And actually carried me further. Because sometimes you read a script and go, it feels like he's like this, you know, and I've not – I've not like written it down or like done a backstory, I just got it feels like that. So, I'm just going to do that. And then you hope that you are with a good director and good actors who – who help shape it. So, I do like big, bold colours like bright yellow, bright red and through rehearsal draw a neat little border around it, you know.

So, yeah, I actually – I think I kind of enjoyed drama school. Like, I've not been back to visit, and I don't think I would. It feels like a very isolated specific time of my life.

But I didn't have a terrible time, really. A lot of the stuff that some of my friends have experienced, like some of their, you know, you'll only play a slave, that kind of shit, I didn't have that said to me.

I did have a few times from other students, you're Black, you'll be fine in the industry, because they always want Black people and it's really hard for white girls with brown hair. And I was like, okay. I have had that a few times. Yeah, I've heard that a few times, which also frustrated me. Because it's like you're going to negate any hard work or effort or talent or skill, and just say because I'm Black, I'm getting – I'm going to get roles.

PJ What drives you? Looking at issues of employability, how do you navigate this?

FA On graduation from Central I managed to get an agent. And then I was just auditioning for things. And then the first job I got was the boy in *Waiting for Godot*, which was a Talawa production. And it was Jeffery Kissoon, Patrick Robinson, Guy Burgess and Cornell John.

It was my first play professionally. And like, you know, little things like learning that on a press night you give people, you know, cards and like I didn't know. I didn't know. So, on press night I was like, getting all these things. And I was like, oh, my God, I've not done anything. And also, I asked our director, Ian, can I sit in on rehearsals because the boy only comes in for like four pages in the play, it is sort of the end of the first half and the end of the second half.

And I said, can I sit in rehearsals? So, I went every day. And I got to watch Patrick Robinson and Jeffrey Kissoon rehearse. And it was like amazing. Because what I saw was two very different approaches. So, Patrick was all about the words, and kind of didn't do anything physically for weeks. But he was like, on the text, like on it. And then Jeffrey was all about the body and the hat and the costume and the shoes and the things. But the words were like, secondary. And then like, sort of during the last week, it was like they swapped. And suddenly Patrick had this body. And it was like, where's this come from? And then Jeffrey was like, bang on with the lines. And it was like, where – how did you – and it was like, oh, that's just your approach to it, that's what you do. That's amazing. And I got to witness that.

And so yeah, so what drives me, I think, to be honest, early on in my career, and maybe up until like, a good few years in, I just wanted to be successful. I wanted awards and acclaim and fame and money. And as a result, none of the work I did satisfied me like in my soul. Because I was always like I need to get – if I do this, then I can get that. And it was always about where can I go, where can I go, where can I go? And I never just sat in the current moment and just went, this is quite nice, actually. It's quite nice here.

And then around like, late 2017 things started to shift. And I started to go actually, the joy is the work. The work is the joy. Like, the rehearsal room is the best room in the world. Because you can like build something with a group of other people. And you can fuck up and get it wrong and get it right and then never get quite there again, and like it's sort of magical. And so what's happened for me personally, is the – the golden things, the golden faces and the golden man and all the gold things have sort of fallen by the wayside.

Now I just enjoy getting under the skin of the people I get to play.

I really enjoy figuring out how to craft a laugh. And being like, oh, okay, there's – there's a grain of a laugh there. But if I pause before I say that bit, and then pitch my voice up on that bit. And I like the technicality of it. And so now the joy from my profession is the work, and all the other stuff is like fluffy now, it doesn't matter. That's like, whatever. But it took me a while to get there, especially when you enter sort of TV and you make TV money, and that's very alluring. And people go, oh, you could be a – you should be – and then you've got all that thing.

But then once you look at – really look and study the people you admire. So, like Philip Seymour Hoffman, for me was one of the greatest actors of all time.

PJ Is your preparation for a role different for theatre and screen?

FA I'm going to be honest; I don't know how to prep for screen, I find it really hard. Because I'm used to rehearsing, I'm used to discussing and figuring it out and talking about it and trying it this way and this way and this way and this way.

On screen it feels like once you do it that once that's it. Now repeat that eight times. Whereas on stage even in *The Glow* – so, in *The Glow* – Evan the historian character. He's – a very funny man, and quirky. And so I was approaching every single scene I had with like, find the humour, find the gags, make it funny. And then maybe like two weeks before we closed, the scene at the end when he sees his mum. That scene, I was always sending up a bit and playing it quite funny. And sort of playing it in a way that was like, 'oh, yeah, it's all a bit shit'.

And then one day, because I was feeling a bit sad in my real life, I just came on, and it was just very downbeat, and very quiet and very to himself. And then the moment he saw his mum, it felt completely different. And you could feel the audience feel it was different. And then when I came off, Vicki (Featherstone, Director) was in that night, and she said, thank you for playing it like that, I never saw it that way. But that is it.

So, for theatre, I do like as much work as I feel like is necessary. And then the real work happens in the room for me. I prefer to turn up and be like, right, what are we doing? And if it means that I need to go away and do – read some books, then I'll do that. But I'd like to sort of turn up on the day and see what happens.

On screen, you don't get that. You don't get to do something for six weeks – and do it differently in week two, differently in week four, and differently in week six.

You don't get to – to let the thing – let it sort of develop like a fine wine, you don't get to do that. You kind of almost have to have all that before you get there.

I feel like filming is like your preview and press night on the same day. And that's it forever. You know, there's no like – you get like a day of rehearsal. And then your preview is your press night. And then it's done.

PJ How do you decide what roles to go for?

FA Scripts …

It really does come down to the scripts, because sometimes you can have a film with really great actors in it. And you're like, oh my God, it would be a dream to work with these people.

Then you read the role, and you're like, I can't pinpoint who this guy is, actually. I don't know who he is. There are too many options. I feel like the best writing is when it's somehow so crystal clear who the dude is and not prescriptive. When that happens, you're like, genius. Well done.

So, like it's got to be in the writing and the story for me. It's not necessarily about size of part or anything like that. If it's interesting or ignites something inside that makes me be like, oh, that's new. That's exciting. Like when I read *The Glow*, I was like this feeds all of my geeky like shit. Like all of my time jumpy, sci fi, medieval shit is in this thing, and I love it. And I'm going to get to do it. I'm going to get to like, be pushed backwards through time.

That's really cool to me. Yes, I'll do it. Absolutely.

And there are other times where there's like *Anthony and Cleopatra* – did not know the play. Didn't know Eros, didn't know at all. But they said Ralph Fiennes and Sophie Okonedo. Yes. Because like who's not going to want to work – all of my scenes are going to be with Ralph Fiennes. I'm going to get to not only rehearse in a room with him, but be on the Olivier stage, just him and I, every day, of course, and he was phenomenal to work with. Unbelievable.

What's the script saying? What's the story saying? And also, can I play this guy? Am I scared to play this guy? Because if you're scared to play him, but there's something in you that goes up, but you could though, that's really exciting as well. Because you don't know, you know. That like, teetering on the edge of like, fear and certainty, is really exciting, I think.

PJ The industry and your place in it?

FA I honestly – I used to be like quite conscious of it. And now, I have decided, for myself, all I require is for my name to be synonymous with a good actor who's really nice to work with.

And that is sort of it. I don't need anything else. I just want to be known as someone who was really fucking good at their job and lovely to work with. Because this industry; I say it often recently, but I love my job, but I hate my industry.

There's a lot of celebration of mediocrity, especially when it comes to Black art, I feel. Like often it's like, this is incredible.

And you're going that's because that's all you expect from us, surely … ?

So the really horrible moments for me – especially when it comes to being Black and gay – and I always felt that from when I – the moment I sort of came out in the industry, that my career was unaffected, because I was managing to work, and I was doing plays and it was all fine.

Then something occurred in 2019 that made me go, oh – oh, it does affect me. Because suddenly what people know of you, counts against you.

PJ One of the recurring issues in the creative industries is the discussion around representation. How do you see your role in relation to that conversation?

FA There's is a lack of – like not even opportunity. There's no Black Queer equivalent Taron Egerton or – I mean, countless people, Josh O'Connor or Jessie Buckley, or – there's no body of that stature who is Black and Queer. And I think that's really sad. Because there are so many talented Black Queer artists working, doing exceptional work, that aren't getting the same notices. And I don't really know what that's about.

And then something occurred in 2019, and that really fucked me up for quite some time. And then it made me look back at other jobs and be like, is that why I wasn't seen for this role and for that guy and for this thing and why I didn't get that, and why I wasn't seen for this even though I'm – like why wasn't – and then, you know, you spiral. Because suddenly what people know of you, counts against you. Because people – more with screen than with theatre. Want the thing to walk through the door. They don't want somebody to act. They just want to see Black man. You know. They don't want to see somebody who's willing to transform or change or act. They want the dude to walk through the door.

Yeah. And if they know that you're gay, and you maybe do something a bit camp in the – in the preamble before your actual audition, they've written you off. They've written you off. Or they won't even fucking see you. Because they're like, I'm not sure he's right.

Now, I've got a really fucking good agent and he'll press. Yeah, he'll press and be like, why? What is it? What is it? Let him show you. Right. So, he's brilliant. But still, prejudice exists. And people have preconceived notions, right? If they know – and it doesn't work in the reverse. If they know an actor is gay, they may not see them ever for anything straight. Ever. They're not going to do it. Right. Because they're like, isn't he, like, camp theatre dude? They're not going to do it. But that shit doesn't apply to straight actors. They'll be like, yes, come and play Liberace. Come and play Harvey Milk. Come and play whoever. It is okay. We know you're not gay. But that's fine. Come and do it. But they don't apply that same metric to gay people. And that infuriates me. Because like I was saying at the beginning, there is no equivalent to – the stars that we look up to.

It's this one out, one in, thing that is occurring, and I don't know what the answer is. Because I go to press nights, or whatevers. And people are always lovely. Like, oh, I saw you in this, oh, you're doing this. Oh, my God, mate, you're doing so well. And it's lovely. And I do feel slightly different because I do get to work a lot. But it also feels like there's a slight like, ceiling.

Like, I do really well in theatre. I don't do too well on screen. And I think that's because I'm a five foot four, northern gay boy, to be honest. And I used to be like, oh, if I was a bit more buff, like so and so, or a bit taller like this person, then maybe I would get the things. But also, I really love being a character actor. I love it. It fills me with so much joy to come in and be like you've only got four scenes but come in and really like unpick the intricacies and do something memorable with them. I love it. I love that. But it would be nice to have some Black Queer people ahead of me. I think that's the thing.

It's like, okay, me and my other Black Queer friends and we're sort of hopefully on the forefront of something.

I remember when Sidney Poitier said – you know, he was the first Black person to win an Oscar. He said, 'It's a lonely place because I'm looking around and there's nobody like me – where are they?' Maybe there might just be a gap in my knowledge. I don't know. But I do feel like where are the other Black Queer actors that are smashing it, that have won the awards and done the things? I don't know.

PJ What pitfalls should actors emerging from drama school aim to avoid?

FA I fucked myself up financially for about four years, because I didn't save any money for tax. I was just spending it and living my life, I had a great time.

But those four years were rough. It was hard. It was hard. I had to borrow money from my mum. All sorts of shit. If somebody would have just said, tell your agent to tell your accounting team at your agency to split your money. And 35 per cent, 40 per cent if you're earning really well, goes into an account that you don't look at and you don't touch until January 31st, right ...?

You just put it over there, because it's never going to be yours. It was never yours in the first place. It's not your money.

Go and get a pension, because when you're eighty, and you can't do it any more, you're going to need that.

PJ What motivates you to want to act and keep doing it?

FA So, I – I mean, really luckily, two shows I shot last year have both been green lit for future seasons. So, that's like really lovely. So, I'll be shooting – I mean, one of them happens at the same time as *The Crucible*, so that will be tricky.

Then *Atlanta* which came out in America last month or the month before. That's coming out in the UK, which I shot an episode of, which was a whirlwind experience.

And that's it for screen, really. I really – like TV money is great, film money is lovely. It's all lovely. But my soul, if theatre paid what TV paid, I would never do a TV show or film again. Honestly, I would never do it again. It's great and it's fun and there's vibes on the set and all that stuff.

But the joy I get from being in a rehearsal room and doing a play is unmatchable, to be honest, I just love it. I love it stressing me out. I love it being really fun. I love it. I love it. I love like the week three meltdown that usually happens where you're like 'I can't act any more'.

Like I love all of it. And I never get bored of it ever. It's just the most alive, immediate art form I can think of.

PJ Who are the actors and directors that have inspired you?

FA Oh, wow. Well, obviously, Philip Seymour Hoffman. But Kobna Holdbrook-Smith, because when I saw him in *Ma Rainey's Black Bottom*, it was really transformative.

I remember when he did that speech in that play. Because he played Levi. And when he does that speech about what happened to his mum, and then he is screaming at God, this man pulled out a pocketknife, ran into the middle of the stage at the Royal Exchange and leapt into the air and tried to cut God.

That's how angry he was. That's how incensed he was. I was like, this is a play. And you're given all of that, it was unbelievable. It was just stunning, like mesmerizing. And then I do my first ever play, *Waiting for Godot*. We go to the Albany in Deptford, and we're doing it there. And I walk out, and he's seen it. He's just seen the play. And he looks at me and he goes, Fisayo Akinade and he says my name properly. And I'm like, you're Kobna Holdbrook-Smith, and he goes, oh, yeah, and I say you did *Ma Rainey's Black Bottom* at the Royal Exchange, and he goes, oh, yeah. I say that is one of the reasons I'm here, and now I'm meeting you. This is insane. And now I consider that man, a friend. Like an equal. I saw him the other day. I went to see *Mary Seacole* at the Donmar. And he was there, and we just had a chat. And like to be able to – to have worked to a point where somebody that inspired me and was like, in my mind, so far ahead in terms of talent and ability and stature. To now meet as an equal. You can't put a price on that.

And he's so worldly and smart and kind. And he always makes time for me. He's a wonderful, wonderful human being, and a brilliant actor. Just brilliant. And he hates it, because I say it every time I see him, but he is a massive, massive influence and inspiration to me. And always has been. Always. He's just brilliant.

PJ If a young Black and Global Majority person of eighteen made the decision that they want to become an actor, what would your advice be?

FA Yeah, it used to be 'go to drama school, get an agent'. That's not the only way to get agents nowadays. You can make a couple short films on your own, be really good in them and send them to agencies.

Drama school is an option. But there are like youth clubs and programmes now that agents go to. It's not the only option. I'd say watch stuff. Develop your own individual sense of taste. Decide what you like, what you don't like. The style you like. You may discover that you want to be in sitcoms, you may discover that comedy is your thing or like drama, whatever it may be.

Find your likes, find your dislikes. Read plays, download screenplays from films you love and read them, read how they're structured, get familiar with them. Decide if you like classics. You know, I don't read a lot of Shakespeare. I've done quite a few. I don't really know what I'm doing. I just sort of like work out what it means. And then say it like I mean it.

But I don't – I don't know about the dum-di-dums and the rhythms and the metre. I don't know, I'll just talk. I don't know. See as much as possible, read as much as possible. And really develop your own sense of individual taste.

Make stuff with your friends. Be certain in what your aims are. And please have aims that go beyond awards, and acclaim. Aim to be good at it. Aim to be well versed, aim to be knowledgeable. Aim to be nice to work with. Aim to be somebody that when your name is brought up in a room, people go yeah, he's sick. Let's get him in. Yes, she's brilliant. Yeah, they're great.

Aim to be that person. Don't aim to be the person that's aiming for awards, because you'll be disappointed forever. Because you get one and then you want more. And more likely than not, you're going to lose then you're going to win when it comes to those things.

So, don't aim for that shit. It's not important. The most important thing is what you do.

PJ Hard-dough bread, Sourdough bread, Chin Chin, Sweetbread, Roti, Sudsa, Bun and Cheese, Nai Wong Bao -奶黄包- Custard Bun or Naan?

FA Wow! Wow! Come on. You threw Chin Chin in there like it was nothing. Oh my God.

I can't pick one of those things. Do you know – do you know me, bread is the love of my life. I love bread. Oh my God, just all four, Hard-dough bread, Sourdough bread, Chin Chin and Sweetbread.

Francesca Amewudah-Rivers

Photographer: Phil Sharp.

Francesca Amewudah-Rivers is a British Ghanaian-Nigerian actor, musician and composer based in London. She made her West End debut as Juliet in *Romeo and Juliet* at the Duke of York's Theatre in May 2024 to critical acclaim. Other credits include *School Girls; Or, The African Mean Girls Play* (Lyric Hammersmith); *Macbeth* (Shakespeare's Globe); *The Kola Nut Does Not Speak English* (Bush Theatre) and *Bad Education* (BBC). Francesca studied Music at Oxford University before training with the National Youth Theatre REP Company. As composer, Francesca was awarded the Evening Standard Future Theatre Award for Audio Design (2021). As a musician, Francesca combines her classical training with contemporary influences informed by her cultural heritage to explore soundscapes of the Black canon.

Pamela Jikiemi – PJ Tell me about your journey to become an actor.

Francesca Amewudah-Rivers – FA-R Music, I guess, is my first love. I grew up learning instruments.

I studied music at university. I did a BA three years. I went to Oxford, it was a very academic course, which was surprising, but I should have done my homework before arriving because all the course information was online. It was hard work, spent most of my time writing essays. It was a humanities subject, so we learnt about the history of music, the psychology and philosophy behind it etc.

I am Ghanian and Nigerian, West African. I felt quite starved of culture in the university environment. And I was like, I feel really uncomfortable here, I'm not enjoying what I'm learning, but I know I love music. So what is it? Where's the disconnect? And over time I realized that it was because I wasn't learning about music that was within me spiritually.

The course that I was studying was very Eurocentric. So music of the classical Western canon, really, which is music that I enjoyed, but I wasn't necessarily excited by and when I think back to when I was little, it was the feeling of peace that I got listening to reggae music, or Lauryn Hill, and what I now understand as diasporic sounds, like Highlife and Afrobeats. So in my final year I tried to lean into more of that energy where I could. I was able to mould the course around my own interests, it gave me the freedom to conduct a deep dive into my kind of music which gave me a foundation within this world. In my coursework essays and dissertation I wrote about Nina Simone, Reggie Rockstone, Childish Gambino, James Baldwin-inspired sound art, I really learnt a lot about my culture. It allowed me to understand where I see myself within the world of music or where I see that I can offer my skillset in the creative industries professionally. I knew that I loved writing music, I had joined the National Youth Theatre when I was fifteen mainly as a musician where I learnt about musical directing and composing for theatre, which I loved. So I thought, okay, great, that's what I want to do, write music for theatre or film or for visual mediums.

And then it got to final year, and all of my friends were applying for jobs, and I was just a bit stuck, I didn't know how, how to actually make this a thing? Because there's not much information around life as a composer or a musical director, or how you sort of get into those things as a young person. So, I signed up to this mailing list called Creative Access, they connect Global Majority young people to arts organizations. I thought, okay, great, cool, something along those lines might be helpful, and I just applied to a load of jobs on there.

One of them was for a production intern at the National Theatre.

I knew that that wasn't really 100 per cent my skillset, but I was like, it's the National Theatre, I love theatre!

So, I just blagged my way, did the interview. Then they contacted me after and said, you're not right for this job, but have you considered music production? And I said that's so funny, because that's exactly what I wanted to do, but I just didn't know how to get into it. And then they connected me to their music producer, who heads the music team at the National. So, I had a drink with him, and he said, why don't you come on board, we're doing an adaptation of Chekhov's *Three Sisters* by Inua Ellams MBE (2019) and directed by Nadia Fall, come and assist the composer and musical director. So that was my first job. I started that I think it was October 2019, and that ran for a few months. I thought, this is it, I've landed on my feet. I'm assisting some incredible musicians, I'm learning about writing music for theatre in a great team and a great space and decided that that was what I wanted to do.

And then lockdown happened.

All the theatres shut, and I was back to square one, really. I was back to trying to figure everything out. And I was doing some freelance composing for some digital projects, one of which was National Youth Theatre. And then I saw that they were doing their rep company auditions. I'm not sure what it was that motivated me.

Maybe it was just being back at square one, or feeling like I was back at square one and having a curiosity around, okay, how can I just maximize my chances of actually doing this as a profession? Because there's no one in my family, no one in my network who has a creative career, I'm not getting any kind of shortcuts into this or any kind of support in that way, I had to make it work myself. So, I was just applying to a load of different things, and the National Youth Theatre Rep Company, that was one of them. And I ended up getting a place on the course. And I just thought, you know what, why not? Why not? It's free, which was incredible. I had already completed a BA degree and would not be eligible for further student loan consideration. I don't have anything else to do since everything is shut, and I lost my job at the National, so why not? And that's how I got into acting.

PJ Training around learning 'the craft'; did you go to a conservatoire drama school?

FA-R Gaining a place on the National Youth Theatre Rep Company, I think I was probably better suited to that model of training. It wasn't as thorough as a conservatoire/drama school degree, but I think, as with all places of learning, it's like they're institutions, and they have their set of values, and they have their syllabus, and they have their structure, and I experienced that at Oxford, and I, I mean, everyone's experiences are unique and different, but, and I think a lot of progress has been made now within these kinds of institutions to decolonize. And refresh the syllabus. But I think I'm also grateful that I trained when I was a bit older. I was in my twenties, I was twenty-three so I was a little bit more understanding of myself. It's still a journey, but I think, yeah, if I'd gone to drama school instead of uni at the time that I did go, I just think it would have been too much, too soon for me. I do think, I think any programme where you can learn is important and is valuable, definitely, but I think it's also important to hold like, who is deciding what we are learning? What are the structures at play here? And how do I feel within this institution? I had some friends who went to drama school, who I met through doing the National Youth Theatre, and they've all had sort of different experiences, but I would say that the majority of my Black friends found their experience of drama school difficult.

So, I did the training programme called National Youth Theatre Rep Company, which is a free alternative to drama school, they say. It's a nine-month training programme for young actors, eighteen to twenty-five, to learn about what it means to be a professional actor, really. I did the course in 2020, to 2021, so it was the year of lockdown. It was really a miracle. Every day it would be like, are we still doing this? We're still going? We had face masks, head visors, squares on the floor, the two-metre rule. It was a real challenge, because everything about acting is connection. But we weren't able to. So, I think, in that experience, I definitely was pushed and encouraged to think about acting outside of what I knew. Because of Covid, and also because we weren't sure when the shows were going to be on, because it was locked down, the theatres were shut. We were rehearsing these shows, and we weren't sure whether we'd ever be able to perform them. So really, every day, we'd check in and just be like, we're so grateful to be here. We're just grateful that we're able to share this room and be creative in this time. And it sort of didn't become an outcome-based process for me, because all of the outcomes were unknown. So, I was really able to tune into the learnings and the craft. That's what started my professional journey. I got an agent from that in 2021 and then I've been working since then, so just over three years.

PJ Talking about your creative career and your commitment towards pursuing it.

FA-R This is a good question. I think when I first started out, there was a projected energy of, 'I should be so lucky', a sort of mentality of scarcity 'there aren't many people who do this successfully' so 'whenever I'm given an opportunity to work, I should take it' kind of thing.

PJ Do you think it was loaded in relation to your being a Black woman?

FA-R Yeah, yeah, yeah, definitely. I guess also it fed into my existing experiences, I'd grown up in white-dominated spaces, and also been in white-dominated institutions, and so the feeling of being hyper visible and the energy of some of the things people have said to me, like, 'yeah, it's fashionable now to be a Black actor', you know, 'agents looking for people like you now', and things like that. It's a sort of feeling that just feeds your insecurities especially if you are already feeling like 'I'm out of place here'. But that was once I was out in the professional world.

Before that, I would say, the National Youth Theatre Rep Company are really great, because they do encourage people from all kinds of backgrounds to lean into their individuality. And I'm really grateful that I did it through that way, because on that course, I really felt very welcomed for me, as a Black woman, and what I could offer. And so I still go back to that training on every job, when I am in the room, yeah, I know I'm a Black woman, but I have all of these other things to offer as well.

So my first job was Merlynn Tong's (2021) adaptation of *Antigone*, at the Mercury Theatre and I was really grateful because that was with Dawn Walton OBE directing, Dawn was the first Artistic Director of the Eclipse Theatre.

I played Ismene, sister of Adeola Yemitan's Antigone, who I trained with at the National Youth Theatre Rep Company. It was a great rehearsal room. I felt very comfortable in that job, because I wasn't the only one. I was seeing myself behind the scenes as well as on stage, and so I felt that there was a level of freedom around being able to be creative and do my job, because I didn't feel that isolation and the alienation which we usually have to navigate. But I also felt comfortable to lean into the ways in which us being Black women impacted the text and messaging. So I was very grateful that that was my first job. Then from that I did *Macbeth* at the Globe Theatre (2022) directed by Sarah Frankcom, I played Witch and Lady Macduff. It was a shortened version that was aimed predominantly at sixth formers who were studying *Macbeth*. And so that was great, because the focus was on outreach. The focus was on, how do we connect a new generation of learners to Shakespeare and to the theatre? That was cool, because I felt like I was representing, I was able to be someone on stage who young Black girls could look up to and be like, 'Oh, if I want to do that, I can do that. I can wear a funky costume and be on this awesome stage and say these words' kind of thing. So that got me through that job just looking out and seeing all of these kids, because it was really amazing.

And after that, I booked Blessing in *Bad Education* Series 4 (2021–2024) BBC Three. That was my first screen job. That was my first journey into television comedy.

I did *Othello* at the National Youth Theatre in training, and that was the show that my agent at that time saw and signed me from. So, I was like, okay, cool, I'm drama and, you know that sort of thing of categorizing myself, and other people understanding, okay, that's what kind of actor you are.

You sort of internalize those things that are put on you to try and understand yourself within the system. Which now I understand, is just so limiting and so backwards.

But coming out of training, I was like I am that kind of actor. And then again with my subsequent jobs, *Antigone*, *Macbeth* ... okay I am that kind of actor.

So, booking *Bad Education* was so odd, and I remember being so surprised, and my agent also was so surprised, because it was a complete venture away from what I had been doing.

But that was probably the best thing that could have happened at that stage in my career. Because, you know, too often we pigeonhole ourselves, and then, we don't realize that we've cornered ourselves off.

Actually, I really learned so much about myself on *Bad Education* because it was a challenge and because it was something different. It's big screen comedy, working in an ensemble, and I met some amazing people.

And I was very grateful for that, for that experience. That opened up comedy for me. And then I played Gifty in Jocelyn Bioh's (2023) *School Girls; Or The African Mean Girls Play* directed by Monique Touko at the Lyric Theatre, Hammersmith, which was definitely a career highlight for me working with Black women.

PJ I directed Bola Akeju as Remi in *IRL,* a multi-award-winning short film.

FA-R Yeah, oh my gosh, Bola, that's my sister. That's my sister. Yeah, so I played her character's cousin, Gifty. Bola is incredible, hilarious, incredibly nuanced and generous. So yeah, that was an amazing experience. Also, because I'm Ghanaian, to read a script that is set in Ghana was brilliant. So I was very lucky on that job.

PJ Oh, so you've switched from the Nigerian side now to the Ghana side now, oh, okay, I see how it is … ma binu …

FA-R Oh no, we're not getting into Jollof wars here, what are we like. So *School Girls; Or The African Mean Girls Play* was Ghana centred which was great but it spoke to all Black women. It was a really special show.

And then I did another season of playing Blessing in *Bad Education* Series 5 (2021–2024) BBC Three, and then I booked my West End debut, which is my most recent job playing Juliet in *Romeo and Juliet* (2024) directed by Jamie Lloyd at the Duke of York's Theatre.

PJ How do you decide what roles to go for?

FA-R So far my career has been quite varied. I'm lucky that I've been able to experience different kinds of sets, different kinds of companies, different kinds of scripts.

But at the beginning of this year, I actually said to myself, this has got to be the year that I decide yes or no to acting.

Because I reached a point at the end of last year where I was exhausted from work and also feeling unfulfilled. It was difficult to explain, but I think I had sort of been just going with the flow, and not really processing each job as I'd done it, and processing, okay, what kind of impact do I want to have? What kind of stories do I want to tell? Where am I going, kind of thing.

I was still of the mindset where I was being led by my insecurities, I guess. If someone says yes, oh my gosh, I have to say yes, because I don't believe I'm good enough, and I might not hear a yes for another long time and money and everything else. And I have to make this work, because I have to prove to my family that this can work.

But yeah, I got to a point at the end of last year where I just felt in myself that I can't continue like this. I have to start taking back agency, and I have to know that this is what I want to do in the same way that I know how I feel when I make music. I know that that feels right to me. Because obviously it takes up a lot of time when you're on set or when you're doing a play, it's like it's your whole life. So I felt like here's a big chunk of time that I've taken away from working at my craft as a musician, as a composer. So, I wanted to be able to better balance my output.

And yeah, really know what it was that I wanted to say, as an actor, as a creative person, because I do believe, you know, as Nina Simone said, 'An artist's duty as far as I'm concerned is to reflect the times. I think that is true of painters, sculptors, poets, musicians. As far as I'm concerned it's their choice. But I choose to reflect the times and situations in which I find myself.' I think it's a privilege to be an artist, and it is a responsibility that I don't take lightly. Because it's incredibly powerful. We have the ability to start conversation, to educate, to interrogate, and I just wanted to make sure that I was moving with intention in that, especially as a Black woman actor. We are visible and we are political in our existence in this part of the world anyway, so it's like, okay, cool. What kind of impact do I want to have? What do I want to say? How do I want to feel? I sort of had a big reckoning at the beginning of this year, and then the *Romeo and Juliet* job happened. So, I've learned so much about myself through this job. It has taught me about the power of community. And also, again, I'm going to quote Nina, because I'm obsessed. She says, 'there's no excuse for young people not knowing who the heroes and heroines are', and it's true. If I am to exist in this industry, I need to know and be inspired by and impacted by and held by the legacies that have come before and the potential that will come after. Because we're all connected, and that's what empowers us all to keep going when society wants us to go all the way away and to stop.

PJ That's the divide and conquer in action.

FA-R Yes, 100 per cent, 100 per cent and I realized that I'd seen the narratives that I'd been told about this industry and Black people in the industry, is that, you know, there's only room for one of us, and we're all each other's competition. And, yeah, we can't all be winning together. We have to watch out for X, Y, Z person. And we're all a monolith, we're all the same.

So, either you have to be unbelievably beautiful or racially ambiguous or whatever the acceptable version of Black is the closer you are in your proximity to whiteness, the more successful you'll be.

So, the way that that production played out, in my experience, really sort of brought those things to the forefront to me, and it being like, oh, this is the world we're in, and it's deeply disturbing.

And I cannot do this by myself if I want to continue, and I shouldn't, because that's what they want me to do.

They want me to feel isolated. They want me to feel like it's the world against me. But I need to do the work to know but it is not that, in that there's a reason why I'm here.

There's a reason because I felt it throughout the whole audition process, there was an energy that was sort of like, okay, I have a connection to this text that I can't really put my finger on, but it is there, whether you want to work with it or not, it's up to you. But like, it's there, and for some reason, it led me to this point. So I knew I needed to honour that. I need to honour that within me, and I need to know that I'm not alone, which just has changed all aspects of my life, really. Understanding that, and really believing that. And there's also a level of, you know, as a young person, you're sort of like, oh, once I get to this point, I'll be happy. Or once I get to here, I'll have made it, or once I get to … whatever. All of those markers, it's all abstract, and I've learned that I can't place my value around external factors. It has to come from within, because I can't control those things. And they change and they morph, and they're different every day of the week. So, you know, it can't be about a sort of like vertical race for me. I have to see it as something more horizontal that is actually about self-growth.

I've been receiving a lot of energy that's like, 'oh, you know, this is a great job for you'. And, 'this is going to do this, that and that', and, 'this is the pinnacle of theatre in the UK'. This is supposed to be what all young actors are aspiring towards. But why do I feel like this? Why do I feel so heavy? Why do I feel like I want everything to stop? So, I really understood that those things that people say are projections, and I've got to be all right inside myself first and foremost, I've got to feel fulfilled otherwise what are we doing this for? And also really understanding that this is a public-facing profession. I think I didn't really fully deep that, maybe because I didn't think that I'd be in a position where I'd be so public facing, but just understanding that, oh, this is part of it, actually. Being so visible is part of this maze.

And so I've got to take control where I can because there are lots of areas that I can't control. And if I want to do this in such a way, I have to understand what I need, and also try not to feel any pressure. I think I felt a lot of pressure to sort of be this beacon of something. When actually it's like I just needed to get through the job, or I just needed to look after myself. And you know, there's a lot of guilt and shame that came around, not feeling like I was doing enough.

But our existence is resistance in itself.

PJ Is your preparation for a role different for theatre and screen?

FA-R It's interesting because before the *Romeo and Juliet* job, I would have said yes, slightly. I think with screen, well, the kind of screen that I've done, there's a level of spontaneity that is necessary that you can't really prepare for within comedy. So, in my preparation for *Bad Education*, I sort of did some background character work and tried to understand who Blessing is as a person, what she cares about, and tried to flesh out her character world. But I also left some questions as questions still, that were unanswered, so that it gave me a little bit to play with on the job.

Whereas with theatre, the aspects of theatre that I love, it's the first week when you do the text work and the character work and deconstructing, the script, subtext, objectives, themes. What are we trying to say as a company? Where are we aligned? Where are we not aligned with the director at the helm? How can we come together and do this? But on the *Romeo and Juliet* job, Jamie, the director, didn't work like that. We had to learn our lines and be off book before we started rehearsals, which was difficult. I was cast three weeks before rehearsals started. So, yeah, it was quite difficult to get it in that time. And then on day one, there was no character work, no table work, nothing, we were blocking from day one, and we were actually told not to talk about the scenes, not to over-analyse them, not to talk. So Tom and I were told not to talk about our balcony scene and not to talk about the text together. We did no character work in that sense.

Jamie very much wanted it to be 'in the moment', what just comes up, in the moment.

PJ Creating a narrative of theatre but 'shooting' it/directing it as for film but for theatre? Which means creating an imaginary world of the text prior to the first 'shoot' day.

FA-R Yes, this play was a hybrid form, because there was this huge screen on stage filming, and a lot of like, close-ups and looking into camera. And we were directed not to look at each other a lot of the time, sort of like, look out and play the internal world, as opposed to playing to each other. In the first few weeks we as a cast joked that everything that we thought we knew about theatre had gone out the window, because this was a completely different way of working. And I think given the context of what happened when I was cast and where I was coming into the job, I found it very difficult being directed in that way, because I wasn't able to separate myself from the character as easily as I can when there's a foundation of context and text work and character work. Also understanding the politics of the world of the play, the themes of *Romeo and Juliet*. It's very rich in thematic material around love, tension, violence, conflict of ideologies, families, you know.

And so I was sort of looking at the world that we were in, not understanding the world that we were creating because we hadn't done that work, and I think that found it difficult because of the context of coming into the show off the back of the abuse and there being so much noise around, why Juliet was Black and I didn't know why, I couldn't tell you, because we hadn't spoken about that, because we weren't allowed to speak about that. So, it was difficult. It was a completely new way of working. It was a challenge, and it sort of taught me about again, my own agency as an actor in preparing for work.

And it being like, actually, I can't, I shouldn't wait for the director to tell me what I need or how to prepare for the job. I need to know what I need to prepare to do my job. And I don't always have to tell the director if I've done X, Y, Z work, but if I need to do X, Y, Z work for me, then I need to do it. But that's what I ended up doing on this job. It was like, I'm really struggling here because I'm losing myself in the work. So I ended up, yeah, coming home and doing a lot of work for myself with the help of an amazing therapist called Wabriya King, who helped me to flesh out the character world, she works a lot in theatre, she's a drama therapist, and she really helped me through this job, to understand myself as Fran, to understand Juliet as Juliet, and that that junction between, how do I get from Fran to Juliet? How do I get from Fran to work Fran? How do I then warm down? Because after the first few shows in the first couple of weeks, I'd come home and be crying for two, three hours, not able to not able to sleep, just still in it. Yes, really struggling. So I had to do that work. I had to do that work because it just wasn't sustainable otherwise. So I learned that actually, at the end of the day, I'm the one that has to get on stage and do the job. So I need to know what I need, and I've got to make that happen.

Because different directors work in different ways, and you've just got to be aware of yourself in the room as well, on the job.

There were lots of things that happened on the job that should never have happened. And it's, you know, we're all as a cast, having to carry those things and reckon with the fact that this was the experience. It shouldn't have been this.

But I have learned a lot, and I hope that it's not always going to be a case where it's like you have to go through difficulties at this scale, to grow and to learn. I'm like, when will it just be do the job? I just want to say my lines and know why and connect and share and play and that's it.

PJ Thinking in terms of how you choose to identify, what do you think are the challenges in the acting/creative industry now and how do you see your role in relation to representation and that overall conversation?

FA-R I was born in the UK so I'm British, but my heritage is Ghanian and Nigerian, West African. Intention is everything and I do worry that representation politics has created oversight without true progress, because it's like, why are you hiring Black people when they're not reflected behind the scenes, or when actually they're not safe on the job, or when actually they're saying that they need something and you're not listening? Or you're not allowing them to speak on their experiences and understanding how that might impact their experience on the job or their experience within the character. To me that feels exploitative, that feels unsafe, that feels disingenuous, I think.

I see my role as lots of different things, but mainly I want to be doing art that is authentic and that allows people to see humanity in ways that are truthful. And I think sometimes, you know, I've had experiences where I've been hired as a Black woman, and they want me to be a certain type of Black woman, and it's like there's a disconnect there. Because, actually, you're not seeing me for me, you're seeing an idea of what you think it is to be a Black woman in London. I didn't even grow up in London, I'm not even from London.

That's something that I've never really been able to really feel like I could be, it's like, oh, we've seen this version of Blackness on screen, on the media. That's how all Black people are. Okay, cool. That's what we want, because it looks good for us to be having Black people. But we're human, like everyone else. No two Black people are the same, and we shouldn't feel like we're being hired to cosplay. It should be if genuine progress and genuine outreach and you genuinely want to dismantle this supremacist structure, then it has to come from a place of genuine care and allyship that is not performative, that is not based on anything to do with ego or anything that is selfish, because then that's where it becomes difficult, I think. And I've definitely experienced those, those feelings on a job, and I hope that much more work needs to be done. Yeah, more work needs to be done to make sure that we are safe at work and we are held and we are authentically represented. That's why it's amazing to see shows like Gina Prince-Bythewood's *The Woman King*, and Rapman's *Supacell*. We can be superheroes as well. You know, all different ages and different experiences. It was really cool to see so much of the Black community represented in ways that were authentic. And even then there are so many other experiences that were not touched on, that I'm excited for the future. It feels like, okay, finally, there is an avenue where we can tell our own stories, and there's some agency of how we represent ourselves. Because I think, yeah, there's definitely structures at play in positions of huge amounts of power that are pulling the strings on that, and that's really dangerous and exploitative, in my opinion.

Yeah, it's a shame that this is even something that we have to navigate. You know, it's difficult enough, but then having to navigate, energies of 'oh, you don't actually care', yes, its exhausting.

PJ What pitfalls should actors emerging from drama school aim to avoid?

FA-R I wish I could have told myself not to worry and to trust in my craft and to invest in the craft, as opposed to investing in external things.

I also feel like sometimes the thinking has been, sort of like at school, okay, I just need to get these grades, and then do my GCSEs, then do my A-levels, and then it's done. When actually, if you want to work at something, it's continual, and it never finishes. I finished rep and I was like, okay, I'm ready, let's go. I'd done my training and I thought I had everything figured out when, actually the training always continues, and I always have to be investing in my craft and working at it and being nuanced about myself as an artist.

I think, also having personal projects are important and something that I sort of put aside when I just graduated, to working professionally. I think, as creative people, it can be quite limiting if we put our ability to be creative solely in someone else's hands. So me just waiting for someone to say yes, to feel that I can be creative wasn't healthy. And so I would tell my younger self to still be excited about making my own art, creating, working on my own projects. And to me, that was composing. Keep on writing music, if you're a writer, keep writing stories, screenplays, theatre plays even if you're not commissioned to do anything. Just keep working at that and keep on reading plays, keep on watching plays, watching screen/television series, keep on investing in that stuff that you can control, because it all feeds into everything.

I'm quite lucky, and I am very grateful the gap between *Bad Education* and *Romeo and Juliet* was the longest time I hadn't worked since I graduated from the rep company, that was six months.

Also, as you have said, Pamela, about journalling, make a note of things as they happen. Don't wish away the job, or don't wish away certain experiences. Because, sometimes I think, oh, the grass is greener, this, that, and that, and it's like, actually, no, just be present. Be present in the moment, enjoy it. There's always something positive to come from everything. Always something, so lean into that.

I think at rep, there was definitely a pressure at the end, when we were doing the shows, to get signed by an agent.

And I was really lucky that I had meetings with a few. And at the time I went with someone who I felt seemed like the most straightforward, and I had a good vibe with. But I think doing research is really important because I think also, yeah, using other actors, asking around people's experiences, also oftentimes everyone will have a different experience with the same agent, because we're all different. But, yeah, sometimes people can definitely get persuaded by big names and things like that. And it's not about the name. It's got to be about your own individual relationship with your agent, and whether they listen to you, whether they listen is such a big thing. It's so important to feel comfortable around your agent, to feel where you can actually be yourself with this person. It is definitely a partnership. It's a two-way thing. Understanding that as well, that it's not just like they have all the power and you should be begging to be signed by them. No.

PJ What motivates you to want to act and keep doing it?

FA-R I want to improve as an actor. I've been doing this professionally for three years, and every job, I've learned something new about myself, and I've been pushed in different ways.

I hope to keep on working at the craft and get to a point in like ten to twenty years from now, where I can look back and be proud of the work that I've done, and see the growth, and see the fruit of the work that I've put in. I hope to also have a varied career. I think that's one of the beautiful things about this craft, that you can move across different mediums and meet so many different people. I hope to have met and been inspired and learned from lots of different people around the world.

PJ Who are the actors and directors that have inspired you?

FA-R Oh, so many. I think maybe because my focus was on music for a long time, I still feel like I'm discovering lots about the industry and people in it now, I'm definitely, inspired by my friends. I'm grateful to be connected to a lot of incredible Black actors, writers, creatives, who are around my age and also doing great things. The first TV shows that I watched, that I saw myself in were *Fresh Prince of Bel Air* and *Everybody Hates Chris*. So its awesome to see Tyler James Williams smashing it now in *Abbot Elementary* which I love! And then, of course, Viola Davis, mother! Black British actors like Susan Wokoma, Sarah Niles. There's just so many, Barry Jenkins's *Moonlight* completely changed my life. That film is incredible.

Or a play that really impacted me was *An Octoroon* by Branden Jacobs-Jenkins. I think mostly on a day to day, actually, it's just my friends, you know, my friends and my family and, and, yeah, meeting people like you, Pamela, and hearing about your work, it's like, yeah, cool. We're all out here. We're all this community, and we're helping each other. It's really great.

PJ If a young Black and Global Majority person of eighteen made the decision that they want to become an actor, what would your advice be?

FA-R I would say it's not easy.

Place your value system on things that are internal, that come from you rather than things that come from outside of you.

Know your why.

Always come back to, why are you doing this? Why have you chosen this? Understand it's a very powerful, tool, very powerful craft that needs to be invested in.

Big up yourself, respect yourself. I think that's so important. It's like, if you don't respect yourself, how can you expect anyone else to? Be your own champion. Be your own agent. Be your own director, your own teacher, your own friend in in the journey. And also, I think it might not always make sense. until you're through it, you're on the other side of it. It's a journey and the outcome is unknown and it's always changing. So yeah, just know your why, and stay rooted in that.

PJ Hard-dough bread, Sourdough bread, Chin Chin, Sweetbread, Roti, Sudsa, Bun and Cheese, Nai Wong Bao-奶黄包- Custard Bun or Naan?

FA-R I love it, I love it, it's like heart versus mouth versus head … I grew up on Chin Chin, I have to be honest, that's my heart, it's like a giant hug, it's got to be Chin Chin, yeah.

Martins Imhangbe

Photographer: Klara Waldberg.

Martins Imhangbe is a Nigerian-British actor who trained at the Royal Central School of Speech and Drama. His presence on the stage has led him to secure historic lead roles such as his recent portrayal of Othello in the 2024 nominated adaptation of the Shakespeare classic directed by Sinéad Rushe. He was commended in the Ian Charleson Award for his role in *The Tragedy of King Richard II*. He is best known for his role as Will Mondrich in the hit Netflix series *Bridgerton* (seasons 1–3).

Pamela Jikiemi – PJ Tell me about your journey to become an actor.

Martins Imhangbe – MI My journey to becoming an actor. I lived in Greece for five years from the age of two to seven. And the first time I was on stage I appeared in a production of Little Red Riding Hood. I played a wonderful tree. That was my first sort of introduction to the stage. And who knew that years down the line I'd get involved, again, at secondary school. And this was in, I believe, year nine. So, it was around the age of fourteen when I got involved in drama classes at school.

And then I went to a Youth Art Centre called Second Wave, which is based in Deptford. And we had the opportunity to do a production of an abridged version of *Romeo and Juliet*. And that was at The Albany, and it was very well received. People were very complimentary. And I thought maybe this could be thing. Maybe I could actually continue to do it. And there were a few people who went there, who then went on to go to drama school.

I just built up the courage, studied Performing Arts at college. And then I applied for drama school. I didn't get in on my first go.

I applied for Rose Bruford, Central School of Speech and Drama (Central) and East 15. The first time around East 15 offered me a different course and Rose Bruford offered me a place on the American Theatre Arts course.

But I knew I wanted to do straight acting. So, I knew I needed to reapply for drama school. So, in the interim, I decided to do a course on technical theatre to keep myself involved with acting and just that whole world.

I did that at Lewisham college, for a year, which was amazing. Because it gave me an all-round appreciation for the technical aspects of theatre making and acting. So, then the following year, I reapplied. And I got into Rose Bruford and Central. And I decided to go to Central.

At Central I did the BA Acting-Collaborative and Devised Theatre (CDT) course. Which I felt was amazing for me because I knew I just needed a bit more. I felt that on the CDT course, I'll be able to incorporate physical theatre, I'll be able to bring myself to the work and devise stuff and write, which I felt excited about. So, that's how I became initiated into acting.

I didn't know much about drama school in general. I just knew that I wanted to train.

And I knew I wanted to go to drama school as opposed to university. So, yeah, I just sort of stuck with that drive, really.

At college, you go through the University and Colleges Admission Services (UCAS). And the assumption was that the next step would be university. I didn't know what drama school was – that you could get a degree, that's a BA Honours. I didn't know that. I thought drama school was somewhere that you just go to train.

I didn't know that it was a validated university degree. So, that was sort of my thinking at the time, I knew I wanted to train. But I also wanted to get a degree, it felt like a good safety net. That if I didn't become a successful actor, I could maybe go into other areas like maybe drama therapy or teaching.

I just felt that it's good to have that piece of paper because it's an accreditation. And people apparently take you more seriously when you do have it. So, I knew I wanted that. And when I found out I could get both, it just felt like a no brainer.

I auditioned for two years. The first round, I had no expectations. Because I just thought it was just like, you just get in. I didn't know that I was competing against the rest of the UK.

I thought – you do your audition, and they see whether you're serious or not. And take you in. I thought there was space for everyone. And that was my sort of assumption at the time. I didn't have anything to compare it to. I was told that you learn your audition speeches. And if you do a good job, you get offered a place. I thought it was a bit like university. Whereas in university, there were a lot more spaces. And in drama school, there's hardly any space.

Out of all the people that auditioned, I know, in my class, there were eighteen people that got through, out of thousands. So, it was a very eye-opening experience, it was very humbling. I sort of coasted through. I took it seriously, but I just didn't think that it would be as difficult as it was. Because, at college people were like, yeah, you're the one. You know, you're the one that's going to go and do it. But at the same time, I knew what I wanted. So, even though I got offered American Theatre Arts at Rose Bruford, I was like, no. I want to be classically trained. I just knew that I wanted to do a conservatoire actor training course.

Well, the light bulb moment came during my Central audition. I had to immerse myself in the work. Because, especially, with the CDT course it's quite demanding physically. And you're asked to throw yourself in at the deep end. And, you know, play and just be open. With some other auditions it was just do your speech, and you might get a bit of redirection, and sometimes you don't – you just do your speech and then that's it.

Whereas with CDT, I felt like I had to really play and treat it like a workshop and allow myself just to be free a bit more, as opposed to just holding on to the speech. And I think that's what drew me to the course. Because I felt like as well as doing the speech, there was a lot more. That I could be physical – there's other ways to story tell as opposed to just like – just delivering lines.

PJ Training around learning 'the craft'; did you go to a conservatoire drama school? Talk about your creative career and your commitment towards pursuing it.

MI Yeah, Royal Central, it was tough. It was really tough. First of all, I'm going into a completely new environment, a higher education institution, that I'm not used to, in terms of seeing people like me, in terms of process. And also, the academic side of it, like, and how much work you had to put in. The reading, the study. And it was just very intense. And you just have to do it, there's no sort of hiding, you have to do it. There was a long reading list. Like you have to get the books, you have to read them. You just had to immerse yourself in it.

So, at first, it was quite hard to adjust to that. Also, I had this confidence, like I went in there and I knew that I had got a place. And I appreciated how hard it was to get.

So, then I was, right, I'm here now. And I had this confidence, where I just wanted to learn. But at the same time, I felt like the class that I was put in just couldn't handle it. Just couldn't handle the fact that I was always willing to go first, so, there was a bit of tension with some of the other students. Because – I don't know, maybe they found it intimidating, because where I come from, you know, everyone just goes for it. You know, we support each other. And it's from a place of love. So, if someone is always willing to go up and it's encouraging because it encouraged someone else to want to step up. But I think the atmosphere at drama school at times was very toxic. It felt like everyone thought they wanted to prove something.

So, it was difficult to navigate because I was used to just going in and being great and start aspiring for greatness. Whereas some people found that, unsettling.

I think it was from a racial perspective. I'd like to hope it was not. But I think there were hints of that. And also, I'm a big guy, I'm like six foot two, quite broad. So, I was, tall, Black and I just thought that, in order to be great, you just had to strive for it. And I was very hungry to learn but at the same time, I noticed that it was maybe intimidating people or people found it difficult. Yeah, that was my experience.

I am a Black African man. That's how I identify. I am a Black African man with British citizenship. That is me. But, I guess, at first, when I came to Central – I was quite unapologetic about who I was, and – open to share that. I never once imposed that on anyone. I just wanted to be my most – my greatest self. And I felt like I had to dim that light a bit at drama school which was frustrating. I had to sort of, take a few steps back. And it sort of knocked my confidence a bit, actually.

I had to constantly make other people feel comfortable around me. And I once apologized for existing. You know, sorry, you feel this way, okay. Which had nothing to do with me. And it sort of got in the way of my confidence and my learning and – and there were times when I just couldn't wait to leave. I just couldn't wait to be rid of that and just fly. And I felt like I didn't have support with that. I felt like I couldn't speak up to anyone and be like, you know, I feel like I'm not being given the space to soar. It's very interesting, because I felt like there were teachers who saw that. And in our second year, we did *Othello* and because the teacher was like, I think like you'll do great in this role. And the students – my peers just found that difficult. For example, the play is called *Othello* and the guys who were playing Iago, were trying to make it all about Iago. And there was this sort of like back and forth about whose play is it. And it's like, why are we not just focusing on the story. It became this place of ego. And it's like, let's just – focus on the story, let's just tell the story of *Othello*.

You see Iago's role through telling that story. And it shouldn't be about who's got more lines. There was a lot of pressure to impress, I felt from people at drama school. It felt like there was so much pressure to do well, impress and get an agent and all those things. And who's going to get the lead roles in the third year. And when you get there, you realize it's not about that. Some of the best roles that I've got to play professionally came from me doing a supernumerary role at Hampstead Theatre, you know, so – yeah, it was hard navigating that sort of toxic hunger. I guess.

PJ What did you get from your actor training?

MI I think there was some positives and there was a lot of stuff in my training that I refer back to now, which I'm grateful for. And there's some teachers – there's a teacher who I'm still in contact with which is great. And she also works as an acting coach, which is good.

But at the same time, there was a lot of toxic behaviour, which got in the way of the learning at times.

I think it's changed now, having spoken to some people. But I think at the time, I felt like the training wasn't tailored. It felt like there was a broad sort of blanket training, as if we all have the same voice, as if we all have the same body. Whereas I feel like if there had been a bit more attention paid to the individual, I think that would have been a lot more beneficial. For example, we have different shaped mouths and tongues, and we all come from different beautiful backgrounds, so that it might be harder for me to reach RP than others, or the French accent or how do we tailor a training that's going to enable you to thrive when you graduate?

What are your strengths? And how do we sort of capitalize on that? And I felt that it could have been a lot better in that respect.

But I also believe, learning the business of the industry, I feel like that's something that I'm learning now. Stuff to do with tax, stuff to do with all sorts like. I feel like acting students should be learning that at drama school, as well. And they have a duty to do that.

Ultimately, I think what drama school gave me was discipline. And I think having that discipline has just been invaluable. I feel I would have just been a bit too, all over the place. But just to have a process and have that discipline is second to none, really.

Acting, it will break you before you break it if you are not disciplined and respectful of the craft.

PJ What drives you? Looking at issues of employability, how do you navigate this?

MI What drives me? I'm drawn to stories. I'm drawn to psychology. I'm drawn to what motivates people to do what they do. So, in terms of acting I just love that. I love getting a role, doing research and understanding why.

In a broader sense, what drives me is the ability to connect. To connect with people. To connect – I'm trying to be more specific, but – doing a play, and being able to touch someone's soul. Or for example, I did a play called *Death of a Salesman* at the Young Vic, and people would come up to me after the show and say, 'thank you', 'I saw my little brother in you', or 'I'm going to call my dad today'. You know, it's those moments that I go, okay, you know, that's why I do it. Our storytelling is having an impact on the world and we're encouraging people to have more nuanced perspectives. So many people who came to see the play were affected in some way. And I think that's a powerful place to be.

And I was going to say, there was a quote that I heard a few years back, and it says that the story is the main character, and it just helps to ground me every time. Because sometimes we – as actors, we aspire for longevity. And we assume that longevity comes with playing the lead roles. So, in the lead role, people are going to see you. And if you do well, it's going to lead to more roles and more roles. But it's about just doing a good job. Just do your job. Go out there, tell the story. That's it.

It's the story that is the key, how can I stay true to the playwright or the screenwriter's intention and create something?

PJ Is your preparation for a role different for theatre and screen?

MI Yes, I think with theatre personally, it feels like there's more of a physical demand. I have to psych myself up. It takes a lot of stamina.

So, I need to be like an athlete. You prepare yourself, make sure your stamina is up and your breath work and hitting your marks and all these things. Even though you have to do that with screen as well. But I think with stage it's consistent. Additionally, there's stage craft as well, like knowing how to pitch your voice, adjusting to each theatre, each theatre space. Some theatres are more intimate, some are larger spaces, so, you just have to adjust, to accommodate to the space you are in, really.

So, if you're doing a play, you know, you're going on – you're going to be on stage for however long, or the show is going to be two and a half hours or whatever.

Whereas with screen you have to sort of tailor it for each shot. So, it's understanding the craft of each shot. And understanding, okay, this is a mid-shot, this is a close-up or this is a long shot or whatever. So, you have to sort of tailor your performance to that. But still be grounded in truth but at the same time there's still all that screen business. Technical aspects, that you have to accommodate.

PJ How do you decide what roles to go for?

MI That's such a good question, such a great question. Because growing up I loved Denzel Washington. And I feel like he plays roles that are very integral and even if he doesn't, he still brings a level of humanity to it. So, even if he plays a villain, you don't just see a villain you see a whole rounded human. He justifies villainy because – you sort of fall in love with it a bit. You know, you're not supposed to because it's him. There's a reason. Yeah, and with anybody else you would go, my man is just playing with evil. When it's Denzel, you think – no, you unpick it a bit more because of what he brings.

And I think that is what I go for. I try to think of the humanity of the character and how well rounded they are. I think if it's on the page, and it's just he's just a bad man, or he's just – what? Oh, he's just a good guy. I always try to see beyond that. And see if what I can contribute to. But also, for me it's also the team as well. Like, are they open to collaborating? Are they open to hearing what I want to bring to it?

And also, I have to be honest with myself, I think that another thing I do as well is I try to be honest with myself. Because sometimes I get sent stuff through and I just go, yeah, I don't know how to contribute to this. And then I just kind of let it go. But I have to ask myself, how can I contribute to this? And how much do I care about it as well? I want to care about the work I do. Because I've done a play before that I just didn't care about. And it really messed with my mental health. Because I felt like I was just doing it, I had no feeling.

I didn't care about it, and it was so depressing to do. So, I just promised myself I never want to be in that position again.

Because Daniel Kaluuya said this thing once, and he was like, your subconscious doesn't know that you're acting. Sometimes.

Yeah, it's so true. And, so, if you're going to put yourself through stuff as actors, you want to make sure that it was worth it. You understand why – why I'm putting myself through that. Like, if I'm doing an Arthur Miller play, I know my overall – my super objective. I know why I'm venturing into this. Whereas if you don't know, and you're just going through the motions, or you're just doing stuff, because other people are telling you to do it and it looks good and stuff like that. It can really put you in a really uncomfortable place.

PJ The industry and your place in it?

MI My place in the industry? I'm still just trying to still be a student, of life.

Because there's so much that you're not taught. So, you have to really be conscious when you're going through it to just to protect yourself a bit. Because no one teaches you how to deal with celebrity or as we call it 'celebrated popularity'. Like no one teaches you how to navigate that. And what that means. You are just sort of thrown in and if you don't have friends who've learnt from it or that can show you a few things, then you can really struggle.

I've been wanting to do TV for a while. And in 2019 I booked my first TV job which was Shonda Rhimes's *Bridgerton*, and it was like, a big one. And it changed my life. It changed my life. A lot more people are familiar with my work now.

But my place in the industry – it feels like a good place. It feels like a place of influence. But at the same time, I have more say in what I do. If that makes sense. Like I feel like I can speak up a bit more. And I can say no to things more comfortably. Whether that's from a financial perspective. But also, just thinking about my longevity. Thinking about what and how do I want my catalogue to look like. What directors I want to work with. I'm a bit more conscious of that moving forward. You know. What I align myself with. And that's also to do with brands and sponsorships and all these things like charities. Yeah, it just makes me think about how I want to be perceived.

It's been interesting, because for example, I have to ask a lot of questions. And quite unapologetically. Now I just ask questions. I'm not afraid to ask questions, if there's any advice I can give to any actor, it's ask – ask questions. For example, with my agents. There's a lot that I'm asking them. And in my head, I'm thinking, why are you not telling me this? Why do I have to ask you about this? You know.

So, in order to get the best out of your experience, I think you just need to be transparent. Which is hard, because no one wants to appear vulnerable or appear like they don't know what they're doing or are weak or whatever. But I think there is strength in that vulnerability, because it's only going to strengthen – it is only going to equip you and make you a lot stronger. Especially stuff to do with finances and stuff like that. I'm just constantly asking lawyers. I only got introduced to the idea of getting a lawyer and stuff like that. So, I just send emails, I just pick up the phone, I am, okay, a friend spoke to me about this, what are your thoughts and – and not being afraid of that. I think it's very important, you know, and also your image as well. Like now you have a profile, an image and people feel like they can extort that or use that as they want. So, you just have to armour yourself a bit because people will take. People will put you on brochures and stuff like that, without your consent. You have to be really equipped.

Because also there's a quote, my friend Nicholas Pinnock, he said to me, 'you know, TV makes you good, but theatre makes you great'. So, I think – yeah, holding on to that, theatre is where the craft really, really is put to the test, I feel, with screen work, you can tweak things and you can shoot things from a certain angle to get what you want and whatever. Whereas with stage, you're there with the audience. There's nowhere to hide – you can't tweak.

PJ One of the recurring issues in the creative industries is the discussion around representation. How do you see your role in relation to that conversation?

MI Yeah. I feel it's important to hold people to account. So, for example, if there is a role that's out there and someone wants you to play it and its historical or whatever, I think, do your due diligence and do your research. And be open to share that. Be open to inform people or to question things. I think as me, I think I'm very open to having conversations, collaborating and asking questions. And if I don't understand something, I just ask for it to be clearer. For example, the role – it's hard not to talk about *Bridgerton*.

But when I got offered the role, I knew it was based on Bill Richmond, a very highly regarded Black boxer in Britain, who existed and one of the things that wasn't clear was his background and where he came from and who he was and his family and information like that. So, they collaborated and suggested that we get a Black historian to also be a part of the process. And they came back with a lot more information, historical information. I think he worked with the showrunner. So, the showrunner was able to come back and give me a bit more historical context, which I must have missed, which was very useful. It didn't make the final cut. But it was really helpful for me to know.

So, to answer your question, I think it's very important to just ask questions. And don't be afraid. I think now I'm not afraid to stand out, I am not afraid to talk about race. I'm not afraid to bring it up. Because some people feel, oh, I don't want to be the one that brings up being Black or race or whatever. But I think it's important. I think it is important to hold people accountable. Because if you want to bring it up, then let's go in there, let's actually do it properly. You can't just do the surface thing. You can't just tick a box and just go, oh, you know, but we've cast so, so and so. But it's like let's do it properly.

I think the industry is trying to change. I think it's definitely trying to change, we just need to continue to hold people accountable. Because otherwise somethings can sort of just disappear. You've got the role. But also, there's a few things that you can help to shine a light on or contribute to just these little details, these little things. You know.

PJ Thinking in terms of how you choose to identify, what do you think are the challenges in the acting/creative industry now?

MI That's a great question. I believe that it takes some adjusting. For example, people have their prejudices, their stereotypes, and some people are not even aware that it is happening. I was joking with my friend the other day, and I was saying how sometimes you can be very polite and lovely, but people don't hear what you're saying, they're just looking at you and thinking, 'oh, my God'. Do you know what I mean? So, I think yeah, and it's hard, because it's such a tough question, it's such a tough question, because I don't know if I'd even know how to answer it well.

At first, I was getting a lot of athletic or boxing roles, which I just completely stayed clear from. And I was aware of how easily you can be put in a box. You can easily be put in this sort of, oh, he's the big Black guy who's going to be boxing everyone. And so, I just sort of stayed away from that. Because also, I have a lot more to offer. You know. It's as simple as that. So, I just didn't want to just because the industry can be very fast. So, the moment they see something that they like, they sort of hold on to it. And that's what they want to see. And I was very mindful of that. Because even on my social media page, there was a lot of stuff from me preparing and boxing or shirtless and stuff like that. So, I just had to – I had to change all of that. Because I just didn't want to be just that guy.

And I was so grateful that in season two, that we got to see a completely different side to my character, we saw him as a businessman.

I was so grateful for that that shift. Because it's so easy to be that person. To just be that archetype or that stereotype. And even now going into a new season you get to see another side. So, I'm just like, this is awesome. This is an actor's sort of a dream to be able to show – just how versatile they are. But I'm also very conscious of my build. And conscious of what my strengths may be and what people perceive my strengths to be. I am very conscious of that as well. So, I just have to be very one. It goes back to that thing of choosing your roles, you know, carefully. Because you can easily be put in a box.

It really is. Because when I auditioned for the part, I think I was only meant to be in three episodes, or four episodes or something like that. And it was just for one season and just come in and do your thing. And then all of a sudden, they were like we want you for like, three seasons. And then that grew again. And then it's like, okay, all of a sudden now we're going from boxer to club owner, and it just – it just started to sort of grow. And yeah, it goes back to what you were saying, Pamela. I just focused on just doing a good job and just serving the story. And yeah. And I think it's so important to hold on to that because the world kind of presents this idea of people need to always be at the forefront or in the limelight or at centre stage to stand out. And that isn't the case. So, we need to dispel that myth.

PJ What pitfalls should actors emerging from drama school aim to avoid?

MI Ego. I think, ego, that's the big one. Because when you get a lot of praise or feedback in all the stuff that book you start to believe your own hype. And sometimes it can just get in the way of the work at times. And it's so interesting that the way the industry is at the moment, it feels like everyone has to be a supermodel or everyone has to look good or whatever. Be on the front of a magazine. And even though that has its currency. That currency has two sides – because at the end of the day it is a business. But at the same time, do not to get deluded by all that. Not to get so carried away that it gets in the way of you just doing a good job. And yeah, putting ego aside. Just be a good person. Just be a nice person, do the work.

Or even if you do a big show, some people feel like you do a big show and everyone's at your feet. And that's not the – that's not the case.

Like I have still got to self-tape.

Because then when you hear, you can then ring your agent, such and such is casting for this, they get you in the door. But they're not across everything. You know. And don't make assumptions. I think that's another thing. It's like some people feel because they're on telly or because they're with an agent that assumption is that people are just going to want to work with you and that kind of thing.

I really wanted to be seen for *Jitney*, because I knew that the part of Youngblood was going. So, I just saw Tinuke Craig at a press night. And I was like, Tinuke, my name is Martins, lovely to meet you. And I would love the opportunity to read, just read the words for you. Because I would love to put myself forward – I spoke to her. And then she was like, oh, my God, of course – yeah, thank you, thank you. And two or three weeks later, she called me, and I had an audition. She called me and again, for a second round. Got the second round, had a chemistry read. Got offered the part. And then it turned out that I couldn't do it because of *Bridgerton*. So, it clashed with – I think their tech days clashed with certain days of filming or whatever. But it's just staying hungry.

Because I think drama school, especially when you're Black, robs you of your superpowers for their own energy. It suppresses you. It contains you. It clips your wings. But it doesn't give you back those clips when you finish. It goes, see ya!

PJ What motivates you to want to act and keep doing it?

MI Life, just life. Life motivates me. But also, I was invited to a dinner a few weeks back and I was sat next to this guy. He was in his late seventies. And we were talking, and he said to me, he has no regrets. I was like, really? Like, not one? And he said, no, because everything I wanted to do, I at least tried. Just to try, just to give it a go, you know, is powerful. So, I think that motivates me. It's okay, I'm just going to give it a go. If there's something I want to do, if there's something I'm going to want to accomplish. I'm just going to try, at least. Because some things it may seem impossible until it's done. So, I think just the opportunity to try, I think motivates me.

PJ What are your broad aims for the future of your screen acting presence?

MI I want to produce. I want to go into production, I want to create a creative space for just like-minded people who want to create, and who have ideas. I just want to be able to collaborate and have a safe space for people who have ideas to come and share and – and hopefully be in a financial and powerful position where I can make that happen. So, if someone says they have this short film they want to do and I'm able to draw a team together and help them accomplish that. I guess that to a degree comes with influence as well. The more you build your profile or whatever, you have a level of influence. And yeah, and you can actually start being the change you want to see.

PJ Who are the actors and directors that have inspired you?

MI Actors and directors that have inspired me. A lot that I've worked with actually.

Producers, like Marianne Elliott is just like amazing, I really enjoyed working with her. Miranda Cromwell, because I get inspired daily. So, I see things and I'm okay, that is awesome. John Boyega had an initiative with Converse, where he was able to work with five up and coming filmmakers and create like these shorts. Like these five short films. And it was sponsored by Converse. So, I thought that was awesome, being able to use your influence to kickstart someone's career, you know. Similar to what you were saying.

So, yeah, I just love that initiative. Yeah, just a lot of homegrown, I love what Daniel Kaluuya is doing. I love the fact that he's got his production company. And he's also writing. And he's producing. And just – just giving back really. Because it's so easy to go, okay, I'm an actor. Let me just – what's the next film? But being able to go,

I'm going to do a film but I'm also going to write a film. I am also going to get it produced, and Letitia Wright is also doing the same thing as well. So, these people like – I've sort of grown up with them and seeing them like start off acting. But now to be in the positions they're in, to be able to give back is just – it's just a dream really.

Because I saw in the US, everyone's just like collaborating. But I feel like over here, we don't necessarily collaborate as much.

PJ If a young Black and Global Majority person of eighteen made the decision that they want to become an actor, what would your advice be?

MI My advice would be – to be clear on why you want to do this. To be clear on your why. I think. Because that's going to give you that anchor. Whenever you feel like giving up or whenever you feel like, oh, I didn't get that self-tape or whatever. You always go back to that, why. You always go back to that anchor, that thing that goes, actually, there is a purpose. There is a reason why I'm doing this. You know, which is beyond someone – someone's yes or no and be really clear on that.

PJ Hard-dough bread, Sourdough bread, Chin Chin, Sweetbread, Roti, Sudsa, Bun and Cheese, Nai Wong Bao -奶黄包- Custard Bun or Naan?

MI Oh, Hard-dough bread. Easy. That's an easy one. Hard-dough bread all day. You see, I didn't even think about it, Hard-dough bread all the time, all day.

CHAPTER 5
NICOLE BREWER, DR KAREN TOMLIN, INDHU RUBASINGHAM MBE, JOSETTE BUSHELL-MINGO OBE, JOEL TRILL AND HEATHER BASTEN

Keywords/concepts: Black-led work → theatre making → opportunity → directing → voice → casting

According to Confucius, we have two lives;
the second one begins when we realise we only have one.

Linda Diggs, *Wu-Tang: An American Saga* (2019).

Nicole Brewer

Photo by Nicole Brewer.

Nicole Brewer is a proud member of the Stage Directors and Choreographers Society. She is critically aware of the impact of racism in the industry and centres her directing practice in anti-racism. Her directing credits include *The Winter's Tale* at Shakespeare Theatre's Academy of Classical Acting; Anna Deavere Smith's *Fires in the Mirror* at Baltimore Center Stage and *The Long Wharf*, as well as numerous projects as a guest director at universities across North America. Nicole is on faculty in the acting department at the David Geffen School of Drama at Yale. Nicole also facilitates workshops on her anti-racist theatre approach to theatres and institutions all over the country, Canada and the UK. She is a proud mother of three and forever grateful for her community whose support allows her to continually pursue her artistic bliss.

Pamela Jikiemi – PJ Tell me about your journey to become a director.

Nicole Brewer – NB I think I call myself an Anti-Racist Theatre Maker. Right, and I think right now, what I get paid to do is directing, and then anti-racist theatre facilitations. And I'm an educator. So I started as an actor in the US and couldn't find consistent steady work in just that field. And so after I became a mom, I became a caregiver. That's when I switched from acting to directing. And I've been doing the directing ever since then.

My father was military; we lived on military bases for the majority of my youth. And I think in a lot of those classrooms, right, it was like one Black person or two Black people are, you know, wasn't a lot. And I think like, again, being dark skinned, we moved, my family moved out of California to Alaska. And when we did that, I didn't really have a lot of friends.

So I just like, ate a lot, I put on a lot of weight for a kid. And so I was chubby. And I think like all of the teasing and, and bullying that I got from my brother, and my family and society kind of developed a skillset on me for humour, like, oh, let me, you know, try to be funny, or let me be really nice, so that I can have some friends or have some kind of safe haven.

So I've always had been able to make friends or figure out how to be a chameleon in a way in order to have belonging. So I think I got into acting.

So, ten years as a director, but, the reason that I didn't stay as an actor is because of racism, in the United States. It's just was impossible for my tall, dark skin fat – fat by the fat-phobic standards of the US, not fat by like any kind of health or realistic settings at the time. But the, like, the fat phobia within the theatre industrial complex didn't know what to do with me, because I was too young to be a mammy. But in terms of my body type, that's probably what they wanted to do with me. And so it was just really difficult to be able to overcome and find work. I was too small, right? Really? Yeah. I wasn't thin enough to be the ingenue, wasn't light enough to be ingenue, wasn't really short enough to be ingenue. But they didn't know what to do with someone you know, who's like, what do I do with you? Your body is solid. And, and we don't know what to do with that story or the narrative around a Black person who is unbent, you know?

PJ Training around learning 'the craft'; did you go to a conservatoire drama school? Talk about your creative career and your commitment towards pursuing it.

NB So I think I got into acting. It was like my junior year of high school, which would have made me about sixteen years old. And I was like, this is amazing, right? The world of the movies is now just so close, closer to me, I started in the theatre, and I'm going to, you know, within the next three years, move to Hollywood and have this life where people will appreciate me and they will see me. So I think it was those kind of basic tenets of wanting to be seen and valued and heard, and was so desperate, right, because I didn't see myself reflected back in any of, like, the teeny bop magazines that were popular in the 80s and the 90s. When I grew up, you know, and then when I would see Black people, more Black women, it was like in a really sexualized way. So I think about all the celebrities and the musicians, and singers and rappers or what have you coming out of the late 80s, in the early 90s. And I just kind of figured, like, if I could get to that level, then I would have the resources to lose all the fat and be considered gorgeous and beautiful. And I would have everything I wanted.

So I think, Pamela, it was from a lot of self-hatred. And wanting to somehow overcome my Blackness to be accepted by the society that I live in. You know, the, the bastard child of the mother colonizer. So, yeah, I think it was like going to historic Black college and attending Howard and really having an opportunity to not be, you know, Nicole the Black girl, but to be like Nicole from California. Because everybody there was Black, you know, and to kind of figure out who I was and to slowly begin to appreciate then love who I am, nurture my talents and my gifts, that that gave me, the shift or the pivot from like, engaging in the craft from a place of belonging and acceptance to engaging in the craft because it felt like hearts work, feels like this place where I can find that creative flow. And there's very few things that I've experienced that sensation in, like, this feels and align with why I have a life right now. Kind of, you know, purpose.

I did end up getting a full ride to Howard. I tried to go to NYU. So New York University is where I applied to, wanted to go to NYU TISCH, and my mother told me not to put all my eggs in one basket. So, she made me apply to somewhere else. And that somewhere else was Howard to get her off my back. So, I didn't get TISCH. I got into Howard with that full ride. And so it's, you know, it's where I ended up going.

I have a BFA and MFA, in acting. My BFA came from Howard University, the MFA from Northern Illinois University.

So yeah, yeah, the MFA, I actually left Howard. Because I'm from California, I was like, basically born there, basically raised except for the three years, we lived in Alaska, in California, so I was like, Yeah, I'm going to go home. And I'm going to make it, do a few shows in the Bay Area, San Francisco, Oakland, Berkeley, and then I'm going to move to LA, and you know, have a life there. And when I got like reality versus fantasy, you know what I mean? Like, I got home; I got to work and got to networking. And I became actually a substitute teacher. And this again, to get my mother off my back, because she was just like, you've got to work.

I've been wrestling with the question of why did I want to be an actor a lot?

I flippantly used to say, I wanted to be, you know, famous and a celebrity. But I think a lot of that is rooted in the racism, right? That I experienced in my everyday life and just not seeing a place for myself.

PJ What did you get from your actor training?

NB I decided I really love teaching. So the next year I became a teacher. And that year taught me I really love teaching, but I don't like dealing with the parents of the children. So I was like, well, how can I continue to teach? What are the pathways? And the answer was graduate school plus, in my acting, I have been cast in, in several plays. And I just didn't have a consistent enough craft, like I have these gaps.

So I wasn't able to recreate. And I think any kind of truthful way the process of becoming or embodying a story. So I wanted to get a programme for both of those things, the ability to teach on the collegiate level, and to shore up my own acting craft, right? In my process in the United States, it just was impossible – the fat phobia within the theatre industrial complex didn't know what to do with me, so it was just really difficult to be able to overcome.

PJ Is your preparation for work projects different for theatre and screen?

NB Yeah, I do theatrical work; I want to move to television and film. So that is on the horizon in terms of a goal. But I haven't figured out how to do it and still be aligned with my anti-racist values. And I'm perfectly fine with working in contradiction, which is, I think, the unnecessary element, this acceptance of contradiction, right, that we work in terms of that entertainment industrial complex, it is racist, right?

So instead of trying to pretend like it isn't, I'm saying, yes, it is. And how do I bring my anti-racist ethos into the work that I'm doing to diminish the contradiction of those things? And the US television and film has so much more money than theatre, that there I think the connection is a lack of accountability, to needing to actually tend to anti-racist practices.

Right, in the US, they still very much centre the product, not really interested at all in the process. They don't care how it gets made, how many people are hurt or harmed, just at the end of the day, does the product gross money?

PJ How do you decide what projects to pursue?

NB I am just now getting to a point in my career, where I feel like I can make my own work, because I didn't take the traditional pathways of, you know, either studying underneath someone in an assistant director position or going to school for it. I didn't really have a network of people who knew me and really trusted that I was a director or had seen my work.

So it took me all of this time to direct enough stuff for that to be something that people like, oh, yeah, Nicole's a director, I'll call her for something. And for the last two years, for sure, like not just an idea, but actively been working on my own project that, you know, I'm hoping will come to fruition in the next few years or so.

But yeah, kind of trying to figure out what my aesthetic is, like, what is my artistic voice as a director?

What are the things that when you see that production, I want you to know that that's a Nicole Brewer show, you know, so now I kind of have what that is. And I can I feel a little more confident or a little more stable in and kind of going after things that I want to do rather than people asking me to do their thing, you know?

PJ The industry and your place in it?

NB I flippantly used to say, I wanted to be, you know, famous and a celebrity. But I think a lot of that is rooted in the racism, right? That I experienced in my everyday life and just not seeing a place for myself.

People will put you in a box, not based on like, oh, I can only cast Nicole as this, but they'll put you in a box if you're doing something other than acting, right. So if I take too many stage-management gigs to supplement the fact that I'm not working as an actor, but I'm trying to be in the room, people will begin to know me as a stage manager, they won't think about me, you know, as something else.

So I was always kind of like, okay, what's, what's the gig that you could do, and still be seen as the artist and teaching, you know, the way that it works here, teaching was the only thing that I felt like that was what you could do. You could teach and still say, I'm an actor, you know, so that's really what kind of pushed me in there trying to figure out how to stay in the industry and be known for acting in the industry.

PJ One of the recurring issues in the creative industries is the discussion around representation. How do you see your role in relation to that conversation?

NB I think, okay, I'm getting older. And I've already put all of this investment into the theatre, and I don't want to switch and do another job. And I worked a lot of odd jobs a lot. And so it's not like I was afraid to do something else. I have that experience of having worked in retail, I have the experience of like having been a telemarketer. And I have the experience of having done manual labour and some of the wineries in Northern California and Napa Valley – like I've done a lot of stuff. I've picked up trash, you know, from the streets and things like that.

So I was always kind of like, okay, what's the gig that you could do, and still be seen as the artist and teaching, you know, the way that it works here, teaching was the only thing that I felt like that was what you could do. You could teach and still say, I'm an actor, you know, so that's really what kind of pushed me in there trying to figure out how to stay in the industry and be known for acting in the industry. But what I found once I became a caregiver, which was of course, something I was not thinking about, like, I don't even think I noticed that people either were or weren't caregivers until I became one, right. Like, it was so civilized. And I think, yeah, for sure. I was aware of the narrative of like, don't have kids be, you know, just don't do that. But I don't think like I had actually taken the time to kind of look around and go, I don't see parents here. Even though of course, they were there.

I'm not even thinking about kids anyway, that I don't even know that's, that's not in my trajectory. Because I'm in the now and I'm doing my own thing. And that's, that's just not, I don't even know why we're having this conversation. So yeah. And the minute you do and, you become that woman with the stroller, for God's sake, then it's you.

Since I became a mom, I was like, Oh, I can't actually keep this up. Like literally, I can't work these odd jobs and try to audition at random times of the day, and call my community panicked. Can you watch my infant child? So I just was like, I'm a director now, like, that is that is literally what I did. I said, I am a director, I had no training, I've never been an assistant director, I had only been an actor. And I was like, I can just make it better for actors. Unfortunately, I was not the best director when I first started out. But I think over time, I have had more opportunities to direct and to act. So I've had an opportunity to stay pretty consistent in the craft, and to think about how space is facilitated. So I think a lot about the design of the space, I no longer think about how talented the people are that are in the space, I think because of all of the isms that we deal with, racism, sexism, ageism, and all of the phobias and all these irrational fears that we have that actually, as you said, at the beginning of our conversation, skill is not something that I need to really put my energy into, yes. Do they have the skill to embody the story? That's an important question to ask. But you know, not the other ones that I think a lot of other folks at the time were wasting their energy, asking, instead, I want to put my energy towards the spaces in which I'm asking these bodies to come in. And these spaces can be strong enough containers to hold the messiness of creation. Right? Yes, that I think that we're not allowed as Black people. And as people of colour, we're not allowed necessarily that same liberty, and freedom of exploration that is necessary to be able to get to wherever we want to be in our own processes.

You know, I really want to work from a place of how do we help each other rise to the occasion. And I think that's just a different orientation. And it's an orientation that requires me as a director, to to be able to attune myself to the energies of the room, but also the need the unspoken needs of the collaborators in the room, because it's dangerous to speak those needs. And that's just the truth of the matter, because we lack an infrastructure to that we lack an anti-racist infrastructure in which to support all people, not just Black people and people of colour.

PJ Thinking in terms of how you choose to identify, what do you think are the challenges in the acting/creative industry now?

NB For me, like looking back into the history of, of the more recent history of the civil rights movement, and watching Toni Morrison's documentary on Netflix, it's called the *Pieces of Me.*

I watched it over the course of three days, because it was so rich, Pamela, like I wanted to stop and breathe and take in the wisdom. So I just offer that to you, to like, I feel like it held its weight. When I kept coming back to it, I was ready to receive more medicine. But I just want, to just like uplift your point of, like, the modelling of that kind of behaviour where Toni Morrison worked as an editor for Random House and brought in Angela Davis as a writer. And you see, Toni Morrison had already published two or three books. And sitting in the photograph off to the side because it was Angela Davis's moment. And she's sitting off to the side as the editor, right. And they mentioned this in the documentary and there's something so beautiful about it, because you can as actors, right? We can look at that posturing, we can look at the body. And we can tell there is not one single iota of jealousy or resentment there – that she is there in support of Angela. And I have to say that those types of spaces in the theatre industrial complex, let alone you know, television and film are so rare.

PJ What pitfalls should actors emerging from drama school aim to avoid?

NB I almost feel like, oh, man, there's a regressive value in me thinking that I have an answer. For someone who's asking me for advice, who isn't myself.

I just think like, the amount of harmful shit that people said to me. When I asked them for advice, whether that was like saying that I was too fat, or I needed to, like never get a tattoo, or don't get too many piercings, or straighten my hair, or always smile, or always be polite. Like, there was just always this thing that wasn't about me about that person's projection of me. And I was so young and stupid and frontal cortex not developed, that I believed it. And I've wasted so much of my fucking time here on Earth, chasing after somebody else's approval, that I think I would like maybe just offer for people to remember what it is that they love doing. And as much as they possibly can to try to surround themselves with people who believe in them.

PJ What are your broad aims for the future of your directing presence?

NB I am just now getting to a point in my career, where I feel like I can make my own work, because I didn't take the traditional pathways of you know, either studying underneath someone in an assistant director position or going to school for it. I didn't really have a network of people who knew me and really trusted that I was a director– had seen my work. So it took me all of this time to direct enough stuff for that to be something that people like, oh, yeah, Nicole's a director, I'll call her for something. And for the last two years, for sure, like not just an idea, but actively been working on my own project that, you know, I'm hoping will come to fruition in the next few years or so. But yeah, kind of trying to figure out what my aesthetic is, like, what is my artistic voice as a director? What are the things that when you see that production, I want you to know that that's a Nicole Brewer show, you know, so now I kind of have what that is. And I can feel a little more confident or a little more stable in – and kind of going after things that I want to do rather than people asking me to do their thing, you know?

So I'm kind of like, I'm at that point for television and film. And I'm like, let's just address the abuse. And that for me is addressing these two cultures is a culture of extraction and a culture of exploitation. Those two things work in tandem with one another, to create the almost impossibility of liberation and freedom from those things. And then of course, we have all the isms that are you know, utilized as tools to reinforce that abuse.

PJ Hard-dough bread, Sourdough bread, Chin Chin, Sweetbread, Roti, Sudsa, Bun and Cheese, Nai Wong Bao -奶黄包- Custard Bun or Naan?

NB I'm very, I'm very much proud that that I am the descendant of enslaved peoples like, hundreds and hundreds of years descendant of enslaved peoples here in the US, and a smattering, a smattering of white in my bloodline like anyone who is descendant of enslaved peoples. So I would say Corn bread.

Dr Karen Tomlin

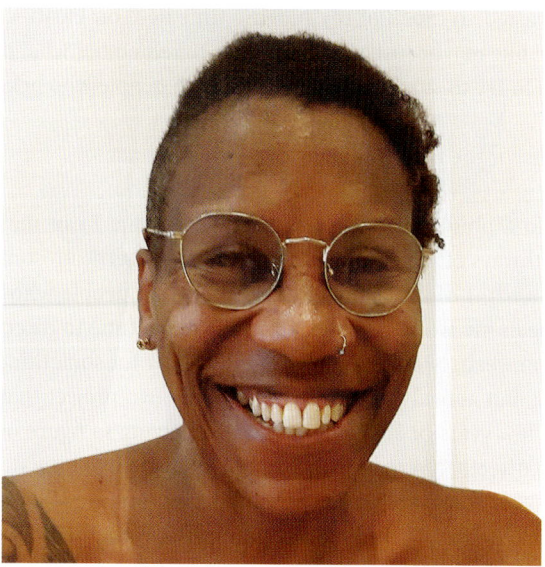

Photo by Karen Tomlin.

Dr Karen Tomlin has worked as a theatre practitioner and artist for over twenty-five years. She initially trained as an actor at LAMDA and has worked for theatre companies such as The Globe and the National Theatre. As a theatre director she is making work for theatre companies such as Paines Plough, Clean Break, The Gate, and Ovalhouse Theatre and the Theatre Royal Stratford East. She has extensive experience working within actor training conservatoires, including Royal Central School of Speech and Drama, Arts Educational, Rose Bruford, RADA, Guildhall Drama School and currently at LAMDA. Her doctoral research at Queen Mary University of London is entitled 'The Body Out of Place: The Conundrum of the Black Female Theatre Director'.

Pamela Jikiemi – PJ Tell me about your journey to become an actor, and then director?

Karen Tomlin – KT I always had a really active imagination – loved playing make-believe, I think it was a way in which I could escape my drab and somewhat dark childhood. I loved those technicolour musicals. *On the Town* was my favourite, the one about the three sailors who get one day's leave in New York, they dance, sing, fall in love etc.

I went to St Martin-in-the-Fields High School for Girls in Brixton. They didn't do any drama and the closest we got to looking at a play was studying Shakespeare in English, which I didn't understand. The notion of becoming an actor was first planted in my head when I had a conversation with a classmate who said that she wanted to go to drama school after leaving St Martin. The idea that there was a place that you could study to become an actor was really exciting to me and it was the first time that I began to consider the idea of becoming an actor for a living.

After some dubious exam results at St Martin, I went on to study at Kingsway and Princeton college in King's Cross to do my re-sits and A-levels. It had a really good drama department and student union that had strong connections with the then named North London Polytechnic. This was the height of Thatcherism and student activism and I was drawn to that, as much as the possibility of studying drama. My parents were also not happy about me studying drama and sociology after jettisoning Geography and English. But I was totally committed to the work, which was academically a first for me. It was the first time that I felt not only good at something, but also enjoyed doing it.

After I finished my studies I was a bit lost and decided that I didn't want to be an actor, as it was just too precarious. I think that this was really about my desire to please my parents. I don't think it was a particularly healthy relationship, they were quite strict and they dominated every aspect of my life. I felt trapped by them and I didn't really know how to extricate myself from them and become more independent.

I wanted my parents to be proud of me. And being an actor was not the way to do it. I don't think it was a thing that I felt they really understood, or they will be proud about. And I wasn't clever enough to be a doctor, I thought, and I didn't want to be a nurse. So, the middle ground was to become an occupational therapist.

I worked for Lambeth Social Services as an occupational therapist assistant, for two years, working towards the idea that after testing the water with the role I would eventually fully commit to the qualifying. But fate lent its hand as my parents decided to retire and go back to Jamaica and so as they left I applied for Drama Schools and got a place at LAMDA.

Which was one of the happiest times of my life.

PJ Training around learning 'the craft'; did you go to a conservatoire drama school? Talk about your creative career and your commitment towards pursuing it.

KT The prospectus. No really, the prospectus. I know it sounds really silly. I'd never heard of LAMDA before, I'd heard of RADA but I really wanted to go to Guildhall School of Music and Drama. Guildhall was in the Barbican, and the RSC (Royal Shakespeare Company) at that time was also based in the Barbican, and it just felt like if I'm at Guildhall, the next automatic step would be the RSC as if by osmosis. I had auditioned for drama school once before. The first time was for Guildhall and once for Guildford School of Acting during my A-levels.

For Guildhall, you had to learn three speeches, and I think I knew two Shakespeare speeches, and the third speech I tried to learn the night before, which is totally mad. I went to the audition. I thought they'll never ask for three. Did the first one, did the second one and they went, 'Oh, can we get a third?' And I thought, boy, oh boy, I thought I'm in trouble now – I'm in trouble because I don't really know it. I had this awful habit while I was doing my A-levels when I was in rehearsals that I, I would always swear when I made a mistake. So I start the third speech, its going well and then I suddenly blank and then shouted 'oh fuck', and all I remember, it felt like the whole panel kind of stood up and leant over the table and I knew that was end of me, I knew I wasn't going to go to be going to Guildhall that year.

In that same year, I was also recalled for Guildford, and the only reason I am mentioning it is because the experience at the Guildford audition profoundly affected me. It was the afternoon session working with the movement tutor. Mid-way one of the teachers came up to me and said, You have no shape. No form. You are just blurrrgh! I was so upset and humiliated by the comments and the retelling of the incident years later still does not take away from awfulness of the situation.

After my parents left for Jamaica, I knew that I wanted to be totally prepared for my next attempt to audition for drama school. So I got myself a private acting tutor. He was an actor who had a little clothes shop in

Battersea. Every week I would go through my speeches with him, I wanted to get in – I really wanted it. And when I was ready I thought right I'm going apply again for Guildhall.

I had seen the RADA prospectus, but it totally put me off. It was this gold-covered prospectus, just gold, solid gold, and on the first page was a list of all the great, good and venerated actors that went to RADA. I just thought, no, this is not for me, I don't even know what this is. I instinctively thought I don't want to go there. There was nothing about it to me that felt I could be a part of this.

The LAMDA prospectus was totally different, it was actually quite beautiful – filled with actors, acting, page after page. Seeing actors in action, and I was so enamoured by it I thought, this looks great. It looks like real people doing, thinking acting. So I applied to LAMDA, auditioned and won a place. Interestingly, I got a reserve place at Guildhall, but I went to the right place. Absolutely the right place, I learned so much as an actor that not only informed my professional career, which still informs the work that I do now as a teacher and director.

I started at LAMDA in 1987 and graduated in 1990.

PJ What did you get from your actor training?

KT I went through different phases as an actor, initially, people thought that I was really, really funny. So I did a lot of comedy stuff and comedy shows and you know, things with John Cleese and lots of television work.

Then I had a bit of a singing phase. Not musical theatre, because I remember after my first ever job, *Little Shop of Horrors*, at the Mercury Theatre Colchester, I was kind of traumatized by the world of musical theatre, even though I thought I'd really want to do that kind of stuff. I realized that if I was ever going to do singing on stage it had to be more a character driven than just song, dance, song.

I worked around the country in repertory theatre, I toured within the UK and internationally. And invariably there were times when I didn't work, I worked out that on average, I would work two jobs a year. But when I say two jobs a year, the two jobs a year could be two massive jobs that took over the whole year, or a commercial that shot for one-day a season at Salisbury Playhouse or something like that. So I called myself a jobbing actor.

The only thing I didn't ever do was film. Yes, I did student films but I was never cast for a feature film. But I think that's also the way that I looked. This is in the 90s, and as a Black woman who didn't look like Thandiwe Newton. This was pre-*Bridgerton*. I was a police officer, I was a barrister. I was a crazy social worker. I was a nurse. All with no character arc, no development, one-dimensional fill-ins for the real characters. In theatre there was a bit more of give and scope.

When I think about another important time in my acting career, was actually my relationship with Theatre Royal Stratford East, because that was the first time I experienced a real sense of community and belonging to a theatre, to an organization that I hadn't felt before. I would do a job and invariably, I would never go back, again barring at the National which I think was just series of flukes. My returning to Stratford East was really down to Philip Headley and the way that he cultivated and supported Black performers. He saw me! He saw me in a way that I don't think I was seen by any other organization before – I was just a Black actor and I wasn't a token gesture or something to be frightened or cautious of. Theatre Royal Stratford East, during his time was definitely a space where Black actors and performance artists, writers, directors were nurtured, and their work was promoted and encouraged in a way that I hadn't really experienced before.

I don't know if you spoke to other actors about it but Theatre Royal Stratford East, it was like you're going to your home. Everyone knew everyone. I mean, the front of house, the bar star crew, the ushers, so many people started out as ushers and then became performers on stage, or in the case of Kerry Kyriacos Michael, an artistic director. So definitely there was a culture within that organization, that kind of culture, but also it was this collision that I love of old East End, white East End charm, and Black, and Indian, and it was just a concoction of all these cultures. That shouldn't have worked, but did. Music hall nights on Sunday hosted by Barbara Windsor comics songs and skits, alongside spoken word and Black performers. How does this work? How does this work? But it did.

One of the happiest times in theatre for me barring being at LAMDA, was being in the Stratford East panto. Who would have thought? I loved being in panto at Theatre Royal Stratford East, I learned so much about acting during that process and I felt like I belonged. This was of course in the late 90s, before the Olympics and the investment into the area. It was a pretty run-down area, as was the theatre – you would be rehearsing in a Portakabin, the green room looks like a bomb has hit it literally, but you really felt that you were part of something – you were part of the community inside and outside of the community. I was a valued and respected member of the Stratford East Family.

I was generally unhappy with my professional acting life – being an actor was not only about what you do on stage, but equally about what you do off it. I think that I was quite naive about the realities of existing, making a living in the profession. I was and still am an awful networker and you just can't be. I struggled to be nice to people who might be able to give me a job, I was an awful self-publicist. Also, creatively and intellectually I found the work I was doing and some of the people I was working with frustrating. Maybe I was the frustrating one!

That's why I think I loved my time at drama school so much. Because I felt like I was really working, really learning and utilizing my creativity you know. I felt like I was expanding and being allowed to explore a range of practices in my development as an actor.

When you're in the profession as a jobbing actor you are the low-hanging fruit, you don't have any kind of autonomy. When you are working on screen, and on a set, it's hit your mark, say the line and in the right order. There's no discussion about your character or trying things in slightly a different way. You don't have that level of creative autonomy, unless you are a lead.

Also, I wasn't prepared to do any television or screen work, when I was training there was little to no training in that area. I was learning about working in front of the camera, on the actual jobs. My first screen/telly job was *The Bill* playing a barrister where I had court scenes arguing my case in front of the jurors etc. But I naively thought when we went on set that we would actually have the opportunity to rehearse. But when we actually got on the set, we would rehearse for the camera positions and then take. I was like, what? I don't think that I was very good.

PJ What drives you? Looking at issues of employability, how do you navigate this?

KT I had a really good agent, I was with Lou Coulson. And she was really supportive regarding the work I wanted to do and didn't want to do. Not that I had that much of a choice but there were times I was offered work and I knew doing it would make me unhappy and I was able to turn it down with the support of my agent. I also took a career break at one point where I asked to not be put up for auditions for a year. I really struggled with auditioning and equally not auditioning. I don't think that I was really mentally cut out to be an actor as I seemed to spend a lot of the time unhappy.

I used to think of the agents being in league. My first agent that I got when I was at LAMDA was probably like, mid-first division, not premier. But then as the main agent he retired and then his partner took over and then the agency dropped down to another division. Then through a series of quirky events and me making the best of an opportunity that came my way via a singing booking at the memorial of the wife of a tutor from LAMDA, I approached Lou Coulson, and she said, What kind of work do you want to do? And I said I'd love to work at the Royal Court.

I had never worked there, theatre was my thing. She went, Oh. She, in front of me, she called the casting director at the Royal Court at that time and got me an audition. And that's when I realized Holy Mother of God. There's a different league and then I had an audition, and suddenly different types of auditions were opening up for me different access to things, different relationships.

Confidence in yourself is so important as an actor

But I also think, I wasn't comfortable in me, because I was at LAMDA in the same year that Marianne Jean-Baptiste was at RADA. So we both started at the same time. And I remember being in an audition at the Theatre Royal Stratford East for Mike Leigh.

So, I was waiting to go in and I heard her audition and she was great, even through a door. She was so confident in what she was doing in a way I could never be in an audition. I considered myself to be a really good actress, but she was telling them in that audition that this was her job, this was her role.

She got the job. She played the show at Stratford, and it was great success. Then Mike Leigh casts her in the film version of the play where she was nominated for an Oscar for the Best Supporting Actress in *Secrets and Lies*.

I remember there was a Black casting director, woman. I think her name was Leo Davis, I remember her saying to me, and it probably was the most damaging things for anyone to say to an actor and it was a Black person saying that it was my look – I would find it difficult to get work because of the way I looked. That's from a Black casting director saying that to you. And I think it's that kind of feeling that I didn't look right, I think informed everything real or imagined in my career.

PJ One of the recurring issues in the creative industries is the discussion around representation. How do you see your role in relation to that conversation?

KT I think one of the challenges I'm just thinking about, maybe what I'm experiencing right now, what I'm witnessing right now.

As a Black female director and pedagogue there is a constant challenge of having to always prove your credentials, where in conversation when they meet me people will start to list their CV as if to suggest you need clarity on their experience, as they assume you're a 'diversity hire'. But you are still always questioned and having to jump through ever multiplying hoops, deflecting/absorbing the constancy of undermining questions and behaviours. There is a fight for who are 'othered' enough. There is a shift, and the thing is who gets lost in those intersections – and I think it is the same, if you're Black and a woman, it is incredibly difficult. It is easier with people who know your work, but you are still always questioned, always questioned. I do feel like that especially as a director in her fifties, a Black director in her fifties, it is really difficult to get work outside of conservatoires because they just don't think you exist. If they don't think you exist, then they don't think you've got any experience, so they don't give you the work and it becomes a vicious circle. That concerns me, there is a level of mistrust towards Black female directors. I feel and maybe this will change, but I do feel the legacy of my experience as an actor there is a kind of a hangover that is still there in my work as a director.

As an actor I think I was in the wrong time. As a director I think we are in a different time and things are changing a bit but …

I'm in the middle of being one of the directors directing, the showcase happening for the third-year students at LAMDA. And so this is the MFA Acting and the BA Acting graduates.

So it's the first time I'm working with the MFA and the BAs in that way. And we just got, we kind of do the surgery, and then you get allocated them. But so it is is quite interesting working with Black students, Black actors, who are using their own their own voice, their dialect in terms of particular scenes, some of the scenes they've written themselves. Also, how do some students react to me as a director, when it's the showcase, which I think might be slightly different, because I'm Black female? So that's the thing which was very different from my experience. Is what we can do, and what voices we can use as actors was very limiting.

When I was training it was all about me losing anything that sounded I'm saying 'Black' in inverted commas. So the idea was, we have to speak using Received Pronunciation (RP), there was a particular voice that was an actor's voice. Your own voice was seen in a negative way. So, for me, one of the major things is that how Black actors or actors, from different classes, are able to own their voice in a way that when I was training, we weren't. It was a very white middle-class kind of idea of what acting was. And that in itself caused a lot of problems for actors in my generation. And me, definitely, that the reality was when you left drama school, you weren't prepared for actually how you were going to be cast or the auditions you were going to go up for.

I remember I had so removed my South London voice. You know, people would go like can you do Cockney, and I didn't know how to do it. And so then I do this weird, weird accent, kind of like mockney accent, because I actually didn't know how to do it.

I didn't know how to do, like, any Jamaican. I had always avoided that when I was growing up. So I didn't have to do any Caribbean Jamaican, but none of that – couldn't do anything. I literally couldn't do any accents that had anything to do with the Black diaspora. Because I'd spent so much time convincing myself that I wanted to just play classical Shakespeare, basically white roles that I was just going to play white roles, essentially or middle-class white roles? Or yeah, so and of course I leave. And they asked me – I'm going for auditions and they ask me to do that. And I didn't know how to.

And then it came to a really weird thing of not knowing what my voice was, what my voice was, a real loss of a sense of who I was. What my actual voice was. I bumped into an actress who I knew trained at Guildhall. And, you know, it was in Brixton – I was, you know, going to the market or something. I met her outside Brixton rec. And she was speaking to me. And I remember thinking, oh, my God, oh, my God. You sound, I can't believe how you sound. You sound so posh. I mean, yet.

It was like, where was the real person, can I check, who's speaking, I didn't recognize this person. And I thought, oh, my God, she sounds like that, how the fuck must I sound. And from that moment, I made a decision to lose my RP accent, and made an active decision to remember how to sound like a South Londoner to kind of undo that. To undo that and to be then be able to do it if required.

But that wasn't my voice, I had to reconnect with what my voice was.

And I have to say, as an actor, I found it really difficult finding what Karen's voice was. And what's so interesting, watching the actors that I'm working with, that it's now the other way. The other way that all these voices, they, all their work is very much rooted in their own voice, which I think is great. But but maybe probably American, they can probably do American now. So there's a more kind of connection with the Black diaspora. And those voices. And of course, then that opens up the work that these actors can do. It was at the first 'Why is Central so white' panel events. And I remember – older – all the actors from our time spoke incredibly posh. They would ask questions, speak like this. And then all the other younger actors just spoke their voice. And I thought, What? How insane is that? You could you feel it, the difference and the disconnect of our own voices.

And I think that really did kind of impact on how you were cast.

PJ What pitfalls should actors emerging from drama school aim to avoid?

KT That's a really good question, but I don't know if I am qualified to say that because of my age. If I am honest I am learning how culturally it is different, even the way that we communicate, even the way that we audition, image is so fundamentally different. I had a student say to me recently, 'I don't want to just be cast as a villain' and I was thinking flashback. Clearly there are certain concerns, the same concerns for Black actors as it was for me and for you. But I could also see the incredible benefits from being a Black actor right now.

PJ Hard-dough bread, Sourdough bread, Chin Chin, Sweetbread, Roti, Sudsa, Bun and Cheese, Nai Wong Bao-奶黄包- Custard Bun or Naan?

KT Jamaican Bun and butter.

My dad was a baker before he came to England. Every Easter he would bake loads of buns for friends and family. I have great memories of those times. No bun has tasted even close to my father's. I never paid attention when he was making it, which I kind regret. I also tried to recreate the recipe once but didn't quite pull it off.

When he baked, he seemed happy.

Indhu Rubasingham MBE

Photographer: Mark Douet.

Indhu Rubasingham MBE is the Director and Joint Chief Executive of the National Theatre. Prior to this, she had been the Artistic Director of Kiln Theatre from 2012 to 2023. During this time, she oversaw a £9 million major capital renovation of the building, which reopened in 2018 as Kiln Theatre. She repositioned the company's mission to bring unheard voices to the mainstream and, in 2021, Kiln Theatre won the Stage Award for London Theatre of the Year. In 2017, Rubasingham was awarded an MBE for services to theatre in the New Year's Honours List, as well as an honorary doctorate from the University of Hull.

Pamela Jikiemi – PJ Tell me about your journey to becoming a director, did you train as an actor?

Indhu Rubasingham – IR I never did. I just wanted to just clarify, I never did acting training. I don't come from an acting background.

PJ Training around learning 'the craft'; did you go to a conservatoire drama school? Talking about your creative career and your commitment towards pursuing it.

IR I grew up in Mansfield in the Midlands. And I got a – just by happenchance just got this experience to do work experience at my local theatre, at Nottingham Playhouse. I had not expressed – been that interested. You know, I didn't know – I'd never been there before. And that's what started the interest really, that's what sparks the passion. And I was working with stage management, backstage.

From that I got very obsessed about theatre, wanting to understand more, going to the theatre, reading about it. And to cut a long story short, I was on a route of sciences, but I changed and then I did a degree in drama at Hull University. And whilst I was doing that degree, again, just to push myself just a tad – I'd never thought about directing. But I made myself direct a play. But in that moment of directing a play at university, I'd found something that I felt very comfortable with or felt very intuitive. And that's what made me kind of think, oh, is this a career? Is this something I can do? And made me really explore that.

When I left university, I worked in the summer holidays with various youth theatres, assisting that. And I then got on an Arts Council bursary to be a trainee director at Theatre Royal Stratford East. And that's – that's the foundations of my training.

PJ What did you get from university?

IR You know, I loved it. You know, for me, it was a true sense of the education. Because I went in and was very intimidated, didn't feel I was going to have a career in theatre, didn't know what I wanted to do.

I was thinking I was just going to use it and then go into journalism or something else and actually, through my education discovered directing. So, it – in terms of an education that opens your eyes and exposes you to things you don't know. I really got that from – from university.

I mean, my parents – there were no artists in my family background, but what was good was that my parents were great in terms of wanting to understand and wanting to engage.

And so though my father was a bit concerned about what is a drama degree going to lead you to, he did his research and – and was very – actually in the end was much more supportive than my school was at the time.

PJ What drives you? Looking at issues of employability, how do you navigate this?

IR I think what drives you changes, doesn't it, as you grow and pursue – as you – you know, I – gosh, it's a very big question.

I think what drove me to begin with was like, is this possible? Is this a career I can – I can make into a career?

Wanting to discover that.

I always found theatre – I just found it magical. I found the world absolutely magical. Be it backstage, be it in the rehearsal room. And I think – and then through – and then it's – and it was also about what – what I loved about theatre, as well was that it can talk about things that – and it can talk about things and really move you in a very different way to other mediums.

And that's what I discovered. That's what I fell in love with. So, I think what moved me – well, what drove me was like wanting to be able to do that. Wanting to be able to move people. Wanting to be able to tell stories, from different perspectives, and challenge the norm. And so, yeah, I think that's what drove me to begin with. And also was I any good? You know, you don't know whether you're any good to begin with, you know.

Can I do this?

And then I think what drives me now sort of old – being older is like, you know – a – what drives me now is being able to make sure that work is enjoyable. To enjoy the people you're with, the company that you keep. Because, you know, things are hard enough, you know, work shouldn't be …

And also the power of storytelling, and how that can change perspectives, change attitudes, change behaviours, and – and whose story are we telling? How are we telling those stories?

PJ Is your preparation for a project different for theatre and screen?

IR Yeah, it's theatre. I don't – I don't do screen, the majority my work is the writing. So, I commission playwrights.

I often start at the scratch, at the beginning of an idea and sort of developing. And that – that can take between a couple of years to five years of developing a play, a script. And what I'm interested in it's basically like I'm led by a good story. It has to have a strong narrative. And a narrative that is specific and detailed, that reveals the universal nature of humanity.

But it's in that specificity that I get really fascinated by, you know, a world.

Being taken into a world. A different perspective, a different culture, a different lens of – of something.

And so, once you've got the script, and you're working in collaboration with the playwright, you then create your team. So, a designer, lighting designer, movement director, however, that creative team is made up.

I then work with that team around storyboarding and looking at how we want to storyboard the play. And then, also, alongside this is obviously the casting process. And then you get into the rehearsal process, which is – with a new play, you're always – it's the first time you've ever seen whether a new play works. You don't know that until you put it up on its feet. And then it's – it's a process of what I call – it's like painting a picture. It's, like, it's sketching the outline. And you go back to the beginning and putting in more detail, and you keep going back and adding and adding and adding more detail.

PJ The industry and your place in it?

IR Well, I think we're in very tricky times, at the moment, it's a very difficult moment. So, we're coming out of a pandemic. People aren't used to going back to the theatre. Audiences – we don't understand audiences' behaviour at the moment and also, you know, the cost of living crisis is really affecting what people spend their money on.

The expenditure is much higher, and the income is being reduced and – and government cuts on funding.

So, all these things converging at the same time. Normally, you have one or two of these things, but we're in a moment of a lot of quite serious things converging. That means that it's a very tricky time for the – for the theatre industry.

PJ One of the recurring issues in the creative industries is the discussion around representation. How do you see your role in relation to that conversation?

IR I mean, it's affected my career right from the beginning, obviously. You know, what we're fighting for is equality of opportunity, and a place at the table. And I think that it absolutely has been something that has been part of my life, but also part of my passion and one of my drivers.

I think when I started I was very interested in what – what the British identity was about, and the complexities of that. And then I got much more interested – in what our global connections were. And when I became artistic director of the Tricycle, which is now the Kiln Theatre, I changed the mission statement, which is the unheard voice being part of a mainstream. And it's about redressing the balance of who – who leads narratives, whose stories are told. So, it's always been in my working and professional life.

But I think what we all strive for is for anyone to be allowed to be an artist, first and foremost, rather than political or representational, or playing – or having to come or play an agenda.

Sorry, not playing an agenda, but having to work on and address an agenda, in the same way that our white male counterparts don't have to address those issues. But we will only get there when there is an equal playing field, and all those stories are allowed and have the same weight. So, it's a long journey.

PJ Thinking in terms of how you choose to identify, what do you think are the challenges in the acting/creative industry now?

IR I think we talk about it in leadership. I think it's really fascinating because I think it's about sustainability. Like, you know, how are we going to – you know, they're really, really difficult jobs.

There's a lot of that – you know, it's about fundraising, it's politics, you know, looking after organizations or leading organizations with a vision, and they're quite lonely jobs. So, how do we support that leadership? And how do we create – you know, I don't – I think when we use phrases like old boys network, you realize they were important in supporting each other.

One of the things I've realized by being an artistic director is how lonely and how small – how there isn't the same network. And how do we create that network to support?

So, I think that is a really – it's sustainability and support is kind of – because I think we'll get people who will get those jobs, but how long will they stay in them? How long will they last? And then – and then what you don't want is like, oh, we tried that. We don't need to – we did that.

PJ What pitfalls should actors emerging from drama school aim to avoid?

IR I mean, the thing is you can't avoid the pitfalls, because that's where our biggest learnings come from like – you know, it's making those mistakes and learning from them and growing from them. But I think what things people can look out for which I think maybe in our times, we didn't have as much is, like, mentors.

You know, not being afraid to go and ask someone to be your mentor or go and ask someone for a cup of tea to get their advice. Also – it's also for forming tribes of like-minded people of your own generation. Because these are the people you will be moving along with.

And not to worry about comparing yourself to what someone else is doing because all journeys are different. And some – I always remember when I was younger, a great person talked to me about careers. It's like a tree and you can be a fast-growing tree that goes really tall really quickly, or a very slow-growing tree that takes its time, but is sturdy. And, you know, it's – it's just really – it's just really important when you're younger, to not feel you have to put those restrictions on yourself.

PJ What are your broad aims for the future of your directing presence?

IR You know, what – I've never had a career path. I've never gone, oh … you know, I love what I'm doing. I loved being an artistic director at the Kiln. And now I also get to direct at the National.

I'd like to have a bit more work-life balance.

PJ Who are the directors and actors that have inspired you?

IR Yeah. I mean, like, you know, Peter Brook. Also, people have been very, you know, kind to me. Oh God, why can't I think? There weren't many because I didn't see many – do you know what I mean? I got to assist Mike Leigh, and I learnt a lot from him.

One of my great mentors was an actor/director called Sotigui Kouyaté, who was part of Peter Brook's company. He was an incredible mentor. I mean, there's people like – I mean, I love Dominic Cooke's work. Yeah.

PJ If a young Black and Global Majority person of eighteen made the decision that they want to become a director or an actor, what would your advice be?

IR I would like go – you know, if you're eighteen I would go get some training of some kind, whether it's going to drama school, getting actor's training, because you learn about working with actors. It is really useful actors' training for a director.

You know. Or you could do a degree in – you don't have to do a degree, but I'm just saying it's just – it's just finding space where, you know, even if you're doing English, even if you're doing sociology or psychology, all these things help you become a director.

Understand – because what directing – it's about many things, but one of them is understanding human nature. It's like what you're trying to do as a director is get the best work out of people that you're working with. How to do that? By understanding what will help them do their best work.

So, from understanding what it's like to be an actor, from psychology, from English, from, you know, the – the research, anything that just sparks your curiosity.

Because the other thing is curiosity, curiosity about humans, curiosity about stories. And so, anything that makes you learn, push, drive, that gives you the space to – to not go I need – you don't need to be a director at eighteen.

PJ Hard-dough bread, Sourdough bread, Chin Chin, Sweetbread, Roti, Sudsa, Bun and Cheese, Nai Wong Bao-奶黄包- Custard Bun or Naan?

IR Oh. Naan!

Out of the Black Box

Josette Bushell-Mingo OBE

Cam Harle Photography.

Josette Bushell-Mingo OBE is the Principal and CEO of the Royal Central School of Speech and Drama. She is a trustee of the University of London, the chair of Equality and Diversity for Conservatoires UK, sits on the board of Hackney Empire, and is the chair of the Mayor of London's Community Advisory Group for Black on the Square, which celebrates Black cultures and creativity in the capital.

Previously Head of Acting at Stockholm University of the Arts, Sweden, Josette is an award-winning actor and director whose career has included performances with the Royal Shakespeare Company, the National Theatre and the Manchester Royal Exchange. She was nominated for an Olivier Award, is the recipient of a TMA Award, and starred in the internationally acclaimed production *Nina: A Story about Me and Nina Simone*, now a documentary film for SVT Sweden.

For thirteen years, Josette was the Artistic Director for the National Touring Swedish Deaf Theatre ensemble Tyst Teater, where her work focused on fostering the understanding, respect and potential of sign language arts and the artistic, linguistic and cultural rights of the deaf. In 2021, Josette was awarded HM The King's Medal 8th size with the ribbon of the Order of the Seraphim by HM King Carl XVI Gustaf.

Pamela Jikiemi – PJ Tell me about your creative journey.

Josette Bushell-Mingo – JB-M My creative journey started as a little girl from the East End of London, I wouldn't call it a creative journey, it was really the arts finding me. I seemed to attach myself to all the things that allowed me to express myself. And that's got a lot to do with the people that I knew at that time. So I think my creative journey started with what we would now call an 'installation'. I directed a production of 'The Owl and the Pussycat' when I was about seven years old, at Creedon Primary School. That's the first early memory I have of an arts creativity, I'd call it really, and there was a chance to do this piece of work. I mean, I'm talking now as a fifty-eight-year-old woman. But at seven, eight years old, I had the idea to make masks for the cat and the owl, we had a boat that was 3D, I had two of my friends sit in it, and they didn't do anything, and then was a little fake guitar and someone sat at the edge of the stage and read the poem.

That was one of my first creative things that I remember. Before then, I suppose creativity came through my membership of the choir, although I wouldn't call myself a Christian in that sense. But I was singing in the church choir, very, very early on directly after that, really. And at my primary school, I think creative writing, drama, acting, after school clubs were quite normal. Another part of that which I'm really kind of spanning between about eight as far as I remember, right up to the teens. I was also an athlete as well, and that has an element of creativity in it. So I was 100 metres and shot put and then 100 metres and relay and then shot put into discus and I almost made it to the England trials as a basketball player and netball player.

So, I learned very early on about teamwork, about on that track, in that game, no matter how poor I was, I come from poor Black working class – it didn't matter. As long as I got my uniform and I jumped higher, I ran faster, I caught the ball, I delivered my lines, there was something that was happening beyond the perception of who I was. And even though I might have been naive at the time, nobody said that little Black girl, she's fast or that little Black girl.

It always seems to be about what Josette was doing. Josette was running higher, drawing, writing. I was producing and directing plays in my secondary school. I still have the scripts, I did the posters. I wrote the programme, I sang the music, and people wrote it down for me.

So by the time I was, you know, fifteen, sixteen, I wanted to be a journalist as well. Because writing for me was a huge part then. I wrote a lot of poetry, I had poetry published when I was much younger than they thought I was at the time, it was called *All English Poets*. And I managed to convince them through my poetry that I was obviously someone else. But when I walked through the door for the first time for a formal meeting, they were like, 'this is a child'! I continued for a while, but I quickly stopped I think they realized that this person is least five years younger than we thought they were.

So, my early journey was one of the arts being an outlet for a family that were dysfunctional to a certain extent, and I have to pay respect because I've got sisters still alive. They won't disagree with it. And music, sport, school creativity, after school clubs, I ran a workshop in my mom's garage, which she was none too pleased about, I had invited the whole neighbourhood and taken all her precious sewing equipment out, I never did it again.

I suppose the moral of the story is that it was always there. It was always – and I'm of a generation where it was so close. We know that the times have changed now. We can see that in higher education, Arts Council cuts, but I grew up in a time where after-school activities, creativity in the places where I learned and studied, together with sport meant that my trajectory was obvious I suppose in one way or another.

PJ Where did that trajectory and those opportunities take you?

JB-M I learned to read very late. And I learned to write very late and actually, I'm dyslexic.

That's what it was in the first instance.

So when it came to the last year, in my secondary school, and as I said, I wanted to be a journalist, as writing I can do, I can write. I was supposed to have the pre-tests you have for the exams, which can give you a kind of idea of how you're going to do and of course, surprise, surprise, I wasn't doing very well, certainly not in economics and maths and certainly not on the written level. But at the same time my involvement in holiday clubs and workshops was just building and building.

At that time that my creativity was at the same height of my education, and I detect even now looking back that I went further and further into my creativity, because the academic stuff was really very wobbly. And then a good friend Avril said to me, listen, why don't we apply for Barking College of Technology, they're doing performing arts there? Which made absolute sense.

I applied and I got into a two-year foundation course at the end of that and, of course, was like Fame, leotard, pink tights, a lot of tap dance ballet, the lot. And again, there I wrote a lot. It was there that I flew, I was home. I then applied and was awarded a place to study for a BA Theatre Studies at Bretton Hall College of Education.

But in that last month, a performance company called Kaboodle Theatre Exchange, which is based in Liverpool, they were Grotowski and Le Coq trained. Those were the days when companies came into institutions, and were resident for two, three weeks. They did workshops and performances in the evening, you know, that rarely happens now. Those were the days. So Kaboodle to Barking College and they did a workshop it was good Grotowski based and as an ex-athlete, I was jumping higher. I could jump off anything, fearless backflips, whatever you wanted to try. I was there asking to do it again.

But at the end of I think more or less three or four days of workshopping as they were clearing up the Artistic Director, Lee Begley, came to me and said, we've been watching in the workshop, and we'd really like to offer you a place in the company. I'm eighteen years old about to go to Bretton Hall!

And I remember giving the poker face because I was so shocked, and then I was just running down the corridor, I ran down and all the doors were open, and I stopped and sat at the end of the stairs and I just sat there. It wasn't a case where you could get your mobile phone and go, guess what? Anyway, I said yes, to the idea of running away with the circus, and it's brought me home all this time, you know, so that's my first foray. But in the midst of that, I did actually go to Central. I went to Central, thought I would try drama school and this looked like one that was really interesting. So, I literally walked up the stairs, picked up a leaflet walked back out again. I mean, it never happened. I just looked at their brochure and thought there's nothing here for me, they don't sound right, there's nothing, it's all posh. No, no, thank you very much. So that's the trajectory. Ironically, I am in a university.

Really, that's how I got there. And extraordinary movement of events and that took me around the world. Kaboodle introduced me to a very strong European way of working which eventually led to Jacques Lecoq, Philippe Gaulier, Rudolph von Laban, a lot of white practitioners in fact. I toured – I did Commedia dell'arte very, very young. I mean, you know, I was touring Italy, France, United States, I did my first stage-management job around twenty-one. And I was in New York stage managing the show for Kaboodle. So, I recognized how my sporting past leant into this as I learned very early on about the team and the work and your place, and you have a huge connection there at the end of the day, you've busted a gut. And now you help stage management to roll the cables.

PJ What did you get from your experiences, how did you navigate the work?

JB-M I mentioned that the early part of my journey that the focus of the companies I worked for were white European male practitioners. I think that my full understanding of that kind of went in and out. I mean, the companies that I worked with were The People Show, Lumiere and Son, Théâtre de Complicité. I worked with Kaboodle and various other companies that were white-based companies that had diverse companies. Did I feel that I was there because I was a Black person? Very rarely at that time. I don't know if that's naivety, or that I didn't give a shit, or because the work for me it was always constructed in a way where I could participate. So, for me, I think when I look at Grotowski's work as I do more and more, I think where is the Black body the Black space in that I never thought Complicité were looking at my Black body being funny. Now, did they understand Blackface or clowning?

That's another question that I grew into. But in terms of me at that time, no, because I was never isolated in that way. And the directors I worked with at that time, none of them went, 'you're Black', and that's why you should do it, or I have a consciousness. Actually where it did maybe come to, in terms of my journey, to be clear, at no point was I not aware that these were all white practitioners. But that wasn't a stop, I was just hungry to know how this would impact my body and my Blackness. And I was still Black at the end of it. Particularly when we were in Europe, where there were comments, occasionally, all my colleagues stood up for me, verbally stood up for me.

I worked with Pan Project, Black Mime, Denise Wong, I mean, these companies that were either Black or diverse. Talawa I worked for, and at no point without, though I am talking about white practitioners, because my artistic trajectory was so diverse, I never felt I lost out.

And therefore when I first started, there was very much about absorbing this and thinking, how did this affect my Black body? What does that look like? I didn't have the intellect to ask it in a kind of intersectional way. But no, I did not think or feel or was made to believe that I was there for anything other than I was a great performer, a great actress, and I used to work in small theatres. And you know, the Blackness was always there and never left me. So I was always a bit confused by that, it was other people.

So, for example, when I was at the Royal Shakespeare Company (RSC) and took over parts there after casting. So, it would have been the same time that Clive Rowe was doing *Show Boat*. And I was taking over from Saskia Reeves, with Hugh Bonneville at the RSC (Josette took over the lead part of Silvia in the RSC's 1991 production of *Two Gentlemen of Verona*). As far as I was concerned, could people hear me, was there integrity in the character, was I delivering that text, was I really in love, I mean all those characters, but it was the press that says 'Josette's performance, however, how can you have a Black person do blah, blah blah?'.

But that only occurred when I went to do the first season and there when I was working with then Phyllida Lloyd on Restoration comedy, and Shakespeare where I played a servant, nobody commented. Because it all made sense. The fact that I stole the scene from Claire Holman is neither here nor there. But basically, that is absolutely in the reviews.

That's also part of growth and change. Absolutely, then is then but now we know we can take Grotowski and push him up against other practitioners, African-descent practitioners, Asian practitioners, then say where are we in that? That kind of analysis is welcome and delightful. But I also think that it's possible to meet that work. The problem is it's not that we only mean white work – the problems we don't meet with our own work, to me is the thing. I absolutely love Shakespeare – woop de doo, where is the rest of it? That's the work. That's the imbalance.

So yeah, the moral of the story, I guess, is very much that the Blackness never left me. It was others that pointed it out. And I always looked at it as if it was something really fucking peculiar. Was it racist? Yes. Was it sexist? Probably, did I feel it? No, because I was too busy getting on with my work.

PJ What drives you? Looking at issues of employability, how do you navigate this?

JB-M These questions are so good. Let it be recorded in this interview that Pamela was really grilling when she asked this question. Right, what drives me?

What drives me is understanding that what I do can change people's lives. That's what drives me. And the fear of not doing that, particularly for my Black community is more terrifying than doing something. Whether it's Nina Simone, taking this job at Royal Central, or whatever it might be.

That's what drives me. What drives me is seeing the agency of the arts and what it gives to communities. I mean, there's no price on that. There's no price on what that means. And that makes the battle to find those spaces of integrity even more important.

So that's one of the things that drives me, in my work, finding those places where I can make a difference. Finding those places where I can do the things that people are uneasy about doing, using myself. It is really interesting, because Elsie Fogerty, who founded Central, she talked about it very early, we can always question what that means, but it is still resonant, which is, service.

Our greatest pleasure as human beings is to be of service to others. I didn't mean a doormat; I don't mean that kind of service. But to know that what you have done has facilitated greatness in somebody else. Hey, I can do that.

That's what drives me and mainly because of my performance-art background, and my community work very early on. Because a lot of the companies did a lot of outreach work, really, I mean, it's a long list of places that I've been, I've now worked with the Sami community, first indigenous Nordic belt, I've worked with Black Nordic-Afro Nordic people; I've worked with the deaf community. In fact, Kaboodle when we first started did a lot of work with deaf and disabled persons. All of these trajectories only shore up my *raison d'être*, that when it's in their hands, or in their space, and they run with it. It's extraordinary.

That's what motivates me, and I think what motivates me is people who fuck around with that, abuse that, that's also a motivation, that motivation to try to rid, clear, spaces of those people. Those are some of the things that motivate me, and the joy of it, because when the light hits it right, it's extraordinary.

PJ How do you decide what direction to travel in?

JB-M I don't have to decide anything. Actually, I just follow the flame.

People keep asking me, 'how are you doing this, what inspires you to keep going?' For me, this is all the same fire. It's all the same joy. It just keeps changing. That's all.

I will still be Josette the Black girl from the East End of London doing *The Owl and the Pussycat*, it's the same person a little bit older, a little bit grey – a little bit. But it's the same person. It's not changed. There have been threats that after a post like this I could go anywhere. But where I am most likely to go is back to Stockholm.

That's enough for me. If I leave the place, seeing itself more clearly and with integrity. That's my job done. I think after this, there has been mooting that I should go into politics. Everything is political is always my response. I'm up to my neck in politics. I walk into a room and that's a political statement in of itself. Oh, girl, girl!

Every day is parliament, you know? Yeah. So in that sense. After that, I'd really like to see that the National Black Theatre of Sweden thrives. It's suffering a little bit with the fact that I'm here. So we've had to go into development while I'm here. I'd like to see that really step up, hand it over as good practice should be. I'd like, after this. I think I'm really excited. I don't know, I've suddenly – because I've identified myself as neurodiverse and I am really curious to see how I can empower the Black Global Majority persons who are neurodiverse deaf, it that area that's of interest to me, maybe because I'm working with Jenny Seeley and Paula from Deafinitely Theatre, they've just pushed through with their foundation course for deaf persons. so let's jump right in, you know, that's good.

Jenny and Paula, they contacted me, but that's because they knew of my work in Sweden, and we have met during the European Union of the Deaf and UN work. So for me, it was, you want to do it with us at Central, are you sure? And they said yes! So let's go one step, let's just do a foundation course.

They've approved the foundation course – that should be end of 2024, then we'll start doing the first cohort for '25, '26. That's okay, we can do that we can get RADA involved and everybody can be part of it, I don't mind. The most important thing is the agency of that community was all on their terms. If they need one million, then I have to take that from my budget to secure interpreters. They need a new fire system so that when the alarm goes off, it flashes and it doesn't. So, this year, we're going to do the first sign language, where they call it a round tables, which is where they invite people, and the deaf community explain their positioning, and then they start to do some of the basic signs. Thank you, tea, coffee central these things before the course starts. Otherwise, forget it. So, you're absolutely right, you're absolutely right. It's, no, more I think it's about the patience, I think it's how you go patiently, I think going back to your motivation question, maybe one of the things is time. Time is a huge motivation, you know, that expandable thing when I think of our lineage and history.

There's a lot of hope with me being in this position. But what they don't realize is that I have a lot of hope.

PJ Thinking in terms of how you choose to identify, what do you think are the challenges in the acting/creative industry now?

The Black part of the Global Black Global Majority community, that's how I identify. And I use Blackness in terms of triumph and glory. I don't use it in struggle, I don't use it in the near in the term of struggle. Of course, if I'm asked to fill in a form, I'll be Black British Caribbean. It's like being Afro-Swedish. You know, we're the only one still describing ourselves to colour without any context. And that's why African British, Caribbean British, although it's cold, is much more in sync. So we'd say Afro-Swedish, African American, but you know, we were still using the term Black. But however, when I use it, I always use it in that context and contextualize it. So people know why I am using it, because people get sensitive about the usage of the word 'Black', particularly in the Nordic region, 'Black National Theatre, what do you mean?' Well, it means this for us, it doesn't mean what it means for you. So that's how I identify.

I think, access to role models. I think that's a huge challenge. I think the balance between what we have absorbed, you know, when we talk about how we absorb the negative image of ourselves, the working against the cliche and the stereotype, I think that's a huge challenge. Because we are strong and we are powerful, and that can be tipped so over into angry and aggressive. This, I think, is a huge navigation. I think the biggest challenges now will be to push against the pendulum swing of racism, that's coming. People have had enough, we've got the woke culture, we've got other things in particular, the Black Global Majority community here, of transgender, all of these things, cancel culture, all of these things, I think, are going to be a huge navigation, particularly Black Global Majority and how to retain the space on our terms. That is also going to be very, very challenging, I think, how to push through racist racism at every level – without – and I think we're getting better at it. But without burning out ourselves. I often say to students I mentor, how do you turn your rage into heat, that it hits, it heats you up and sustains you and doesn't turn you to ash? How do you do that? Which is what I think about when I'd say because I don't talk about being angry any more. I talk about rage. For me that's a very important way of articulating an internal clock when we're talking about heat, and all of this. So, I think those are going to be some of the challenges ahead. If that makes any sense.

I think taking up your sports analogy. that if you take sport, then you need to train, we have stamina, you need to go back when it doesn't work, you need to find your new tech and you need to go forward. But we also need to communicate. And also I think our global network is something we really underestimate. We are not alone. And we're never alone. I'm not just talking about Black Britons, I'm talking about from the Caribbean, from New Zealand, transgender, these are the alignments we need to have with each other. And it's certainly something that I say to my Afro-Swedish colleagues, we're not alone. We never were alone, they made us think we're alone and we are not.

PJ What pitfalls should actors emerging from drama school aim to avoid?

JB-M Avoid assuming that what they learned at drama school is real life, it's not. Because people come out going, 'aha, this is exactly the same as my classroom'. No, it's not. It's not. And the other pitfall is that they think it's very much about what they've learned. But I think a pitfall is to lose yourself against what other people think you should be and its something that you and I have spoken about, which is, you can be whatever you want to be and get there however you need to get there. Your training is just part of that journey. That's it, particularly in the times we're living in now.

PJ If a young Black and Global Majority person of eighteen made the decision that they want to become an actor, what would your advice be?

JB-M Get on with it. Never forget your lineage, have courage, question, get on with it!

PJ Hard-dough bread, Sourdough bread, Chin Chin, Sweetbread, Roti, Sudsa, Bun and Cheese, Nai Wong Bao -奶黄包- Custard Bun or Naan?

JB-M Roti … yeah … ooohh … Bun and Cheese is quite good … the Bun and Cheese tipped it right over, yeah, Bun and Cheese a little bit of the sweet cheese and bun. Hate Sourdough, yuck, you need to have plantain on the list, okra and rice, c'mon – but definitely Bun and Cheese though.

Joel Trill

Photographer: Ajamu X.

Having worked as an actor, **Joel Trill** trained as a voice coach at the Royal Central School of Speech and Drama, a course he now guests lectures on. While training, he was awarded the VASTA Diversity Scholarship. For the past six years, Joel has been running accent workshops with Diaspora Accents for Actors (DAFA). These workshops specify in accents ranging from the Caribbean, to North, East, West and Southern African regions. Joel has coached on a variety of urban and multi-ethnic British and American accents. He has sustained a career spanning more than fifteen years as a voiceover artist. Television and film credits include *Here We Go Again, Mr Loverman, Call the Midwife* and *Murder is Easy* (BBC); *The Crown* and *Queen Charlotte* (Netflix); *The Ballad of Renegade Nell* (Disney+); *The White Lotus* (HBO); *Riches* and *The Confessions of Frannie Langton* (ITV); *Gangs of London* (Sky); *Citadel* (Amazon Prime); *Drift, My Name is Leon, Empire, The Ancestors, Queen & Slim*.

Pamela Jikiemi – PJ Training around learning 'the craft'; did you go to a conservatoire drama school? Talking about your commitment towards pursuing a creative career?

Joel Trill – JT So, my creative journey started at the age of sixteen. When I went to college, and I studied A-level Theatre Studies, I studied half an A-level in Contemporary Dance, I didn't know why it was half an A-level. And I went off to Poole and Bournemouth College, which was obviously a separate entity from my school. And that was cool, it was called the Jellicoe Theatre. And I hadn't done any school plays and wasn't you know, a child, actor or anything like that. I was more interested in sports. And anyway, I went to Jellicoe Theatre, I was taught by a guy called Dr Charles Lamb who taught me all about mask work for theatre, he, himself had a doctorate in masks for theatre. Dr Charles Lamb was partnered with Fran Denley, who was a voice coach, and I had no idea about a voice coach even existed until I went there, and I was about sixteen, seventeen. And I had a bit of a crush on her then, I was the other way those days, and I had a real crush on her. So, because of my crush, I became interested in what she did. And she trained at Royal Central School of Speech and Drama, where I went. And so, I became aware of the sort of two aspects of theatre: theatrical theory, or I don't know what you call it now. And then also the practical stuff with the voice work. And then my tutors at Jellicoe encouraged me to audition for drama schools, I auditioned for lots of drama schools. I didn't get into a lot actually. I nearly got into Guildhall. But I lost out, I was gutted. In the end, I went to Rose Bruford. I was here for three years from 1998 to 2001.

So I went to Rose Bruford. And one of the attractions was obviously the grounds – Rose Bruford is set in parkland outside of London. I grew up as part of a trans-racially adoptive family in a green and leafy white middle-class town in Dorset, so it was a sort of intermediary transition before going into less green and more diverse London; ironically, it was rumoured that Sidcup was, at the time, the location for the BNP headquarters. However, I do not recall experiencing any direct racism from locals. And so, I went to Rose Bruford. I did the acting course, but I really struggled there, because I was quite full of myself and not as good at acting as I thought I was, and at the same time quite arrogant because I wanted to mask the fact I was scared I would not be accepted, i.e. I would not be seen as Black enough and certainly not white enough by peers or by the tutors. I wanted to mask the fact that I had an undernourished relationship with my Black identity and the fact I was incapable of satisfying their racialized assumptions about me. People that sit only inside of the European white psychology seem to assume that Black people are all moulded to be homogeneous at birth, meaning we share the same ideas, intellects, customs, expressions, politics, ambitions and pain, and that we are all bound together by the threads of global oppression, but that was not how I thought about myself, I didn't grow up having access to Jollof rice, I got 'Jerk nuttin', let me put it this way if I had, had to take a test for being stereotypically Black, I would have failed, hands down …! I was also taught by my white parents that being Black should not be a barrier to achieving what I wanted. So I felt like I inherited the moniker of 'Black' through other people's labelling of me, other people's gaze, even my parents, who meant well! So I had this contrasting character of who was, like wildly entitled but at the same time totally inadequate as a person and unconfident, as an actor. I was often confused and felt incapable of delivering on other people's expectations of me. This had a big impact on my confidence as an actor at this time. Up until this point, I had largely ignored this fact that by assimilating so deeply with a predominantly white European society, I had neglected a healthy, informed and embodied relationship with the notion of Blackness that sat outside the lens of identity politics. I did not know about what Blackness was – Black Consciousness, history or philosophy. Rose Bruford was my first sort of introduction to all of that and I remember being selected to play Othello which was, weirdly enough, it was one of the, one of the roles I got the most sort of positive feedback from peers and students and staff. I sort of wondered, is that just because, it's a Black role, or is it because I'm good and all that sort of thing? But I struggled at Rose Bruford, particularly in the middle year, like many people who do in actor training. I thought acting required a surface-level investment and then realized it required much more of me as a person. I'd started to wonder if it was what I wanted to do.

And I blamed the school and not myself, as one does. And then I got through and I think I played Paul in the John Guare's play *Six Degrees of Separation* in my third year. Will Smith starred in the Fred Schepisi film adaptation of the play in 1993. All the way through this period of my life, and through my childhood and through sort of making stories up in the school playground and going through the Jellicoe Theatre, and through going to drama school, the voice was the one thing that I had, that I could maybe use as an influence on others, i.e., I could maybe shift people's perception of what they thought I was going to offer, because of my voice. It was about simulating a voice, that was unruffled, clear and confident, I guess. Let me put it in that way. Yeah. And then I graduated from Rose Bruford.

Diversity at Rose Bruford in the late 90s was not great, but that was much the same at other schools. There were two, there was me. I'm not going say the name of the other person, it was another actor of my year who was Black, two of us basically that was the late 90s, oh, yeah, there was an African American woman. I think it was three of us – three or four of us. But we were very much in the minority. But you know, for me, because I grew up in a white middle-class family, it wasn't such a jarring thing for me to kind of navigate this stuff. What annoyed me, though, was the fact that people assumed that I was 'putting on' an RP-ish accent, it had not occurred to them that maybe it was part of my actual lived experience growing up, perhaps my relatives spoke like me. The process of having to constantly define who you are because others refuse to accept the peculiarity or uniqueness of your embodied-story is so draining. At this time it felt that people were happy to accept you if you represented a type of Black identity that was totally urban (e.g. London/Birmingham) and or regionally British (e.g. Essex), but it had to be disassociated with what they understood to be the most esteemed form of British white speech … RP, so a Black man with, for example, an aristocratic accent was somehow unacceptable to them. I remember one comment that was made by an actor on the course to another actor, and this actor was from an upper-middle class family, he was always going on about it. And I remember him saying to this other actor who reported back to me, 'so you know what, Joel thinks he's all of this and all of that. But I'll tell you what, he'll never have it in his blood'. Looking back, I feel sorry for somebody like that, someone who thinks they have a monopoly on a style of expression due to their racial identity.

PJ Wow! Wow!!

JT Interesting. I'm not trying to be anything other than what I am. What I lacked in exposure to Black culture and heritage was plugged with white middle-class thinking, white history, middle-class aspirations and Christian values, so when I say I grew up within the belly of a white ethnocentric beast, I mean it.

I left home at eighteen. And I went to Rose Bruford, and I was there until I was twenty-one. It seems like a long time ago now. At Rose Bruford I did the Carleton Hobbs Bursary Award radio competition. I remember Marina Calderone, coming in and teaching us radio, it was the first experience I had of recognizing that my voice could transport me beyond the narrow parameters of racial identification. Not just racial identification, but also sort of perceptions with social class, intelligence, and all these other component parts that fit into it. Because you can't see the person, so, you're just left with the voice. And so that, for me was a big light-bulb moment, I was like oh, wow, I can actually do this, I love this stuff. And then when I left drama school, I got an agent, I don't know how, but I somehow managed to get in with a large and prominent agency. I was represented by them for about three years until I got booted out. It was a useful sort of exposure into going into the performance industry. There were meetings in a smart hotel with well-known directors. Access to exciting scripts from studios, you know how it works, Pamela, you get all this stuff. And it was great, and it was fun. But I don't think I really understood what acting was! And I don't think I really understood how to be the Black character that agents, castings directors, and directors wanted me to be, I was put up for roles that were, urban London, or Caribbean and all this kind of stuff and, and I wasn't that. Of course, one does the research and character biography stuff, but the roles I went up for and my unruly lack of confidence made many auditions an uncomfortable experience. Hope that makes some sense. I mean I would be thrown into auditions, when I left drama school, with the brief of being this African character, no distinction of which African country, and then there would be a jump to Caribbean, and I genuinely didn't, I didn't have that lived experience to rely on. I didn't grow up with a Caribbean granny to ask for pronunciations or cultural references.

My native accent was a kind of Dorset RP hybrid. I remember a well-known coach, I talked to her the other day, a voice coach, she taught me my first year at Rose Bruford and she told me I had a 'Contemporary RP' accent. That's what she said, I was very put out by it. I felt like I had been given a conditional definition due to my Blackness. I thought she was saying that my voice was somehow not good enough in some way. I didn't understand it. It fed into my crippling sense of low self-worth. We've all got it at some point. Isn't it like that? We never feel that we quite make the grade. Or sometimes, whether it's us perceiving or whether it's them doing it, I think it's probably a combination. We always feel like that we just need to work a bit harder or just do something a little bit differently to be accepted as an actor or to be accepted within the body of acting. And for me, for much of my early career, all my career really, it was a white middle-class heteronormative profession, and I felt like an outsider almost everywhere. My Black presence seemed conditional to the status quo, and the caveat was that I should conduct myself appropriately and show gratitude without rocking the boat.

I'm sorry, I don't know what other people's experiences were, but those were my experiences. But anyway, I would be put up for all sorts of jobs, and I would feel slightly back footed, and I would feel less than Black, you know, I would feel that I had somehow gone down a route of lived experience that wasn't validated or wasn't recognized within the industry. Because people had a sort of template, if that is the right word, but an idea of Blackness that was static, and that was fixed, rooted within stereotypes.

PJ Nurse, prostitute, mugger, Huggy Bear UK style/type character (African American actor Antonio Fargas played that character in the original *Starsky and Hutch* US television series in the 1970s. Huggy wasn't a pimp, you never knew what he did, but he was always in the know), but without the styling or dialogue, drug dealer, all of that. We didn't have to buy make-up. Yeah.

JT Oh, Pamela, that's pretty funny! And so, this conversation is helping make me realize something. I was so at odds with what people were expecting me to do. And I think that's probably one of the reasons why I became a voice coach, because I sort of felt, well, I want to try and help other people maybe navigate that journey through the work of voice work, i.e. as Paul Gilroy calls it the 'potential double consciousness' that we all have around being Black and British and bring Black and African or Black, whatever else, you know. I mean, all of these, these multilayered identities that we have, being both inside a culture and outside of culture, being accepted, but also rejected within a culture within an industry, do you see? And so, I think that my lived experience and struggles as an early actor, inspired me wanting to be more instructive or more … influential on drama training culture, you know, more of a teacher, someone who used their work to help others flourish within the frame of whatever identity make-up made them unique.

PJ What drives you? Looking at issues of employability, how do you navigate this?

JT They kept me on for two to three years. I was put up for loads of stuff. But, because I didn't know how to bridge that gap between what was expected of me and what I had to offer due to what I had been exposed to growing up, I didn't necessarily have a footing, I didn't understand all these cultural references in scripts and was sometimes ashamed to ask. I think I am dyslexic, although I've been told I'm not dyslexic. Back then there wasn't the same kind of awareness around reasonable adjustment then in drama schools. So, I didn't necessarily have any support around understanding why I was very anxious about reading, and this is the irony, I struggled with exposing my difficulties with reading, I struggled with that. For instance, reading a play in class, I would stumble over lines, often. I remember, you know, and a lot of that was accompanied with feelings of shame. I think, an embodiment of my feelings of shame were linked to a feeling of displacement too my feeling of being 'less than', throughout my drama school training and also in the early years of my career.

However, I pushed through this skills deficit (reading issues) by working in voice-over, I forced myself to become a better reader. I was a voice-over artist, I still am. Voice-over is like, for me, the most spiritual, most, most enjoyable, most accessible medium for my expressiveness. I felt I could be myself or transform myself into something from myself in a way that was autonomous, to some degree, obviously, you've got direction and guidance. And that's probably why I did voice-over jobs and I have not cared whether I got paid for them or not. The freedom I felt was payment enough. That's the truth. Sometimes I still feel like that, because I enjoy it. Voice-over allowed for me to be both my authentic self and also to transform expressively without self-censoring or the desire to people please, or to appease other people's discomfort with my tall Black body being in the space.

PJ I feel the same way, whether it is commercial work or gaming, you can play.

JT You can play and I never, I never had that, as an actor, you know, this is really interesting. I've never talked about this before. I stopped acting in about 2008. I did plays and I did stuff. But there were three reasons why I stopped.

One, because I didn't feel like I was getting where I wanted to be, even though I was working, I wasn't getting where I wanted to be. And the roles, you know like *Holby City*, you know, whatever, in *The Bill* I played a gangster or something, whatever, which was fine. It was work, but it wasn't what I wanted to do.

And two, and three, because I've always had this feeling of having responsibility to create social change, I became an actor, partly because I wanted to broaden, interrogate, or challenge societal attitudes around culture, politics. And that was a massive instigator for me. And once I found out that you had to go through so many hoops to get to a position where you were able to make the decisions to choose the work that would eventually broaden interrogate or challenge, what I perceived to be narrow thinking in other British society minds, it all seems like a mountain too steep to climb through the lens of acting. I thought maybe this isn't for me, acting, it's not the right way for me.

And then I just decided to leave. And the thing that allowed me to leave was this sort of feeling that I didn't deserve to do it, because I felt like I wanted to do it, like so many actors do, regardless of whether they're any good. And it's – there's this ugly entitlement that comes with the attitude 'I deserve to do it because I want to do it'. Do you know what I mean, I didn't want to be like that or be around that energy any more.

So, then I went to work in schools with kids who have behavioural difficulties. I worked as a teaching assistant. I continued to do voice-over, because that was kind of too much fun to let go and paid better than acting on stage. You've really made realize, in this conversation, that voice-over work was so integral to my sense of wellbeing and identity, and it's always run through my life because of this fact, it gave me creative agency and self-love. Then I worked in schools, and I was going to train to be a teacher, but I didn't because I wouldn't have fit well within the traditional education system. I perceived that the schools weren't actually designed to serve the students – they were there to babysit, so parents were able to contribute to the state coffers by working. I was working at the pastoral end too, which was about helping children with behavioural issues, and not, the curricula end. I used to run an initiative with Southwark Children's Services about social emotional wellbeing. And I came across a lot of Black and Brown kids in that as well, a lot of kids, you know, some who hadn't got any parents or, you know, were from abusive backgrounds. And it taught me a lot about humility and patience. It taught me a lot about meeting people where they're at, without judgement, you know.

The reason I mentioned that, was because I realized that actually, that was another light-bulb moment for me, that I wanted to go into a profession that would enable me to support people where they are at – help them to accept themselves. But I also realized, that I would also need to do something that was connected to performance as I still had an enjoyment of the performance field. On Saturdays I would help run drama classes in Bromley to keep that part of me satisfied. And so, I applied for the voice course. There was Birmingham, then, I think, it was just Birmingham and Central then. I applied for it, and I didn't have any financial means to pursue it. And I asked people, family and obviously, rightly, they said, no because they'd probably given me enough money. So as part of my application I wrote about what I wanted to do with the voice work, which was around addressing the limited cultural representation offered in accent and voice work by offering accents from the African diaspora. I didn't know much about accents, and certainly didn't think I would be an accent/dialect coach. I managed to get on the voice course at Central, but I didn't have the means to pay for it. And I applied to the Equity Charitable Trust[1] [https://www.equitycharitabletrust.org.uk/retraining-and-education/]. And they gave me like, five grand, and that was like a spur to encourage me to pursue the course at Central. It was, a message from the universe, that this was the right thing to be doing.

And I think this is really important, because, you know, I was very fortunate in that I was aware that number one, there was a thing called a voice coach. And number two, that I had some experience of what it meant to be an actor, and I had some experience of the kind of arc of conservatoire training. So, I had some understanding of what a voice coach might well do and what it might entail. But I recognize that the reason why there's a lack of diverse representation in voice coaching is because the only kids that will go into the voice work are the ones that have been exposed to going to the theatre that have had the connections with the business. I realized I was really fortunate in that way. I went on the Master of Fine Arts (MFA) Voice course at Royal Central, and that was the period of my life that's probably the most transformative, both personally and I think in terms of my career trajectory.

I did the MFA Voice, which is two years, incidentally. Central's position was, this is what we're offering, as a training, around voice, pedagogy, and theory, but your perspective, and your experience as an actor is going to be invaluable in you supporting the work that you're doing. So it wasn't just that I was getting a new skillset to try and evolve myself, but also what I was bringing with me, this was of immense value, all of the challenges I'd had all of the questions I had around Blackness and what it means to be Black and Black identity, that was a catalyst that got me reading books, got me reading Na'im Akbar's *Breaking the Chains of Psychological Slavery*, it got me reading. I mean, I've always read but all of these books are particularly around Blackness, and, Franz Fanon's *Black Skin, White Mask*. They made me aware of what I had experienced, and contextualized it for me through the lens of critical race theory. And it's like, oh, wow, if only I'd known this when I was younger, I probably wouldn't have, struggled with depression. And I wouldn't have struggled with thinking that I wasn't good enough. And I wouldn't have maybe asked so many questions of myself.

I thought that that academic world was for other people. And I never thought of myself as being remotely academic or anything. I've always been interested in politics, though. I would always have my nose in a broadsheet newspaper on a Sunday, because I was turned on by politics, culture and ideas. I've always been interested the way that people think and operate and the actions that manifest from these elements. On the MFA voice course, I was exposed to this whole world of different ideas around not only voice, but voice and identity, voice and philosophy, voice and biology etc.

Patsy Rodenburg's book *The Right to Speak* was quite useful in terms of how, you know, lots of people have lots to say about Patsy Rodenburg, but, I think she sort of promoted the idea that voice existed as a reflection of social, political and personal landscapes, not just as a tool for telling stories or putting on of plays. And as a Black guy working in this business, it was really a very exciting invitation to explore. Of course, I was curious about the sounds that make up a voice and speech system, but it was the notion that social conditioning could influence the voice, things like identity, sexuality, psychology, sociology and politics, that really interested me in voice work.

I suppose, my approach to the work it isn't just about learning sounds, it's about understanding why those sounds are made and for whom they are intended. It's about understanding why we take space sometimes and why we don't take space. And again, going back to my lived experience, I've been able to sort of excavate that and sort of look at things that might well be useful in terms of exploring voice and cultural identity.

I mean, I really relish the discussions and energy that comes from interactions with other people in the business, due to my work. I mean, just speaking with another Black British practitioner, us giving space and time to each other, is, so important to me. I think it's so important because what I've realized is the reason why other coaches who are not Black, are not having these conversations, is because they don't experience the same things, or they haven't experienced the same kind of violence that makes them question their very purpose place and plausibility on a daily basis. Perhaps I am assuming too much here, as we all have challenges. And I don't mean physical violence, but like in terms of the trauma, so they don't have the need. It isn't about survival for them in the same way it is for us, perhaps.

PJ It's like, going back to drama school, when you all go to the pub, and everyone's drinking and you have to make the choice because you know, at some stage that conversation will come around to you and what you look like, and someone will make some throwaway comment, a microaggression. But you have to suck it up. But at the same time, that's when they decide they want a pint and a double vodka and such and such, everyone orders something and it happens to be your round, and no one seems to want a 'top-up' when it isn't, the rules and tithe of inclusion to white world. And you're supposed to handle this hostile, alcohol-fuelled environment and bounce back, like you have been doing all day but without alcohol greasing the wheels, it's just pure, unadulterated hostile environment.

JT I feel comfortable in this situation. I'm in the process of talking to you, and sharing what I've experienced, I don't feel like you doubt me or think I am talking hypothetically, it makes me feel that I exist and that my perception is valid. I do not feel that I am risking anything of my career by having an honest conversation with you.

But I think this does raise the questions of 'why do we not support each other in this country, in this industry as Black practitioners?' The risk sometimes of supporting someone means that you may lose your place with your industry-ecosystem, by trying to address iniquity or marginalization. And, sometimes I feel maybe people are nervous about that. And so, what I'm saying by that is, if you perceive that you have safe place or are established within your field or career class, then you may feel that you've earned that and you don't necessarily want to upset the applecart, because you have worked hard to maintain that safe place. Staying in this game intact is tough, I understand why people prefer to keep their heads down.

In this country, and I think in our business, it's so much about, recommendation in terms of getting work, it's so much about people's perception of you and so much about associated projects that you've done, that are higher on a spectrum, as opposed to less than. Therefore, people are loath to try to challenge the establishment, they're loath to try and change things. And being part of a visible group, which is galvanized around a certain issue, politically or socially or culturally, is for them sometimes, risk, I mean, we're not just talking about, whether or not if you upset the applecart in layman's terms, doing so could be actually mean that you don't get any work. I've already had situations where because, I grew up in a family where, we say what we think if something's unfair. And it's probably cost me work in some way. And I've heard that from so many of the people who've been in the same situation of being held back for speaking truth to the established order. I've lost out on work. I mean, there is also a financial element here, which is about survival, so speaking out does have very real consequences. So, sometimes I think the risk is too great for people. Do you know what I mean? And, I think, with all due respect, I think there's another sort of element to consider here, that also prevents people challenging the status quo or inequality. I'm trying to think of how Paul Gilroy puts it, something like 'the complexity of experiences means that we can identify under the umbrella of Blackness'. Sometimes we underestimate the complexity of other people's experiences and the attitudes that emanate from that, we can assume they are aligned with a cause because of the fact they have melanin. There are lots of different experiences and attitudes towards what it means to be Black. I'm saying and sometimes we don't always value that. And I think sometimes that's the thing that makes people feared, you know, they'll be subsumed into some kind of fanatical totemic ideology, which negates the uniqueness of their lived experience. Whilst we may face similar issues in the industry, there will be variation in our interpretations, actions and experiences. Diversity initiatives should acknowledge there are lots of different experiences of Blackness, I have learnt to respect that beautiful fact. The work has to be about finding, not assuming common ground.

PJ One of the recurring issues in the creative industries is the discussion around representation. How do you see your role in relation to that conversation?

There's a lack of representation in the voice world, and that is partly to do with, you know, a lot of voice coaches don't necessarily come from backgrounds that would be able to afford to train and do a postgraduate qualification.

I am not sure I fully get the complexity of the issue, but I do know that we should always want the most suitable person for the job, due to their uniqueness, their perspective, their skillset and capacity to imaginatively embody and realize their craft for the purpose of best possible outcomes. I also think, you know, that within that process of finding people within the creative industries, we should acknowledge the very tangible socio-economic, locational and educative barriers that prevent getting as diverse group of candidates as possible. Also, we need to accept and share the personal limitations and biases that we may hold that may prevent us, ourselves from making, rational, informed, and equitable choices in recruiting and mentoring. As part of this great mission of inclusion, we all must do work on ourselves, none of us come out unscathed!

For my part I have been trying to broaden voice and accent learning curriculums, by offering a pedagogy and language that incentivizes actors and students to value the complexity and uniqueness of their heritage in voice and accent work. I mean I have been delivering accent and dialect work, alongside coach Hazel Holder, under the umbrella term 'Diaspora Accents for Actors' aka DAFA. The term diaspora relates to accents of but not limited to the African diaspora and seeks to provide accent and voice training, mostly for actors, interested or invested in learning these accents for performance. Our workshops, so far, we have explored: African American varieties, Nigerian, Ugandan, South African, Jamaican, Trinidadian and South Asian, and we hope to explore South Asian and South American diasporas shortly.

We had initially wanted to broaden voice and accent learning curriculums within drama schools, by offering workshops, but soon recognized the inherent value of pitching diaspora voice work to trained or untrained professional actors, who had expressed how marginalized they had felt, during their training, due to a lack of diverse accent training within voice curriculums; which occurred largely before more progressively inclusive practices were embraced by several well-known training institutions. So, we decided to start running some workshops at Bristol Old Vic Theatre School, with the support of the former head of Voice, at Bristol Old Vic and Mono Box, that actor training enterprise and theatre archive resource.

The fear around accents for many accents is sizeable, some folks say that public speaking is their number one fear, however, I am sure that for many actors, it's the ability to maintain a believable accent and character, whilst simultaneously connecting to other characters on stage.

So, the diaspora accents for actors' workshops aim to untangle some of the complexity and anxiety that surrounds learning accents, by offering practical, accessible and fun accent learning. The diaspora accent workshops bring actors of all types together to explore voice and accent work, that is pertinent to their casting opportunities and sensitive to the lived experiences within the room. One of the underlining principals of these workshop has been to offer people a place of 'radical openness', a space in which people feel safe enough to share, participate, flounder, discover, and enquire together, without apology or censorship. This approach has successfully helped participants in honing their vocal skills and enabled some to reaffirm their commitment to the skill and craft of acting self and performance through the lens of voice work.

One of the things I also sometimes do, to promote, um, inclusion or to expose potential voice teaching candidates to the voice work is to invite them into an MA/MFA Voice Studies workshop on. I will bring in, usually an actor from the BIPOC community, who's interested in becoming a voice coach. So, I've got them in the room, and I say to them, I'm not going to pay you, but you're going to be in the room, and you get to see what a voice coach does. And also, I'm going to introduce you to the course leader in case you make an application to the course so they know who you are. And you get to be in a building and get you some free accent coaching as well. I'm bringing more diversity into the field in a way, I suppose.

PJ Thinking in terms of how you choose to identify, what do you think are the challenges in the acting/creative industry now?

JT As a person. I choose to identify in relationship to the political strand with which I'm exploring. So for example, I don't always think about myself as a cis male, unless I'm asked to think about being a cis male. I don't think about myself as being Black all the time, unless I'm in relationship to talking about issues of race or politics or inequality or culture, or speech systems, do you know what I'm saying, I don't think these terms are sufficient to describe what I am, as being a human is broad. I don't think my starting point, as a conscious being is an awareness of codified identity category, but I understand that these terms function as symbols of a particular social positioning.

I read books around you know, critical race theory and so all sorts of, sociological books, book on behaviour and neuroscience and all this rest of it. I try and understand what I'm experiencing what others might also experience. Also, I want to explore how that knowledge can further my practice and support people and make people feel more included within the work, essentially.

And one of the books that I've been reading, which is Paul Gilroy's book I mentioned before, which is *The Black Atlantic*, which is all about exploring the relationships, histories and evolutions of Black culture that have arisen as a result of the metaphorical and literal movement of people during the transatlantic slave trade. So what it's kind of made me aware of is a much broader understanding of what I'm experiencing that relates to being both inside and outside of culture, that relates to being both Caribbean, being African, being European, being all these things combined, and how they kind of inform not only the way in which you interpret your lived experience, but also how you understand the relationships you've got in your life. Thinking about this dual consciousness, 'continual aspiration to acquire authentic, natural and stable, rooted identity' (Gilroy), is perhaps a motivation for me to remain and educator a voice teacher.

Out of the Black Box

I think one of the things that inspires me is my own quest to find an identity that feels stable, that feels valued, that feels natural, whatever that means. And then there's also something that's about trying to offer work that offers others validation and reflects stability and acceptance as well. So to try and do voice and accent work that feels authentic and embodied and supports the actor or the artist in telling the story that they want to tell in a rooted way, in a way that feels authentic to them, a way that feels, embodied to them, and that's part of, that's part of my quest, really.

I was very aware of coming into this business, that I was doing it at a time where there was lack of ethnic and racial diversity in terms ideas of representation. So, basically as an actor, there were lots of gaps that I didn't have, as I talked about earlier, I would go to sessions, and I wasn't being taught the speech systems of the particular character that I was working on. But I also recognized that I wasn't being taught in a way that would help me unlock and feel connected to those speech systems. So that's another influence on my style of teaching. And a lot of the work that I have done in accent teaching, and particularly voice teaching is physical. A lot of voice, all voice teachers work in the psychophysical plane, yeah, because that's what acting is, right? But I think I've been quite explicit in helping people understand the relationship that we culturally have as Black people, to the physical nature of rhythm and tone and melody of our speech. As opposed to a cognitive-semantic one, with more European ideas of communication.

I was teaching other day, and some of the actors were doing Nigerian accents, and some of them were doing Sierra Leonean, and I was just saying to them, you know, one of the things that I think people forget or fall back from, is that as Africanist people, we communicate much more with melody and tone and rhythm and intonation. You know, when someone goes ':eh heng' and 'un-hun' all that kind of thing, and we know exactly what is meant by the utterance, we know whether, for example, if they are dismissing us or approving of us as the listener. Which is different from the very subtextual and often covert message being sent through, for example, British utterances. And so, Pamela, you've got to really dive into that when working on for example Sierra Leonean. But what I find fascinating about my approach is I've not lived with any Caribbean of African speakers. I didn't grow up with that exposure, but I have learnt to recognize the value of these details in recreating authentic and embodied work. I grew up with middle-class, white RP speakers, some Dorset speakers, you know. But I have somehow digitated that, or synthesized or assimilated that in some way into my teaching. That means that I think the value in my work is that I understand actors particularly from the Black and Brown Global Majority – access the work much more from understanding tone and melody and rhythm. That's what I'm kind of interested as a voice coach, in exploring why that is. The feedback has been very, very positive from actors, saying, Wow, I never thought about thinking about the rhythm in this way, or thinking about the tone in that way.

I was working with an actor recently and I said, listen, if you're doing Nigerian you go to a Nigerian barbers. Nigerians take up space and time. Yeah, they don't apologize. The English sensibility is the opposite. If you're going to play a Nigerian in the context of speaking to another Nigerian, yeah, it has to be, it has to be, I said, you need to go to the barbers to understand the registers of Nigerian speech in a more animated situation. Nobody is waiting for permission to play their instrument; they just riff off each others' energy. At first it may sound like an argument is happening, but it's a carefully curated cacophony of jazz instruments imbued with respect and passion. You've got to understand when you come into a space, there are two things happening here that sometimes as an actor in training that you're feeling that you can't take up space and time, yeah? Because that is how most drama school buildings operate. But actually, you know, in order to really do justice to the character, you're going to have to take up more space and time, you're going to have to. It's the same with Americans, they have the same thing. They take up space and time, my job as a coach is about getting the actor to hold onto that very necessary phycho-physical energy when speaking.

PJ What pitfalls should actors emerging from drama school aim to avoid?

JT Thinking that they ever know enough, that's number one. Losing the lust and thrust of inquiry, as it were, we haven't talked about it, but I think a lot of people want to be actors, and they think that the wanting is more important than asking the questions that arise from wanting and needing to be a creative and an artist. I think that fundamentally, a lot of people think that they should be actors because they want to be an actor, rather than thinking of themselves as a craftsperson with a burning question.

That's the kind of the end point of the goal, I'm not saying it's that thing about, I'm an actor and I can't do anything else, but it's having a burning question. To be an artist, you have to have a burning question. And I think what I'm saying is, in this sort of age, there's a 'disembodiedness' that goes on. There's a detachment, and there's a fragmentation that happens when people sort of, just want, because they think they've got a desire, like, I want ice cream, so therefore I'm having an ice cream. It's like, that's not enough. There has to be a burning question that sustains you through the times where you're not able to work, that sustains you when you don't necessarily understand the complexity of the language, that sustains you when, you're forty years old and you haven't got to where you want to be, there has to be a burning question. That's what, I think. That's what separates for me, you know, people who say they want to be an actor, and really, real actors, real artists.

Losing the ability/inability to take risks, number two.

Thinking that they don't have something to offer, number three.

Undervaluing technique, practice and rigour, number four.

PJ If a young Black and Global Majority actor of eighteen decided that they wanted to become an actor, what would your advice be?

JT My advice would be, to do it, and to understand that one might well have to make sacrifices. And that also to understand that in the same way that the thatcher has to develop their skill as a craftsperson, as does the carpenter does, and, so should the actor. It's, lifelong learning, and that's the joy of it.

PJ Hard-dough bread, Sourdough bread, Chin Chin, Sweetbread, Roti, Sudsa, Bun and Cheese, Nai Wong Bao -奶黄包- Custard Bun or Naan?

JT Interesting. Interesting, okay, and what's interesting is I would have gone for Sourdough, yeah? But that's just because I'm bougie, because there are other assumptions that people made. I didn't grow up with Bun and Cheese, but I do like Bun and Cheese, so I say Sourdough, Bun and Cheese. So, I would say Bun and Cheese as the main course, and Sourdough is the starter. Excellent.

And I'm going to say that, thank you. Just thank you so much for number one, asking me to contribute, whether you use it or not, whatever. But thank you, and also, thank you so much for giving the space and time. Because, yeah, I feel like a million dollars. Because I often go through this thing. We haven't talked about it, but I go through this thing, I'm going to stop doing voice coaching. I can't be bothered – the pushback, and rudeness of people with having to prove myself, with having to justify myself in the space. And this conversation has made me realize why I need to still keep doing it, because we're pioneers in lots of ways it's never going to be easy, but thank you.

Heather Basten

Photographer: Sarah Harry-Isaacs.

Heather Basten is a Royal Television Society nominated casting director for film, TV and theatre. She is best known for casting the A24 and SHOWTIME Emmy®-nominated TV series *Dreaming Whilst Black*. Heather has cast for notable directors and producers such as James Watkins, Jada Pinkett Smith, Matthew Dunster, Luca Guadagnino, Lynette Linton, Kwame Kwei-Armah and more. Theatre credits include: *Shifters* for the Bush Theatre (Dir. Lynette Linton), Harold Pinter's *The Homecoming* for the Young Vic (Dir. Matthew Dunster), *Red Pitch* for Soho Place/Bush Theatre (Dir. Daniel Bailey).

Pamela Jikiemi – PJ Training around learning 'the craft'; did you go to a conservatoire drama school? Talk about your creative career and your commitment towards pursuing it.

Heather Basten – HB Growing up, I didn't know about the role of a casting director. I was the type of person who would watch something and wanted to know who the people were. I was always very curious. As I got older, I would then be the person who was on Google after watching something, and obsessing over who the actors were. When I was eighteen, I did a work experience placement at Theatre Royal Stratford East. And that was my first exposure to the professional industry. It was there I met the wonderful Jan Sharkey-Dodds, who I am sure many people know and love; Jan has launched many careers. I told her I was rather curious about actors, and she explained the role of a casting director to me. And I replied, 'Okay, great, well, how do I do it?' And she told me to 'go and live my life, and try to immerse myself around the art'.

So I went to Royal Central School of Speech and Drama, on the BA Drama, Applied Theatre and Education academic course. I knew I did not want to be an actor, I was quite terrible in fact.

However, I was always very good at working alongside actors. I had read books and studied how to make and facilitate theatre and performance. In my final year I was on a placement at the British Film Institute

(BFI). There were about 120 of us in a year group, 119 placements were theatre based, and only one was a film placement, theatre placements and one film placement. That was the one that I wanted to get.

I think the stars had aligned at that point. I was tasked with organizing a casting masterclass for their emerging director's cohort for that year. I had found myself liaising with casting directors to organize this masterclass. I met casting extraordinaire, Jeremy Zimmerman (*Hellboy*, *Moon*), who had just landed a big TV show with NBC, and he was looking to take on a new casting assistant. I put my name in the mix for that, did some work experience with him, and then here I am today over a decade later in 2024 with my own casting company. That was the start of my career.

I owe a lot to Jeremy because he is a true ally. He has launched a lot of careers, he has helped a lot of people get their foot in the door, so I am very grateful to him. Jeremy, Jan and Noel Goodwin, formerly at the BFI, were instrumental people in developing my career.

PJ How was your overall early career experience, what did you get from it?

HB It wasn't what I was expecting. I think people have a perception of casting from the outside, and when you're in it, it's very different. Bizarrely, there's a lot of math involved, deal making, negotiations, all on top of the auditions and creative brainstorming. I spent a long-time making coffee and teas as an assistant. And actually, I used to relish that as an unofficial opportunity to really listen and learn. Whenever I'm talking to the next generation who are coming up in casting, I always say staying humble and making lots of coffees and teas is the best way to have opportunities to listen and learn. You can learn the language. I didn't expect any of that. Once I got into it, I realized that this is what I love and this is what I want to do.

PJ How many Black and Global Majority casting directors are there now? When I graduated in the late 80s, there was only one, Leo Davis in the UK.

HB Not many, but I think things have progressed. I had never even researched it when I started, because I just had no idea what the industry truly was that I was stepping into. Jeremy Zimmerman's office was always incredibly diverse. And that is a testimony to his ethics and his drive, in people that he would give a leg up to in the industry. I still walk into spaces now, which are all white. So, seeing that very early on in my career, helped shape my confidence and my self belief.

PJ What drives you? Looking at issues of employability, how do you navigate this?

I believe education plays a big part in everything that I do. I try to keep myself well informed. My job is working with humans and trying to replicate the truth; to capture human stories. And so I think it's so important to be connected with the real world. That is what I'm trying to put on screen on stage. I tightly hold onto that human aspect of casting; connecting with actors, connecting with stories, finding parallels in the fiction and the real world. All of this is with a goal of ultimately getting the best performance out of an actor, and to serve the story and to serve the production.

PJ In your role at Heather Basten Casting is there a difference for you between casting for film or theatre roles?

HB Theatre is a new space that I found myself in within the last few years, and it is both different and the same. I believe the core of it is the same. Ultimately, our intentions are to seek out the truth.

The process however is slightly different. When you're casting for stage, you want the actors to be fully in their own bodies and physically present and active within the space.

For film TV, we tend to frame with a mid-shot for a first casting and it's really about the actors emoting. It's quite vulnerable. I find myself switching between both, which I love. Ultimately, the person who feels closest to the character will normally get the part. I shape shift myself to best serve the actor in making them feel fully comfortable and trusting.

PJ What projects do you decide to connect with?

HB I'd always wanted to cast theatre, it was difficult to get my foot in the door – especially after doing screen for so long. But I knew I could do it. It was then I realized it was about opportunity. And an opportunity came up, where Lynette Linton, Artistic Director of the Bush Theatre asked me to cast Ella Road's (2021) *Fair Play* at the Bush directed by Monique Touko. And I remember her calling me and saying, 'Heather, I know you don't usually cast theatre BUT', ever since then my phone hasn't stopped ringing, it's been great. It was a chance and opportunity. However, in tandem, I wasn't actively going out networking in those spaces, which in hindsight I should have been doing. Because how can I expect an opportunity to just land on your lap like that?

PJ The industry and your place in it?

HB I am very committed to the projects that I'm on. I don't stop until I find the perfect people – or so I am told! I believe that is how I have cemented my work ethic in this industry. I think my passion for the casting process shows, my love of actors, and my love of finding new talent as well.

PJ One of the recurring issues in the creative industries is the discussion around representation. How do you see your role in relation to that conversation?

I am someone who truly cares about the projects that I'm on, and I believe that care shows. I always try to put conversations about representation at the forefront of everything I do. I always try to integrate it into any casting process. It's one of the first conversations I have with the director and producer. And it's normally met with a lot of warmth and reception. I'm very conscious of it at all times. There's never a moment when I'm sort of like, 'oh, well', you know. So I'm very conscious of representation. I'm always trying to be creative on how we can do more. And how we can see more on screen and on stage. So, I don't wear an activist hat as such, but like I am always striving. I think activism naturally comes with who you are as a person anyway, by default, but yes, more so probably in my job. I try to be very conscious and active about representation.

PJ Thinking in terms of how you choose to identify, what do you think are the challenges in the acting/creative industry now?

HB Our voices are being heard more than they were when I started. I'm feeling more empowered now, to be able to speak up and speak out and talk about things when it comes to representation. There's more visibility now and there's more opportunity for me, for example, to be part of productions, which are telling stories connected to myself. I don't feel like people can write stories about us, without us being involved at some point. So I'm very grateful to have opportunities now to be part of productions where I can relate to the story or align with some shared experience. I will always say that more can be done. And I'm very conscious to keep being part of that movement. What more can we do? How can we do it?

PJ What pitfalls should actors emerging from drama school aim to avoid?

HB Actors emerging from drama school should emerge with the knowledge that they are a freelancer and that they are a business. And so getting clued up on things like taxes and other 'freelancer' bits, such as making an IMDB account, being mindful of any named social media etc. is really important. Unless I am wrong, I feel like there is a lack of knowledge for third years in how to survive as a freelancer. Students emerge from drama school without a real sense of what life is actually like as a freelancer and how you should operate.

Be prepared to dive into that side of things. Be prepared that as an actor, your name is your brand. And so when you post things on social media, and it's public. It can be very difficult to see your peers landing roles, if you're not landing any, or even worse, you're in the same casting waiting rooms as them. So naturally, you will build up resilience. But equally I would say it's also okay to feel sad, it's okay to feel something about that, and to keep moving forward. It's very easy for people to tell you to not give up as well. But this industry is very, very difficult, say, you will find the pathway that is right for you.

PJ What are the broad aims for the future of your professional presence?

HB I would love to cast more TV. I'm very grateful that I'm in a position where I can choose what I want to do. I think that's a very, very privileged position to be in. And so, I would love to just keep handing the opportunities to the next generation of casting people. I'm always looking to nurture people and to build a strong and resilient team around me. We've just started to build departments within my office, like we have a dedicated theatre department, we have commercials department, we have a screen department. And so just to really keep building on that.

PJ Who are the writers, actors, directors, producers or showrunners that have inspired you?

HB I think it just has to be some of the close people that I work with. Because I owe a lot to them. Lynette Linton from the Bush Theatre, who gave me that first opportunity. Jeremy Zimmerman, he was an amazing, incredible casting director, I am in awe of all the projects that he's cast over his time and he still continues to cast now. Adjani Salmon from *Dreaming Whilst Black*, that was my first TV show with A24. We went from a small readthrough at the Pleasance Theatre to A24 and Showtime, and his trust on that whole journey from it starting out as a baby seed to what it is now was immeasurable. I look up to Bernard Telsey in America, as he has built this casting model that I'm trying to strive for in terms of growth. I think it's admirable. I always have to say I'm in awe of all the actors that I meet every day, because without them, my job wouldn't exist and wouldn't be necessary.

PJ If a young Black and Global Majority person of eighteen decided, they wanted to become a casting director what would your advice be?

HB The Casting Directors Guild (CDG) runs a casting internship once a year, so keep a lookout for that. And the CSA also runs a fellowship for people who want to get into casting. The National Film and Television School have a casting course, which is also a great pathway into casting and networking. Whilst you're networking, try to email casting directors perhaps to do some work experience. Really, really build on your knowledge in the background while you wait. I can't tell you the amount I interview people, and my first question is 'who's your favourite actor?' and they can't tell me, I go well, this job is about actors … and so you gotta be ready with a handful of ideas.

Out of the Black Box

PJ Hard-dough bread, Sourdough bread, Chin Chin, Sweetbread, Roti, Sudsa, Bun and Cheese, Nai Wong Bao -奶黄包- Custard Bun or Naan?

HB Hard-dough bread and Naan. Hard-dough bread – it's really bad – I just dip into it. Naan – I usually have with a curry or a stew, it's normally there for a reason – to be paired with something.

CHAPTER 6
SHEILA ATIM MBE, KIT YOUNG, SARA ZWANGOBANI AND ABRAHAM POPOOLA

Keywords/concepts: Theatre work → craft → audition process → play → pitfalls → roles

Empire Road … when Horace Ové came in to direct some episodes in the second series, that immediately introduced a different voice … And so all the structures of English acting that we had been using went out the window and, suddenly, we were doing big arm movements and using West Indian language in the way that we do back home. That was a wonderful experience.

Norman Beaton in *Pines* (1992), 116.

Sheila Atim MBE

Photographer: Yellow Belly.

Sheila Atim MBE is an actor, singer, playwright and composer. She was nominated for the BAFTA EE Rising Star in 2023, awarded the Chopard Trophy at the Cannes Film Festival in 2022, named as a Screen Star of Tomorrow in 2021, appeared in Variety's '10 Brits to Watch', and awarded an MBE for services to drama in 2019. She has won two Olivier Awards, a Critics' Circle Award and the Clarence Derwent Award. She has also been nominated at the Evening Standard Awards, and for two NAACP Image Awards. Sheila's film credits include A24's *All Dirt Roads Taste of Salt*; *The Woman King* starring alongside Viola Davis; Netflix's *Bruised* alongside Halle Berry; Marvel's *Doctor Strange & The Multiverse of Madness*; and Robert Zemeckis's Disney live-action adaptation of *Pinocchio*.

Pamela Jikiemi – PJ Tell me about your journey to become an actor.

Sheila Atim – SA I was always in the school shows and I did drama up to A-level. But I never thought it was going to be a career prospect for me until I literally started acting, professionally. So, I thought I was going to be a doctor. I was going to do a medical degree, but I didn't get the interviews to university, which was very frustrating because I had the grades, but they just didn't get the interviews. And it was a crossroads moment in my life, where I was trying to understand the world more broadly outside of school, and all the things that you're told at school, you work hard, you get the results – and understanding that that wasn't quite as linear an equation as I had been led to believe. So, a teacher of mine kind of suggested that I should maybe consider an artistic vocation instead. He actually said, 'I think it's a sign'. And in that moment, I thought, Oh, I'm going to be an artist. And I thought I was going to be a singer. Because I also sang and I'm a musician.

So my plan was to go to university to study a Biosciences degree, which I did do, I did Biomedical Science at King's – and during that degree, to learn about music in the music industry. So that by the time I'd finished my three years, I would be spat out of uni, and I'd be ready to be a singer songwriter, whatever that meant. And in my journey to understand that landscape, of course, there's a crossover with music and acting and a lot of the places that I attended, were offering classes for both. So, I would go to singing classes and I'd go to music classes and I'd also go to the drama class, not because I thought it would be something I wanted to pursue but just because I enjoyed it.

PJ Training around learning 'the craft'; did you go to a conservatoire drama school? Talk about your creative career and your commitment towards pursuing it.

SA The place I went to was WAC Arts. And I want to be very specific in mentioning that I went to WAC Arts at the time of which Celia Greenwood was CEO. It was an amazing place. So many people have come through there who people would know, Michaela Coel.

PJ What did you get from your actor training?

SA I think the bottom line, there's two bottom lines. One is money, right, money to live. But yeah, for me the more pressing bottom line is to have a good time. I think sometimes it's just that simple. You know, it's about pursuing whatever it is that makes you happy, makes you feel fulfilled and engaged and stimulated and sparks something within you, and it's great if that can also make you money. But there are lots of people who make lots of money, who don't have the other side of it. And they struggle. So it's a balance between the two, right, because on top of that, nobody wants to be the starving artist. It's not fun, however much it gets romanticized or glamorized, it's not fun. And I think for me, as somebody who could have gone down the scientific route but found this pull towards the arts to just be too strong to ignore – and it felt like I was definitely being guided back towards where I was supposed to be, you know, I think it's also about wanting to look back on my life and say that I followed my nose, and that I lived as truthfully as I could, and that I enjoyed myself while doing it, and connected with people while doing it. And that's why even now that I have been acting for ten years and I'm continuing on in my career and have some experience, I'm really trying to put a priority on the kind of experience I will have in any given project or job. I don't just want to make work that has critical acclaim. And I don't just want to make work that brings in a nice pay cheque. I also want the experience of making the work to be valuable. Because when you get to the end of your life and you look back on it, that's what you're left with, you're left with the memories. And the muscle memory as well, and the feeling of what it was like to do something that you felt mattered and do it in a way that allows you to connect with people in a kind of wholesome way, you know?

PJ How do you decide what roles to go for?

SA You do. And you don't know. And that's the point. And that's how it will always be if what you are pursuing is what I've just talked about, which is something that's quite ethereal. If what you're pursuing is much more black and white, and I don't judge that, but if you are trying to save for a mortgage, for example, it's clear (because you know what your fee is) that you are not in that space, and you're pursuing other things at that time in your career. And it can change throughout your career as well, which is important to note.

Then it's partly down to the script. It's partly down to the people who are attached to the project. So directors, producers, other actors, studios, production companies. I do try to do a bit of research and vet some of those things if I'm completely unaware. That's partly what your agents are there for as well. Your representatives should be there to tell you the truth about what they may or may not know about a company, or any experiences that they've heard, or things on the grapevine, to give you the context because it's a lot to consider, when you are the actor being asked to potentially join a project. There are so many moving parts, particularly in these larger scale studio blockbusters. And even in, you know, smaller theatre projects, when you're starting out, it's just hard to understand the context of everything and how you fit into that. So having people who can support you and understanding how all that works is really important. And then, yes, going by your gut, I've had so many instances where there's been a job that looks perfect on paper. But something about it just hasn't quite made sense to me. And invariably, almost every single time I've been right. And the thing that wasn't right about it wasn't necessarily foreseeable. And it also isn't necessarily as black and white as the job being good or bad. It's about what works for you. And what works for you at any given time. Some people might want to join a big TV show, which is going to run for ten seasons. And that is their contract for the next ten years of their life. And they're locked into that. Some people don't want to do that – some people want to have the freedom to move around. You know, again – if you have a mortgage to pay, that can make sense at a certain point in your life. If you don't and you feel like you can ride the waves of what that freedom comes with, which is a degree of uncertainty, that's also fine. But it's about really understanding who you are, and what you want in any given moment, and then seeing if the project fits in with that. And whilst there's never going to be a definitive yes or no answer with anything, there's always clues. And then sometimes it makes sense to do something that on paper doesn't look like it's right for you at that time. But something in your gut says you want to do it. And maybe the job doesn't pay that well. And maybe it's not that big a role. And maybe there's not lots of flashy stars in it. But something about doing that project is calling to you. And that can be a very personal thing as well. Some people have found working on certain projects healing. It's been for them something they felt they needed to do. So as long as you're in touch with the reason as to why you're doing it and you're staying in line with that, more often than not, you can figure it out, I say all that to say there will inevitably be times where you may end up on a project that you thought would be one thing, and it ends up being something else. And that is just a part of the job. So it's also important to learn how to manage what that feels like. And I think everybody should have one experience like that, at least. Not to wish bad experiences on people. But I think it's a great training ground for understanding yourself, understanding what you want, and understanding how to navigate a workplace that you find yourself in.

PJ Is your preparation for a role different for theatre and screen?

SA It's the same. It starts with a text, or whatever the source material is that you're working with, if it's devised, then the conversations you have about the project or the character. And you go from there, I try and just let my imagination lead me. And my instincts lead me, you know? So if you are trusting that your instincts and your imagination are strong enough and are valid, then you will just get ideas about how you want your character to sound, how you want them to look, any idiosyncrasies that they have, any features that they have.

And then you'll do some research if necessary, and then you will dig into that context of the time or the setting or, you know, whatever other clues that you're given by nature of the script and the project, and whatever the director tells you, the given circumstances, I guess.

And then I just let it roll. I try to uncomplicate the process for myself as much as possible, because human beings are very good at getting in the way of themselves. And I know this doesn't work for everyone, there are lots of people who like to do a lot of preparation. For me, my preparation is about having a few foundational things in place, and then allowing everything else to emerge as and when it needs to. So, if there's an accent, I'm nailing that accent, if there is some defining feature of the character that is non-negotiable, I'm focusing in on that. And then everything else can sit in around that in a way that makes sense to you, as an individual, artist and person, because how you are will impact how their character is, right? So, yeah, I don't dig into lots and lots of research, unless it's a project that requires me to. If it's a project that's set in a very specific time and place, and there's all this context that I need to be aware of, I'm all in. But even then I try to be specific, I try to be lean.

And then, linking back to your actual question, if you are agile, then you can traverse between mediums much more easily. Because whilst I believe theatre acting and screen acting are fundamentally the same thing, there are specificities about the mediums that require some tweaks to the skillset. Just an awareness of the fact that 'camera angles' is a thing, you know, and that 'eyelines' is a thing and that there might be a boom next to your head, and that you have to try and find your light, and you have to hit your mark. And you could be doing the best acting in the world but if you don't hit your mark, you're out of focus. But you know, the nuances of working on a screen, which can see every single thing versus working on a stage – any stage, even if it's a fifty-seat theatre means there are differences there, which do require that agility. And what you don't want is feeling like you're gonna get thrown off in either medium because you're too rigid with the way in which you work. I've seen examples where people who do a lot of screen find it hard to do theatre, and I've seen the opposite as well. And if you just want to be someone who focuses on one, that's fine. But if you do want to be able to work in both, it's important to allow yourself to trust yourself, to know that you've got this and that everything else is within the context of this individual project that you're working on.

You then funnel your fundamental skills and expertise through the prism of that project. And you go, 'this is what is needed for me in this moment'. If you're working on a soap – I've never worked on a soap – you are shooting a huge amount of scenes within a very short period of time. That is a very different skillset to having five, six weeks to mull over what you're going to do for a performance that could last months that you'll have the opportunity to repeat and go over and over and change and tweak and 'okay, that might wasn't so great. So I can chuck that away. But it's cool – come back stronger tomorrow.' You don't have that when you're filming. And then if you're filming a film or a TV show with a different format, then you're somewhere in between all of that. So, yeah, agility is absolutely the word that you've picked up on, that I would really stress because you just don't need the aggro of getting into your own head.

On top of that, there's going to be things that annoy you. There's going to be a note that changes at the last minute, script changes. Or they are going to change the blocking on press night, someone's going to do something, you know. Or you're trying to get a shot and you're doing everything right but the camera operator just can't quite get it in the right thing, and you have to go again, and you have to go into overtime. And your co-star is doing something that you didn't plan on, but you have to go with it, because you need to make it make sense. That's why it's important to listen when you're acting, you know. So I think having the fundamental basis underpinning everything, you'll be alright. And then just allowing yourself to again, try and have fun. Where possible.

And sometimes it is also just about getting it done. That's something that I think younger or newer actors, you know, it will really help them to understand that sometimes it's just a bit of 'bish, bash, bosh'. And that's not to be derogatory towards those projects that require that. But sometimes you will just make your life easier if you just roll with it, you make some choices and you go for it. It's the same with self-tapes. You could sit there for a million years do 3,000 takes and agonize over every single inflection that you did and every single eye movement that you did. Or you can make some strong choices, you can send it to the casting director and they can see that you've got potential. Sometimes, it's like that on the job as well, where it's like, I'm just gonna go for this thing, and then we'll figure it out. Not everything has to be, like, angst.

So some of the small choices that you agonized over, it's not that they're not appreciated. It's not that your effort isn't, you know, valid, but they [casting directors] might not need all of that, at that stage. They just need to know that they can see you and hear you, that you can read, that you can make decisions about character and that you've understood the brief. And then there will be a whole bunch of other things that has nothing to do with you, that you unfortunately cannot impact or change. That could be height, that could be something about the tone of your voice, that could be something about your aura, you know, or your energy, or just the sense of you. Something inexplicable. it could be your, your fame level as well. 'We need some, need a big name in this'. These are also some of the things that go into this decision making. So, you know, just make it easier on yourself. And don't take it all on sometimes.

I've had quite a few roles where the role was absolutely not written for me. But I did it. And then the team changed their mind and they tailored the role around me. I've had that, I think once, for race as well. And not only did they change the race of the character, but they referenced the fact that the character was now that race. So originally, it was a sister within a white family. And then she became the adopted black sister, and the context of that in 1930s Duluth in Minnesota changed the story. And so sometimes it's still worth turning up.

Because just know, you have the potential to do that. You have the potential to make an impression. You have no idea how the creative team actually feels about the project that they're working on. Some people are like, 'this is what it is' – very rigid, don't want it to change. Some people are still in the process of developing and taking inspiration for the characters. And for even the story itself. You just have no idea. And you can't second guess that. So you just do your best, right? And you say, look, if I was to play this character, this is the version I would be, so what do you think about that? You know, I also think it's just worth doing good auditions. Because even if you don't get the job, you make a good impression. People do remember you, second chances can come around, or different projects can come around, it happens all the time.

But also, I think it's good practice to try and be consistent in your craft, whether you're working, whether you're auditioning, whether you're meeting, whatever it is. As an actor, setting a standard and a bar for yourself, trying to meet that at all opportunities, I think is a good thing to do. That's not to say you need to put pressure on yourself. But there's still a level of consistency in terms of how you respect your own craft, you don't have to take yourself too seriously. But you take the craft seriously.

PJ One of the recurring issues in the creative industries at the moment is the discussion around representation. How do you see your role in relation to that conversation?

SA I have talked about it in the past and as my own career develops, but also as my understanding of representation, its importance and its function develops. I think for me, my role and goal is to pursue what it is I want to pursue, in the hopes that other people can see that and know that that's possible to do. I like to do a variety of things. I have a variety of interests, I want to play all different types of roles, I want to be in lots of different types of projects, work with different types of people, I want all of the variety. And that should be available to us. So, for me, when it comes to the representation conversation, that's where I think I sit in. Personally, you know, I'm a Ugandan-born Black woman who grew up in a very white Essex, in a working-class environment. So I was already meeting up with family on the weekend, and having some, what some would call 'unorthodox' music tastes. I had different cultures coming at me at the same time. I'd go visit my family in East London, and there was a much larger Black community there. And then I'd go back home to Essex, and then it was a predominantly white community there. And I kind of liked that, you know, I liked that I knew about different things.

Similarly, with my career, starting out as somebody who wanted to be a doctor, doing a Biosciences degree, then wanting to be a musician, then wanting to be an actor. I'm like, don't box me in. Because I also don't know what I could become. I didn't know at the time what I could become in the future, I didn't anticipate I'd be an actor. I didn't anticipate I'd be a writer. And who knows what else is in store for me. But that's why I think representation is important, not just because, oh, I can see myself represented. I also want you to see the versions of yourself that you didn't know you can be represented too. Because it's one thing to reflect the same back at yourself. It's another thing to have ideas of yourself challenged by somebody who looks like you, and have those ideas expanded as well. I think that's what representation means. Because to put it bluntly, white people have been allowed to do that for so long. You know, the monolithic stranglehold that gets placed on marginalized people, of all different groups and categories, is, to me one of the most corrosive aspects of how that discrimination can work. Because it doesn't allow you to even postulate that you could be so many other things, you could have so many other experiences. And 'variety is the spice of life' to use a very overused cliché. So I think for me, that's what's important. Allowing people to just relax into the idea of exploration, exploring themselves, exploring possibilities, embracing other cultures, as well, and other people connecting and empathizing. That's where I think I sit within it.

PJ Thinking in terms of how you choose to identify, what do you think are the challenges in the acting/creative industry now?

SA I'm a trustee at the Old Vic. So I was helping out with some of the anti-racism work that was happening from 2020 onwards, and I'm still involved in their inclusion work. And terminology is one of the big head-scratching topics that makes everyone's brain hurt a little bit. Because everyone feels differently about it. And I don't think it's something that can be solved. I don't think it's a solvable thing. It's always going to evolve. And it's going to evolve in line with the context of the wider society and the times that we're in, how people feel about history, and themselves in the present, and the future, in comparison and in parallel with other groups. It's just the nature of how it's going to work. But one of the things that we landed on as a general consensus is less about definitives around terminology, and more about an approach towards defining yourself or other people. So why am I saying all that long-winded answer, I try and be as specific as possible. So, I'm a British Ugandan. That is just a fact. Yeah, I put it that way round. Because I'm a Ugandan first was born in Uganda. The fact that I'm British is an adjective, so to me, I'm a British Ugandan. But I am a Ugandan.

And then there can be no confusion.

I think the challenges are that fundamentally, the industry is still white facing. And so sometimes, even in the corners where there is a real desire to embrace others, there's just a real lack of understanding and people just not getting it. Actually, it's almost harder when you're faced with somebody who thinks they do get it, because then you have to argue with them about why they don't as opposed to somebody who's like, 'I don't get it. Let me know what we got to do', you know? So, in the midst of people trying to be more proactive and take responsibility and be allies, I guess, that can be great on one hand, can also be quite obstructive, because those people are still coming with quite a forthright attitude that is born of entitlement. So yeah, that for me is definitely one challenge. Then there's the people who just are deliberately obtuse and don't want to understand.

Then there's the wider system, which we're seeing, which is how the industry views what is 'successful' or 'valid'. That is something that I think is underpinning a lot of the dis-ease in the industry at the moment. People feeling like, you know, studios and executive producers, how they perceive us, how they value us, what price do they put on us? How lucrative do they think we are for each of their projects? What do they want to pay for? What do they want to remunerate? Or not to remunerate? What do they think is without value, even if we think it is, even if we know it is? That's a big issue because we're in a time where people understand that representation is important. But some people only want to understand that as a kind of nebulous concept, that doesn't mean anything to them at its core, and it's just a marketing ploy. And when you're engaging with those people, it can be very difficult to actually make work that speaks to the truth of that particular representation.

So it's a bit of a Trojan horse, where you're let in the door but then you got to deal with all this shit on the other side of the door. You're still like wading through and you're almost like 'it was kind of easier outside of the door, actually, when I wasn't even in in the first place, just dealing with the stuff that I kind of know and understand'. I think that's a big problem. And again, is born out of a lack of understanding – people not wanting to understand or not thinking they need to understand. Just wanting to rush it wanting to just get it done.

Another thing about when I was working with the Old Vic – we were trying to be really methodical about how we implement changes and have these conversations and do this reform, for lack of a better word. Because anyone can do a 'flash-in-the-pan' something, and it will have no sustainability. And in the process, you'll probably end up offending a lot more people. You can't make everyone happy all the time – the proportion of people that you will upset is probably greater. And we just have to stop – we have to accept that there are lots of different people in this world, and all of them are valid. And we need to start engaging with each other properly, at least trying to. But as long as we keep trying to commodify representation, it's not going to work.

PJ What pitfalls should actors emerging from drama school aim to avoid?

SA The reason why it's important to know yourself and to trust your gut and to listen to yourself is because there's going to be lots of advice that flies around from lots of different people, and lots of different places. And some of that will be great for you. And some of that will be not so great.

Because, it's a freelance gig economy, right? So everyone is hustling and trying to work for the same jobs or similar jobs. And there's all of this comparison going on. And I know that that can be particularly intense, when you're just about to leave drama school, or have just left drama school. And you got to find a way to just cut out all of that noise and to accept that you are on your own singular path. Don't read reviews as well. I feel like if you really want to read reviews, read them right at the end of a run, and probably read them if they're good. I just I don't think it's valuable to you. And even good reviews in the middle of a run can be detrimental if you read them, because you start to change your performance based on what you've read. So, I tend to avoid them. And then there's one other thing – when you have an audition, throw it away. Do the audition and leave it and if it comes back, that's wonderful. And if it doesn't, don't let them live rent free in your mind. And that's the case with so much of your career. You absolutely want to be retaining experiences, for learning and for, you know, nice memories and all the rest of it. But if you're just becoming a sponge for negativity and all the things that you can't control again – slippery slope down to somewhere very unpleasant.

PJ Who are the actors and directors that have inspired you?

SA Oh, I'll speak about the people that I've worked with, because I've got to watch them in action. So, Viola Davis, obviously, because, you know, she's Viola Davis. But also, when I worked with her on the *Woman King*, she was an actor and a producer at the same time undertaking a tremendously all-encompassing role on an all-encompassing project. And a very ambitious project, as well. And for me, the thing that really stands out about her as an actor is not just because she's 'Viola Davis', but because she takes the craft seriously. And as I was saying earlier on, you set yourself a bar, you try and meet that bar, and she's consistent. So, when I say or there's no huge difference between screen and theatre other than the nuances of the techniques that require you to adapt to the medium, she epitomizes that. Because she's still turning up, learning her lines, we're having conversations, the same kinds of conversations that you would have if it was a theatre script.

We're trying to understand intention, we're trying to make sense of who the character is, and what they're trying to do to the other character, all of these things are happening. And in that respect, when we're on set, there was no hierarchy. That was particularly notable to me – that when we got there, on the stage together in front of those cameras, we felt like peers, we felt like sparring partners. And that's absolutely how it should be. Because the skills that you learn as an actor, whilst they obviously develop over time and over the course of your career, they are timeless, you always go back to the basics. And that's the same, I think, with any craft, particularly artistic craft. You've always just got to know the fundamentals and the foundations. And you can always lean on those. So she really showed me that, because she's somebody who is so highly respected, and highly regarded in the acting community, who has such a wealth of experience, who is the generation above me. But to be able to watch her in action, and demystify all of that and go, 'oh, she's great, because she cares' was so important for me.

If I think about all the people that have really inspired me that I've worked with, they're the same. Halle Berry was the same – she was acting in a film and directing it and it was her directorial debut, *Bruised*. And again, I had to watch her fight. You know, she was – she was fighting for these characters. She was literally fighting as well, as an MMA fighter, doing her own stunts. Same with Viola. *The Woman King*, we did all our own stunts. Halle Berry had two broken ribs, and she got those cracked ribs at the beginning of the shoot. So she did the rest of the shoot, acting and directing and doing her own stunts on broken ribs. But she just kept on going, you know, kept on asking questions. Barry Jenkins – director – Gina Prince-Bythewood – director – Che Walker – director – I could, I could go on Lashana Lynch – actress – all of these people were just there, they're on their game, and they're about their shit, you know, and they're all lovely, as well. So I know, everyone's got their own process, but it doesn't require you to be some kind of intense, unpleasant person to be around, in order to engage with your craft to the highest level.

I don't think it does. I think it's something that is very possible to achieve, whilst also having some humanity and some personability, and some respect for those around you, which is what it comes down to. And all of those people, they conduct themselves with the utmost professionalism, and make great work.

They're all boundary pushing as well, which for me in particular is very important, because that's what I want to be. That's the kind of work I like to be involved in. And speaking back to feeling like a bit of an oddball, and feeling like I was in between worlds when I was younger, and having always felt that way in so many different ways, it helps to be to feel affirmed, in seeing people doing things that are ambitious, or against the grain or something that people told them couldn't be done. But they just do it. They figure out a way. Anybody who's doing that is very inspiring to me, and that's people who are older than me, younger than me, across generations.

PJ If a young Black and Global Majority person of eighteen made the decision that they want to become an actor, what would your advice be?

SA I would tell them to focus on two things. One is their mental health. And I hate this term because I think it's overused and bandied about in the wrong way, but 'self-care', and actually not even self-care – 'self-preservation'.

Because in certain corners, it's getting better. But this industry is notoriously neglectful in that respect. So, if you're waiting for people to look after you, or to recognize that you're in trouble, or to recognize that something is challenging for you, a lot of the time, even if they do recognize those things, it might not be in their interests to help you.

So you might be met with a lot of inaction. If you're expecting to just look in someone's eyes, and for them to give you that extra day off that you needed or give you that compassionate leave that you needed, or, you know, have a conversation with an onset therapist or whatever, you've just got to be forthright and say, 'these are the kinds of things that I want, need', whether it's something that the production itself provides, or something that you give to yourself outside of production hours. Yeah, be front-footed with that. Not aggressive, but front-footed.

Actually, I'd say three things. The second thing I'd say, which is connected to that point is to be prepared to advocate for others and stand up. I've seen bullying happening. And I've had to say something, and I've done it in a particular way. I'm not saying you have to jump in and get punched in the face or whatever. But you know, there's a variety of ways that you can address a situation. And that will always depend on the context of the project and who you're dealing with, on the production team, on where you're at, at that time on how high up you are, what capacity you have – all of these things come into play. So absolutely factor those in. But advocacy is really important, particularly in this industry, because as we've seen with the fallout from the many abuses that have been rife within our industry, and many others, they work in plain sight, actually. And they are dependent on our silence. And when it comes to us, as Black people, marginalized people, Global Majority people, we're at the bottom of that list every time when it comes to somebody standing up and speaking for us. So, we need to try and build up some courage to be prepared to do it for others as well when we see it, in the hope that we can also receive it.

And then the final thing I'd say, isn't connected to both of those things and this is just a life lesson, really. But try and build a strong sense of who you are, as an individual. And when I say 'who you are', I don't just mean who you are as an actor. I mean who you are as a person. Because that will give you a steer when it comes to your foundations, your principles, your ethics, your work ethic, and that will guide you throughout this whole process. It will guide you when it comes to making choices, both in terms of your career and the jobs you pick and also just your characters. It will help you with your professionalism. It will also help you with the two previous things, the self-preservation and advocating for others, because you will have a better understanding of yourself when it comes to knowing what you need and knowing how you want to conduct yourself and knowing how you expect others to conduct themselves around you. And the reason why it's so important to be robust with that is because this industry is notorious for gaslighting as well. So you need to make sure when you leave the house every day that you've just had a little check in with yourself, of like 'who am I?' Right? So that I know that if I'm experiencing something or seeing something that isn't in line with that, I can get out of it. There's so many things that will convince you that you need to incentivize yourself to stay in dynamics or situations that are not right for you that are not healthy, that are corrosive, that are hurting you or someone else. You need to know where your line is. And the only way you can know that is you really know who you are. And then you can make the choices for yourself that actually allow you to continue on this path. And I think the reason why I said it's so important for people of the Global Majority, is because there's not many people trying to do that for us and trying to help us on that journey. But also, we're just dealing with so much in work, and in society. And generationally we've inherited a lot of stuff as well. So we just need that little bit extra. We need to be told, and we need it to be reinforced in us that that's something that we need to do. We can't just take for granted that we're already doing it, we need to be intentional about. And then if you're a woman, there's even more – Black women we have to be so on it.

On the topic of Black womanhood, female presenting people, that solidarity and community is incredibly important. Because there are very few people in the world who are going to understand us. I talked about the barriers to understanding earlier on if you're a Black woman that is compounded, and magnified, 10-fold, 100-fold, right? For all the reasons that would take a whole other book for you to explore.

So find your community be open to that community. And that's why knowing who you are is even more important, because there will be times where you might feel that isolation. So you need to know that you can stand firm in yourself. And I think one thing that Black women are up against is that we find it hard to blow our own trumpet. I think a big part of that is patriarchy, and all of the other things. But, make sure that doesn't impact on your confidence internally, sitting there thinking 'I'm just little old me by myself'. You're not. Keep your head down, do your work, but know who you are. Sometimes there are situations that will be out of your control. That doesn't mean you have to relinquish your power; control and power are not the same thing, necessarily. They're connected but they're not the same thing. So always be aware of the power that you have inside you.

PJ Hard-dough bread, Sourdough bread, Chin Chin, Sweetbread, Roti, Sudsa, Bun and Cheese, Nai Wong Bao -奶黄包- Custard Bun or Naan?

SA Well, annoyingly, I'm gluten free, so all of them will give me a bit of a bellyache, but if I'm ignoring that … you know what, I'm going to add my own, which is actually quite similar to, I think it's like Puff Puff in Nigeria. Mandazi, it's the East African version. It's like Puff Puff or Festival, it's kind of like a variation of all of them, sort of small, kind of doughnutty, kind of a bit sweet. Yeah, that's me.

Kit Young

Photographer: Pip.

Most recently, **Kit Young** can be seen returning to his starring role as Jesper Fahey in the Netflix fantasy series *Shadow and Bone*. Film credits include *The Beautiful Game*, Netflix feature *School for Good and Evil*, and the Oliver Kassman-produced horror, *The Origin*, written by Frank Cottrell-Boyce. Theatre credits include starring roles in *Macbeth* (Sam Wanamaker Playhouse, 2018); *The Prime of Miss Jean Brodie* (Donmar Warehouse, 2018) and two plays for Nicholas Hytner at The Bridge: *Julius Caesar* (2018) and *A Midsummer Night's Dream* (2019). Kit trained at RADA, graduating in 2017.

Pamela Jikiemi – PJ Tell me about your journey to become an actor.

Kit Young – KY I wanted to be an actor pretty early on.

When I was about three, I wanted to be an astronaut. And then I saw *Apollo 13*, with Tom Hanks, where they get stuck in space. And I was like, nope.

And then I think I wanted to be an ice cream man, but then realized I couldn't eat my own stock. So that went out the window pretty quickly.

And then funnily enough back to space. My dad showed me *The Empire Strikes Back*. I saw *The Empire Strikes Back*, before I saw the original *Star Wars*. I was probably about maybe five, and that was the point where, yeah, it's an escapist fantasy thing. That's amazing, your mind runs wild. But I think that was the first time when I realized, oh, that's someone's job, someone has to do that. They get to dress up and play with light sabres and thinking all that stuff was real. They get to go to space and make a movie. And I was okay, maybe I didn't quite have it all together yet. But I knew that I wanted to kind of be part of that.

I was always a very musical child, I was always a dancer and a singer and played instruments quite young. So, I think performing was kind of inevitable.

What wasn't was whether I'd be any good.

I was part of lots of youth group stuff, and I did all the school plays. I kind of did it all. And I had like my first professional gigs between the ages of eight and ten, doing Oxford Playhouse pantos. I did that for a few years in a row. That was cool, because I was doing that for free and as a kid you're doing that for half the week.

But I was around, you know real actors. Some of them incredibly jaded, because it's a Christmas show. But I was with real actors, and then going back to school and doing homework and stuff and having that weird duality. And this kind of escapist life thing that I realized was something I wanted to be a part of.

Towards the end of my school years, after there were no school plays left to do. I thought about applying to drama school because I was looking at uni. And I liked some of the uni courses we were looking at. Places like Exeter had a good drama course and I think Warwick did as well. But my issue with the uni thing was the contact hours. It was like seven or ten hours a week, and I was like, I'm going to have a lot of time on my own. Technically, I might have more time acting if I created a extracurricular thing at university.

And then I kind of discovered the drama school thing quite by accident, because I think there was a prospectus for RADA, in the drama department in my school. It was not even a proper brochure, it was just a leaflet. And I was like, what is that?

And then I started looking into drama schools. I had then applied, and I got into the National Youth Theatre. And then that's when you meet a whole host of kids that also have the same idea, right? So suddenly, I was learning from all these other kids. So, at that time. I knew about three, I would say, and they're all really random. I knew about RADA, I knew about LAMDA because it sounded similar. And I knew about Rose Bruford, because that's where I was doing my NYT course. I applied to Rose Bruford through UCAS, and I applied to RADA and those were only two I applied for that year.

I got into Rose Bruford, I didn't get into the RADA BA (Hons) Acting course, but I got the foundation course. Also, I wasn't quite sure if I did want to do it. Because also, I'd had an agent beforehand as a kid for some of the jobs I had done before and thought that maybe I should just get out there in the world there and just do it.

But then I decided to accept the foundation course offer at RADA, and I quickly realized that this is something that I need to do.

I then reapplied the next year, and I did RADA, LAMDA, Guildhall, Bristol and maybe a couple of others. I did the circuit, as much as my pocket would allow. It was much cheaper back then than it is now. But listening to others talking at the NYT, at auditions, 'what do they teach such and such a school?' 'what's good about the Drama Centre? Why is it nicknamed "the trauma" Centre?' Trying to capture those comments and colour code it my head as checklist.

But I knew it was what I wanted to do so reapplied.

By this time I had already been at RADA on the foundation course for the better part of a year. And so, every other drama school that I walked into to audition felt really weird.

I remember my final round in the RADA audition process.

Because I was on the foundation, all of my audition rounds were like really close up. So, I had my second round, third round, fourth round, all within the space of about three weeks. I had the third round on the Friday, I found out I got the final round on the Saturday. Sunday came down with tonsillitis and had never had it before and didn't know what it was, I couldn't speak, I was coughing up blood and was shipped back off home to Oxfordshire to recover for a week.

And then came back to London, the RADA audition. I was ill and I was the last person to audition in the last fourth round of that year. So, I technically got I guess, the final place. It was also the last chance, I had to choose between accepting RADA and going to one in Bristol.

And so I just had to make that choice of this is where I want to go, I know RADA already. So I was fortunate enough to get that.

PJ Training around learning 'the craft'; did you go to a conservatoire drama school? Talk about your creative career and your commitment towards pursuing it.

KY And then I was in for three years. And it was – it was a little bit odd at first.

A twelve-week term takes you about eight weeks to actually settle in and stop, either, pinching yourself that you've made it there, or wondering about the group politics of the class, and for it to kind of stop being a hobby, and for you to get to the point where you walk in on Monday and go, I don't want to do it today, like it's become a job.

And because I'd already been there from the year before, I was a little bit out of sync at first. And a couple of the teachers were like, don't race ahead because you think you know, just focus on breathing. And I was like, what? We didn't touch a script until like the second term or whatever it was. And I remember getting really confused and quite frustrated.

And I think it was only once I went into second year, which I think for most drama schools are famously known as the really hard year, because you're just so busy. That was when I hit my stride, because I was forced to do stuff. And it's high turnaround and being busy and doing that. But I still found it hard.

It was when I got to the end of the second year when we had our first audience in the Shakespeare for Schools tour. Then the third year when we have audiences, when it really clicked, when I went oh my gosh, I'm meant to do this for people, and not to people who are critiquing, right, because you get used to that.

If I'm playing this guy, I probably shouldn't be thinking about my Alexander Technique all the time. Or, you shouldn't be thinking about what so and so thinks because you want their approval, you shouldn't be comparing yourself to whatever, blah blah, whatever that thing is that gets in the way. Soon as you have an actual external audience there, that kind of don't care, and just want to have a good time, and they want you to not be bad, suddenly everything's switches up. And that's when it made sense to me. And that's when it became fun again. Not that it wasn't fun, but there was a certain amount of pressure because it was all we did all the time.

And after nearly four years there, I was getting to the point of, oh, yeah, this is what it is. And I was able to have fun doing shows, even when there was the pressure of agents and all of that stuff, get an agent, that's the goal, move to the next level.

I was still able to find a way even if I was stressed to go out and have fun. I was fortunate with the roles I got to play in third year, but I asked for every single one I played, directly.

I was like, I want to play this part in this play, for these reasons.

Couple of them I was a shoo-in because it was like you're the one guy we were going to pick given your skin tone. But a couple of them I really argued for and like. And so yeah, I felt like I was able to navigate my third year really in the way that I wanted to and the best way I possibly could have, because we don't get to pick what the plays are.

But I remember, like, one of the shows we did. We did the UK premiere of Pearl Cleage's *Blues for an Alabama Sky*. And it was a whole situation to get the rights for it. Because it was like the school got in touch with Cynthia Erivo who was a RADA grad, Cynthia got in touch with Oprah Winfrey, who got in touch with like the writer Pearl, because she doesn't fly, and then we got the rights to it. And basically, RADA got really excited because basically, they had never had enough Black actors in a year to do that play, or to do lots of plays. There was no production of August Wilson's *Fences*, or *Jitney* or anything like that. It was a five hander. And what was great about that play was, like, the play's not about race. It's about relationships, aims and ambitions.

In a lot of ways, it's kind of like an African American *Cabaret*. Like story wise, it's about the social commentary, snapshot of things, because it's Harlem everybody is Black.

That was one of the highlights of my time as an actor at that point. Because also we got reviewed, drama school plays don't get reviewed, we got four stars in *The Guardian*. It felt like it was a natural transition into the real world. I played Guy. And I loved it. It was genuinely one of the best characters I've ever got to play. I had the best time with it.

And then the next play I did was *A Bitter Herb*, which is Kwame Kwei-Armah's first ever play, which I think up until that point had only ever been done in Bristol. We did it and I played basically a younger version of Kwame. He put himself and his family into the play. And the play's a kind of comment on the Stephen Lawrence case and I played a character largely quite unlikeable, because it's basically as close as you get to any sort of reverse racism, he's really aggressive, and people really didn't like me. The audience were really confused about it, a lot of white people really upset. And it was great, because then that literally was the thing that got me a job.

Nick Hytner was starting the Bridge Theatre, and he came to see *A Bitter Herb*. I thought I was auditioning for *Julius Caesar*. And I walked in and he said, I'd love you to play the part and I was like what? Because up until that point, the cast announcement was Ben Whishaw, Michelle Fairley, David Morrissey and David Calder. It was like *Paddington Bear*, *Game of Thrones*, *Walking Dead* and me. But then I had to wait ten months for the theatre to be built before he started. So I was like, wow! But, I've had quite a linear, I think, trajectory in a lot of ways. But to me, it's still surprising how unpredictable it is.

Because everybody has it differently. Most of the things that have been in my career I could not have predicted really, but at the same time, one of the things I'm most proud of, the job that's given me a lot of what I have today, being *Shadow and Bone*, for Netflix.

I can track back to the email that I sent at Christmas break in my third year saying, I want to play this really despicable character in *A Bitter Herb*, please.

And that led to that thing, that led to that thing, that led to directly over a two and a half year period. Sure, other things might have happened, I probably also had to be good at my job along the way. But I was like, wow, if I didn't give it a go and ask, I know, I wouldn't be where I am right now. And if I were, it would be different. And I think sometimes you ask and, you fall on your face. Like I love the kind of comic book staff and all that kind of thing. And I was really early, when they were like, they're making a Joker film. And I wrote to my agent being, get me seen for that. And they went, I think they're going with Joaquin Phoenix, and he's probably going to win an Oscar, it's not going to be you and I went 'cool'.

Sometimes you fall on your face. But you have got to ask. People take you seriously when they think you have something to contribute. If you don't, why are you there? Surely, you have to want to do something?

PJ What did you get from your actor training?

KY I think the tricky thing with the drama school training is you need a bit of distance afterwards, for you to actually be able to look at it.

Because it's such a kind of hurricane in the eye of the storm type of thing, you can't see the wood from the trees at all.

And it's only after it's done. And probably a while afterwards, you're able to go, oh, that stuff was really useful, or that, I should have done better, or, you know, you're able to actually kind of like reflect on it properly.

Obviously, there is stuff I learned, right, physical stuff. There's types of theatre that I now know about that I didn't know before, I kind of have an idea of how to approach a lot of things. But that's a starting point, really. I learned to work really, really well with groups of people.

But each time you do a job, you have to start that again. Unless you're working with people you already know.

But it gave me the tools to understand that this is all a collaborative thing.

Because the thing with drama school that is so important, whether it's RADA, where you have four rounds to get in, let's be honest, when you get to the third round, chances are you are someone that they are thinking that can act, it's then about, do you fit into this cohort, because you're kind of building the cast of sorts. And sometimes you fit and sometimes you don't. So, I learned really how to work with a group. I also think I gradually got to know what it is that I bring to the table. What makes me unique.

I also learned not how to do a play, but how *I* do a play. For instance, if I'm in a show, I *know* the play, I know the whole play. I'm not saying I know everyone's lines, but after a while you probably do, because you hear it.

But honestly, what I mean is I know the play, meaning if I come off from the scene, I know exactly how long I have to go to the toilet, get a coffee, all that stuff, all those things and that gives you security. If you're on stage and there's a continuity error or something goes wrong, it's your job to fix it, you are part of the solution.

Then moving into the screen territory is a completely different thing, which I feel like I don't really think I was prepared for. Most of what I've learned in the screen field I've learned on the job. I'd say ninety per cent. Just in terms of how it works, what all the lingo is, who all these people are, you know, it's very easy for, people to identify actors on set. Because our headshots are in every office, we've got character and a number on the call sheet. And we're probably in some flamboyant costume. And then especially if it's cold, you see a sea of people in puffer jackets and beanies, and you don't know who the director is, who costume is, who the Sparks are, what some of those jobs mean.

And they – and there are some that you'll never have heard of, because it's specific to that job, right? Like, took me a while to realize that 'stunts' isn't the same as a fight choreographer in theatre. And there are typically different people that do those things. Some things are transferable, some things tend not to be.

The sheer size of a production changes how you feel that you fit into it. That's something I wasn't ready for from drama school. I don't think I was prepared for that at all. The training could have prepared us better and the pandemic had a big impact, the theatre industry collapsed and suddenly everybody was at home watching Netflix or whatever and that was very useful.

For me, I was very fortunate at that time, nobody was working. And I did three movies during the pandemic, I was lucky. But at the same time, it's because the streaming platforms needed and wanted to make more content.

I think the training should address an understanding of, like, what your job actually is, meaning on a film set, you might be the lead, you might be a day player, you might be there for five seconds, five months. But you're a cog in the machine. You are not the storyteller, you don't have as much agency, your job is to fulfil a certain function.

And also, my first filming experience I did, I gave all the options and gave one to ten. And then I'm surprised at which bits they picked. Because there's so much to choose from, of course they are not going know what that is. Whereas in theatre, you're encouraged to do that. Because you have agency. And I think being made aware of *how* an actor actually, day-to-day fits into a production and what they need to fill and what they don't, is very useful. Because one of the things that can get quite annoying on set is actors who chip in on stuff that just isn't their job.

Yeah, I'm sure a collaborative atmosphere at times, perhaps, is, fine, but still stick to story. But there's all sorts of different politics and stuff. There's code, there's all these different like sayings and things. I spent ages on a set, not knowing what going for a ten-one means. And I was like, 'what's that?' And people were like, basically, we don't want to say on all the comms, to hundreds of people that I'm going to the loo. And I was like, I wish I knew that. I wish I knew that stuff. I didn't know anything. I couldn't read a call sheet. Because it looks like a bunch of telegrams.

Whereas like a call sheet for theatrical rehearsals is pretty simple, it's a list. With screen work you need to understand the call sheet, there are so many more moving parts, the training needs to support the understanding of who all the people are on it and how they fit into it. Your cast number and what that means in relation to your characters scenes, which bits are useful to you and which bits aren't for you.

You don't need to go through looking through the health and safety of the locations department. You might get sent it, but it's not about you. So, basically, knowing what lane you're in, something that I learned through trial and error, that I kind of wish maybe at drama school we'd had a little bit of time to finesse and work out.

Because the right thing was that we got taught about acting, which is the point. But with screen work there's all these technical elements you kind of learn obviously through acting, obviously your lenses and your sizes and what shot you're fitting into. But also on some level, you're already doing the acting, what you need to learn is the technicalities.

I learned that through trial and error, and I'm really glad I did in a way, because I learned quickly. And then, because I didn't know, I also asked lots of questions. I was like, what is that? What do you do? What's that dial you've got? And they're like, well, without me, we don't see you. And I'm like, cool. Good to know. I'll be your friend.

So, really learning what those roles are on a set and how you fit into it, because you can just go yeah, the cast and creative. If you don't know what different elements of the crew are, you need the differentiation, for it to make sense. And I don't think I got that until I was out there in the field.

PJ Is your preparation for a role different for theatre and screen?

KY I think inherently, you're probably different for every job. But, on a base level, yes, because there's more in common with theatre and film than there is with television.

Because quite often, you'll sign on to the job. And you can't prepare in the same way that you will with a play because you don't have all the scripts. So you literally don't know where it's going. You don't know what your arc is, you might have been briefed, you might not have.

With a play, you can do so much in-depth work, you're creating an entire arc before you even start.

Also, you learn about it together in the rehearsal space and on your own.

On screen, you have to have done that solid amount of work yourself, and then show up and play. So I think inherently you come at it from a slightly different approach. My main thing is because also scripts change a lot, sides change, lines change, if I can work out who the person is that I'm playing, and how they respond to things. That's the most like it is in theatre when you really understand the character.

With screen work when it comes to the actual dialogue. And where this is happening. That stuff is in flux. So, basically, with theatre you do all the work, all the work that you can think of, you can do it. When it comes to screen work, there's some stuff you can do and some stuff you're just going to have to find out. And that's great, because it keeps you on your toes. And it's exciting, but it is also a little bit like daunting.

When it comes to rehearsal, the rehearsal with screen is minimal, it depends on where you are in the foodchain. I've realized that with a lot of screen work that I've done, there has been some rehearsal, but it's literally mainly for blocking sake. It's so the cameras know where to be. I've also been fortunate enough in the food chain to have been able to kind of like, maybe snag a bit more extra time. But largely most of it was just the actors going do we – do we all know the lines, let's run the lines. That's mainly what it is.

The first take is your rehearsal, in a way, then it's just a question of how many you get. But I also think it really depends on the scale of the production. There was a large film that I did, the scale of it was huge. I was the villain in the movie. And I was basically just in the finale really. I did the whole kind of like villain monologuing thing, 'everything that's happened is because of me'.

And it was seven pages of monologue. And then a huge action bit. We shot that scene for eight days. My previous experience in television was two scenes a day. So I was monologuing for days, so they could get all sorts of shots. And then they started blowing stuff up and like all of this stuff that has to do with the scale. So really, by the time I was getting into close coverage with some of the monologue stuff, it's like I've done a week of shows. Because I got chance to rehearse it, there was lots of blocking and all that kind of stuff. But because it was a proper like acting scene, with two people that was quite lengthy. It was just like watching a scene in a play. And then you get to the end and you actually mourn it in the same way that you do with a theatre job.

It's like oh, we I've done it so many times I don't get to do that any more. Whereas with some things you don't get attachment because it comes and goes. I think it's really dependent on what that production has time for.

PJ How do you decide what roles to go for?

KY I don't think I have actively had the luxury of just outright choice. I think that I've had things come my way and I've gone, Oh, that is something I've always wanted to do. Or it surprised me and I've gone, maybe I could be the guy for that.

And then quite often, it's surprising. I also think it takes time for you and your agent or you and your team, whoever it is, for you to really work out and align yourselves with how they see you and how you want to be seen.

There was a long time where, like, all the stuff I went up for in theatre was largely kind of Shakespeare and classical stuff. That was great because there's certain, like, lexicon there, and a kind of set of roles that you just go, that makes sense. I'm prepared for this. I've come out of perfect place for this.

And then on screen, I was always going up for the nerdy hacker, who is kind of cool. Basically, the Rami Malik – *Mr Robot* archetype, that wasn't really my thing, or wasn't something I naturally was gravitating towards in a that's what I always wanted to do thing.

And then when I booked 'Jesper' in *Shadow and Bone* who's literally like, the Han Solo archetype, it's this kind of like lovable rogue and I went this I can do. And suddenly everything I was getting through after that matched that, and the people around me went, Oh, maybe you're the guy that does these things. And I was like, sorry, have we been miscommunicating, have we not figured that out yet together?

But I think now I've got to a place where I'm now more comfortable with saying no to things I don't want to do.

If someone asked me, what do you want to do? I can't honestly tell you that. I can probably tell you what I don't want to do. And the reasons for not doing it are, I probably just did it, or it might just be I'm not interested in doing it. I was offered something where I was playing the new boyfriend of someone that turns out to be a kind of a horrible guy. And I thought, I'm good with being a villain. But I don't want to be like just a douchebag. And I went, you know what, actually, that isn't something I want to do, I've decided I don't want to do that.

I've never been the lead in anything. I'd love to do that. But also, that's not the way I'm seen.

So I have to choose things that surprise people.

And the thing for me is I choose things based on what I haven't done. And you haven't seen me do that. And you probably don't think of me when you think of that thing. So let me go do it. First thing I did after a massive kind of budget fantasy show was a really weird, indie, prehistoric horror movie in a made-up language. I was so happy that I got to do something that was so different. I'm terrified of being pigeonholed. So, if I can be the opposite immediately, I can play this game with people where they are always guessing.

But really, as much as that's, you know, a joke. We all seek a certain level of versatility. I think you know, you can't be everything. Everybody wants to be everything. You can't be everything, you're not going to be good at everything. It isn't all about you, basically. But if you can choose things that keep you interested, then there's a reason that you do this for a while. Because if you did everything you wanted to do you do, you would do it in five years, you would move on to something else. We would all release an album, and do paintings and go on to the next thing. So for me, it's yeah, it's about picking things I haven't done. You work out the things that you've missed and have always wanted to do and start aiming for that.

If I've been pigeonholed for anything, it's the best pigeonholes I could be in.

Do you want to be the really cool fun guy, with the cool skills and the jokes, who's everything, gets the cool costumes, and I go, yeah, of course I want to be that guy. If I'm going to be stuck as that guy, that's fine.

If I get stuck as the guy who's playing the stalker, murderer, a serial killer, I'm going to have problems walking down the street. And that's the thing too, if people recognize you, they want you to be that thing. And so that gets weird, too. But, um, yeah, if pigeonhole's nice it's, okay, but you always want to break out of it.

PJ One of the recurring issues in the creative industries is the discussion around representation. How do you see your role in relation to that conversation?

KY I think it's kind of always changing a bit. I think you're kind of aware of, like, the actors in your circles, like your stages, right? There's almost mini generations. There's people I kind of came up with, they all came out of drama school at similar times within, like, there's like a five-year generation, you know about, the two years above you and the two years below, maybe a bit beyond that. So it feels like the people who are the next level above dealt with that question a little bit differently. For me, and I feel like the people who are at drama school right now are probably at the newer stage of that.

Because, when I was coming out of drama school, I was the Mixed-Race kid on some level. But also, I was just like one of the Black ones in a way, right. One of my favourite things about castings was that I would go into lots of castings and not get recalls. I wouldn't get cast for anything, but I would make an impact, not because of any acting. It's because they'd look at my headshot, and they'd be like, looks like he's Black, and then they would hear me and say ahh but he sounds white, where do we put him?

And I'd be, well, at least they can remember. Right. And so on some level, at first, there was a little bit of a kind of a need to stand out and forge your own thing.

Because you're constantly trying to forge your own identity, but also, you are still part of something.

If I'm in a production, like this horror film I did, it was all Mixed-Race actors, because it was prehistoric, the idea is that we don't know where people came from. So, it'd be a whole mix of things, and that felt really important to the storytelling, even though it wasn't the point of the film.

And there were a couple of roles that are played where like, the book source material says, He looks like this, therefore, it gets to be me. But then I also did a book to screen of *The School of Good and Evil* where the character I was casting for, he was described as having alabaster skin, and like spiky white hair and sparkling blue eyes. And then they cast me. So sometimes it feels like they're making a diversity choice. And sometimes it feels like you just happen to get it because you might have been their best choice.

Morgan Freeman's character in *Shawshank Redemption* is asked by another inmate 'why do they call you Red?', to which his character Red replies 'maybe it's because I'm Irish', because in the book, he is Irish, he's a white guy. But I think that conversation is interesting, because you get into tricky conversation with people. There's a whole wave of Black actors really doing well, when I was coming out of drama school, I noticed it was around the time when John Boyega was in *Star Wars*. And then what was quite funny was like mates of mine – Black actors would be, I'm being seen for the very white Irish play in the West End, and I'm not going to get the job. And I don't really feel like I should go in. But it feels like there's a quota and all that stuff. And people kind of re-navigate that stuff. And then I felt like it got a bit different, again, when BLM came around, and I got into tricky conversations with friends of mine, because they were like, 'why aren't you posting stuff?' I was going on marches, but I wasn't posting stuff on Instagram all of the time. And well, it isn't news to me, if it's news to you, fine. But I don't have to take part in your learning in the same way. And because I have a platform, quote unquote, it's, it's not up to me to do that for you. I'm an actor, I get to represent something, but at no point should I be the spokesperson.

I am down for having conversations, but I'm twenty-eight, I'm a youngster on the block. Talk to the person who's been around, talk to the person who's, like, seen it, and the person who can actually tell us what's going on and how it is changing or isn't changing.

It's very hard for me to see how it's changing year by year, but I'll be able to look back in ten years and go, there it is. Some jobs, it's not a thing, at all, it never comes up. And sometimes you're hyper aware of what it means. I was shooting a film in Rome as a football film, and the team was six of us, seven of us. Three of us were Black. We are in Rome. We were all really aware of our Blackness, right? I love certain cultural things. When I work abroad, I'm very aware of it. But that isn't about representation that's just about racism, or prejudice. And so, I feel like basically, long story short, the way that I navigate it, I think is constantly changing based on people's expectations always being different.

Some people want to talk about it, and make it the cause and make it the point of the thing. Cool. Some people are like we're going to pretend this doesn't exist, but we're going to kind of address it as well. They'd be like *sotto voce* 'he's Black but we're not going to say it', well, you can see me so … You just kind of got to take it as it comes, yeah …

PJ Thinking in terms of how you choose to identify, what do you think are the challenges in the acting/creative industry now?

KY I identify as Mixed Race. Actually when I was at RADA, I had a bunch of people tell me what I was. I remember being at the pub, and I remember getting to all sorts of conversations with local punters where they were getting really interested in it. It was around that time when everybody got really interested in terminology, and phrasing. And terms were floated around and people would say, you can't say that any more. It's offensive. And I was is it, for you? Okay, cool, fine. And then someone was like, well, I think you should be called Dual Heritage, and I was like, well, lucky for you, I am. But if I was three, that doesn't work. So Mixed Race makes more sense. My mum is Black, My dad is white. My mum's from East Africa, she is Ugandan-Kenyan, my dad from Scotland. So it's quite simple for me, because also, I think when people think Mixed Race in this industry, I'm the most obvious version of it. A lot of people go, you mean Black and white, right? Not everybody when you say Mixed Race is thinking, you know, Black and East Asian?

Yeah, I think people, find it very easy to place me if they are willing to think beyond one box. But I think it's the way I've always identified, because it's made the most sense to me.

PJ What pitfalls should actors emerging from drama school aim to avoid?

KY This kind of goes in two parts.

One of the greatest pitfalls I think actors have when they get into drama school is to think that they've made it, right. Because it's hard to get in. It's very selective. It's very exclusive. And you are one of a lucky bunch. Yeah, you feel like you did it, especially if you've tried it more than once, right? It was a journey to get there. When you leave drama school, think people can be fooled into thinking that they have completed it. Right? They got 100 per cent on video games done. I've done my learning. And now I am Master Jedi. No, this is literally where the learning starts.

Because even if it's something you know, really, really well, it could be exactly in your wheelhouse. You could be the Shakespeare guy, and you're doing the play that you know like the back of your head. But you have to learn a new way of working, I have to learn these new people. You have to learn whatever version of this painting this is and you go, Oh, my favourite scene has been cut, deal with it, you've got to, you've got to work with whatever vision has been put in front of you.

I think another pitfall is that there's a fine line between you have a right to be in that room, because you were picked to do the job. So, you have a right to speak up and have your voice be heard. And also, excusing my French, when it's not your turn, shut the fuck up. It's not always your place. I think a lot of people in drama school are empowered to create and to kind of take charge of stuff and take part. But there will be times when you're with a more accomplished actor. And if you're not in that scene, don't talk. Let them do their work. Don't get involved in everything. I think those are the main ones that come to mind. I think the learning isn't done is the main one.

If you're working/rehearsing and someone's always getting a note and then they stop getting notes it means the director may have given you that note five times, you haven't taken it, so they've stopped.

When it comes to notes, I have worked with a lot of directors where actors start to freak out when they're not getting notes. And it's because they're not worried about you, you're doing it fine. They'll give you a note if something is wrong most of the time. The other thing is people looking for feedback, wondering what the audience thinks. The British audiences largely are pretty nice, if they liked it. They might say something, if they didn't like it, they'll probably just ignore you. And so when an actor starts getting international recognition where people will come up to you and go hello, you were that person in whatever, that was terrible, that"s actually a kick in the teeth. But it's also quite charming that it happens. Don't go seeking feedback. You can from your peers, in a way if you want. You can't go seeking feedback from the audience, you'll just find out. You'll see, you go like, Oh, wow, it's been reviewed really badly. But tickets are selling. Critics don't like it, but audiences do. It's a mixed bag. It's always, always confusing.

And also, you know, actually, this is to the point of when it becomes unpredictable. If you think you know how it's going to go, you're probably wrong. Because you don't know, nobody knows. A mate of mine, recently come out from school. And he's, he's not that far up, and he just became incredibly famous in the last six days. He doesn't know what's going on. And he's looking at me going what's going on? And I'm, like, mate, it's happening to you, I don't know. It's completely your own thing. And it's unpredictable.

So don't think because you think you've worked out drama school and finished it. Because now you have got to do your life. You're not going to finish that in three years.

PJ What are your broad aims for the future of your screen acting presence?

KY I haven't finished it yet. I mean, I'm one of those slightly annoying people that I do kind of say, I want to do a bit of everything. But also I don't love horror films, never liked horror films, always freaks me out.

Did a horror film, loved doing it. I kind of want to dip my toe into every genre I can. I also, you know, if it were a video game, and you can play as multiple different characters, I kind of want to replay it and do it through different perspectives. There are some places I want to do more, and some I don't ever really want to do, but I might change my mind in ten years. I also like that there are things out there that I'm not ready for yet. And so, well, it gives me a sense of longevity. *King Lear,* yeah, not there yet. But I think there are some things out there that it's okay to have them as distant things and bucket list things almost. But also, think about, like the older actors now, the kind of kings and queens of actors right now. The seasoned pros, you know, people like Ian McKellen. What did the industry even look like when he was my age? So, what will it look like when I'm sixty? This whole thing will be very different. And I'm intrigued to find out what that is. Unless I've gone, you know, I've had enough, I've done enough, goodbye, because I've decided I'm going to off and save the planet. I'm probably going to be acting though. I just haven't completed it. I've got more stuff to do. It's all about play. And it's all about collaboration. It's all about communication.

PJ Who are the actors and directors that have inspired you?

KY I worked with and now is a kind of great mentor to me and a friend, Laurence Fishburne, he has had a huge impact on me. We are kind of part of each other's lives, actually. But what was great was when we worked together, we didn't really work together. Because the film that we were doing, the whole point was when you saw him, you didn't see me. It's kind of he was the Dumbledore, I was the Voldemort kind of thing. We have this one bit together where I had this epically long scene, but he had one line at the beginning. So he had to sit to one side and watch me. He could have left, but he watched me and he saw me do my thing. And he really empowered me and kind of passed on the baton. And it meant a lot to me. And we've kind of kept that going. And also, he's, you know, he's in his sixties now, and he's got this kind of great gravitas and sage-like quality about him, but he's still very youthful and very, playful. And he came up to me going, what do you think I did? I don't want to mess it up for you. And I'm, like, you're asking me? Oh, this is collaborative, I thought I was following you. And that was really amazing to work with someone that way who was so established, so knows what they're doing. And has been making movies, he did *Apocalypse Now* when he was fourteen. He doesn't need to take anything from me. But it felt really amazing to have someone bring me in in that way. So, that's a real one.

I think also working with Nick Hytner twice, as a director. He's such a brilliant director. He's got it all down he's mapped it out and he goes, basically, you're going to be there. And then we'll kind of work out what it is. And Nick's also great because he also he's like, 'I don't know anything about acting'. And I'm, like, what do you mean you don't know anything about acting, you've directed so much stuff?

It's really good stuff, he's like, I don't really know anything about acting. I know if you're going to get bad news on the phone, pick it up like you're happy, and then flip it around the other way. And I was like, actually that's a really good piece of advice. But I think working with people who have a sense of play, but also just really, really know their bit. Basically, if you have a director on a set and the DoP on set, and all these people that really know their stuff, I'm not going to worry. It's like if you're on a plane, and get turbulence and the flight attendant is chill. You're like, Oh, we're going be fine. But if they're like losing it, then you're, like, well, maybe I need to do more. And then that's never the answer, because you can only do your bit. But I think working with people who really know their stuff and love their stuff and want to keep making stuff. Those are my favourite people. People who can't stop working, you know, people who don't need to work. But they still do three things a year. I'm, like, you're cool, yeah, that's what I want to see. I never want to do this type of thing, really. But Tom Cruise cannot be stopped. No one can stop him. No vehicle, airborne or underwater, whatever, will stop him. But he's all about the experience. He has such a commitment to that. I'm, like, how does that not just inspire you genuinely to go out and do stuff?

PJ If a young Black and Global Majority person of eighteen made the decision that they want to become an actor, what would your advice be?

KY I think people will tell you what they think very quickly.

I think you can afford to work out what you like by just trying stuff. And I've been really pleasantly surprised by where that takes you. I'd say to them, just try stuff. And when you find something that you like, lean into it. Because the stuff that you like, will be the things that kind of really feed you, there'll be the things that you want to see, want to make and want to do. It's the stuff that gives you longevity. If you like watching stuff, stuff that you really enjoy, try and imagine a way to bring that to life.

Out of the Black Box

I would say, don't be afraid to ask questions. Just give it a go. And question if people put you in a box because maybe you're more than that. You're probably definitely more than that, because I know everyone I care about is, and I know I am. So why wouldn't you be?

PJ Hard-dough bread, Sourdough bread, Chin Chin, Sweetbread, Roti, Sudsa, Bun and Cheese, Nai Wong Bao -奶黄包- Custard Bun or Naan?

KY I mean, for me, I'm like, I'm looking at that and I'm like there is one for every day of the week almost. But I mean, and this is this is actually kind of boring, but I'm not the most amazing cook, but I really do breakfast well. If you give me a piece of Sourdough. I will make that meal and prevent you from spending £30 on brunch.

Sara Zwangobani

Photographer: Alex Vaughn.

Sara Zwangobani is an Australian actor who grew up in the Australian capital, Canberra. Her heritage is Zimbabwean and Irish. She graduated with a Diploma in Drama from the prestigious Victorian College of the Arts, and later completed a Bachelor of Arts at the University of Sydney and a Masters in Teaching at the University of New England. Most recently Sara starred in the Amazon Prime blockbuster 2022 TV series, *The Lord of the Rings: The Rings of Power*, playing Marigold Brandyfoot. She has appeared in numerous popular Australian television series, as well as US shows *The Starter Wife*, *Monarch Cove* and *Nightmares and Dreamscapes: From the Stories of Stephen King*. On stage, Sara has worked with numerous Australian theatre companies.

Pamela Jikiemi – PJ Tell me about your journey to become an actor.

Sara Zwangobani – SZ So, I did want to be an actor from a very young age. It was around eight. And it actually stemmed from my love of fantasy, really. I was watching a show that was a fantasy show that had Merlin in it and all sorts of stuff. But prior to that I had read lots of fairy tales. I was into Tolkien. Didn't understand hardly any of it at that age, but still it was like dipping my toe in those waters. Loved to read. Loved language, because my mum's an English teacher.

My grandfather is an English teacher. Lots of English teachers on my mother's side, the white Aussie side. And so, just loved fantasy and was watching this show about Merlin, and it was like a light bulb. I just went, oh, instead of seeing it as a show about fantasy. I suddenly saw that it was actors performing a show about fantasy. And I went that's what I want to do, I want to do that.

And from then on, that's all I wanted to do. Now sometimes I go that's just crazy. Why? You know, from the age of eight. I know that happens to a lot of people. But it was very clear to me, but how to do that, I didn't know. I just knew that's what I wanted to do.

PJ Training around learning 'the craft'; did you go to a conservatoire drama school? Talk about your creative career and your commitment towards pursuing it.

I did the things that kids who were interested in arts do. I – you know, made up plays with my friends and liked to try dress ups and did a lot of imagining, and all that sort of stuff. But it wasn't until I was in high school that I started to realize, oh, this is how you go about it. So, I did all the dance competitions, and I did all the plays, and I did all that sort of stuff. And then followed the trajectory that in Australia is probably the clearest trajectory or used to be. Now things are changing with streaming and all sorts of stuff. But it was to go to acting school.

I applied to Victorian College of the Arts (VCA), I really liked the audition process because we had five different things we had to do. I'm sure we had to do a Shakespeare, definitely had to do a monologue, and probably a storytelling thing. There were a few different things. I really enjoyed it, I think because I was just so excited and at that point, hadn't had enough rejections to be nervous. I genuinely didn't think I would get in. Partly because of my youth actually. And so, it was low pressure in that sense. And I definitely chose it because my brother was there. That that was a big – it – ended up being a big plus for me, because he's older, he's an actor. And he was very much a shelter for me during the years of being a VCA. So, it was definitely the right choice even though National Institute for Dramatic Art (NIDA) in Sydney was the more prestigious school. Also, I just like Melbourne.

And so, I went to the Victorian College of the Arts (VCA). I didn't try for NIDA in the end, I was going to – and I thought no, I'll try for the VCA first and see what happens. Partly because I had a brother living in Melbourne, at that time, and I was still a very small-town girl in a lot of ways. I mean, I was really quite nervous about leaving Canberra. And so, I auditioned for the VCA. And I got in straightaway.

I think I was seventeen at the time. About to turn eighteen. And Australian acting schools generally take people older or prefer applicants being a little bit older. And I think part of the reason why I feel in retrospect, I was a bit young, though all things are meant to turn out how they did. So, it was probably good that I was still very small-town. And I think also that thing about going into a big city and being a person of colour and entering that field of acting. Yeah, maybe just didn't quite know what I was getting myself into. But yeah, that's what I did.

The first year was difficult. I was very homesick. Very, very homesick. And I felt probably out of my league. I didn't have the confidence in myself, that came later. And so, that was challenging. And there are a few little things getting back to race that were a bit difficult.

I went, at one point, I went to Africa to see my father and I got braids for the first time. And it was just so culturally fulfilling to get a traditional African hairstyle for the first time in my life. And it was a really joyous occasion as well, because it was the first time I was sitting in a Black hairdresser's with all the Black women and the aunties and the music and the whole thing. I was in Africa. And, you know, because we don't have – unfortunately – I've now seen that in America. And I've seen it in England that those – those kinds of places exist. But they don't exist – or didn't exist in Australia at that time. So, it was an amazing experience. I got the braids.

PJ What did you get from your actor training?

SZ I won't name and shame. But I – there were several comments about the hair. Several. And there was one day in particular, when we were doing head massages, it was voice class. And we were doing head massages.

And the other actress, Sophia Laguna, who came and did my hair. She sort of said to me, I'll be gentle because of your braids. Which was great. And I said, oh, thank you, you know, fantastic. That's it. But the teacher overheard and basically made an example of me in front of the class about vanity – about, you know, do I want to be an actor? Or do I care more about my hair?

It became this whole diatribe. And of course, now with the knowledge that I have, and the more we talk about these things, if that happened to me today, I would say this is about culture. This is about a lot of other things than vanity. This is an expression of who I am.

You know, all that sort of stuff. Then, of course, I was very young. I felt all those things. But didn't know what they were. And I just felt myself being absolutely shamed and humiliated in front of an entire class of white actors. None of whom, of course, either – and – and what made it worse in retrospect is probably some of them were thinking, well, why is the hair such a big deal for her? And not able to explain that.

So, Sophie Laguna, bless her, after the diatribe was finished. And this teacher said, you know, get on with it. She leant over and whispered to me, I'll make it look like I'm doing it. But I'll still take care of your hair. And I thought, you know, that's an ally right there. Of course, I didn't know that at the time.

PJ What drives you? Looking at issues of employability, how do you navigate this?

SZ So, it's really interesting. I think – what drives me? I mean, what drives me is my passion for the craft. I mean, it's really interesting to me how many people along the way have actually left the industry that I travelled with. And I think that's absolutely a legitimate choice.

And it's a bold and brave choice in its own right, that you go off and decide to do something else and live a different dream. But I think for me, the passion has outweighed the negativity, because I'm still doing it.

There were definitely days where I would just go, why don't you just stop? Particularly before *The Rings of Power* came along. But I just have such a passion for it. So, that's why I keep doing it.

Issues of employability, it's funny, because it's not just about being a Black person. It's about being a woman. And it's about being an older woman, now. You can feel each year as the age creeps in, the ageism and stuff.

I think, the truth is, though, for a lot of the time, until recently, I couldn't really worry about it so much, as just hope that I just get an audition. Like you're just waiting for the next audition in a lot of ways. I think that when I was in my twenties, I railed a lot about the unfairness of things. I really, really did. And I had a lot of times where I would break down crying in tears about things.

But I think there was somewhere in my early thirties, where various things happened in my agency and a new person came on in my agency, Monica Keightley. And she and I had a really long and frank discussion. I think for the first time in my career, one of the most frank discussions that I've ever had about race, ageing, and all sorts of stuff. And she was sort of – her basic thing was and she's – she's white, but from a Spanish background. But white, well, actually, I won't speak for her – what she calls herself. But she said to me, we can't control a lot of these things. But what we can do is empower you as much as we can. And so, this is what I'm going to do. I'm going to look for moments where I can empower you. And she said, one of the things I'm going to stop doing is sending you for roles that are just, you know, the junkie – well, I didn't really go for the junkie, but the pregnant Fijian girl or whatever. That was one thing. But the second thing she said was – we're going to try and find you more classes, more training, more – more training that speaks to you, not just training for training's sake, but training that speaks to you. More ways to feel that you have some power over what is happening to you. And that was incredibly helpful. And actually career changing. Because after even that conversation, it was a little bit like, without getting sort of woowoo about it, putting it out to the universe, that I wanted a different path. And what I actually think happens in that when we talk about putting things out to the universe, what I actually think happens is, it's a shift in myself so that I start accepting certain things and not accepting other things. And I think that all of that happened around that time.

And I started doing classes with people who then actually started calling me in for auditions. So, it might also have been about actually, I'm not going to just do this class, I'm going to do this class with this person who has some influence in this way, who I've seen cast women, older women, Black women, non-Indigenous Black women, in this way. And so, making those choices.

PJ Is your preparation for a role different for theatre and screen?

SZ Not really. I think at the basis, they are very similar. They start with the text, first and foremost and looking for the clues in the text. They start with world building for my character internally; they start with creating an imaginative and rich life for my character. It then goes on to what do other characters say about me. How do I interact with other characters? All those basic things of acting, I think they're – they are inherently the same. I think they start changing once you get past all that initial preparation as to how that then is conveyed. And I think that's where the changes start happening.

Obviously, in theatre, it's a bigger art form. Also, I feel like in theatre, you can be a bit crazier with your choices. Thus far in – in the screen work I've done, you know, I can't go as wild as I might go in theatre. And that's what's great about theatre, you can go really wild in your choices, and then learn which ones work and what don't and pare them back. You can do that to screen in some extent. But you've – you're much more on a time crunch, as you would know. So, the choices have to be probably more – more – they have to be smarter. That – that you can't – you don't have the time and the luxury of making a whole lot of choices and seeing what sticks. You have to really start paring down by yourself before you get there.

And to that end, for screen, I get outside help. And again, that's part of – stemming from that conversation many years ago, I didn't for a while. But now I do. If – if – especially if it's important to me, or it's a big monologue, or it's a big scene, I will get a coach, or I'll speak to a friend if I can't afford a coach. I'll grab another actor and say, hi, what do you think about this? I will get help. For screen I definitely get more help. And I think it's invaluable. And I don't see that any more. I used to see that as like failing somehow, if you couldn't work it all out yourself. And now I'm like, no, the more the merrier.

If it's your idea, and I can implement it, great. What does it matter? I used to be so worried about the fact that if I don't come with all the ideas, I'm not a good actor. Now, I steal from everybody and anyone.

PJ How do you decide what roles to go for?

SZ So, again, it – this is an interesting question, because it's come up a bit too in the junket for *Rings of Power*. And I think the idea that you've got agency in what roles you go for – I mean, certainly in Australia, you kind of don't for a lot of your career before you get to a certain level. I think a better way to for me when I think about this question, I definitely went for pretty much anything that I was asked to audition for. But there were definitely roles where I was, like, this isn't for me.

I'll do the audition. Because you know, I just need to get work. But I could feel it wasn't for me. And that is probably a better way that if I think about this question is that there were roles that I felt like I fit and roles that

I felt like I didn't. And the roles that I felt like I didn't were often roles that – well, they were tokenistic. That obviously was some of them. Obviously, but it was some of them. And others were where I could feel like I was ticking a box to come in and be present. But I wasn't, like, why am I going for this role? It's like a different age. It's a different this. It's a different – you know, like that sort of thing. And sometimes there were just roles that to me didn't have any written – I can't quite describe it, richness I want to say, but it's not that – it's roles that were two-dimensional, especially of women. Now, I'll touch on gender again.

But two-dimensional female roles that didn't have a life and an agency and agenda of their own. You can be as – you know, I know that you're very aware – you can be a small character, but still have incredible depth and agency.

PJ The industry and your place in it?

SZ Ah, that's becoming really interesting. I'm navigating that right now; I think in a really big way. I'm navigating in being an actor of colour in a massive fantasy series that hasn't had actors of colour in it before. And some of us, such as Ismael Cruz Córdova or Sophia Nomvete are more prominent, are being held up – are being pushed more prominently as the spokespeople for that. But obviously, I am an actor of colour in the show. And I have feelings around that. And trying to navigate that. And what I want to say about that, and what I don't want to say about that, is – has been really interesting.

In part, because I also don't want to only always talk about everything to do with myself as an artist through the lens of my colour. Because I think as much as that's great, and I want to be a spokesperson for that, at the same time it's still boxing me.

It still means that all you see of me is my colour. Before it was in a negative way. Now, it might be in a positive way. But it still means that all you want to talk about is my colour and still not seeing us as whole human beings. And that's something I'm definitely navigating right now.

In (other) interviews, I've been quite circumspect, because I'm still trying to navigate it. And I know once you say certain things and they are out there in certain spaces you can't take them back. And it might open a can of worms that you're not necessarily wanting to open. I want to be very considered.

Also, I'm Australian, so I'm coming from a very different place in terms of colour than my American cousins and my English cousins on the show, and just in – in the world of acting. And so, all of that I'm navigating.

On the flip side of that, being at the forefront – not the forefront, because there's a lot of other actors of colour out there before me. But certainly being part of the zeitgeist right now is incredibly gratifying. It's really gratifying. It's gratifying not to just be watching it from outside and cheering on, which is something I've been doing for quite a long time.

It's amazing to now be amongst it. And not just for myself as Sara. But as an example, as we're discussing for other actors out there. Young actors. And also, just for people of colour, generally, and the Global Majority, generally. For my daughter, you know, that she will now see people like me on screen, and that I'm part of that. She will see me in this world. She will never be like me, who is constantly looking for a bit of representation anywhere.

PJ One of the recurring issues in the creative industries is the discussion around representation. How do you see your role in relation to that conversation?

SZ 'black' with a small b, probably.

Because of course, talking about race, even now in Australia is very fraught. And so, it's not like I was out and proud. Though, you know, internally that is what I was. Now, what's happened in the last maybe ten years or so, is that people are awakening more to race in Australia, which is great, and just generally, which is great. But what I found really interesting is that from being told, from a very young age, what I was – everyone else called me Black and called me slurs that were associated with being Black. And then I – you know, that's what I identified as. Now I find that when the conversation is happening, it's great. But I still find that now people are telling me what I am. And it's something different. So, when I say that I'm Black, there's a lot of people that go, well, you're not really. And I'm like, well, okay, so I'm Biracial. And so, then it becomes this whole thing about – or I'm a person of colour, which is all fine. I absolutely do identify with those things as well. But I guess what I found really interesting is I'm still being told by outside forces, what I can and can't call myself. And now – and fortunately, I've found in the last few years, I sometimes get confused now. Because I'm not sure if saying that I'm Black is okay any more. And what's really hard to explain in five seconds, and of course, I wouldn't, is that well, when I was growing up, there were no other Black people. So, I was as Black as it got. And – it has created, unfortunately, again, another kind of identity crisis in me, not a very deep one. I know who I am now, because I'm older. But another kind of identity crisis about what am I now allowed to call myself? Again, because of what other people say. And I find that all frustrating at times, that you're constantly having to as a person of colour, reassess, or justify what you call yourself. Rather than just being allowed to exist in a space. But yeah, I still like to say Black. But I find often I say now, person of colour. If that all makes sense.

PJ Thinking in terms of how you choose to identify, what do you think are the challenges in the acting/creative industry now?

SZ This is again, an interesting question. I always identified as Black. And as African-Australian when I was younger. And primarily – well, because my dad's from Zimbabwe, for starters. But also, because when I was growing up, and particularly I was growing up in Canberra, it was incredibly white. So, now we've got a lot of Sudanese Africans coming out. So, the African communities are growing in places like Melbourne, particularly. Some in Sydney. Quite a lot in Adelaide as well. But back then it was very, very white. So, it was Black or white, and I was Black. That's it.

I think the amazing thing about the Black American experience, which I have been following my whole life, because I grew up in a country that was a white majority, as a Black kid. And we look to America, because that was the most prominent visual example of Black people living in a white-majority country.

So, I knew a lot about Black American history. I actually studied it at university; I was that fascinated by it. Always equated with Black characters on shows when I could find them. What's interesting now, as the conversation is opening up, much, much more, is I'm now trying to find space and trying to find out the nuances of what is it like, with the Black American experience as quite a dominant force in this conversation.

What is it now like for those of us who equate with that, and there's some similarities with that, but also have our own separate experiences of being part of the Black Global Majority that are not from America. And that could be for those who are African actually coming from Black-majority countries but trying to enter these spaces. But it also could be those from white-majority countries. And what are our experiences of being Black actors and – and Black performers, that differ from Black – the Black American experience.

And that's what I've seen on the *Rings of Power*, even in these conversations, where some people are much more confident in just talking about this stuff openly at any kind of interview. Whereas as I said, I am a bit more circumspect, because I'm still trying to work it out. And I think part of that also comes from where I come from.

PJ What pitfalls should actors emerging from drama school aim to avoid?

SZ Definitely avoid thinking, as I said, that that's the end of your training. You'll be training all your life. I don't know about avoiding, but I know about things that I think that people should do, maybe I should speak about in a more positive light. I think that – look for your mentors, look for your support system.

Talk to your other actors, talk to them, talk to them, talk to them, and open those conversations. Control what you can, which is usually the text in front of you. That's usually all you can control. Don't be terrified by the fact that there's only twenty-four hours to get in a tape. I'm still terrified by that all the time. And then I just think, oh, you just do what – you just do what you can do. It's all you can – all you can do. Just do what you can – just pick a flavour. Make a choice, and just go for it. And all – and this is so easy to say because I'm terrified of it myself. But don't be afraid of failure.

Even the interview I did this morning. The fact that I was echoing all the way through it. Of course, at first, I was going, oh my God. And then I had a bit of a giggle. And then I thought, well, now I know, if I feel like I hear something funny, instead of just being polite and thinking, oh, they'll sort it out if there's a problem – just stop and say, hey, can you hear me properly? And there you go; I've got a little lesson. So, failure is not a bad thing. It can teach you things as we all know, but it's worth repeating.

And what else?

Oh, I think there is one pitfall actually, we talk a lot about being creative producers now, as an actor, we have to have all these different strings to our bow. And I think that's true. But I think that there is a pitfall in feeling like you're not doing enough if you're just an actor. I think that there are some people who are just going to be actors. And I think that that is okay. But if that's the case, then make sure that that's what you're really good at. That you work really hard on that skill and that craft. I think some people end up feeling like they're no good, because they're not writing and they're not a singer, and they're not dancing, and they're not, you know, juggling, and they can't speak three languages. And like, Jesus, give yourself a break. Like there's only so much time in a day.

I still believe that old adage that going out and living a life will actually give you so much more for your craft than anything else. I mean, after I became a mum, that was another thing that changed my whole craft entirely. Took it to a whole another level. And that had nothing to do with having fifty million different things that I can do.

I had a baby and it changed me, so therefore it changed my craft and made me a better human. So, I think that's a pitfall. I think it can – or can be a pitfall. I think it's great to do all those things if you can. Awesome. But don't feel like you're less than if you decide to just focus on one thing.

PJ What motivates you to want to act and keep doing it?

SZ Oh, communicating and storytelling is just the best. Telling stories is so important to me. Because that's how hopefully we as a society grow and change.

We as humans grow and change. We watch stories. And we either think, oh, wow, I've never thought about that before or – which is really important for people of colour and the Global Majority – is that we see ourselves, we see that we belong, we see that we're undeniably present. And that is incredibly important.

And also it just teaches us what being human is all about, I think. That we're not alone. So, in representation, but also just in existence. We're not alone. There are other mums out there. There are other older women out there.

PJ What are your broad aims for the future of your screen acting/directing presence?

To keep being seen not just for myself, but for all the – all the minorities that I am.

The female getting older. Black. Actually, Australian, you know, for the Aussie actors out there. To keep being seen for myself, but to keep being seen for all those people that I represent. All those minorities I represent, all the majorities I represent as well, you know.

To keep being part of a bigger conversation. And to just keep telling really rich stories, that even if one person watches something I do, and goes away, feeling empowered, moved, changed, happy, uplifted all those things, then – then that's what I want to do, for sure.

PJ Who are the actors and directors that have inspired you?

SZ Oh, wow. There's a lot of obvious ones like Viola Davis, for sure. Denzel Washington, just my whole life I've loved watching his work. But then I'm also interested in people like Markella Kavenagh, my daughter in the show always talks about Saoirse Ronan, I'm really interested in watching younger actors now, how they navigate spaces, because I find them quite brave. I find them quite brave in their choices and brave in some of the things that they choose to speak about. So, I'm quite fascinated by a lot of younger actors coming up.

Younger women, like Jennifer Lawrence, I found her quite fascinating to watch. That she will just be 100 per cent herself in interviews and things like that. And then she'll choose these incredible, rich roles to perform that are quite different from her persona. And I find that really interesting.

PJ If a young Black and Global Majority person of eighteen made the decision that they want to become an actor, what would your advice be?

SZ My advice would be, go for it. Definitely. We need more of you.

My advice would be similar to what I was talking about, just generally, for young actors, any actors, find your supporters, and find your allies. Don't be afraid of speaking to other actors of colour, who are more experienced than you.

I think most of us would welcome it actually, to be able to pass on advice and share ideas. You know, even if it's for five minutes, even if it's just like this, we get to chat for an hour and then we might never see each other again. Or we will see each other years from now. But like we've got stuff out of it. I think that would be definitely my advice in that – in that sense. And also look for those things – if you can't find them in your personal life, look for them online. Look for the interviews, also support – support – go to the movies, go to – go to every, you know, Black and Global Majority movie that you can, and not just about Black people, but about Mexican people or films from the Middle East. Films from Asia, go and see it. Because I mean, I remember that the Oscars, I think – was it last Oscars or the one before that had *Minari* and *Parasite*, there was like six or seven that were basically a whole bunch of different minorities.

PJ Hard-dough bread, Sourdough bread, Chin Chin, Sweetbread, Roti, Sudsa, Bun and Cheese, Nai Wong Bao -奶黄包- Custard Bun or Naan?

SZ Sudsa. But I'm pretty partial to some Sourdough to be honest. You know why? Because you can put Vegemite on Sourdough …

That's the Aussie coming out.

Abraham Popoola

Photo credit: Yellow Belly.

Abraham Popoola is an actor and writer from Hackney, London. After stints at the Young Actors Theatre and Identity Drama School, Abraham earned a place at RADA and graduated in 2016. Abraham's debut role out of drama school was as Othello in a touring production, for which he won the Stage Debut Best Actor award. Abraham has been working on stage and screen since.

Pamela Jikiemi – PJ Tell me about your journey to become an actor.

Abraham Popoola – AP I grew up in Hackney, single parent household, as the oldest of three children. And I remember I was in primary school; I must have been like eight years old, I remember when I first realized, oh, this is something I like. We were rehearsing a school play. And it was actually quite heavy; it was *The Passion of Christ*. And I was cast as Jesus. And – and I always find that very peculiar because I wish I had a time machine to go back to see what the teacher saw in me before I realized. You know, why he would cast me as Jesus.

But I remember – one of my earliest memories is being in a playground, and the teacher was trying to block the scene. And I – it was – I was interrupting him saying, no, they should stand over there. And I should be over there. And I saw the teacher look at me and see something. And at that moment, I realized that I had something. I was way too young to understand or conceive it, but I was like, oh, there's something here.

So, between the ages of eight to eleven, when I got to secondary school I realized at that point, oh, it was acting. So, as a kid, I'd be watching mainly cartoons. But I'd watched the Saturday kids' TV shows – I remember seeing, like, a very young Reggie Yates in, you know, all these kids shows and things like that. But at that point I was like, okay, I want to be in these TV shows. I have no idea how to get there. I couldn't ask my mum, she's – you know, she was an immigrant from Nigeria. We barely spoke the same language. So, she didn't understand it either. So, I did school plays whilst I was at secondary school.

I went to St Aloysius' College in Highgate. And something that's really interesting is at the time I was there, a couple years above me – when I was in year seven – in year nine was Daniel Kaluuya. In year eleven was Arinzé Kene. So, what was really interesting was in our secondary school, in year seven, there was a drama department. But by the time I got to year nine, there was no drama department. So, I couldn't pick drama as a GCSE in my secondary school, the funding wasn't there.

So, that led me to asking kids that were a bit more privileged than me – I'd heard about a drama school called Anna Scher. And by the time I went there, I think I was in college – sixth form, by the time I got to Anna Scher. And by that time, it was called the Young Actors Theatre. So, I was there for a couple of years. And that's when I learnt what agents are. Around that same time, I was also doing writing. You know, I'd write plays and like short scripts and things like that. I don't really know why I was writing them. It wasn't even necessarily to get them made; I just was writing these things.

And I think I remember there was a point when I was studying at the Young Actors Theatre, I think I must have been like sixteen, seventeen. I was at the Young Actors Theatre, and a director had come in from Poland, who was looking for an actor. And I remember this director was sent to my house through the Young Actors Theatre to come and talk to me about a role.

That was the first time anyone had ever come to talk to me about anything. I remember thinking, oh, is this how it works? It didn't work out that way. But I then realized that the Young Actors Theatre had an agency. So, that's when I was like, okay, cool. I need an agency to get into the industry. I need an agency to get me jobs, auditions. And so, I would do things like try and go to open calls, nothing ever really worked out.

Then I went to Identity Drama School. I just turned eighteen when I joined there.

It was marketed as the UK's first and only Black drama school. And it was run by Femi Oguns, and I think at that time, I was there at the same time as Letitia Wright and John Boyega. They had started maybe a year or so before me, and were agency actors. I never made it into the class where the agency actors were. And that became something I was fixated on. I was, like, I need to get onto this agency. I didn't understand the business then. And something that I found was my experience was – it was hard to determine whether or not – at the time, I thought I wasn't getting into the agency, because I wasn't good enough. And then I started to see people in the agency that hadn't trained at the school as long as I had. They just looked different. And that's when I realized, oh, there's a business element here.

Identity Drama School have a pipeline of young Black actors coming in. But of course, as a business, and unfortunately, as I saw at the time, there was an oversubscription for people that looked like me. And there were people that were coming into the drama school, who at that time looked different enough and could just go straight into the agency. So, when I learnt that I was like, okay, well, I feel like I'm not getting any better at this school. I've been there now for three years.

And with money, yes. Sometimes I'd have to like miss, a term, because I couldn't afford it. And I would go back again. So, at this point, I was, like, I need something else. I'm not getting on the agency. And I'm also not getting any better. I think I've peaked.

The teaching at Identity had some limitations. I think it was great for someone just starting out. But if you were taking it as seriously as I was taking it, you realize that they couldn't teach me much more. So, I needed more. And that's when I was like, okay, what about America? I'd heard about Tisch Art School and things like that. And at that time, I was at university studying English Literature. So, I was doing Identity part time, whilst doing this English Literature degree in Westminster and I realized I just want to get better. I'm not learning any more. Surely, there is some place that could teach me better? And I researched at that time, the actors that were most visible to me were American ones. So, I find where they trained. And they'd been at these, you know, big American, you know, conservatoires. And I was like, okay, cool. Let me apply to these American schools. Oh, $25,000 a term. I said, well – I asked my mum. My mum was like – bless her – she was like, I can't do that. But, you know, let's pray. So, I was like, okay, cool, that's definitely not going to happen. And that is when I found out about drama schools in England. So, I was twenty, when I found out there were drama schools – conservatoires in England.

My Mum said well, tell me someone we know who's doing that and earning money?

She would just tell me, Black people can't do this, is what she'd say.

My mum never saw Black faces apart from Nollywood and she didn't want that for me. So, she would tell me like, no, it's not going to happen. And my mum and I really fell out actually over this. She categorically thought that I was throwing my life away, which I'm sure is a common theme.

And I remember the second time I was applying for RADA. Obviously, she found out I had dropped out of university. So, that was another layer on top. But I remember I wrote her a letter – a plea – I wrote her a letter saying, hey mum, I know you don't think it's a thing. But look, I went to school at the same time as John Boyega. And he just did *Attack the Block*. And I think he's about to be in *Star Wars* around the time I was writing this letter. I went to school – and there's a guy called Daniel Kaluuya who's doing really good things. And if we're talking about Nigerian people, there's an actor for David Oyelowo and, like, these guys are doing this thing, mum, I promise you. Like they're older than me and they have done it. And they all went to drama school. And my mum, I thought, wasn't listening. She kind of just dismissed me, in that Nigerian mother way.

From my high school play *Lord of the Flies*, that was the first time I started to learn about, I guess, very loosely, techniques. It was very much at a very elementary level, but there I found I was able to judge how good I was based on the responses other people were giving me, compared to everyone else. Which was – which was my only source of affirmation, that I was not only good at this, but I could be exceptional at this. Because that was also really important for where I was coming from. I couldn't be average. Otherwise, mum was right. The only way I could do this is if I was incredible.

PJ Your actor training, where you trained, if you trained, why you chose to go there, how did you find the audition process – talking about your overall actor training/initial acting experiences of drama school?

AP So, this would have been 2012, when I first auditioned for drama school. And I got to the final round of RADA. Second round of Guildhall. Didn't even get past the first round of LAMDA.

And the process of going through RADA, the four rounds of auditions was the most immersed I had ever felt in acting in my life. I was around the best actors I'd ever been around in my life. And the expertise and the things I was learning, especially in the third and fourth rounds, where the third round is – you know, was a half a day workshop.

And the last round was essentially a full day of school. And that was just exhilarating. Fast forward, I didn't get in the first time. And I had dropped out of university. I didn't tell anybody. And my plan was to tell my mum, hey, I've dropped out of university, but I'm going to drama school. But that didn't work out. So, I had a year of hell. But I resolved to apply again the following year. And I got in. So, I got into RADA in 2013. I left in 2016. And I've been working ever since. Yeah.

I got into RADA at the age of twenty-two – I was able to stand out because of the experience I had up until then. My general experience of RADA in terms of the training was, I loved it, I had the best time. Because I completely surrendered to what I was being taught, I had no resistance to any part of it whatsoever. I just said, these guys know more. I just want to soak it all up. And I think because I knew I was there for three years – and I was seeing John Boyega doing things and Letitia Wright doing things. And Malachi Kirby – the people that I was walking around the same corridors with, I was hungry to join them. And so, I was like, I'm going to take every last drop of this training.

And it was amazing learning all of the different components that go into it. I didn't know there was so many classes you could take for acting. So, going there knowing there was voice and then there is movement, and then there is an amalgamation of the two. And then there's screen, and there's acting and improvisation and all of these things – dramaturgy. And I just soaked it all in. It felt like I was at Hogwarts. That's how I felt. Like I was in Disneyland. It was the best time. It was such a stark contrast to my home life, which is very much like in the ghetto.

Poverty. Like I used to have to – to shower in the morning, I would have to go to the kitchen and boil a pot of water on the stove and carry it up the stairs to shower. And that was where I was leaving and coming home to.

So, being at RADA was a holiday for me. And I think it meant that the sort of adversities, you know, in terms of, I guess, identity or psychology, mental wellbeing at RADA, I never felt them because all of it felt like – in terms of, I never felt like I was under duress – all of it felt like a holiday for me. Not that they weren't difficulties. I worked very hard. Like me, along with another guy, would always be the first ones there and the last ones to leave. And we worked incredibly hard. But it wasn't something that – I never went home upset because of school, you know, in terms of the training.

What also was interesting was, of course, the racial element. And it's still something – I'm thirty-one now, I started drama school when I was twenty-two. So, you know, almost a decade later, I'm still learning about how different I was to the people that were there. The majority of the people that were there, the types of people that have come in, the people that were teaching us. I think my views then and I guess the nature of my personality meant that I was very bull-headed, and I just sort of would do anything I needed to do to get by. So, a lot of those things kind of bounced off of me. But when I look back – I had to get the training, if this doesn't work I am back to square one.

It is like this – this has to work not only for me, but my family are relying on me. Do you know what I mean? I don't have time. But still, I was constantly calling things out, often on my own. And then thankfully, I met Joan Oliver, who was a big support to me in terms of like, when I called things out racially. And I would try to organize and get people to see, oh, look, we need to be treated the same here. Because my main motivation was like, it's already going to be hard for us when we leave. So, we need to make sure we get the same training as our white counterparts, especially when it comes to third year and the shows we perform. They get to show off in shows catered to them, and we have to fit in – fit into their thing, you know. So, I think the consequence of having a hard upbringing meant I had no fear telling people exactly how I felt about what I thought and what I saw. And I think that definitely also helped with my training. And I know we'll get there in terms of now in the industry, every other job, I'm constantly talking to producers and things like that about how we can improve what you're doing. That's always been my personality. So, if there was any sort of, you know, difficulty it would have been that path, the fight. But again, that was still a vacation compared to what I was going through at home.

PJ What did you get from your actor training?

AP So, I personally had a wonderful time at RADA. And I also believe, because of the way I carried myself and how outspoken I was, I not only got the best – the most out of the training, I was also able to benefit from it when it did get to the third year. You know, I was able to get good roles, often that were kind of similar to the outspoken nature of my character. You know what I mean? And, yeah, I think my experience of RADA was great. I saw what other experiences were, and I understood why they had them. But my own was – was great, was cool … And I think the first – the first role I got out of drama school was playing – playing Othello. And that was, for me, a great thing because one, I was put in a position to play a role with a degree of difficulty. Nowhere near as hard as playing Jesus, but a degree of difficulty, which – which meant that after finishing *Othello*, I said to myself, as an actor, I know with a bit of work there is nothing I can't do. And that came from RADA, you know. RADA gave me something, and *Othello* allowed me to prove that what I learnt works. And so, since then, there's nothing I feel I can't do. That is such an amazing gift. That my journey through drama school has given me. And, you know, going forward, that's the thing that I think I carry in my back pocket all the time, is that I can do anything if I – if I put my mind to it.

And what's been really nice is a couple years after graduating drama school, I got to work with David Oyelowo. And I told him, I wrote a letter to my mum, and I used you as an example. And he completely understood because he had been through his own version. And I sent a picture to my mum, with me and David saying, I told you. And what was really sweet is, I think it was earlier this year, she told me that she still had the letter. She said, she kept it. She kept it under a bit – under her mattress, which is, you know, really nice. But I think those are the things I think Black actors from certain backgrounds have to go through as well, even before the struggle of getting to the industry, is getting the support from your – your primary carers.

PJ What drives you? Looking at issues of employability, how do you navigate this?

AP How I navigate it is, pouring a lot of energy into creating my own work, and writing my own stories. And that's something that is very important to me and something I've done throughout so, the whole story I told about my acting career, I've been writing since I was sixteen, too. So, in – in the pandemic, I got a writing agent and I've been having endless general meetings, and I've had a couple scripts optioned. And I'm developing some now. And I have representation in America for it. So, those are things which all kind of feel like I'm in another school for that now.

You know, in regard to learning, okay, cool, this works, this doesn't work. And also seeing very, very blatantly, the very obstacles for creating Black art. Because when it comes down to it, the further up you go, eventually you are going to meet the person who has to make the decision. And they're invariably white, and rich as fuck.

I think I have to acknowledge the privilege I have at this moment in time, partly – a lot down to the hard work I have, and the talent I have, where I was able to get representation that meant that they understand my concerns, and they understand what I want to do. And the obstacles I will face as a Black actor.

I think that's imperative for anybody, any Black actor that's trying to get into the industry, and is at a point of getting an agent. If you don't have an agent that understands that you need different treatment as a Black actor to succeed, then you're relying on luck. You're relying on a lot of luck, essentially, you know.

And I think being able to be comfortable knowing that my agent will be very aware when a breakdown comes, which might be something like stereotypical, or a lateral move when it comes to like the types of roles I'm playing. And when they see an opportunity for me to play something that isn't necessarily written with my ethnicity in mind.

PJ Is your preparation for a role different for theatre and screen?

AP Yeah, it is. And it is also different from role to role. So, this is the thing that I love telling people is that going to drama school, if you soak it all up – and I remember a tutor at drama school saying this to me, I think they were talking about Anthony Hopkins. And how, Anthony Hopkins would have learnt the sort of Stanislavski method where you write it all out and … and they said, you know, but when you get to a certain age, you can just read the script and not have to write things down. It just happens in your head. And I remember at the time thinking, there's no way. No one can be that good. And you realize it's actually not that. Once you've soaked it all in, I think my – what I've realized, again, is from role to role you require different things. And part of the training is learning to trust that you know what requires what. You know, so there is some roles I've done, where I've had to do that work.

But sometimes there are some television roles and a couple of theatre roles I've done where it's like, oh, this isn't required for this role. And the thing that's made me feel like an actor more than anything else, is me trusting that I know the difference.

So, that's been one of my favourite parts of my own journey, is understanding that I've got my own method, and I'm a professional. I know, I'm no longer – I don't feel compelled to do work as if I'm in drama school. I have a – a keen eye for the project, and what is necessary and what's required. So, yeah, I guess the short answer is definitely, each thing requires different preparation.

But even within each medium, different roles require different preparation as well.

PJ How do you decide what roles to go for?

AP At the beginning, I'm at the mercy of the gods. I'll take what I can and as for theatre, because I started with *Othello* and then I was in some really high-profile productions.

I have been able to turn down more work than I take. And that's because of the privilege of – also what was incredibly important was my second or third year out of drama school, I finally was able to get a voice agent.

Again, a voice agent meant I was having income through acting, which meant I had – I didn't have to go and do a part-time job. Also, at that time, I was getting paid more – I was working consistently as an actor but I was getting paid more for voice work at that point than I was for theatre work.

So, all of my decisions about taking roles will be a balanced decision on timing. You know, do I have the space and time to do this? Will it take me out of action for something that can be better? Will it raise my profile? Or give me a really good experience to learn from?

Sometimes I've done things which don't pay very well, and won't be known. But the experience is invaluable. So, my agent will say, let's go for this, because you're going to learn something about this. So, I feel so blessed I can even have these conversations. And I'm nowhere near the point where I will get to eventually where, you know, I have – I open my door and there's a line of producers, you know, pitching the scripts.

PJ The industry and your place in it?

AP I guess, the short answer is it is all based upon building my career. If I can help it, I will say no to things. But also, if money has to be made, I will do that.

You know, but getting a voice agent was an incredible, incredible asset, which meant I could just make choices at the beginning of my career, where without that, I'd have to do things I didn't want to do, you know. Yeah.

PJ One of the recurring issues in the creative industries is the discussion around representation. How do you see your role in relation to that conversation?

AP I've always been someone that felt comfortable speaking out. And one of the reasons I speak out is because I know not everybody has my personality. I know a lot of people that I trained with, who didn't have that personality, who couldn't speak up for themselves. And I felt like they deserve to be able to have the same treatment as someone like me.

So, I think the challenges are always, I think what we have got to do is just look at any poster for any TV show or film and you can see where they put the Black people. We're always – if there's five characters we will be like, back, left or back, right. And that's generally what it always is. And that's always been something so stark to me, the fact is we're still – before we weren't there, then we were there, you know, in a very menial capacity.

And now it is a combination of that and the sidekick, the person who legitimizes the hero, all of those things. And I always see this industry and the stories we tell, I see it as a cultural war, what we do is war. Because there are people in parts of the world that have never met a Black person, but will know how to treat me based on the things they've seen. And that's why it's so important for us to be telling the right stories and to be failing in the right place, in the right way.

So, as a Black male actor, some of the difficulties I faced again, is sort of like the assumption of how intelligent or otherwise I am. Always having to overcompensate for being perceived as intimidating, being perceived as scary or stupid. You know. And if I show any signs of intelligence that is so – can be so overwhelming for someone that it almost creates an even bigger intimidation.

PJ Thinking in terms of how you choose to identify, what do you think are the challenges in the acting/creative industry now?

AP Yeah, the hope, of course, is to be able to choose roles purely – purely on the art. Purely on the content of the script. At the moment, I have an amalgamation of that. But I – the hope for every actor, of course, is to be able to say, hey, which one speaks to me the most, which one could take me somewhere.

But very few actors get to do that on a consistent basis. But that's – that's the goal. And in regard to how I see diversity right now, and my – my role and relationships – in relation to that is, for me, it's always about speaking out.

So, having to navigate those things and having to be able to – how do you be yourself without scaring people is I think a conundrum that Black people and as a Black man, I find are very much not something I want to do. I don't want to do fake laughs and, you know, hi hi and ha ha, if people don't like me, but there's a certain element of having to learn how to – I don't like the phrase, play the game. But I guess be aware of the game. Being aware of what – of what's at hand and how you are being perceived. I very rarely get to be in a space as my complete self. You know.

And that is something that I really crave working with other people like me. That's one of the big reasons. I think I've been in one production where I did a Netflix Christmas movie, which was an all-Black cast, and that was the first time I got to be me. So, those are the – I think those are the challenges of being a – of being a Black male actor. And of course, you know, not wanting to be pigeonholed, not wanting to be stereotyped. I do think things are changing in that regard. I think it's not as easy to get away with like raising stereotypes. But there's still a lot of work to be done. Because again, like we're – I want – I want to see more people like me, like us, telling stories about what it really is like to be us, you know, as opposed to a white fantasy version of what Blackness is.

PJ What pitfalls should actors emerging from drama school aim to avoid?

AP I remember thinking that people at drama school, they were like timid, white boys who wouldn't say a word, but they'd have the best experience of drama school because they were being catered for without having to say a word.

Whereas if I was quiet, I wouldn't have got what I got out of drama school. So, in the industry, my role is to continue to say things and use whatever power I have. And I think as an actor, and I think specifically, as a Black male actor, I think it's different if you're female. I think as a woman – Black women, especially, have a different experience than that. I think, as a Black man, the privilege of being a man, I use. So, being able to say things, and for people to listen and take it on board. So, I always try and do that wherever I go. And not just about race. I talk about, you know, gender politics, specifically as well wherever I can and basically trying to be the change wherever I go. So, from project to project, I'm able to leave a mark, not just on the actors around me, but more specifically, the people that make the shows. So, I've had conversations with executive producers, and, you know, the writers of the show, the crew, the cinematographer, all of those things, and just saying, when I'm in this space, when Abraham is here, there are certain things that cannot be tolerated, because he will say something. And that's kind of my – the little thing I do, which I think can make a big impact, essentially, you know. And I make it very clear, very early on what my position is. So, that's been really helpful.

I think, it's better – and I know that young actors starting out, they are not going to believe me, because I wouldn't have believed it either – but, it is better to be unrepresented than to be repped by a bad agent. Now, I don't even know if I would take that advice if I heard it, but it's true.

PJ What are your broad aims for the future of your screen acting presences?

AP I want to win all the awards. I do. I want to take it to the absolute pinnacle. I want to do it all. And I think the thing with awards; I think awards are really a shorthand for working with the best material consistently in the highest quality production.

And being able to be recognized as a brand. A brand meaning that's a good actor. You know, that's an actor that's going to – I would love for people to say, oh, Abraham is in this, I'm going to watch it. I don't even need to know what the story is about. That's my aim, you know. And – but to be able to do that across genres is the thing I want to be able to do.

PJ Who are the actors and directors that have inspired you?

AP So, Ryan Coogler. He's a young African American director who made *Black Panther* before that, and did *Apollo – Creed*, but before that he did *Fruitvale Station*.

Oh, of course, the one I recognize most is Spike Lee, like he was the first person I ever saw, who was doing this, and his films are always incredible, always compelling, always so interesting. And always so bold. The fact that he did *Malcolm X* and at the end of *Malcolm X*, he did *Nelson Mandela*, you know – you know, and it's just like, he's – he's someone that gives me courage in terms of the stories I'm telling.

He can do both. I think there's a – how do I articulate this, there's a thing around artists having to hide their true intention, so people listen. And Spike Lee does both. He will – he will put it in a film. And then at the end of the film, say, by the way, this is what I'm talking about, you know.

Viola Davis is an actor that I really respect. Denzel Washington. And of the ones who are coming now, I'm actually a really big fan of Idris Elba. I think his performances early on in his career specifically, were just – he must have done so much work, to stand out the way he's done. To build a career he's done especially with like, *Luther* specifically. I think we've kind of gotten used to it. So, remember going to see a test screen of the *Luther* movie and it blew me away. And it just reminded me of how nuanced that performance is. It is something that could have been very stereotypical. You know.

PJ If a young Black and Global Majority person of eighteen made the decision that they want to become an actor, what would your advice be?

AP I would say, do it with everything that you have, every part of the body do it. And constantly be in touch with why you love it and how much you enjoy it. Because if I think back of all the things, the joy was the thing that allowed me to go through like – especially before RADA, the constant disappointments of trying to – it took me between the ages of eight to twenty-two to get to a space where I was doing it consistently.

It was a joy that I'd find in even the small moments when I do, like, you know, a fringe play somewhere. Or I did a YouTube series. It was a joy that carried me through continuing to, like, pursue this thing. And I think if the joy isn't there, then you've got a big problem, actually. Not just whether or not you'll make it, it's harder, I'd say. But even if you do make it, I don't think you'll have a good time. It's been really interesting being in – I am in Hollywood right now. And it's been interesting, speaking to young actors in Hollywood, because there's a completely different school of thought here.

The young actors are all about how can I be noticed, so I can make it? Whereas from my perspective in the UK, it's how do I get good enough to be noticed? You know. And I think joy, the joy of what you do, will allow you to get better and better at it.

I think for Black actors, find other people to talk about this stuff with. I think that's super, super important. And I guess specifically pitfalls. I think when you're asked to name one; I think your – your gateway into the industry, being with the right agent, that's where most of the pitfalls will come from.

If you're on a production and an issue comes up, you need to know that your agent will understand and back you. And your agent will trust them enough to put you right if you're in a wrong.

But if you're in a situation of paranoia, it's not going to be good. You need to have some sort of safety when it comes to dealing with this big old world. They are the – they're the point of contact you have; they are the gateway.

PJ Hard-dough bread, Sourdough bread, Chin Chin, Sweetbread, Roti, Sudsa, Bun and Cheese, Nai Wong Bao -奶黄包- Custard Bun or Naan?

AP My actual favourite absolutely is Hard-dough bread. I put it in the microwave with some jam, and some butter and I am – I'm in heaven. And I have been known to go through whole loaves in one night. So, that's why I've said I can't – I can't do Hard-dough bread any more. Yes, Hard-dough bread.

CHAPTER 7
JENNIFER LIM, CYRIL NRI, CORNELL JOHN AND LEO WRINGER

Keywords/concepts: Film → character → writing → training → people → imagination

Never does a story tell only a singular tale. Look closer. Closer. A story is a story of many, and the tale it will tell is one that spans ages.

Esmie Jikiemi-Pearson, (2023) *The Principle of Moments*, p. 115.

Jennifer Lim

Photo by Ivan Weiss.

Jennifer Lim is an actor, filmmaker, theatre maker and artistic director of Moongate. Theatre credits include *Worth* (Arcola/Storyhouse Chester); *Dreamers* (Omnibus); *The Key Workers Cycle – Midwives Story* (Almeida); *Freedom Hi!* (Vaults); *World Factory* (HOME); *Citizens of Nowhere* (Edinburgh/Southbank Centre); *Wild Swans* (Young Vic and American Repertory Theatre); *The Good Person of Setzuan* (National Theatre) and *Into the Numbers* (The Finborough). Film credits include *British People – The Uncertain Kingdom Anthology, I'm Not In Love, A Monster Calls, Hostel, Act of Grace, When Evil Calls, Piercing Brightness, Code 46, The Monster Beneath* and *Leviathan* by award-winning artist filmmaker Shezad Dawood. Television credits include *Holby City, The League of Gentlemen, Spirit Warriors* and *Strangers*.

Pamela Jikiemi – PJ Tell me about your journey to become an actor.

Jennifer Lim – JL I did part of my growing up in Singapore, and part of it in Britain. You know, at the time, I think when I was growing up there was this film called *The Joy Luck Club* and there were these amazing women that kind of look like me on screen. And you just think, 'Oh, that's amazing'. But then, it was a bit like, you know, it comes around once in a very, very blue moon, English-speaking Asians on screen. Do you know what I'm saying? There was Tsai Chin, I will say that she was like a role model – well, not a role model, but she was there, she was very, very visible, and you can count on your fingers who else. And then there were people like Lucy Liu, and Ming Na Wen, but it's still very western-centric. And then, of course, also, I love Chinese films as well. There's Gong Li in those Zhang Yimou films, and so Gong Li was like, for me, Oh, wow, I want to be like her. Then the reality bites, you know, the kind of work and roles that you get offered here in the UK, you will very rarely get an opportunity to do those kind of roles where you are put front and centre of things. Where it's all about you, portraying a slice of humanity. And so it was just kind of weird, really, there's a dissonance with the reality of the work you get offered. So yeah, I mean, those were the sort of like, people I kind of looked up to and think, Oh, I don't mind having a bit of that.

I mean even now, there are still people that I kind of look up to, some of them are for me more inspirational in the sense that it makes me feel like, Oh, it is doable. And some of it there's still that kind of, like, Oh, is it, like, a bit of a pipe dream? How can I kind of make that happen? You know?

So Tsai Chin, she's had a remarkable career. She was one of the mothers in *Joy Luck Club*. And before that, this was way before my time, and I didn't know until much later, but she was in those Fu Manchu films playing Fah Loh Suee. And her range is just remarkable, you know. And the thing about Tsai, I had the good fortune of meeting her by chance in Singapore. one time when we were out there, and she was staying with someone we know. And she knows Daniel, by the way, she helped Daniel with his break in a way. He was doing a play at the Etcetera Theatre years ago and she came along, saw it and I think, put him in touch with an agent or something like that. Anyway, when I met her, she was just so refreshingly wonderful and honest. And, you know, she was, like, she said to me, she said that 'look, you know, the thing is …' when she was younger Brando made a pass at her. And she basically said 'No!' He said something like 'Do you want to do some rumpy pumpy?' and she's said, 'No!' I just love that she's aware of who she is, as a woman, and yet she's also aware of the power of 'No'. That is so amazing and remarkable. And she has had an amazing life. I think at one point, she ended up like waiting on tables in America, you know, before she got *Joy Luck Club*.

PJ That's funny, the power of 'No', which is diametrically opposed to how Asian women were historically portrayed in films.

JL I think the power of 'No', it's just so potent. I think people don't realize that enough. Even as actors, as actors when you say 'No', that's the power you have. People think that actors are at the bottom of the hierarchy. But oh no, you actually have the power to say 'No', 'No, I'm not going to do that piece of crap'.

And with young actors as well, they could get blindsided by the fact that 'oh, you've got a casting with a very well-known casting director, but you're going to play a bad stereotype or you don't have any lines' … Actually, you don't have to take the role if you don't want to. You can say, 'No, thank you', and that is your power.

Also, there's something about doing something you don't want to do eating into your psyche. As an artist, it can eat into your soul. I have turned work down in the past. I remember a BBC TV series that I got offered. And it wasn't a great part. So I basically said no, and also because I had a real problem with the programme itself, with the script, with the portrayals of Chinese people and the white gaze of geopolitics. And I was like, no, I don't want to do it.

Recently, someone got in touch regarding a short film. I read the script, and they said, they couched it in a way … telling me, 'so the culture and language play a central part, it's a lead role'. I read it, I thought, what a lot of bollocks … it is basically playing a brothel madam, in a very stereotypical way, and there is this whole kind of like, hyper sexualization of women. And I was like, No! No! No! I feel that at the very least, you walk away with self-respect, you know, and that's so important as an artist, and as a woman of colour.

PJ Training around learning 'the craft'; did you go to a conservatoire drama school? Talk about your creative career and your commitment towards pursuing it.

JL So I studied Theatre Studies and Drama at A-levels and then took the route to drama school. I was given an opportunity go to Bretton Hall, which was then part of the University of Leeds; and I went to Bretton, and found that it just wasn't for me. There were lots of elements about being at Bretton that just didn't work for me. Apart from the fact that you're so cut off from everywhere else. Don't get me wrong, the people there were great – people were nice, but I was like, the only East Asian person in my group.

I stayed for about three or four months. I was doing Theatre Arts at the time. The course included devising, commedia dell'arte, making theatre … We also did a lot of text work on Shakespeare. I felt it was very, very British. The training felt very focused on technique, history and the theory side of things, which I found really interesting. But I found it quite challenging when it came to doing lots of devised work. I think devised work is such a tricky art form anyway, you know, it depends on the kind of people that you're in the room with, especially so if they're not people you've chosen to work with; and when these people tend to be quite cliquish as well, then it can be very difficult you know, you feel that your voice just isn't heard. And I think it's very hard to work in that way, when you feel that you're always fighting to get your voice heard, or when you kind of, like, seize the opportunity to say something, and then it gets dismissed or disregarded. I find it really tricky. Yeah.

And I didn't gel at the time, you know, with the whole kind of like, the culture of, you know, hanging out at the Student Union bar all the time. And, and I found it really difficult. I had a very tough time settling into Bretton. So I ran away to London, I literally ran away and I caught up with some friends who kind of managed to find me a place in Bayswater. I literally just turned up in London, a friend of a friend said, oh, there's this place going, you know, Bayswater, should I take you over to see it? And then you can see if you like it.

I then enrolled myself into the Lee Strasberg Studio in London, because prior to that I did a couple of years at a drama school in Singapore, which was run by teachers from Britain anyway. So, it was a very British drama school kind of model in terms of the way they ran it. And I was very interested in finding out more about the American stuff, like the method system of acting.

I stayed at the Lee Strasberg Studio for three years, it wasn't like a strict drama school system where you have to turn up every single day. I was turning up three to five times a week for scene studies, stage combat, voice classes and all that. I kind of stuck with it, because it allowed me, at the same time while I was taking classes at Lee Strasberg Studio, to actively find work as an actor. So, I found that that supported me at the time, because I was able to kind of keep my acting muscles, constantly, actively being flexed. And to me acting is like a muscle. I was in that studio, whereby I was able to kind of still be in training and at the same time enabling me to go out and find work because I was just so impatient. Pamela, I was so impatient to work. I just wanted to land a job, do you know what I'm saying? And I thought I was such a know-it-all and I was like, Oh, wow! I can do this, you know.

And I feel now that I was a bit of a maverick, you know, but obviously at the time, I didn't think of myself like that. I was literally hustling all the time. Do you remember *PCR*? I remember *PCR*, I was constantly looking at *PCR*, *The Stage*, you know, trying to find work all the time.

And at the time, I was with an agent. The agency name was so mad, right? I mean, this agency was called Oriental Casting and now they would never have got away with it, with a name like that. And it was really interesting. I started getting quite a bit of work. You know, through them, mainly commercials, some short films, I got a few feature films as well. And then I felt like, I wanted to move away from that kind of ethnic casting bracket, not for anything else, but simply for the fact that I felt like I was just being seen for my ethnicity.

I wanted more than that, I wanted to do theatre, but they weren't very keen on me doing theatre. So I made a deliberate choice to kind of move away from them, and I found another agent. So then, this other agent was great and lovely from LWA, she's not there any more, she retired and passed me on to another agency. I was still not getting much theatre work. And then I ended up doing this film called *Hostel*, it's a horror film, you'll know it if you're into horror, it has kind of become a cult classic. I felt at the time that they weren't very supportive of me. There was a phase back when East Asian actors were kind of flavour of the month. And they just ended up bringing on lots of other East Asian actors on their books for that and then getting rid of them when the work dried up.

I was like, can I do more theatre please? Nothing, nothing. And then I kind of moved away from them. I wrote and found another agent. And moving agents is quite a traumatic process for me, because I don't like moving agents. And then I found my current agent, who I've been with for a long, long time now. Who's great. And she has been very supportive. She is the first agent and the only agent that I've known who actually allows me the autonomy to have control in the sense that I don't have to do anything I don't want to. She gives me the choice, which I find very refreshing because for once I suddenly realized that I'm being treated like an adult here. You know, because oftentimes, I think we have a very unequal relationship with agents. And it's like you think you have to accept everything that they pass on to you. She is the only agent I know who actually says to me, 'Oh, darling, this has come through for you, would you like to do it?' So I actually have the opportunity to kind of say yes or no. And that's great. She has been very supportive. So in that time, I have also started producing my own stuff and doing my own work and she's been great about it. So, so that's my sort of, like, journey in a potted history. And I'm kind of, like, doing lots of various things at the moment.

PJ What did you get from your actor training?

JL Do you know what was really interesting was the fact that at the time, I found the Lee Strasberg work quite positive, because I felt like it kind of helped me access my emotions. And I needed that because I find that although the British system is great, it tends to get very head bound, it's about analysis and all that stuff. Or maybe it was just me finding my way, finding my own way in acting itself. And I found the method useful in the sense that I was able to access emotions and working it with text although at the same time, I had real problem applying some of the teachings. I didn't quite understand how sense memory could help me when I'm doing a scene, it just felt like, it's going to take me out of the moment. And so in terms of the exercises, it was good; it kept me in shape, it gave me the chance to be with other actors. But I didn't really find my own 'system' until like, five or ten years ago, really. I suddenly realized, ah, this is what acting is about, it takes twenty fucking years, you know, when you finally understand what it means to be an actor, and what works for you and not to be afraid to actually say, you know what, something's not for me, thank you, or I'm going to borrow a bit of it. … I'm going to be a magpie, I'm going to take this, and I'm going to adapt that, and I'm going to make it my own. But at that time, I just wanted to experience everything, really. In hindsight, that allowed me to kinda have a global picture, and then after that I feel you're able to say, Ah, okay, this is for me. Or that's not for me.

PJ What drives you? Looking at issues of employability, how do you navigate this?

JL I think deep down innately I love acting. I've always wanted to be an actor, you know, I think the joy of inhabiting a character, of being someone as far away from myself as possible; I mean, that's what really, really drives me … getting to grips with challenges, or something that kind of pushes me beyond my comfort zone.

I think that drives me too. I set sort of little challenges for myself every single time – little things that only I am aware of, you know … it might be a character thing. It might be an accent thing. It might be something I want to do, something that pushes me, that takes me beyond what I'm comfortable with. That's what drives me, or doing something that I've never done before, that I'm afraid of … I think fear. Fear drives me as well – what can I do to actually surmount that fear? Like exposure therapy in a way … It's a fear that I can't do it, a fear that I'm not good enough, you know, a fear that I'm going make a fool of myself. A fear that … actually, do you know what? … I can live with that fear of not being good enough as long as I take the plunge. At least I know, for myself … I think it's the fear that I'm never going to experience it and I'm never going to find out. So I think that answers your question? That's what gets me up in the morning. And why I still want to do it is the fact that I also deep down even though I think the situation in terms of diversity has moved on a little, I think there's still room to go further. And I think, I think that's something that I'm really, really interested in kind of pushing, as well.

But from an acting point of view, I think is to go into new territories, so to speak. For the first time in my life, I finally acted a role in a northern accent.

So, it's just sort of pushing myself beyond my own comfort zones. Also when lockdown happened – I had never read an audiobook before that, and then I started doing audiobooks. It didn't even cross my mind that I could do it before then. And then it was like 'Oh actually, I can do this', you know, and I also believe that whole Bill Gates thing about '10,000 hours of practice' …

I think deep down the very, very bottom line for me is that my craft is really important to me. So, I think the driver is how to hone my craft and make it better and better. And I would do 10,000 hours of anything, if that kind of you know, pushes me forward; and if that makes me a better, more rounded performer or actor or creative.

PJ Is your preparation for a role different for theatre and screen?

JL Yes, and no, I think for me, I always start off with the character. That's homework I can always do by myself. Research – in terms of the character, what they do, and also the world of the play, or the film … These are the areas that cut across both theatre and film and there's learning my lines, obviously.

I think the privilege of doing theatre is that you get to do it again and again and again, you've got the rehearsals and all that, and then you get to play in front of an audience and you're able to flex your performance every night and make it slightly different, being alive in the moment. So that is great. I think for theatre it's about how do I stay 'live' in the moment, every single time, you know, and be aware of the other actors as well. I think for film, beyond the initial stages of research and knowing your character and learning your lines and all that, for me it's more like, because everything is shot out of sequence – how do I preserve that focus, that concentration and not get pulled in other directions and get distracted? Which can be quite difficult sometimes. It's that focus of centring yourself, when you're on set. Obviously, with the cameras, changing lenses in between and depending on how it's shot, whether the scene is shot continuously with no break like in a Bela Tarr film … then you just do it once, Or if you are doing the usual with a master, close-ups, reaction shots and all that; then you have to do it again and again. And then there's shooting out of sequence as well … So keeping a sense of continuity in your mind, knowing what comes before and what comes after, which you don't have to take care of when you're doing theatre.

PJ How do you decide what roles to go for?

JL You know, that's a really good question to ask, because that implies 'choice'. And I think there are times when you don't get a choice or it's Hobson's choice? It's what is presented in front of you.

I know very well what I don't want, but I also know very well what I do want. You know, I think I – I'm always looking for a three-dimensional, rounded character. I don't care if it's a protagonist or antagonist … If it's nuanced, if it's a three-dimensional character, and if it's well written. I think the script is really important. So that's another strong criteria for me. It's got to be a really well written script. And who's directing it? You know, like who the team is? Yeah … and I guess in terms of finances, that probably plays rather low down on my list, and I probably shouldn't be saying this … But those are the key considerations for me, when it comes to decision making.

PJ One of the recurring issues in the creative industries is the discussion around representation. How do you see your role in relation to that conversation?

JL About ten or so years ago, we set up a little company called Moongate. And, and that was in response to the whole RSC production of the *The Orphan of Zhao*. And also, you know, the year before that I was in *Wild Swans* at the Young Vic, where it was the first time we had, like, a full East Asian cast on the main stage of a major London venue, and then for the RSC to do that after was very regressive. So, we decided to form our own theatre company, and we produced a play called *The Fu Manchu Complex*. And so I think, from my point of view, as a creative, as a producer, my place in it is to kind of, like, ensure that I do my part in keeping that going in my own little way?

I remember that when we ended up producing our second play *Forgotten* 遗忘 about the First World War Chinese Labour Corps written by Daniel York Loh, I had a fight with the director because they wanted to bring on a non-ESEA lighting designer without even wanting to consider this very talented lighting designer who's East Asian and female. And she's very, very good. So I fought for her. I had a huge row with the director to get her to be considered, and we ended up employing this very exciting East Asian lighting designer. And this lighting designer has since gone on to win awards and she is in high demand right now. So I guess my place in it as a creative is to constantly open doors when I can, when it's within my power and allow other East and South-east Asian creatives to come through. My place as an actor … of course, as an actor, you're far more limited in what you can do in terms of the power that you have, but you still have power. I think, to actually say 'no' to certain parts … I think that's the only way I can send a message out to say 'that is not good enough' and I don't want it. And I think, also as an actor, is to kind of ensure that this whole diversity conversation grows and evolves, right? I think that we have to grow and evolve with it as well, and get in with the nuances of it. And actually, not settle for just quantity. But for quality too. What is 'quality diversity', you know, and what is 'quantity diversity'? Having a stage or a screen full of bodies looking like you does not mean that it's 'diversity'. Sometimes, on the contrary, it's down to the kind of parts you play, the type of parts you play, and how do you affect the narrative … And I think we have to ensure that we don't get complacent. I know there are admittedly more doors being opened, but deep down are they real changes that you want to see? And more perceived 'opportunities' don't mean that we've 'smashed the ceiling'. We haven't and we have to keep on at it up to the point where there's absolute parity.

There are productions like *Miss Saigon* and *My Neighbour Totoro*. It's great. Lots of people get employed, but then that is not the apex of the representation that we need. Actually, within that diversity, we need diverse offerings of that diversity. There needs to be more representative stories, the stories we need to see more of and they need to capture our presence more truthfully and humanize our portrayals.

Out of the Black Box

You know, usually when it comes to ticking boxes and all that about identity the choices are East Asian, or Chinese and it kind of negates the complexities of our identities. Because what does Chinese mean, you know? I'm ethnically Chinese, nationality wise, I'm not Chinese.

By that I mean, I've got roots in Singapore, I'm Singaporean Chinese. I think ideally, I would like to identify as a London-based Singaporean Chinese or British Singaporean Chinese. Yeah.

PJ Thinking in terms of how you choose to identify, what do you think are the challenges in the acting/creative industry now?

JL I feel like there's a lot of, sort of lip service being paid, you know, to diversity. I still think that there aren't enough roles for East and South-east Asian people, you know, across the spectrum in terms of ages. So I think one of the challenges is that … I seriously think about longevity, as an actor, especially as a female actor. I mean, we probably get lots of offers, you know, in our twenties, or we have to wait till we're sort of like in our sixties or seventies … but in between, sort of like the thirties, forties, fifties, even …. I don't think there are enough presentable roles. And also, in terms of our own stories written by people from our own communities, so to speak, the East and South-east Asian communities are actually very diverse … I mean, at the moment, if you look at what's happening, you know, on our stages at the moment, I mean, it's like, why can't we commission a South-east Asian musical theatre writer to write something? Why not? Do you know what I'm saying? So it's like, writers are not getting that opportunity.

PJ There's a whole funding thing as well, you know, who they give the money to … And I think there is a bit of divide and rule politics going on … So how do we ensure that all stories get a level playing field in terms of funding and getting them told? I think that there are quite a lot of complex challenges coming up, you know, in terms of the East and South-east Asian sector, I'd say.

No, I tell you what I mean, Pamela, because I said to you that I recently did this thing where I had to use the northern accent? So I did a lot of research and watched a lot of stuff, like dramas set up north, and I ended up watching *Happy Valley* and *Gentlemen Jack*. And I was like, 'Wow, they are amazing!' Admittedly, *Happy Valley* is a great series. But where is the representation in the actors? Chinese and BESEA actors never ever get parts like that and it upsets me. You know why? We never ever get parts like Catherine Cawood, and there was only one tiny part in series one for a BESEA actor, Micky (a Chinese character) was a friend of Catherine Cawood. But he was just such a tiny character. I couldn't believe my eyes. I was like there's barely any Black characters in it. You know, barely any Chinese as well … You know I was like … I mean it was a sort of moral quandary for me, because a part of me really likes the writing. I really like the drama, but at the same time, I was like, it's not representative. Truly integrated casting is still very, very rare.

PJ What pitfalls should actors emerging from drama school aim to avoid?

JL Okay … I feel that actors just emerging from drama schools are actually in a pretty vulnerable position. You know, albeit, that is a very exciting time for them … And I'll say that one of the pitfalls is, actually … going back to what I said earlier … have a sense of who you are, what you want to do. And don't let your agent run your career, not to be afraid to say no to certain stuff if you're not comfortable with it. Not to be afraid to speak up if needs be and not to feel obliged to say yes to everything, you know, and literally be strong about it and know what you want. And try to find a way …

If I were to answer that question in a direct way, I will say that, in terms of one of the pitfalls for me personally when I first started acting … is the fact that, um, try not to have your identity too tied up with acting. You're actually a complex being, you're not just an actor. Be a creative and enjoy doing other creative stuff as well. You know, to feed you, to feed your soul. And, also because when you tie your identity up so tightly with acting, when rejections inevitably come and they come to every single one of us, that will affect your mental health and you need to look after that.

PJ What motivates you to want to act and keep doing it?

JL What motivates me is partly because I don't know how to do anything else. This is what I have wanted to do since I was seventeen … what motivates me is to have the opportunity when it comes along, to escape into other characters. And acting on stage, on screen, is a little like a drug, isn't it? I feel like you know what I'm saying … when you've been on stage or on screen, it's like 'wow, you're so wired'. You don't need to sleep for three days, you're high on it … I think it's not very healthy. But knowing the pitfalls changed it for me in a way … So now, I kind of like, ensure that I've got other things around me to ground me. I know that when it comes I'll enjoy myself, and then you know … and then I'll just have to wait until it happens again. But in the meantime waiting, during the resting period, I've got other things to occupy my mind, you know, and hopefully continue to do something creative.

PJ What are your broad aims for the future of your screen acting/directing presence?

JL My 'screen acting presence' is such a lofty term (LOL) … if I have a choice, I would like to play some really interesting complex characters, you know, and if I have to write it myself, I will. And if I have to shoot it myself, and find the money and get a crew together, I will. So that's what I'd really love to do, something fulfilling.

PJ Who are the actors and directors that have inspired you?

JL Gong Li … there're so many others as well. I mean, recently, from a creative point of view, honestly, someone like Shonda Rhimes really kind of like inspires me, her as a showrunner … the fact that she created *Bridgerton* – I think that's amazing, to kind of buck the trend, actually takes risks. I mean, she basically changed the whole way we perceive period drama and the place that people of colour have in history. She did that through *Bridgerton*. And I think that's amazing. How many people would dare to do that, you know?

So, um, she's definitely one of them. And other people that I look up to are people like, Claire Denis, she's a French film director. She's in her seventies. But she's still going strong, she still makes films. And I love that … And Juliet Binoche, as an actor. I love her. I love French films because I love the fact that they make films with middle-aged women who are still seen as desirable, or maybe not desirable, but they can still have sex. We see humanity being portrayed on screen that is so often ignored, you know, on our screens a lot of the time.

I love French films … that celebration of womanhood and not being afraid of ageing, and all that. And just because I've been watching so much Sally Wainwright at the moment … I do think she's a fantastic, phenomenal writer. But I think she needs to do some work on including representation. In terms of implementing more diversity and presenting more diversity in her work …

PJ We should approach her, Jennifer.

JL Yeah, maybe I should drop her a line? (Laughs)

PM If she doesn't get any feedback from anyone else saying, Oh, we love your work, we would really like to see more representation in the casting choices, she probably thinks that she hasn't got the audience, of that demographic, but she would have if the actors in the roles were more representative, I'm a mum, not a Black mum?

JL Yeah, no, you're absolutely right. Yeah. I will. (Laughs)

There're so many, you know, I mean … I love films by Bergman, Haneke, Yorgos Lanthimos, Tarkovsky, Kieslowski … But yeah, there're quite a few people who inspire me.

PJ If a young Black and Global Majority person of eighteen made the decision that they want to become an actor, what would your advice be?

JL My advice would be … have an open mind, be willing to experience as many things as possible. And I'm speaking from experience here, because many, many, many moons ago I wrote a script. And I sent it to a producer, who at the time was at a company called Spirit Dance. I think Forrest Whitaker had something to do with it. Yes. I sent it to Johanne … And he read it over Christmas. And he got back in touch with me. And he said to me, I love your script. I would like to put you in a room, in a writers' room. And I was terrified. And I said, No. I said, I'm an actor … And I should have said Yes! You know? I know … I know … And then I think what I learned was that about ten years ago, ever since Moongate, I started saying yes to things. I started saying yes to producing things – I curated an exhibition in Singapore, I became a filmmaker as well. I became a hyphenated, you know, sort of, like, hyphenated identity. Yeah. And that does not make me less of an actor … Also, keep an open mind, be open to as many experiences as possible, because they feed into you as an actor as well. You need that reservoir of experiences to draw from, you know, when you're playing a part. And to say yes when it feels right, and have the courage to say no when it doesn't, or when you're asked to kind of compromise yourself in any way, as an artist or as an actor … like if you're asked to put on a silly accent, or you're asked to play a stereotypical part that is going to cause more harm, you know, than good for the wider community … Then that's what I'll say and also fill your life with lots of creative activities to feed your soul.

PJ Hard-dough bread, Sourdough bread, Chin Chin, Sweetbread, Roti, Sudsa, Bun and Cheese, Nai Wong Bao -奶黄包- Custard Bun or Naan?

JL Ha! It's got to be Nai Wong Bao. That's Cantonese custard bun. Oh, Pamela. I mean, I hope to see you at some point, I will bring one for you. It's to die for actually … Or a cocktail bun which is filled with coconut filling, but coconut or custard …

I love custard. So Nai Wong Bao is great for me. Yes, that's the one.

Cyril Nri

Photographer: Tyler Fayose.

Cyril Nri's work spans film, television and theatre. Cyril can be seen in Netflix's *Queen Charlotte: A Bridgerton Story*, as well as Amazon's *The Power*. In 2002, Cyril played British TV drama's highest ranking black police officer, Superintendent Adam Okaro, in long-running series *The Bill* and won the 2003 Best TV Actor EMMA and 2004 MVISA Best TV Actor awards for the role. Cyril's film credits include Thea Sharrock's *Wicked Little Letters*, Robert Zemeckis's remake of *The Witches*, and James Gardner's critically acclaimed *Jellyfish*. Cyril has worked in some of London's most renowned theatres including the National Theatre, the Young Vic and the Royal Court, alongside a multitude of exciting, talented directors including Nancy Medina, Richard Eyre, Tinuke Craig and Simon Godwin.

Pamela Jikiemi – PJ Tell me about your journey to become an actor.

Cyril Nri – CN I started at school; I had done stuff at school even when I was in Nigeria as a very little kid.

We – me and my sisters took part in a Nigerian programme, which was akin to the British television programme that was shown here, which was called, *Why Don't You Just Switch Off Your Television Set and Go and Do Something Less Boring Instead* (in the UK it was produced by Kirstie Fisher and Pam O'Brien and directed by Russell T. Davis). So we used to be in the alternative to that programme in Nigeria – I was less than six, like a four-year-old or whatever. I wasn't really interested in acting or performing or anything, I was just a kid going along with my sisters to take part in whatever.

And then, arriving here. I was at school. And I wanted to do a production. I was at Holland Park at this time, in secondary school. And I had taken part in a production of *Zigger Zagger* (written by Peter Terson), as one of the members of the crowd, and the leads were played by the sixth formers.

Out of the Black Box

I remember at the end of that show – I think it was only on for less than a week, four days or something like that – at the end of the run they had a party. And I really wanted to go to the party. But I was still a little kid, I was eleven. My mum wasn't going to have me go with these seventeen-year-olds, to a party! So, I wasn't allowed to go. So acting as such, that just went to the back of my mind.

A couple of years later, I was thirteen, when my parents were splitting up, and my dad had come over to England, trying to get me and all that sort of shit. You know, just parental break-up. He was still in Nigeria. My dad he's Igbo, he's from the east. My mum whose Bajan (Barbados) was here with us. So all that happened. And it was a major trauma in my life. Anyway, I used to go to school early, having done my paper round. And I would end up just sort of crying in corners of the school, you know, pre eight o'clock in the morning. And a teacher saw me one day and wondered what was wrong and started inquiring, and I wouldn't tell him much. But he said to me, well, whatever it is, you'll find examples of it within the pages of this book. Why don't you have a read? And it was the complete works of William Shakespeare. Anyhow, I read a couple. And yeah, he was right. Every single human condition is within those thirty-six plays, and that got me interested. I then started doing after-school drama with that teacher, Tony Fagan, and Linda Oakley, who sadly passed on. And then I was in my fifth year at secondary school. By then, I was sixteen or something like that.

And they had an audition for this thing called *The Threepenny Opera* (written by Bertolt Brecht). Which I still have the poster for it hanging on my wall.

I went and auditioned for that. And I got the lead, Macheath. And it sort of started from there. I had a whale of a time, and suddenly, I was out of wanting to do sciences and become a pilot. I was doing Drama and English, and – much to the annoyance of both my parents it must be said, but particularly my dad who came over and you know, wanted to read the riot act.

Yeah, you know, with Nigerian and Bajan parents. That doesn't wash. So – in either accent, it doesn't wash. The joy of that was that was though they'd been deeply in love and then not deeply in love – not hate really. But you know – whatever, so the fact that he disagreed meant that she was okay.

And my attitude towards him was, well, you know, who are you? I don't know, who are you? You know, you haven't been around in my life for years, you know.

And now you are trying to tell me what to do. I don't know you. Other than an attempt to kidnap me at eleven, you know, basically I don't know who you are. So – so, yeah, so that sort of decided that. And I went on from there.

I joined three youth theatres, the Royal Court Young Activists, the Old Vic Theatre – Youth Theatre, and also the Young Vic Theatre. That was me three nights a week, I was out, you know, and doing that. And then eventually, just before going to drama school, in fact – about a term before going to drama school, I got into Anna Scher, which had a long waiting list and stuff. I sort of went, yeah, you know, feast or famine. And I was fully in this business.

I got into three – I tried for three drama schools. And I got into all three. At that point, you know, you couldn't – I mean, I was poor, you know, having gone from quite – I suppose quite a rich sort of status in – in the early 60s in Nigeria, you know, very middle to upper class, I suppose. To refugee status here. Living in, you know, Shepherd's Bush then, Barons Court in Fulham. You know, and single mum. But she managed to get us all – all of us through, to university education-type stuff. And so, I was – I was a bit of an anomaly, you know, deciding not to go to uni and deciding to go to drama school.

So, was doing my paper round and my Saturday job, which was mainly to buy me clothes that, you know, I wanted to wear. Because single mum, you know, you got Woolworths best.

PJ Training around learning 'the craft'; did you go to a conservatoire drama school? Talk about your creative career and your commitment towards pursuing it.

CN I auditioned for Bristol Old Vic Theatre School (BOVTS), because my sister was at Bristol University, then I auditioned for LAMDA, and I auditioned for Central and yeah, RADA. I met a girl that had gone to RADA and I didn't like her. So, I thought I'm not going there, It's obviously full of I don't know what …

But, anyhow, at that point, I was getting into a little trouble in London. So, I decided I was going to BOVTS. I also thought BOVTS was the best audition. You know, it was the only one that I could see where they actually decided on you, you know. Because they had the weekend school and I remember it cost £13, the others cost £10, at the time. I don't know what it costs, now. It's probably hundreds to audition now.

I remember thinking, well, the difference is that LAMDA – they did a recall. But it was only like half a day. And Central did a recall but that was like, hardly anything and then BOVTS did a whole weekend where they took you through – with most of the teachers there, and then they decided and I thought, you know, this is a serious school, and they decided on you. They are seeing how you're working across the board, then they are all discussing it, and I thought, yeah, I'm going there. And also, I wanted to get out of London because I was getting in little bits of trouble you know, I mean, yeah, it was just where I went to school, you know, it's Holland Park – Ladbroke Grove is up the road, Shepherd's Bush down the road, everything's – had the potential to start getting a bit serious.

And mum had a couple of mantras, one of which was don't bring police to my door.

And I just thought, yeah, it's time to get out of London, do something somewhere else. And – and I just thought the school was classical. It was almost a way of saying, okay, mum, okay, dad, I have chosen not to go to uni. But look, it's a classical training. It's a serious school, My eldest sister was at Bristol University. So, I stayed with her on that BOVTS weekend long recall. And it was cool. It was a good place – it was a good place to go. There were bits of that, that I regretted later, about BOVTS. But there were also great bits too.

PJ What did you get from your actor training?

CN I would say, I had to rebel to succeed. In those days – and I talked about this at a talk I gave at BOVTS. In those days, really, there was one Black male, one Black female per year.

I remember being told when we did a group exercise – and there were, I think eight males in our group of thirteen, something like that. Anyhow, everybody else got to have a go at the lead in this particular exercise in this play that we were working on, a vast thing.

And I got to be the brass salesman. And when I said, why am not getting a go at the lead part? They said, oh, well, you won't be cast in that part anyhow. And I went, what?

And they reiterated that I wouldn't be cast in that part.

And I thought, okay. So, I bunked off …

I went and did a play externally. I joined the Bristol University Student Union; I'd been there, watching plays at the university drama department. They had put on a play. And I remember being in the audience, and there was a guy called Jeremy Brock, who later went on to write the screenplay for John Madden who directed (1997) *Mrs Brown* and co-wrote the screenplay with Peter Morgan for Kevin Macdonald's (2007) *The Last King of Scotland*, as well as various others.

Anyway, he was watching this show, too. And we both left at halftime. We met in the pub. And I said, oh, you were in the audience, he said, yeah, I thought that was shit, and I said, yeah, I thought it was shit too, you know. He then said, I have written this play, you should come along and audition. And I said, where? And he said, at the University Student Union. I said, yeah, okay. I'll see, you know, if I am free. And, I went along.

There's a guy called Simon Curtis who, you know, was directing at the Royal Court later on, and I'd met Simon in London before I had gone to drama school. I'd audition for Peter Gill, at Riverside for a Tunde Ikoli retrospective. They were doing a series of five Tunde Ikoli plays and I had gotten the part. But then I had the dilemma of I'm about to go to Bristol. Because they (The Riverside) had left it a long time, I was in the school play which I'd written part of, a play called *Regarding the Label, Displaced Person*, which was about war children, refugees. I'd written quite a lot of this play in relation to be Afro and Nigerian.

And I was in this play. And because they had taken so long at Riverside, I was in this dilemma. Do I go and do this thing, which could possibly get me my equity card, with Peter Gill who is a proper theatre director, and Simon Curtis assisting and, whatever else and – or if I do that, I let down all these guys at school. We've rehearsed and rehearsed and rehearsed and rehearsed this thing, you know, and my mum said to me, you gave your word, your word is important, no matter what. Other things will come along. But you gave your word and that is really, really important. Stick to your word.

And so I went yeah, okay, I've got to do the school play. So, I went and did that. So, when I saw Simon – he's now at Bristol University, having assisted Peter Gill. And, he said to me, oh, yeah, Peter was really upset about that. He thought, you know how stupid of this boy to not take, you know, parts that could have added to his Equity card and all the rest. Because in those days, it was difficult to get it, an Equity card, you had to have done – your time.

Anyway, I went in and auditioned for the play Jeremy had written. And I got the lead in that. And that was a play called *Breaking the Ice*, which I also have the poster for on the wall up here. So, I basically, bunked off BOVTS for a little while. And I went against their rules. Because they told me, well, I wasn't going to be cast in any leads in the way I am being cast in this play. And I thought, I came here for a classical education, if I'm not going to get it, or if I'm going to get a lesser version, then I might as well be doing something with my time that's right for me.

And then in the break – at the end of that term, we took *Breaking the Ice* and *Empire* – to the Sunday Times National Student Drama Festival, up in Hull. And I ended up winning the Sunday Times Best Actor Award. And there it was in the papers, you know.

So, I couldn't deny BOVTS where I had been. I wasn't 'unwell' any longer.

Anyhow, I came to BOVTS the following term. And I thought, oh, here we go, I am going to be hauled over the coals now. I've gone against all their rules, you are not meant to do outside work, all the rest of it. Because it had said that I was a student at the BOVTS, in the paper and everything. And Adrian, who was the Deputy Principal called me in to his office, first day of term. And I was thinking, okay, here you go. So, this is where you get kicked out of drama school. Don't worry, people have been kicked out of drama school before, it is okay. And I entered his office, and he said, oh, Cyril, well done, well done. We have got some great plans for you. You're going to be one of the knights in *Murder in the Cathedral* this year, and blah, blah, blah … and I am looking at this man, like, what (Cyril gives a lengthy kiss of his teeth) what, what?! So, I thought this is how you go on, okay. So, this is how you play this game is it?

I thought, yeah, sometimes you've just got to go, yeah, thanks a lot. But, you know what – no, thanks. I am better off sticking to my stuff.

They wanted me to be half a person, you know. But that's the way it was back then, you know, so I – yeah, it helped me.

And because of going to the National Student Drama Festival, I had met both Anthony Minghella, who had been one of the judges, and – Bill Alexander, who was one of the directors at the Royal Shakespeare Company (RSC) and Joyce Nettles, the Casting Director for the RSC. And they both said to me, would you like to come and audition for the RSC? And I said, well, no, I couldn't because, home wise I couldn't justify leaving a three-year educational course, my mother would – you know – there would be death …

And so, it was towards the end of my second year, and they called me in again. And I thought, okay, well, I'll go along. I got in, I thought, well, it starts in my third year, like a term into my third year. And you're doing five plays here. And you'd be doing five plays at the RSC. And there's not that much difference, but you are being paid. You'll be learning in this atmosphere a proper professional environment.

And so, I decided. I was a little way into my third year, and I was suddenly going off to be at the RSC. It was fantastic in many ways and – and terrible in other ways. So that's how I ended up there. I talked about it at Bristol – I went back and I had a talk with them after doing the British TV comedy in (2015) *Cucumber*, when I was in Bristol doing – a David Hare play – *Absence of War*.

And they invited me up to the school to talk to some of the pupils. And, you know, the great thing was that there were a few Black pupils there.

PJ Staff as well as students? Or just students?

CN No, no Black staff. Black students, they were like, six, seven. Which was great. But, you know, I suppose, because I'd been nominated for a BAFTA for *Cucumber*, the talk was packed.

PJ What drives you? Looking at issues of employability, how do you navigate this?

CN I think I have been lucky – I am interested in telling that story. And I think at each point when I used to get low about it, something has come along, that same spirit of – I was surrounded by strong women, you know.

My mother, who sadly has now passed was a strong bloody woman. Brought up four kids and when I think of her travelling the world. She ended up here from Barbados at a very young age, you know, studied, did all the rest of it, met my dad – really educated my dad in the ways of the world, really. Because he was first generation from Nigeria, you know.

PJ Is your preparation for a role different for theatre and screen?

CN It differs all the time. I don't subscribe to any particular method. I mean, it's always important to learn the lines. You know, but then the underneath preparation – what I call the psychological experience of the character, what drives them I think is equally important.

For example for Cassius, I started looking at the way he acted, and somebody put me on to manic depression so, I looked into that. And he was a classic manic depressive in all his actions. So I went and studied that and looked into all of the symptoms of that. And gave him those things, and I think Shakespeare wrote that before we'd even decided on any of the Freud or the Jung or the whatever. And that was a brilliant help.

It made it just different with Polonius, that thing of being a father, a single dad, and caring passionately about – and trying to protect his kids at all costs, particularly around privilege.

PJ The industry and your place in it?

CN I just care less now, you know about that shit. Because I just go, yeah, I will survive this shit, no matter what and this isn't the end of the world. There are important things in life. But, at the end of the day, I'm being paid to play cops and robbers and doctors and nurses, and all sorts of roles. But I was doing that in the playground at seven and, actually, you know what, most probably the kid who fell after being told 'Bang! Bang! You're dead' is probably the best actor in the world, it's just that they're not getting the chance to show it.

So, when I get as good as that kid, then I'll really start caring. But up until then, this is all a game.

I had the pleasure of doing a feature film, working with Olivia Coleman who was also in it. And just watching her, you know – the joy – the innocence and just having fun. And I thought, wow, you can't teach that shit. That's death in the playground shit. That's just – that's just gorgeous to watch.

PJ One of the recurring issues in the creative industries is the discussion around representation. How do you see your role in relation to that conversation?

CN I have said to BOVTS and to the Council of Drama Schools, if you don't make yourselves relevant, then people will just skip you. Because people don't need to go along to learn their technique at drama school any more.

Most of them are going into film and TV. They're learning that stuff, without you. And so, you need to be so much more relevant. You need to be right on board. You need to be doing the film and TV stuff as well as the theatre stuff in equal measure. And doing it to a standard that is, you know, unparalleled.

It gets difficult. But I use my phone and I do my little self-tapes, and the fact is that, my piano room becomes my – voice-over studio because I have all the sound curtains and whatever that come up. And I've got my little self-tape studio upstairs, so it's all there.

Now, it just – they're in a different world. So, I'm really appreciative of the fact that, I do think that there is a legacy from us older actors, of having just stayed the course, and done it, appearing every so often. And every so often, a younger actor will acknowledge that.

Not the very young but you know, the in between, that's – that's quite pleasing, to see and hear that. To see that they've acknowledged that.

In my day, you know, we definitely acknowledged the fact that, people like Norman Beaton, Rudolph Walker, Corinne Skinner-Carter, Mona Hammond, Yvonne Brewster, Horace Ové, others that had gone before, all these guys. I talked to George Harris not long ago, who actually played the first senior, Black cop on TV. You know, he was, plain clothes. But when he did the TV miniseries (1981) *Wolcott* playing a Black policeman who has been promoted to the CID, I remember looking at that and thinking, wow, wow, that's possible, you can do that. And, yeah, all these guys and there was definitely a looking up to these guys and thinking, wow, they're doing it, they're really doing it.

It was much, much harder for them. And then, my generation came along and hopefully we have passed something down just by even being here, just by still doing it, you know. At sixty-one, to be still doing it.

There have been times – you know, in '88 I thought I was going to give up. And, luckily, for whatever reasons, George said to me at that time, 'why would you give up doing something you hardly ever do?' That generation they didn't butter you up, they just told you straight. So, yeah, even if you end up not doing it, you don't need to go and talk to anybody about it or tell them you're giving up.

And then of course I booked Ariel in *The Tempest* and a role in David Hare's film, *Strapless*. And, suddenly I was thinking, okay, well, I am relevant.

Because I'd been thinking, the problem with this profession is that it's a bit like they were saying at drama school, was that I wasn't being cast in what I call the intellectual or emotional kernel of the piece. I was always on the outside, I was always the visitor, I was always the guy ringing the doorbell, I was always the outsider somehow.

And I thought, no, I want to be:

- in that central family that's promoting the intellectual and emotional kernel of this piece
- central to telling the story
- part of the story line that becomes part of the catharsis that people experience when they go to watch a piece of art or a piece of storytelling that they take away with them.

I don't want to be on the outside of that, because that seems to be irrelevant.

PJ Thinking in terms of how you choose to identify, what do you think are the challenges in the acting/creative industry now?

CN You know, we had all these discussions, at the National – and Rufus Norris came along and talked about, what the building was doing, and all the opportunities that were to be made available to make sure that we were fully in. At the end of some of those – I found myself saying, well, that's great, that's fantastic, but are you expecting us to say thank you for that? This is stuff that should be going on anyhow. I worked for every regime bar Peter Hall, you know. So, that's a lot of years. But I'm here on merit. I'm here because I'm a good actor. And I give to this process. Ain't nobody doing me a favour.

Nobody is doing me a favour by employing me. So, thank you very much. But you know – I said thanks for doing what you should be doing anyhow.

I am glad you have all caught up, I'm glad y'all caught up. That's fabulous. Yeah, nice. And …? So, there's a long way to go before you actually catch up.

PJ What pitfalls should actors emerging from drama school aim to avoid?

CN To be honest, I don't know whether I know the answer to that question.

I think – well, ask more questions, I don't know that people would have the time for all the questions I would have asked. But yeah, be less scared. Don't take yourself too seriously, read more, don't believe the hype.

Don't believe the shite that they tell you. One of the joys is watching people like Michaela Cole, grab her world and do it. That's not taking, I can't do this or somehow that's another person's world. Because there was some of me that still believed that you weren't going to be cast in that way. And I would just go, yeah, cast yourself. Just do it anyhow. And I think there are bits of me that wish I'd just gone off and – there were points where I thought, oh, God, I've got to do this rather than going off and bullfighting or doing some other shit, you know.

I've only actually had two agents, you know. And I'd also say don't be scared of them, they're agents. They're making money out of you, yeah, remember, they are making money out of you. So, you are the important thing there. So, do what you want to do and – I would also say try not to be too typecast, mix up the roles. I try not to go back too often to the same thing, try something different.

PJ What motivates you to want to act and keep doing it?

CN I think the joy, the staying power. And I think that's thanks to, not just the strong women that – that have been right next to me in life, you know, like my mum and my sisters.

But also, some of the previous generation and Tony Fagan, you know, on that morning when he found me tearful at school, he was so right. I think I have been lucky. I am interested in telling that story. And at each point when I used to get low about it, something has come along, that same spirit. I was surrounded by strong women. My mother, she was a strong bloody woman, you know. My mum and dad both sort of scholarship kids. But they met here. She then went back to Nigeria, you know.

And that was a difficult thing to do. My mum faced a lot of obstacles there as well. Being I suppose semi-light-skinned. Yeah, I mean, you know – I will show you a picture.

That's her in her Angela Davis phase. This strong woman, she – she didn't give up. She did the stuff, even in Nigeria. My mum she ran a magazine, which was like a cross between *Woman's Weekly/Woman's Realm,* she did that. Then she was a PA for the head of Lufthansa Airlines. She did lots of stuff. She was this woman who just didn't stop. When we got back here. The Nigeria-Biafran War happened. It was '68 when we came over, just less than a year before the end of the war. You know, my dad had been setting up radio stations as a civil engineer and stuff for Biafra and – you know, so he wasn't around a lot. And, she managed to keep us together. And when we flew out, and lived in Lisbon, Portugal for three months, and then here. And, this single woman, got it together, got a couple of jobs and did the stuff and did the stuff and did the stuff. And, and then she worked in under-fives nutrition. Then she was an aerial photographer for a while. She worked as a secretary at an ice cream place, Milo's, Chiswick. And then she was an accountant for Texaco and Shell. And, you know, she just did, did, did, and then she started Wandsworth Black Elderly, out of nothing, you know. And raised all that money and did all this stuff. This was a woman who didn't have any idea of, you sit down and give up. So, having all that behind you, you just go, yeah, okay, I have got no right to give up, I have got no right to sit down and go poor me. No, you know, F that.

Because, I'm a Chelsea supporter. When I was growing up Chelsea fans were a racist bunch of shits. I lived around the corner. And often, I do still come up against that. And every so often, I just have to go, yeah, okay, cool. Yeah, yeah, I'm still going to carry on. And you know, it's been interesting because – I don't want to talk about specific productions. But, I remember, you get in these situations where you have white males telling you – how they think you should be Black. I had the that in one show, I'm going well, yeah, yeah, the thing about it is, is that I'm playing a Black Nigerian male who is around fifty something. And I happen to be a Black Nigerian male around fifty something. I ain't got time for that shit. I'm holding down, my mum didn't have time for that shit. I'm holding down two jobs and doing all sorts of stuff, just to keep the food on the table.

I ain't got time for that. And I have got to react in that way. And so sometimes I find myself going, alright. Okay, you know. Okay, well, maybe we have to agree to disagree. And if it gets too much, well, we have to part, you know. But that's fine, you know.

The other thing is, I suppose, I've always had the attitude of you ain't going to own me. So, you know what, if it comes to it I'd rather leave, there's other shit to do, you know.

PJ What are your broad aims for the future of your screen acting/directing presence?

CN When we did the RSC (2021) production of *Julius Caesar*, it caused a storm. It was, brilliant, and all the rest of it. But it didn't get up for one award – actually, no, I tell a lie, the *Manchester Evening News* gave Ray Fearon, Best Actor for Mark Antony. I think that was the only award that it got or was up for. There was a point when we were in Stratford, and it was outselling *Matilda*, in terms of ticket sales. And that was on word of mouth. It wasn't publicity. There was no publicity for it, you know, it was all word of mouth. And it did something different. And it showed, yeah, look at all these fucking talented actors at the height of their stuff, who don't get the chance to be out here doing their shit. It came like a surprise to the RSC that it was such a success. Because I think, at the end of the day, there was a bit of ticking a box. Everybody went, oh my God. Yeah. You see what happens.

Yeah, these people have fucking loads and loads and loads of fucking experience. So, what a surprise that when you allow us to turn it on, it can be turned on. But if you ignore it, if you don't have it in the Evening Standard Awards, if you don't have it in the Oliviers, if you don't – don't have it in the blah blahs then what happens as the years go by? They'll only look at the same list. They will forget that that happened. They will forget. So, it's not recorded. It's not there. And those careers didn't take off in the way that for that production they should have done.

PJ Who are the actors and directors that have inspired you?

CN Tony Hopkins, just brilliant. Brilliant. Brilliant on all fronts. Again, simple, joyous, free – yeah. Wow. Norman Beaton was a triumph of an actor. Just – again, Norman was – yeah, he was like the bullfighter, he's just went out there. Doing it. Living it for the second, for the moment. Brilliant. Yeah, I mean there's so many. So, so many. American actors, well, there's so many that just hit that spot. Obviously, Sidney Poitier and various others. Yeah, I can't – I can't even begin to go down that list of, you know, classic actors, you know. There are loads. Yeah. People like George Harris. I remember Daniel Kaluuya at the Royal Court and just watching this young man, you know, who only had like two scenes in the play. And you just looked at him and go, wow, he – there's something hot about this one. Look at him, on fire, just great, brilliant and watching him go on, you know, getting over and over. And, you know, that's fantastic. So yeah, there's hope, and I'm always grateful – to the universe that has given me what it's given me. And to allow me that chance to have passed on some stuff.

PJ If a young Black and Global Majority person of eighteen made the decision that they want to become an actor, what would your advice be?

Out of the Black Box

CN I'd say, yeah, go for it. If you really want to become an actor. Not just wanting fame because that's a different thing. That may get you all the places you need to go to.

But if you want to become an actor, if you want to tell stories, go for it. Because, you're not going to have a stronger pulling. If you really want it, go for it, enjoy it. Like I say, don't let anybody tell you the bullshit of what you can and cannot do. Keep going and do it. You'll enjoy it.

PJ Hard-dough bread, Sourdough bread, Chin Chin, Sweetbread, Roti, Sudsa, Bun and Cheese, Nai Wong Bao -奶黄包- Custard Bun or Naan?

CN Oh, well, I would say Roti. But – yeah. And I try not to eat too much bread now because I can't afford the gym time!

Cornell John

Photographer: Maxarella.

Cornell John is an actor, writer and director. Film credits include Bishop Lumumba in *The Pope's Exorcist*, Arnold Guzman in *Fantastic Beasts: The Crimes of Grindelwald*, Curtis Gayle in the Hood Trilogy *Kidulthood*, *Adulthood* and *Brotherhood*, and the centaur Glenstorm in *The Chronicles of Narnia: Prince Caspian*. Television credits include Joseph Singer in the hit sky Atlantic series *Gangs of London*, Didi Mputu in *Five Days II*, Sid Lejeune in *Inside Men*, and a series regular on *EastEnders* as Sam James. Stage credits include Pozzo in *Waiting for Godot*, Malcolm X in *The Meeting*, Satan in Steven Berkoff's *Messiah*, and Paul Cranmer in *The Rubenstein Kiss*. In the West End, he originated the role of King Mufasa in *The Lion King*. He was the first Black actor to play Javert in *Les Miserables* and he won an OFFIE award for his portrayal of Memphis in *The Life*.

Pamela Jikiemi – PJ Tell me about your journey to become an actor.

Cornell John – CJ Oh, my God. I'm going to start with what you just said there, work. Part of the journey with me and why I'm still in it and how I managed to probably push to where I am now, was – as I said, that this, is the only job I will do.

That was part of my drive. So, when somebody would say to me, what do you do? If I'm not working, I say I'm unemployed. In other words, I don't work at McDonald's. I don't wait at tables. I have never done that. I've always pushed in the industry and that was part of my driving mechanism to keep me going.

So, I would keep it real. If I'm not working, I'm unemployed. You know, when people say, what do you do? I'm an actor. Are you working? No. Then what are you?

Out of the Black Box

I was happy to keep that, the idea that you talked about work. If I wasn't working, I was unemployed. I wasn't working in McDonald's. I wasn't serving tables. I wasn't being distracted. So, the only thing my focus was on was getting back into work. So, that was part of my early drive.

I didn't have a plan B. When I got the bug, this was it. And it kind of drove me, simply because that kind of mindset has kind of pushed me through.

PJ Training around learning 'the craft'; did you go to a conservatoire drama school? Talk about your creative career and your commitment towards pursuing it.

CJ First of all, I haven't trained. I've done all sorts of things. I've done radio, I've done presenting. I've done dance. I've done singing That's my first thing. I'm one of those rare beasts. Well, back in the day, there was loads of us.

Well, part of my journey was – Colin Salmon. Colin Salmon was a busker in London, and there was a show called *Buddy*. And somebody saw him busking and told him to audition. He auditioned. And he got the role. Then while he was doing the role, Helen Mirren came along and saw him and wanted him for *Prime Suspect*. And they said, okay, they let him go to do *Prime Suspect*. And they asked me to come into the West End, to replace the role. And so, the journeys are really funny, overlapping. So, yeah, I came into West End to do *Buddy*, because he left. I'm just joining the stories together.

Yeah, and again, it was one of those things. Because they wanted me to do it. And I don't play an instrument, I was raw in those days as well. I was quite raw. I said, yeah, well, I'll do it. But I was having a child as well at the same time. So, I said, I'm going to need two weeks off, so there were two people, because I said, I'm not going to learn an instrument. Get somebody in. And they said, okay. So, they obviously liked me at that point.

I had worked for the company, it was EMB, I think it was. I'd done a few shows for them. And – and yeah, they loved what I did. Funny enough. At the same time, I was doing radio for the BBC. I had my own show.

I did dance for a long time, from way back when I was six.

I remember there was a panto audition in Birmingham. I went along and started to do auditions. And they – they picked me. I'm like, well, okay, can I stay for the next one, because I'm here. And it started from that, really. So, I worked for the company on that. And they got to know me, and all the kind of madness I was doing at the same time.

Then I had my own dance company and all that kind of stuff.

Going back to how I really got into the acting world. I'd split up with my missus and was in a real state. And that's when I went into acting. I started doing acting classes. And that was my therapy. And that was my way out. So, for me, I always say that people who get into this, we are mad. Because, in life, look at it. In life we avoid rejection, we try to avoid rejection. But the fact is, that to do what we do, that's the first port of call, rejection. So, I think anybody who gets into acting, actually – there's a screw loose because you're putting yourself up for rejection. So, that's the first standard thing that we all do, no matter what colour you are, in our profession, we put ourselves up for rejection. And in life, the first thing we don't want to be, is rejected.

I taught myself to play the piano a bit, and that led into singing, and I started crossing over. I had a voice. I had a good vessel for singing, and I got into additionally creative stuff. And then, from that point, it was about the parts with singing in musicals. Sorry, I'm doing all these time leaps, because it's so long ago for me.

I then started doing musicals, getting small parts which led to bigger parts in musicals, where you had acting and singing. And then I started booking bigger and bigger roles. But then I stopped, because musicals for me at that time they weren't truthful. So, I decided to stop doing them for a while, and I went back to doing more studying. Because I wanted – again, my thing was about – truthfulness. And what I learned through study, and it wasn't about the genre, it's what you bring to it. It's the truth you actually bring to it. So, then I was able to go back into musicals again. And then – I suppose for me, then I started doing the mix. I would do a musical which paid you great money. Then I'd have to do a play for my soul.

Then I would do little bits of TV or little bits of film. So, again, it started to overlap, and I was jumping genres and I was doing all these things. But take me back anywhere because like I say, I'm spinning and spinning and spinning. Because for me it wasn't a simple journey.

I think the crossovers are kind of crazy like that. But going back to the idea of craft. Again, I think for me, I knew a long time ago, when I started, I didn't want to do nine to five, I think that's the thing with me. I didn't want to do nine to five. So, it was anything to avoid that. I think there's a couple of things, talent is one thing, and I think I had talent. But then it's the other things that go with it. And that's craft. And, you learn that, or you experience that. Somebody who can be 99 per cent brilliant one night and can fall to 76 per cent the subsequent nights, you're better off getting somebody who's – who's a constant 85 per cent plus.

So, talent – talent will take you so far. Then you have to be consistent.

That's also part of the growth in this, I mean, like I said, I have studied. I did loads of classes, I've studied techniques. And I am always working and learning on the job.

I went to the Actors Centre, I would do workshops all over. I went to America for a bit and did a few classes over there. I have studied Uta Hagen, Meisner, and again, so, because of my personality, and what interested me, it was just about being truthful. I mean, that was the whole point of it. And it's trying to find out how to be truthful in what you do. Some people will say which method, but it's a simple word, the truth, trying to find, to connect to your own truth. So, when you appear on stage, that's what you seek, basically.

And so, for me, I brought a different standard in terms of musicals, especially. Because that was the most important thing for me. It wasn't about the fact that I had a good singing voice, but I'm not a singer, if that makes sense. So, I would use the words to express whatever. So, in terms of learning my craft, I spent most of my crafting in the musical world, learning how to act, basically.

So, that's why I was able to segue between the two. Quite easily. And I've had some interesting breaks along the way. So, part of my journey has been doing traditionally 'white' roles. But because my quest is truth – the problem I have with them is because they're not written for us.

For instance, I have to work out how this guy in the 60s is with this woman. And so, my truth was trying to find a way into this. So, it's like a burden on top of a burden.

Because again, I suppose – and that's the thing about not getting the formal kind of training, where it's just – ignore these little things and just play the character. But no, the first thing people see – for me when they walk in the door is my colour.

And there's me doing what is traditionally a 'white' role. The love interest in *Sweet Charity* is basically what the role is. It puts an added burden on top of you as well. But for me, it's not the added burden, it is the fact that like I'm saying, I have got to justify how this guy lives in this world, and how this connection happens. This is the 1960s.

I also – here's another example of the same thing. I was offered the role of Luther Billis in *South Pacific*. Which is again, it's a traditional white role. Because he's the head of the sailors. And the whole piece is about racism. And so, my challenge to the director, at the time, was – do you realize that he's the head of the sailors and this play's about racism? I'm Black, yeah, so, I'm saying this, if there's any stuff that needs to just slightly twist a bit to make sense here. Please help me.

Because for me, it wasn't just about turning up and doing what it says on the page. You couldn't, because like I say, the first thing seen is your colour. And if it's a traditional role, the first thing the audience are seeing is, this guy is Black.

So, I've done a lot of crossovers in that respect. So, on my journey, I've had the extra burden of carrying that. I did Javert in *Les Miserables*. Now, I didn't even look at this role because – it was clear. Twenty years or twenty-plus years, there were no Black people in *Les Miserables*.

PJ I used to work at the Palace Theatre restaurant before I went to drama school, at the time making salads with this mad wonderful chef called Maureen (who had a very good-looking Australian husband, Malcolm), Mohammed who ran the bar and Rita, the manager, who ran everything with a rod of iron. Yes, the whole West End theatre scene in front of the curtain was very white at the time and I wondered how was I ever going to get look in?

CJ So, I was the one. So, my journey has been really interesting. There's something about me, I don't know, that had this crossover thing. That's the only thing I can say, there was something about me that had this crossover appeal thing, which made you look at yourself again, going, what's that about?

PJ What drives you? Looking at issues of employability, how do you navigate this?

CJ I think because back in the day there were always only two Black people that were allowed through, one man and one woman. I think that you were just striving and just doing your own thing really.

So, for me, what drives me is, that simple quest of truth. Finding out – making sense of roles. It was the challenge to make sense of this for me, I think. Because I didn't go to the formal training of drama school where it's ABC, where maybe you get to tackle these roles there.

I have a wider view, a worldview, I suppose. And I think a part of my personality at the time, which was open and – and pretty much positive, helped. It helped me navigate those times. Until of course, the industry batters and bruises you and you get a bit scarred and stuff like that. But I think it's my energy and my optimism and my naivety, I call it as well. Because I wouldn't conform to the norms, because I was guided by a simple thing. I judge people in conversations based on my parents. If my parents wouldn't talk to me a certain way, then I wouldn't allow anybody that I've known for two minutes too.

PJ Is your preparation for a role different for theatre and screen?

CJ Yeah. I think I've had a couple of gifts from God, and one of them is I have presence. So, on the stage, I have a huge presence. And so, it's about how to find out what their thing is, and how to use it.

So, for me, I wrestled with having to use this thing, because again, if I have presence, and I have presence on the screen, then I have to work out how best to use that. Whereas I personally want to try and push boundaries.

I have to guide myself to do less rather than push, especially on screen. Because I have a very expressive face that I have to control a lot more.

On stage, I appear huge, people tell me. So again, these are gifts that are given to me that I have no control over. It's making sure that you can guide them to your best advantage. Because if not – if you have huge presence and you're constantly working hard, then that's going to be too big for us. And trust me; I've done too big on occasion.

I am still learning, and I'm long in the tooth. I think for me, I don't know about anybody else. And I think that's why people have to continue; I call it filling the bucket. You have to fill the bucket. I don't know whether you take up knitting, whether you take up something else, you have to.

Because every time you go into the bucket or well and it gets dry, then you lose your energy, you lose that passion, you lose that.

PJ How do you decide what roles to go for?

CJ I look at a couple of things really.

I look at how taxing it's going to be.

How much of a challenge it's going to be.

I did a role recently, that wasn't me – it wasn't my wheel house. Because when you read something, you see a person, you can see – and in the end, I did it.

I just did my thing with it. It was basically a character that was written nerdy. He was unkempt, he was a paedophile hunter.

So, it was like nasty. It wasn't a great role in that, you know – and I wasn't going to do research for that. A paedophile hunter.

In the end, I decided I'd do it because again, I just wanted to test myself and I'm glad I did. I'm glad I did. Because again he reminded me of my strengths and what you can bring to a role and where you're at.

PJ The industry and your place in it?

CJ I think the industry and my place in it, that's an interesting question. I say to most people this; there are only a handful of people in our industry that can have a career looking forward.

Most of us have a career looking backwards. In other words, you look back to see what you've done, to say you've had a career.

For most of us, our career is viewed backwards. So, in terms of how I'm viewed in the industry, I look at my CV. And my CV is quite strong. In that I'm employable, is the best way to look at it. Because of the ups and downs in the industry, I suppose, and because of the times that you're in and out of it. I look at the industry, and it's now completely different, it's changed. And I think it's more technical, it's a very technical industry now, I would say.

And Black actors, producers, directors of our generation are valuable, but our worth isn't fully coined, simply because we have different generations now in charge of our industry. And so, it's for us to enjoy – I enjoy the new blood, it's not about passing on anything, and it's really just about enjoying the jump.

PJ One of the recurring issues in the creative industries is the discussion around representation. How do you see your role in relation to that conversation?

CJ I had concerns way back. I played Mufasa in *The Lion King*.

That was – way back in 1999, when *The Lion King* came here. And basically at that time it was – and still is a massive show. But you had six kids, Black kids, who were suddenly thrust into the limelight, eight shows a week, 2,000 people …

And they can only work for three months. And then they were tossed back out in the street, so to speak, they return to civilian life. So, you have generations and generations of kids that have done *The Lion King*, who were introduced to this business, at an early age, I'm talking about, it's probably, I want to say probably around ten to twelve.

They are suddenly thrust into this business and then tossed out again. My concern at the time was that you've got these children; you've given them the taste of this. And they are at the top of the tree because they're playing the 'lead', inverted commas. And then three months later, they're just thrown back into their normal life.

I enjoy watching youngsters who have come through (today) without that burden.

PJ Thinking in terms of how you choose to identify, what do you think are the challenges in the acting/creative industry now?

CJ I think now it feels as though there's more opportunity, it's still hard. It's still incredibly hard. You see, for me, if the industry admits that it's never been a level playing field, then we can have a conversation about representation.

Going back to the things that you've said about, opportunities. You didn't have a run-up to this opportunity that you get, you'll suddenly get this opportunity, and you have to jump up suddenly and rise to this challenge, my observations are hopefully, a lot more people have come through the challenge of that.

And there are a lot more people getting, more regular work under their belts. So, when a huge challenge comes to them, they're actually prepared for it rather than putting them in a situation where they're doomed to fail. Because of lack of experience, lack of, environment. Because for me it's always been hard, changing genres and getting used to the environment if you suddenly have to do this one again. And it's making the adjustments to environment and all the technical elements around it.

I still think it's hard, very hard. But I'm heartened by the training I've seen some of these actors come with now. A lot more of the generations have gone into drama school. Good drama schools and have taken on the craft, the work.

I would say to those young people entering the industry from drama school, just remember who you are in terms of your culture, your base, and who you are. That gives you an added bonus. Because if you're British, I was born here – if you're British, and born here, you are the same as everybody else that's British and born here.

We also have a different heritage as well, which you can always tap into. And that's a spiritual one, that's a physical one. And so, use your advantages. Don't just set them aside because you've gone to drama school and trained.

No, use your advantages to guide your own journey.

PJ What pitfalls should actors emerging from drama school aim to avoid?

CJ I think that there are too many pitfalls. So, the only thing I would say is that they have to be determined. Find out what their strengths are and push for that, focus.

Take someone like Susan Boyle. Susan Boyle is a prime example for anybody in the industry. And that is this woman since she was probably six to ten got up in the morning sang whether it was in the bathroom, the shower. So, she was able to sing the shit out of one song. She went on to a programme and – didn't look like she could do anything and sang the shit out of the one song she could sing.

So, I tell people, focus – if there's something that you really like to do, if it's a Shakespeare then focus on that. Because then if you put your energy into that, you'll get it.

PJ What motivates you to want to act and keep doing it?

CJ I've got lots of bruises and scars now, which eventually you get. The longer you're in this business, what you will get, and experience can be a double-edged sword. Because experience makes you question. Whereas in our business, it's better to be naive and just go.

Experience can be a bitch simply because it comes with too much information. You know, a child sees something on the floor, just goes for something on the floor.

And I think – it's always trying to remember that – that simplicity.

So, like I say, that simplicity is the key to all this. The deeper you get into it, the more heavy you get – forget that, go for simplicity. Think like a child.

PJ What are your broad aims for the future of your screen acting presence?

CJ It's kind of an interesting thing for me. I'm very spiritual. And I think the world is very spiritual. There are loads of times, when I'm like, I'm ready, I'm cooked, I'm over, I'm done, roll me over, lay me down, I'm over this.

And this has happened to me several times. And I'll walk down the street, and then somebody will come up to me and say, excuse me, I just want to say, you're brilliant. You inspired me. Please keep up the great work – it's ridiculous. The amount of times I'm ready to just call it a day and take up fishing or whatever.

It's a reminder for me that I have some sort of gift – it's my job to keep going. I've managed to touch quite a few people in this industry. It's hard. It's broken me at times. But again, it's all I do. It's all I know.

So, for me, I look for the next challenge. And hopefully it's one that's going to interest me because, like I say, if it's not interesting, I'm not going to rise to the challenge.

PJ Who are the actors and directors that have inspired you?

CJ Oh, God inspired me. Berkoff. Berkoff is mad as a hatter. Julie Taymor. Again, her visionary stuff was great. I've worked with loads that actually inspired me – and allowed me to grow and develop. I think a good director will allow you to grow – or push you, or get out of your own way or encourage you.

And also, I remember – and this may sound arrogant, but it's not arrogant. Again, it's a simplistic way of looking at things. We have to remind people; a director is there to help you. A director is there to help you, especially in theatre.

So, if you look at a director, rather than, oh, my God, it's this person – you should look at the director as someone who is going to help you in the role. How can that person help me? Is a better way to look at it.

So, that person is here to help me be great. As opposed to I've got to kowtow to this person, it's the other way around because you're the one that's going to be up there doing it. So, it's a small twist on the prism. But it's a different way of thinking about the same situation.

These folk work for you, not the other way around. These folk are here to help you be the best you can. And so, how do you do that? And how can you get them to help you? Rather than I'm here to please you, the director. You do your work and say how they can improve it. And these are these are hard lessons.

PJ If a young Black and Global Majority person of eighteen made the decision that they want to become an actor, what would your advice be?

CJ I would really ask them, is it your passion, why do they want to do it? Is it their passion?

Because it needs to be your passion, if it's for anything else, you will find lots of pitfalls. If you're driven by it as your passion, then it goes without saying, I don't need to say anything else. So, my question would be, is it your passion?

If it's not your passion if this is not what makes you get up in the morning, do something else. Because there are too many, too many pitfalls that will drive you to stop. It has to be your passion. It has to be your passion. Not your wish to be famous. Not your wish to be known. Not your wish to be – no, it has to be your passion. Because if it isn't – you're fooling yourself.

Remember, it's a business. And when that business is in play, the only thing that's going to sustain you is your own passion. So, you have to be passionate about it or forget it.

Networking, I couldn't do that. It's hard work. So again, I would just say, these guys are here to help you be your best. A director's job is to help you be your best. To remember that. Not the other way around. You're not there to impress the director. They are there to help you. That's their job. So, anything that falls outside of that, question them. It's a hard thing to remember when you're in the maelstrom.

But yeah, if you'd have met me years and years ago, you would have loved me because I was mad as hell.

Because again, it's when you have that energy, and it's about cracking this code of this part of this person. And so, that's what the focus is. So, it's not about me and my ego. It's just about – if that doesn't make sense, making sense of that, making sense of this. The craft itself.

And again, if you can enjoy the craft, then you're in heaven because you're enjoying what you're doing. And then hopefully, at some point, you get paid well for doing it. And that was what was driving me, helped me get to where I am as well. Enjoy what I did, and eventually – keeping the focus on that – and eventually somebody will pay you well for doing it. Because I'm enjoying what I'm doing. If you're enjoying it then you're digging, you're searching, you're improving, you're getting better. So, yeah.

PJ Hard-dough bread, Sourdough bread, Chin Chin, Sweetbread, Roti, Sudsa, Bun and Cheese, Nai Wong Bao -奶黄包- Custard Bun or Naan?

CJ I'm going to go Hard-dough. I want to go Hard-dough bread. Because that's kind of sweet as well.

Leo Wringer

Photographer: Simon Annand.

Leo Wringer is a winner of the Shakespeare Prize from the Guildhall School of Music and Drama. His acting CV has seen him perform nationally and internationally, in Shakespearean productions from *Romeo and Juliet* to *King Lear*, *The Fantastic Follies of Mrs Rich* for the Royal Shakespeare Company, Stool-Pigeon in August Wilson's *King Hedley II*, *Our Lady of Kibeho*, *Perseverance Drive*, James Graham's *QUIZ* and *Two Horsemen*, for which he won a Time Out Award for Best Actor. Television and film credits include *Domino Day*, *Anthony*, *Sitting in Limbo*, *Urban Myths – The Trial of Joan Collins*, *Heirs of the Night*, *Black Earth Rising*, *The Moonstone*, *Gangsta Granny*, *Silent Witness*, *Nighthawks*, *Death in Paradise*, *The Kitchen Toto*, and Thomas Peters in Simon Schama's *Rough Crossing*.

Pamela Jikiemi – PJ Tell me about your journey to become an actor.

Leo Wringer – LW Okay. So my journey to becoming an actor started a very long time ago, though I may not look or sound that old.

The idea of acting probably first began to take hold of my psyche during an English lesson at the secondary school I was attending in Tottenham, North London. The school had recently transformed from being a grammar school to becoming comprehensive. I was probably fourteen.

Anyway, some magic must have entered the room while this particular English teacher standing up in front of the class read out a scene from the Scottish Play, in one hand the script and with the other he gestured freely and in so doing clarified subtly what was being said. The effect for me was captivating, and I fancied that I understood that mysterious ancient language called Shakespeare. At the time, it was an issue to actually know what was being said, but because of the way he communicated, I felt I understood everything that was being said in that little passage of text. The way he did all the gestures in such a way that it sort of came off the page and started to take shape.

Then what else? It became customary for me to be in one of the school plays. And at the same time, outside of school, I was invited to play Romeo, for an amateur dramatic group called The Mermaids, which was run by an indefatigable woman, Ivy Calvert. She took me under her wing, and awakened my desire to make a go of being an actor.

Incidentally, I was in touch with her when she celebrated her 100th birthday, we've regularly kept in touch.

However, when it came to having the career discussions with one of the sixth-form teachers at the school, and even though there was the distinct impression that one could do so much better than becoming an actor. He did his best to persuade me to think of another profession, or at least to go to university with languages because French and German were two things that I that really became fascinated about. I don't really understand why but languages did mean a lot to me. I think his idea was go to university to do languages and a bit of drama at the same time. I didn't want to do that. I was in pursuit of the real McCoy, and I got a place at Guildhall School of Music and Drama.

PJ Training around learning 'the craft'; did you go to a conservatoire drama school? Talk about your creative career and your commitment towards pursuing it.

LW I applied to a few drama schools, including RADA and Guildhall, as just mentioned, in terms of the auditioning. Hard to recall in real detail the differences in the process. Since we're talking the mid to late 70s. I didn't know if that chimes. I seem to remember that RADA was pretty thorough, but seemed to lack certain warmth, leaving one a little intimidated by the end of it all.

Whereas Guildhall was the opposite. No less thorough, but far more warm and welcoming. That helped me a lot. Now, maybe that was because they were trying hard to be seen to be diverse. Although it wouldn't have been termed in that way then – probably more accurate to say they were engaged in tokenism, like many other institutions at the time, because each of the three years only ever showed off one Black actor as far as I could see. So in my year, there was only me. So that's what I mean about tokenism. I think there was a general sense at the time.

However, I was pleased to have chosen Guildhall, not only because of the drama department, but also because of the music part of the school. I was developing an interest in classical music. I remember at 8.30 in the mornings, happily walking down John Carpenter Street to enter the building, that's where the school was at the beginning because it moved after that. And long before arriving at the gate, down the street, you could hear the blended bars of the opera singers' voices, either warming up or practising bars of music and instruments, striking up fragmented lines of notes, it was a wonderful cacophony of energy of sound, always pleasant and invigorating that set me right for the day. That was so wonderful, and it made a deep impression on me. So, music became important. When the drama school took up residence at the Barbican in Silk Street. That happened one and a half years in. So, everything was much more modern – polished surfaces, glass and steel and you know, it was very impressive. I would sneak into the concert hall and sit at the back listening to them practising. Usually it was the orchestras practising some piece then I would run upstairs to the library to investigate that piece further, for instance, Dvořák's *New World Symphony*. What I'm trying to say is that Guildhall School for me, gave me the best of both worlds, the way the two worlds came together was just amazing for me. And then in terms of the overall training for the actor. I felt grateful for it. It gave me and

I think this is true, a good grounding in classical acting and other styles of creating theatre. Especially the physical aspects, in fact, all the elements that involve just doing and not thinking before doing, I enjoyed much more. When they start analysing scripts in a way that seemed to get bogged down, it became less enjoyable for me. That has always been the case for me. It put me in touch with some of the most wonderful and supportive people among my classmates and my tutors. There were some amazing people. And then after three years, I was awarded the Shakespeare Prize. They could not have given me anything more like a lodestar because most of my work since has been in Shakespeare. So that topped it off for me nicely.

PJ What did you get from your actor training?

LW I was looking forward to going to Guildhall so much. And, I mean, there were – there were aspects that didn't work for me. But, you know, it didn't traumatize me in a way that stopped me from evolving. That has been a basis that I draw on all the time. They couldn't have provided me with a better start really. So I'm very grateful, very grateful.

I went there with nothing, they clearly saw something in me. And felt that they could encourage me to develop.

I was such an empty vessel, you know, just had a desire to do this kind of work. It was nothing more than the desire to be doing work that involved Shakespeare. But when I say I came with nothing, what I mean is that I didn't have the intellectual apparatus to be able to, to analyse a text, for instance, all I had was the raw, raw material to be worked on. And that's what I liked very much about Guildhall, that they were able to work on the raw material that you came with, and shaped you into, being able to express those texts. And what they also gave you is the knowledge that you will never quite get to the end of that. I mean, I think I might refer to it later. But there's always more to mine from the texts, and all they did was to give you the tools to allow you to study prepare your body, your mind, your heart, your imagination, to be at the surface of those texts. And that's what I liked so much about them about their way of developing us as actors.

The school was keen to give us a variety of tools and all disciplines, whether that be dance movement, or handling texts. And for me, it was priceless. It gave me a lot of confidence in my abilities and worth, especially the work that the voice department did on our voice.

At the time, I clearly had a voice that contained Caribbean cadences, because my Jamaican mother kept on prompting me to talk English, 'no man, talk English'.

My parents are from Jamaica. Well, my father is no longer with us. But they came over in the, in the 50s. And sent for me. As you know, that's, that's, that's a common story. And and so my father came first and set up, you know, the house and then sent for my mother. And then my mother. Once my mother and father were a little settled, at about the age of about four to five, they sent for me and my aunt.

I was born in Jamaica, and I think it was round about when I was one they left to come to Britain, and then sent for me when I was nearly five. So I was with my aunt for all of that time. And then when we finally came to Britain. I, for a long time, thought my aunt was my actual mother. And because in that kind of society at the time, you know, there was this sense of extended families, nobody really said that that was your mother, that's your father. So nobody was really specific about who was doing what.

It just wasn't clear, so I thought my aunt was my actual mother. And I didn't know until I was probably about ten, we were living all in the same place in North London, I think it was when it became clear that there was a difference between the two women. So for a long time I just didn't know. I didn't even think about asking, you know. And then at some point, my aunt said, you know, the woman downstairs, because my aunt used to live upstairs. She had a room and then she, you know, she had her children, three children. By the age of ten, I had brothers and sisters. She said, you know, the woman downstairs is actually your mother, and I thought, what?! It just was a thing that I just couldn't compute. I couldn't compute, and then gradually over a period of time, I was able to make the adjustments, but I'm sure that deep down there must have been some, some scars, some psychological scars, there, have to be, to deal with it, you know. So, I've got three brothers and two sisters. And, and there is a sister outside of the family who is older, and we all get on brilliantly.

My parents, they were so supportive, I think they were just glad that there was something that I wanted to do. I mean, it was the relief of 'oh God, at least we don't have to worry about him too much, now'. My father did say, you know, if things don't go well, you know, we're always here. So, I mean, they were positive, but they didn't really understand this need to pursue that kind of a life.

And, even worse, to have produced a son that was fascinated by Shakespeare. That was just, where did he come from? So yeah, it was, it was weird, weird for them. But they were positive in terms of glad that there was something that I felt that I wanted to do.

Because I mean, I have a son, who was trying to work out what it is that he wanted to do. And my partner and I were thinking at the time, how much do you push? How little do you back off? What do you do? How do you handle someone that's evolving into his own person? How do you guide them towards doing something that's going to be positive for them? But you, in the end, maybe you do very little, because in the end, they have to be the ones that guide, they have to be the ones that, you know, find the way forward? So, when I think about my boy, I think back to what must have been happening, you know, the discussions that must have been happening between my mother and father in trying to bring me up, and my brothers and sisters, I mean, they had it even harder, because there was no support system, then really.

I said that Guildhall was keen to give us a variety of tools and all disciplines, whether that be in dance movement, or handling texts. And for me, it was priceless. It gave me a lot of confidence in my abilities and worth, especially the work that the voice department did on our voices. This is the bit that I think I need to share. So at the time, I clearly had a voice that contained Caribbean cadences, because my Jamaican mother kept on prompting me 'talk English, nah man, talk English', she was always saying that to me. Indeed, at the time, wherever the actors came from, we were encouraged to iron out the differences and to adopt a more standard RP accent – theory being so that you can move the voice in any direction when is called upon to do so.

So, so vigorously did most of us apply this directive that little did we realize, a sea-change was coming ten years or so down the road, when the clamour would now be for authentic voices, voices that declared and celebrated where they were from. This actuality threatened to leave me high and dry. It meant I had to get back in touch with my Jamaican-ness, and I was always worried whether I'd lost it. Or whether as one of my brothers would taunt me, 'it was too diluted'. After drama school, I made my Jamaican-ness one of the tools to draw on when I want to distinguish between playing more than one character in a production. I thought it was important to mention that.

PJ So very important, Leo, I'm glad you did. I think, especially being racialized as Black. It's not just about the voice. We believed it was about the voice. For me. I mean, I went to drama school later than you, but there were other things at play that for me anyway, we didn't have – I didn't have the tools to understand what they were. So I thought it was a level playing field.

LW Yes. Indeed, but it wasn't. And, and it's looking back … I mean, at the time you don't see it, it's just a problem. You just don't see it, one isn't conscious enough to see it. I mentioned the word conscious. But I think that I mean these days it's different, I think absolutely different people. Everyone is much more conscious and more ready to know, how to go forward on issues. But at that time, it was all new, it felt all new, there was no roadmap to, guide you to what the right path was in a number of these – these things, especially in terms of from, where you came from, and how you should be celebrated. And given space.

PJ I know, my mum was Jamaican and my dad was Nigerian. So, with the Jamaican it was the English speaking and sounding, you know, don't be like me, don't speak like me, we want you to sound English, not 'back a yard, country gyal'. So you have that, but you've also got that with the speed. People were always saying 'you speak so fast' even though, I didn't think I did. Even though I was born in London my mum was keen to iron out 'rough talk' and anything that might suggest that I wasn't born within the sight of standard flag-flapping full mast at Buckingham Palace or something like that, because that was the BBC sound and a clear speaking voice that most definitely meant you could advance in life. I was really good at toasting over reggae dub plates, I was a good mimic. And then you start to lose that to a gradual degree because you're not asked to use it, it becomes frowned upon. Drama school does not recognize Sam Selvon or Barry Reckford, only Terrance Rattigan and Harold Pinter, you move in different circles to forge a career and you become acutely aware of the perfomative connotations of sounding 'Black' courtesy of stand-ups like Jim Davidson. But I think it does psychologically affect you because you then, become like a bat, as my dad used to say neither bird or beast and you are in danger of losing yourself.

I am so glad that you shared that, Leo. That's really important. Especially for younger people who adopt various accents now and dialects and speech systems. And they move fluidly. It's not just code switching, its taking ownership of a key aspect of their identity, they know who they are and have a much clearer idea about aspects of classical training in relation to vocal work and RP. They are now quite clearly saying, thank you, but RP is an accent not a way of life for me.

LW Exactly. Exactly. Yes.

PJ What drives you? Looking at issues of employability, how do you navigate this?

LW I was underway with my work as an actor from the 80s. At the time, there was a keenness to have one Black face in ensemble companies, any more than that would be surplus to requirements, it would seem. Like at the drama school, I found as the only person of colour for a long time in the early and middle part of my work. As a consequence, there seemed more than enough for me to do. So that's the point I was trying to make in terms of employability the first fifteen years, I think it would be fair to say that I was prepared to take anything. Yeah, I was prepared to take anything in order to work and build up contacts and stamina. After that, I was determined to accept only leading roles, and especially those not specifically written for 'Black' actors.

I wanted to be treated as an actor and also not fall into the trap of being typecast as one type of Black actor. Most of the opportunities were among Shakespeare's protagonists such as Petruchio, which are played – Petruchio, Brutus, Lear's Fool. And then I've got one that wasn't, which may be of interest to include.

One that wasn't Shakespeare was different. It was a restoration comedy called *The Fantastic Follies of Mrs Rich* (or *The Beaux Defeated*) written by Mary Pix at the RSC in the Swan in 2018, directed by Jo Davies. I played the Country Squire, for the most part upstaged by a couple of setters. I had to come on with two dogs, which took all the interest in that scene.

One or two of the reviews didn't see the funny side nor past the colour of my skin, and wondered out loud if this was more RSC box-ticking quotas. So that kicked up quite a scandal at the time, 2018. I didn't realize how much of a storm was being kicked up, because Greg Doran got in touch with me and said, 'do you know you're at the centre of this thing?' Because this particular reviewer said that I was miscast. Could it be that the RSC and the Arts Council are yet again, at their box-ticking exercise, quotas or something like that, I can't remember exactly what was said. So yeah, so that became quite an issue. So to answer the other part of your inquiry based on that incident, what drives me is the need to be part of that movement in art that shows how we can or must look beyond our narrow borders and embrace difference.

PJ It wasn't that long ago. And how did you – how did you feel about that? I mean, did you let it affect you? Or did you brush it off?

LW No, I wasn't able to brush it off. I did respond. I think they approached the RSC and I gave a lengthy response at the time. So yes, I did respond, and I don't really want to go into it because I don't really want to awaken those thoughts about that moment. It had a profound effect on me.

So it was fascinating, fascinating on one level, that yes, we haven't moved on. I mean, there's a lot that has been done. And again, I will refer to it as we get further into the conversation. But yes, so a lot has been done. It's not right to say oh, that nothing has changed. A lot has changed.

PJ A lot has changed. And some sometimes it's the more things change, the more they stay the same.

LW But, I think we have to also give space to what has changed as well, because sometimes you can get the impression that nothing at all, you know has changed. I'm always looking for balance, Because, too often it's only the negative, and that can be so oppressive in its own way.

PJ Yeah, sometimes you can't get up, I can't see anything. But bad badness, and then you feel it your body and everywhere. But then actually, when something happens, or you think of someone who has helped you, or something that connects to the reality of you, you can summon the strength, the ability to turn the ship around. It's hard, but we do it, we must, because we've always done it, and we have to keep doing it otherwise. I don't know what the flip side of it is, because I've never looked that deeply into – because I can see it's an abyss. And that's not where I want to be.

LW I'm with you. I recognize that. Yeah.

PJ Is your preparation for a role different for theatre and screen?

LW I think the short answer is yes, there is a difference, right.

I mean, obviously, for theatre, and most of my work has been in theatre. I appreciate the fact that we get typically four to five weeks to rehearse, right, so that I like a slow build up to being ready to do the play for an audience. I think it's priceless.

The process allows you to layer in different aspects of the character, which enables you to continue deepening them right up to the end of the run, should you wish. So, in contrast, because for screen everything is more circumspect, you know, you're expected to have everything buttoned down, by the time you arrive to shoot, there's really not any rehearsal time, where you can argue back and forth about the direction of a character, and how they might relate to other people in the scene, typically.

And then, it's only maybe by the, the third take, if you're so lucky, that I really begin to relax with this thing. So a lot of thinking and practising needs to be done as soon as it's feasible, you know, you may not even get the script until a week before you have to go and shoot.

There are many reasons why there's a big difference. For me, I haven't done very much on screen. Because most of my work has been on stage, that might have been also a negative, too. Because, you know, it may be that I'm just not suited for the screen in one sense.

But I'm sure that if the environment was different, where you could be allowed to develop over a period of time. I think it wouldn't be such a problem but because everything has to be so quick.

For various reasons, I don't think it works for me. It doesn't readily work for me, even though I've done quite a few things. But I don't see my future on screen. And then on the positive side with screen work there is something refreshing about once it's done, you can forget about it and move on, so that's a positive side.

PJ How do you decide what roles to go for?

LW I mean, it all depends with roles. It really just comes down to the quality of the material. And that plays a big part in my decision.

Also, who the directors are, I mean [in the] earlier days, I was keen to get experience, have a wide range of work with any director who would engage me.

Now, the only reason why I might consider doing a play in which I might not play a leading role would come down to the director engaged on that project. Yes, so I mean, for instance, I've worked with Deborah Warner. And so, if she was to ask me, I played a couple of cameo roles for her in the past, I would always be open to working with her again, just because of how much I enjoy working with her.

I think the main thought of that answer is about the material, the quality of the material, is it challenging enough. Is it something that I've done before? And won't want to do again, or I should do it again, because I didn't quite do it well enough the first time. Like with the Othellos, which I have done four times, I always think, there's more to mine. And as you evolve as a person, you see more, you feel more, you're able to bring more. So that will be one reason for going back to it.

So it's the material, and the director, content and venue in that order. I mean, the venue would be important as well, the profile of the venue in a way. Does that make sense?

PJ The industry and your place in it?

LW I said once fortunes fluctuate from month to month, year to year, decade to decade, so it's hard to say where my place is in the industry.

Suffice it to say that I'm an established professional actor. Although the industry is changing, to accept more people from diverse backgrounds, it doesn't mean that it's changing in a way that includes actors from the older generation, on a consistent basis.

Out of the Black Box

For one thing, we are likely to be at a distinct disadvantage with technology now that the rate of auditions are turbocharged by having to do self-tapes, not something that I feel comfortable doing.

Of course, the saying 'adapt or die' comes readily to mind. So, since I'm not technology minded, it hasn't been easy but I am getting there.

I'm not a fan of how things have evolved. You know, with self-taping, but as you say, you have to somehow find a way through. And of course, in time, you will develop the facility for it. No, that's absolutely as it as it will be. But the point is, is that it just seems alien to how you want to be able to be in a room where you can actually look in the eyeballs at that person across the table and really find some kind of connection you want to be in the room with that. With that creative energy.

PJ One of the recurring issues in the creative industries is the discussion around representation. How do you see your role in relation to that conversation?

LW It suddenly went to another level, this question of representation, post-George Floyd's murder. And so many places, such as drama schools and other national institutions started to have fundamental and long-overdue talks about change. Or in a few cases, they actually speeded up their deliberations and actually put into place structural change now, as part of their *raison d'être*, not a dignified spectacle, the wholesale scramble onto this new bandwagon to do the right thing by Black and Brown actors. But then, I guess whatever it takes, no matter how ugly the process. Groups like Talawa were engaged to lead programmes, give advice and guidance to address unconscious bias, and the lack of diversity and inclusion. As for my role, I happen to be a member of a panel that is part of the global conversation.

I also teach, and at the British American Drama Academy (BARDA) I am a faculty member. And we have regular meetings with the Dean, who is keen to put into place regular meetings throughout the year to monitor that structural change, and to make sure that structural change does take place – and we're doing brilliantly, I think with it. So, yes. That's my contribution to it. And I think it's moving in the right direction. It goes back to our conversation a little earlier about change, whether anything has changed. This shows that there are steps taken to change, because they've looked at the structure and practices and are making the change. So I'm more hopeful, and I can see evidence of it even on television. I don't watch television that often. But I can see evidence of it too. I can see the way my friends who are white, saying, 'Oh, but we're not getting as many jobs as we used to get, you know, we don't go up for as many'. Yeah, because they now realize that there's priorities given to a degree to people of colour, to actors of colour. It underscores the fact that change is happening. Maybe not as fast as we all wanted, but at least I want to recognize that it is happening and the fact that it should not take the death of a man in America in such terrible – in such a terrible manner. And then the outpouring and clamour for something to be done. To me it's, it's a case of pre-George Floyd and post-George Floyd is the era, so two eras. I don't think we can go back to pre-George Floyd in many respects, you know, in any way now.

PJ Thinking in terms of how you choose to identify, what do you think are the challenges in the acting/creative industry now?

LW One of the challenges will be to continue for some time to effect actual and sustained change in all areas of the arts. And for us, as Black artists to be this change, so that our audiences can see themselves reflected on the stages of the country. We need a pool of diverse practitioners. The myth and misconception that there's only one type of Black man or woman needs to be challenged by actors having the opportunities to be in productions, on screen and onstage that shows a multilayered character who can be vulnerable as well as powerful and rich, and that needn't be threatening.

They can be lovers as well as warriors.

We can be thinkers as well as doers. Fathers who are conscious of how they are bringing up the next generation, whether that is within or outside of a family unit.

However, when it comes down to getting work, there still persists a marked distinction between we in the UK and actors of a colour in US. We seem to look to that continent for our opportunities, understandably. I think going forward over the next decades, the challenge is going to be how we can lay down equitable foundations here that can give UK actors of colour the best opportunities and support to build a pyramid of work that sustains and grows and endures.

What tends to happen, and that's pretty much of my generation, is the sort of stop start, stop start, as most of my decades have been about. So I'm saying that I'm hoping that no longer applies. Because of the kind of generation we have now. This generation of actors, wonderful actors, wonderful crop of actors. And because they're so conscious, and so ready to put down structures. I think it's going to be different. It has to be different. Yeah, those are my thoughts on that question.

PJ I agree. I've had other actors and generations saying every ten years, I get remembered what a good actor I am. It goes in that cycle. And I felt really sad because they're all actors when I graduated from drama school I was working with and I thought, wow, this is the standard and the work they were doing. It was invariably male – Black men – not women, which was quite interesting, which I'm sort of working to unpick in a way. But it's mainly the males and then to see you pop up once in a blue moon, I think there's something wrong because these guys taught me a lot. But it was the positivity and the strength of their focus, whereas others seem to fail upwards, which upset me deeply. People like Maynard Eziashi, Mo Sesay, Valentine Nonyela, Buki Armstrong, John Adewole, Louis Mahony, I mean, John, Louis and I used to do quite a bit of BBC Radio together and I didn't know John had gone to Dartington Hall and Louis had gone to Central School of Speech and Drama. He was of a generation where they used to let them go at the end of their second year, so they didn't get to do a third year showcase for industry, because it was deemed at that time, 1975–76, 'that there were not enough parts for Black actors to go around'. I discovered this while doing research for my PhD, I came across that and I was I was horrified, because I had had a very difficult time at drama school and I realized my experience, I was at the tail end of that kind of thinking. So there was a lot of actors that I crossed paths with, that I connected with that I thought would take the world by storm and others who I wouldn't cross the road for that did momentarily take the world by storm, but whose careers for some reason were not developed. The opportunities for me were few and far between, but I then did not understand the hierarchy of agents.

PJ What pitfalls should actors emerging from drama school aim to avoid?

LW My thoughts on this is this has been a trend which I think one has to be wary of, but then maybe I'm out of touch to a degree now. But I thought to go straight from drama school into the mechanical media could put you at too much of a disadvantage ten years down the road, when you want to give your *Hamlet* for instance, of course, everyone is going to have a different set of challenges to deal with, and different opportunities placed in front of them.

But a pitfall might be in one's eagerness to be seen on TV, for instance, and then letting too much time go by before doing that rigorous work on stage. But then, you know, what I thought about as well is maybe some people just don't want to do theatre, maybe that's an old-fashioned idea?

To me, it would be a pitfall to leave drama school, and/or just or to be encouraged at drama school to go into the mechanical media. Because once you start its difficult to come away from there, to try and do your work on stage. I think it's the wrong way around. So that's the pitfall I would say.

As for actors of colour, the one thing that is common to all, perhaps, is the drive to succeed often on one's own. And I think this was part of the generation where we're talking about, my generation. And that could be a pitfall because you need to have a society of like-minded people looking out for you, mentoring you, supporting you during bouts of micro aggressions of a racist nature, for instance, that needs to be called out and not put up with in silence, which is what we used to do. Being able to talk it through with others will be an important rebalancing. But yes, I've identified a couple of pitfalls.

So one is not to overlook the stage working on the stage before getting swept up by movies and television and then think oh, I should go, I should do some stage, but it would be nice, if all things are equal to have it the other way around. And, for people of colour to find more community to support one another really, because there must have been a lot of … the fallout from the disappointments in the preceding generations of actors must have been terrible, because we don't hear about it. And because again, it's only been within the last ten years or so, this business about speaking about your mental health, it's come on the scene, up until then, it wasn't really encouraged really.

PJ We weren't even encouraged to be friends with each other – there was too much divide and conquer. I've said this to my daughters I said there's some people who I met, Black actors who were positively you know, territorial, blocking, overly assertive pushing me back or keeping me back. And at the time you're sort of scratching your head, thinking is that what I think it is?

LW Yes.

PJ Then you have friends who are white who were actors, and you realize just like drama school, they all get together in the pub, talk about who's doing what and I've heard so and so is casting that. I would sit on the edge listening and thinking who am I talking to? And then when you pipe up and ask for clarity on a valuable production contact detail, they would sort of waft you away with their hand and say things like 'they are not really casting for Black actors' or 'it's not a Black play' and you sort of go 'oh okay … yeah right'. You felt you were constantly running around the outside of the circle.

LW Exactly.

PJ We didn't seem to have those networks which I'm really keen to foster. I mentor a lot because, if I can open the door, even just a bit. I have found that we, if anything, we were subjected to harsher treatment, we had no allies. We were too separate.

LW Yeah, I think that is it absolutely. You identified it brilliantly, I think. But you see, as always, it's when you get to this point, when you look back, you can really see it. And, and identify it. And, you now know that it's inadequate, it can't be like that for the future. And so with your mentoring, with my mentoring – is to encourage, yes, a different approach.

PJ I wish I tried harder to keep in touch with you. Oh. But again, I didn't know. I didn't know that's what you do. I was inherently caught up in the system, you get an agent so you can get work. And that's what you do. I didn't have that same understanding that the white actors innately had, plus there were so much more of them graduating each year than there were of us. I didn't understand what I had to do or how I was supposed to do it, especially in terms of networking.

LW I'm with you. There was no roadmap to tell us.

PJ Our family training and background didn't encode that kind of 'pub/drinking' social interaction, my parents didn't go to the pub. They didn't socialize at the bistro, no, we didn't go out in the same way. So that was a new thing. Plus, when you did join the group for a 'few rounds', the conversation would come around to race and you always felt singled out, parrying micro aggressions, thinking I don't have all the answers. I want to talk about what you're talking about, in the same way you all are.

LW I think we were at a distinct disadvantage for certain. And we just had to make it up as we went along. Just try and do the best we could, with our arms tied behind our backs most of the time, or one arm, or both arms. And then, then we realize when it's too late, that we're being a bit of a fool, oh, if only we just done that, or this, you know, or looked at it in a different way, or been a little bit more assertive in our need to obtain, you know, turn the corner. And yes, indeed. But I think we were at a disadvantage, but I feel that the future is different now for this generation. Wonderfully, I just feel more positive for them. I certainly do think there's so many things in place now. Because the way you're talking, I'm talking, the way others are talking, the way the structures are changing, to enable this generation of actors to go forward in a positive way, and with all what they can learn and hand all their down to the next generation. And so that's why I think it's, it's very positive, really, the future is very positive.

PJ What motivates you to want to act and keep doing it?

LW Not an easy question …

The need to be involved with like-minded creatives who want to tell compelling stories, and bring them vividly to life in a way that touches others and they can see aspects of themselves in it, this thrills.

One of the productions that did this for me was August Wilson's *King Hedley II*, directed by Nadia Fall at Theatre Royal, Stratford East I played Stool Pigeon in that and this was just before the before lockdown. I think it was towards the end of 2019. We did this production. So that was thrilling. Also, when I see productions like Ian McKellen's most recent *Lear* at the Duke of York's, they reignite my passion to do more Shakespeare.

Then I did Cush Jumbo's *Hamlet*, directed by Greg Hersov at the Young Vic. I played the Grave Digger, so that in answer to the question that motivates, makes me want to do more of that kind of quality work.

I think that's what motivates me, you know, is to have the right kind of group around me, and that's always so difficult to get that right. I mean, what is the right group? Yeah, who knows what the right group is, but something happens, you know, chemistry happens that ignites the story and the audience, then, then get something from it, something that can be profound, or just, you know, tickles them or, you know, whatever it is. That's when I feel for instance, in the *King Hedley II*, you know, there were nights when the audience audibly responded to moments, you know, audibly I think that's thrilling, that is thrilling. And that's why you want to absolutely be involved in that. To actually hear gasps, you know, because of a moment that, you know, because the tension is building, building, building and then whatever happens, provokes that response. That is theatre and it's happening live in front of you.

That's what motivates me to be able to have more of those opportunities to involve the audience in a way that that makes you feel, oh, we're getting through. On behalf of the writer, we're getting through.

PJ What are your broad aims for the future of your screen acting/directing presence?

LW I've got a crop of wonderful roles that included *Sitting in Limbo*, which was a critique and part of the UK government's Windrush scandal, and *Antony*, a drama about the racially motivated murder of Antony Walker, brilliantly written by Jimmy McGovern. I played Steven Walker, his father. And in his actual mother Gee Walker, who collaborated in the storytelling to produce an emotionally steering story, it was almost impossible to watch. These are the kinds of material I'd love to do more of.

I've long since stopped fooling myself that I will suddenly become the action hero like say a Tom Cruise, or Idris Elba, or Denzel Washington. To persist with that delusion will probably see me in A&E more often than I'd like. Well, that is if there's still an NHS to go to. You can tell from the ones that I've selected, like *Sitting in Limbo* and *Anthony*. Because actually, again, like the stage work, communicating something on a human scale again, you know, that we all can identify with that.

PJ Who are the actors and directors that have inspired you?

LW In the movie world it would have to be the late Sidney Poitier, who to my mind was a kind of a pioneer, showing the way with a range of barrier-busting films that could only be called a special kind of activism. I mean, he was the light for me in so many ways. When I was starting out on stage, one of the actors that I looked up to, was certainly Norman Beaton. So, he was in the generation ahead of me, consummate Shakespearean, amongst other things, he was playing Angelo in *Measure for Measure* directed by Michael Rudman at the National Theatre, and I was down as a mere Angelo's Lieutenant, so it was great to be with him. There was also the late and much-beloved Mona Hammond with whom I worked in Dennis Scott's *An Echo in the Bone* directed by Yvonne Brewster, this production and the people in it provided an important first step on the ladder of consciousness for me, because it was done quite early, it must have been in the 80s and I was only just beginning to work out what the hell was going on in the world. My list must include the series of productions that I did under Tim Supple's direction at the Young Vic London in the 90s. And one of them was Orsino in *Twelfth Night*, at Bristol Tobacco factory under the direction of Andrew Hilton I played Petruchio in *The Taming of the Shrew*, Brutus and Caesar, Aaron and Othello. Also, James Dacre, another director with whom I felt I could have, I could give a good account of myself both in Roy Williams's play about Marvin Gaye called *Soul*. And in *Our Lady of Kibeho*, about the three Rwandan girls who claim they could see and speak to the Virgin Mary. The Vatican have since said, yes, they did. In that, and this was under Nadia, as well as from Theatre Royal Stratford East, in that I played the Bishop, with his eye a little too focused on earthly matters. Lastly, I must also mention my good friend Basil King, with whom I shared the stage in the two-hander, *Sizwe Bansi is Dead*, written and devised by Athol Fugard, Winston Ntshona and John Kani, a blistering critique on the racist apartheid regime that was in full swing at the time in South Africa. Basil inspired and moved me with his raw, uncompromising power, emblematic of the black South African who wanted to be free and would wait no longer. I think there's just something about his raw power that was incredibly inspiring.

PJ If a young Black and Global Majority person of eighteen made the decision that they want to become an actor, what would your advice be?

LW Firstly, what else can you do? It's got to be serious. It's pointless attempting to dissuade an actor from their path, as I know only too well. Nor would I seek to but instead to put the emphasis on having other things to fall back on when the going gets rough as it will do. However, if you can come out of the blocks and establish yourself, as soon as feasibly possible and become the talk of the town in production, or screen projects, then that will increase your bargaining power.

Lastly, to consider writing projects that you can take the lead in, perhaps that could lead on to forming your own production company.

Whatever you do, enjoy the ride as it will be on a roller coaster of a fairground.

PJ Hard-dough bread, Sourdough bread, Chin Chin, Sweetbread, Roti, Sudsa, Bun and Cheese, Nai Wong Bao -奶黄包- Custard Bun or Naan?

LW At every single point, it has to be Hard-dough bread. And especially when it's just baked. And because I love the chewy quality when you toast and butter it, it's the best thing in the world. I love it because it reminds me a lot of when you eat dumpling because that's another favourite of mine – is dumpling. And I love the chewy quality of it. So yeah, Hard-dough bread definitely.

EPILOGUE

What the black actor has managed to give are moments – indelible moments, created miraculously, beyond the confines of the script; hints of reality, smuggled like contraband into a maudlin tale, and with enough force, if unleashed, to shatter the tale to fragments …
To prevent this, the black performer has been sealed off into a vacuum. Inevitably, therefore, and as a direct result, the white performer is also sealed off and can never deliver the best that is in him either.

James Baldwin (1976) *The Devil Finds Work*. New York, p. 554.

Speak kindly to and be kind to yourself, celebrate your wins big and small.

Take creative risks, don't allow yourself to be pigeonholed. The life of a creative artist will never be easy. It will always be hard. But we can choose our hard. Pick wisely.

To truly understand ourselves and how to situate and construct an explanation of the present experience, the past needs to be interrogated and truly understood. The future is in our hands, hearts and minds, and as my dad would always say 'one step and then another the long journey will be completed'.

Think big. Take risks. Get it done.